Cultural Anthropophagy
The 24th Bienal de São Paulo 1998

Lisette Lagnado and Pablo Lafuente (editors)

With additional essays by Mirtes Marins de Oliveira, Carmen Mörsch and Catrin Seefranz, and Renato Sztutman; interviews with artists Dias & Riedweg (conducted by Line Ellegaard) and Andrea Fraser (conducted by David Morris); and texts by Oswald de Andrade, Andrea Fraser and Paulo Herkenhoff.

Exhibition Histories

Exhibition Histories

Afterall Books presents *Exhibition Histories*, a series dedicated to shows of contemporary art that have – since the first documenta in Kassel, Germany, in 1955 – shaped the way art is experienced, made and discussed. Each book in the series draws on archival material, bringing together numerous illustrations, texts from the time and newly commissioned essays to provide detailed exploration and analysis of selected exhibitions. The shows under consideration have all responded to and influenced artistic practice whilst provoking debates about the meaning and importance of art within culture and society more broadly.

The history of modern art has conventionally focused on artistic production, emphasising the individual artist in the studio and the influences on his or her practice. *Exhibition Histories* complicates this approach by arguing for an examination of art in the moment and context in which it is presented to a public. Exhibitions offer art its first contact with an audience, and in so doing they place art within explicit or implicit narratives and discursive frameworks. Every decision about the selection and installation of work, the choice and use of the venue, the marketing strategy and the accompanying printed matter informs our understanding of the art on display. The various agents and diverse factors that give form to an exhibition and determine its subsequent influence are addressed in these books from multiple standpoints: the voices of artists, curators and writers are all brought to bear. In some instances the shows selected for study already have established reputations and our work involves analysing why this is so and whether it is justified. In other cases the opportunity is taken to illuminate lesser-known exhibitions that have, nonetheless, suggested new paradigms and that can stake an equal claim to historical importance.

This series is the result of a research project initiated by Afterall at Central Saint Martins and it benefits from the collaboration of the Center for Curatorial Studies, Bard College. Through archival study, interviews, symposia and seminars, we have amassed the materials to allow us to select exhibitions for examination and to give shape to the resulting books. The findings, analyses and narratives we propose are by no means exhaustive; rather, we see these books as a spur to further research into the exhibition form, and ultimately as a contribution towards a better understanding of contemporary art and its histories.

Front cover image:
Laura Lima, *Sem título* (*Untitled*), 1997–98, and Edgar de Souza, *Sem título* (*Dois corpos*) (*Untitled (Two bodies)*), 1997, © the artists and Arquivo Histórico Wanda Svevo/Fundação Bienal de São Paulo; photography: Juan Guerra

Back cover image:
Regina Silveira, *Tropel* (*Throng*), 1998, on the façade of the Ciccillo Matarazzo Pavilion, © the artist and Arquivo Histórico Wanda Svevo/Fundação Bienal de São Paulo; photography: Juan Guerra

Edited by Pablo Lafuente and Lisette Lagnado

First published 2015 by Afterall Books in association with the Center for Curatorial Studies, Bard College

***Exhibition Histories* Series Editors**
Tom Eccles, Charles Esche, Pablo Lafuente, Paul O'Neill and Lucy Steeds

Managing Editor
David Morris

Associate Editor
Line Ellegaard

Research Interns
Rafa Barber, Alice Ciresola, Piotr Florczyk, Ella Lewis-Williams and Irene Rossini

Afterall
Central Saint Martins
University of the Arts London
Granary Building
1 Granary Square
London N1C 4AA
www.afterall.org

Editorial Directors
Charles Esche and Mark Lewis

Publishing Director
Caroline Woodley

Copy Editor
Deirdre O'Dwyer

Research Assistant
Ambra Gattiglia

Design
A Practice for Everyday Life

Print
Industria Grafica S.I.Z.

Distribution
Koenig Books, London
c/o Buchhandlung Walther König, Köln
Ehrenstr. 4, 50672 Köln
Tel. +49 (0) 221/20 59 6 53
Fax +49 (0) 221/20 59 6 60
verlag@buchhandlung-walther-koenig.de

UK & Eire
Cornerhouse Publications
2 Tony Wilson Place
Manchester, M1 5NH
Tel. +44 (0) 161 200 15 03
Fax +44 (0) 161 200 15 04
publications@cornerhouse.org

Outside Europe
D.A.P./Distributed Art Publishers, Inc.
155 6th Avenue, 2nd Floor
USA-New York, NY 10013
Tel. +1 212 627 1999
Fax +1 212 627 9484
orders@dapinc.com

ISBN 978-3-86335-554-8 (Koenig Books, London)
ISBN 978-1-84638-149-5 (Afterall Books, London)

British Library Cataloguing-in-Publication Data
A catalogue record for this book is available from the British Library

Exhibition Histories was initially developed with Teresa Gleadowe as Research Consultant and as a Series Editor with Stephan Schmidt-Wulffen and Sabeth Buchmann

Cultural Anthropophagy

The 24th Bienal de São Paulo 1998

Exhibition Histories

Contents

8 **Anthropophagy as Cultural Strategy: The 24th Bienal de São Paulo**
— Lisette Lagnado

63 **The 24th Bienal de São Paulo 1998**
68 'Representações Nacionais' ('National Representations')
78 'Arte Contemporânea Brasileira: Um e/entre Outro/s' ('Brazilian Contemporary Art: One and/among Other/s')
100 'Roteiros. Roteiros. Roteiros. Roteiros. Roteiros. Roteiros. Roteiros.' ('Routes. Routes. Routes. Routes. Routes. Routes. Routes.')
114 'Núcleo Histórico: Antropofagia e Histórias de Canibalismos' ('Historical Nucleus: Anthropophagy and Histories of Cannibalisms')
174 Catalogue covers

176 **The Epistemological Leap of Anthropophagy After the 24th Bienal de São Paulo**
— Mirtes Marins de Oliveira

188 **Out of the *cantinho* — Art Education at the 24th Bienal de São Paulo**
— Carmen Mörsch and Catrin Seefranz

206 **The (Re)turn of the Anthropophagites: Reconnecting Oswald de Andrade's Proposal to Amerindian Art-Thought**
— Renato Sztutman

222 **Manifesto antropófago**
— Oswald de Andrade, 1928

226 **Anthropophagite Manifesto**
— Oswald de Andrade, 1928

230 **Incomplete Glossary of Sources of Latin American Art**
— Paulo Herkenhoff, 1993

248 **Reporting from São Paulo, I'm from the United States: Five Broadcasts on the 24th Bienal de São Paulo**
—Andrea Fraser, 1998

268 **Interviews**
268 —Andrea Fraser in conversation with David Morris
272 —Dias & Riedweg in conversation with Line Ellegaard

280 **Afterword: For What, For Whom**
—Pablo Lafuente

284 **Authors' biographies**
287 **Selected bibliography**
290 **Picture credits**
292 **Acknowledgements**
293 **Index**

Anthropophagy as Cultural Strategy: The 24th Bienal de São Paulo
— Lisette Lagnado

The analytical tools required for appraising art biennials are distinct from those required by other international exhibitions. They involve extra-aesthetic criteria, such as the relevance of theme, the sophistication of the display and a consideration of the exhibition's historical character: biennials have to consider what has been achieved (or not) by previous editions while giving an account of history in the most contemporaneous mode – a contradiction in terms. Parallel activities, which have evolved to become central features of biennials, add a further set of complicating factors. To ensure the event's singularity, there is now a general culture of seminars and films, artists' residencies and workshops, interventions on a public-work scale, partnerships with schools and universities, educational projects and publications, and so on. This trend has led to a decline in the significance of the *sine qua non* condition for exhibitions: the exhibition itself. At one event after another, the curators of the more ambitious biennials pursue evermore elaborate aims, taking on the ambiguous mission of upscaling their project in order to achieve the desired major event, while having to struggle against its dilution into the supply chain of globalised cultural tourism. Few initiatives are able to withstand being ground down by the economic and bureaucratic force of this pounding anti-Promethean machinery.

It is in this context that Paulo Herkenhoff's curatorial plan for the 24th Bienal de São Paulo in 1998 takes on the mythic proportions of an insurmountable event. Such a phenomenon was observed only once before in the history of the Bienal de São Paulo, the second oldest exhibition of its kind,[1] when Pablo
p.58 Picasso's *Guernica* (1937) arrived in Brazil for the second Bienal in 1953.[2]

—

[1] The first art biennial was the Venice Biennale, in 1895. In the genealogy of international biennials, few studies have included the 1896 Carnegie International, perhaps because its name, format and periodicity were altered several times in the second half of the twentieth century. Until the eleventh edition of the Bienal de São Paulo, in 1971, the exhibition featured a section of architectural designs as well as displaying artworks; the independent Bienal Internacional de Arquitetura de São Paulo (BIA) was established in 1973.

[2] '... since World War II had broken out in Europe at that time, the mural and studies remained at the artist's suggestion on extended loan to the Museum [of Modern Art, New York]. In 1953 at Picasso's request, the mural was sent to Milan and to São Paulo; in 1955 to Paris, Munich and Cologne; in 1956, to Brussels, Amsterdam and Stockholm.' See '*Guernica* to go to Madrid's Museo del Prado' [press release], Museum of Modern Art (MoMA), New York, 10 September 1981, available at http://www.moma.org/momaorg/shared/pdfs/docs/press_archives/5928/releases/MOMA_1981_0059_60.pdf?2010 (last accessed on 4 March 2015). The second edition of the Bienal, and particularly the inclusion of *Guernica*, had such a strong impact on Brazilian cultural self-worth that it remains an exemplary horizon for what an international exhibition can achieve. On this point, see the masters dissertation by Ana Maria Pimenta Hoffmann, 'A arte brasileira na II Bienal do

As time passes and memories of the exhibition as a whole fade, it is Herkenhoff's 'Núcleo Histórico' ('Historical Nucleus') – which was subtitled 'Antropofagia e Histórias de Canibalismos' ('Anthropophagy and Histories of Cannibalisms') and developed sophisticated art historical arguments from an astute Brazilian perspective – that is confirmed as the high point of the 24th Bienal; other sections are much less remembered. To what extent is this retrospective evaluation contradictory for assessing the magnitude of a biennial by its museological component (and particularly at a time when, elsewhere in the world, biennials were increasingly focused on activities beyond the exhibition display) rather than its display of contemporary work? Or should the content of contemporaneity be gauged by other signifieds inherent in the exhibition, given that this edition of the Bienal had, according to Julio Landmann, president of the Fundação Bienal at the time, a 'clear political project' with its 'point of departure' specifically located in Brazil?[3]

pp.114–73

This prompts another issue to be examined: since this biennial not only plumped for a Brazilian perspective but also announced that its agenda would revisit the colonial process and highlight Latin America more broadly, what are its critical implications for the present? In particular, bearing in mind Herkenhoff's ambition to rewrite art history, is it possible to verify in subsequent publications of art theory whether this edition of the Bienal transformed the national narrative and international perspectives on Brazilian art?

The 'Núcleo Histórico' focused on establishing points of contact and transference between artworks from the sixteenth, seventeenth, eighteenth and nineteenth centuries, yet it also featured recent works that scrambled the notion of chronological, linear artistic development. A shrewd advertising campaign had billboards printed with the figures of van Gogh and Tarsila do Amaral as spokespersons, beckoning visitors to 'view historical and contemporary dialogues between Brazil and the world', posing blunt questions such as 'Are we all cannibals?' or making categorical statements, for example, 'Only anthropophagy unites us.'[4] Press releases emphasised the appeal to historical revisionism and contradicted the Bienal's long-standing commitment, since the 1950s, to keeping Brazil up to date with the latest developments in art.

fig.2–3

—

Museu de Arte Moderna de São Paulo: o prêmio melhor pintor nacional e o debate em torno da abstração', available at http://www.bibliotecadigital.unicamp.br/document/?code=000236176&fd=y (last accessed on 4 March 2015).

[3] Julio Landmann, 'Apresentação do Presidente da Fundação Bienal de São Paulo' / 'Fundação Bienal de São Paulo President's Foreword' (trans. Veronica Cordeiro), in *XXIV Bienal de São Paulo: Núcleo Histórico: Antropofagia e Histórias de Canibalismos* (exh. cat.), São Paulo: Fundação Bienal, 1998, p.18.

[4] From the first paragraph of Oswald de Andrade's 'Manifesto': 'Only anthropophagy unites us. Socially. Economically. Philosophically.' O. Andrade, 'Manifesto antropófago' / 'Anthropophagite Manifesto' (1928, trans. Adriano Pedrosa and V. Cordeiro), in *XXIV Bienal de São Paulo: Núcleo Histórico: Antropofagia e Histórias de Canibalismos*, *op. cit.*, p.536, and this volume, pp.222–29.

However, visitors to the much-publicised historical core of the Bienal in 1998 were not greeted by art's influential figures immediately upon entering the Ciccillo Matarazzo Pavilion in Ibirapuera Park, home to the Bienal de São Paulo since 1957.[5] To reach the top floor and the exhibition's air-conditioned pp.114–73 space, where the promised cultural banquet of the 'Núcleo Histórico' was waiting to be devoured, visitors had to climb the vast, swooping ramps of the huge, 33,000-square-metre building designed by Oscar Niemeyer, and then pass through the other sections of the show, which presented installations by artists more likely unknown (as ever) to the general public.

The three sections complementing the 'Núcleo Histórico' were: 'Arte pp.78–99 Contemporânea Brasileira: Um e/entre Outro/s' ('Brazilian Contemporary Art: One and/among Other/s'), curated by Herkenhoff and his associate pp.100–13 curator Adriano Pedrosa; 'Roteiros. Roteiros. Roteiros. Roteiros. Roteiros. Roteiros. Roteiros.' ('Routes. Routes. Routes. Routes. Routes. Routes. Routes.'), an international show involving ten curators and arranged by continent; pp.68–77 and the usual 'Representações Nacionais' ('National Representations'), a selection of artists from 54 countries. In addition to the exhibition itself, comprising these four sections, there were two further pillars supporting the curatorial design for the project overall: an educational programme headed by Evelyn Ioschpe and a publications project coordinated by Pedrosa. It was the first time that the Bienal de São Paulo had an editor in charge of its publications and a director exclusively for its educational programme.[6]

With the 'Núcleo Histórico', the Bienal was clearly mooting a rewrite of art history, indeed questioning the discipline as such. In the context of globalised biennials, what is to be expected of an iconology-related narrative tradition in art history? Given these issues, how are we to interpret the following statement from the president of the Fundação Bienal at the time: 'Perhaps the most important role for the Bienal of the future is to focus exclusively on the present [and to be] a thermometer for the present once again. São Paulo no longer needs a temporary museum'?[7] After all, what was the key

—

[5] The first Bienal de São Paulo was held in 1951 in a makeshift building on the Avenida Paulista site where the Museu de Arte de São Paulo (MASP), designed by the architect Lina Bo Bardi, would be erected between 1957 and 1968. With pavilions designed by Oscar Niemeyer and landscaping by Roberto Burle Marx, the Bienal building in Ibirapuera Park was inaugurated in 1954 for the city's fourth centennial. Since its fourth edition in 1957, the Bienal has been held in the pavilion originally known as the 'Pavilion of the Industries', subsequently renamed in honour of the Bienal's founder. The use of this municipally owned building was transferred to the foundation under a loan arrangement.

[6] The detailed report compiled for the 'Public Education and the 24th Bienal' project is now held by the Arquivo Histórico Wanda Svevo / Fundação Bienal de São Paulo.

[7] J. Landmann, quoted in Vera de Sá, 'O banquete antropófago', *Bravo*, no.13, October 1998, p.3. Landmann's vision for the event's future seemed to find a different echo in the institution's official publications. Agnaldo Farias, for one, concluded that 'the Bienal de São Paulo is a much needed museum'. See A. Farias, 'Um Museu no Tempo' / 'A Museum Inside Time', in *Bienal de São Paulo 50 anos, 1951–2001 / 50 years of the São Paulo Biennial*, São Paulo: Fundação Bienal, 2001, p.38. Except

mission for this strange combination of historical and contemporary work? Would the 24th Bienal merely be a stage preceding an already announced future – a future aiming for pure contemporaneity? The argument that São Paulo had no need for yet another 'temporary museum' hardly squared with an exhibition featuring Tarsila do Amaral, Gustave Moreau, Auguste Rodin, Joaquín Torres-García, Lucio Fontana, Yves Klein, Maria Martins, Piero Manzoni, Yayoi Kusama and Robert Ryman, to name just a few of the selected artists. What, in 1998, was the contemporary dimension of these names?

These questions only redouble the oddity inherent in analysis of that year's Bienal – the oddity of judging the whole by a part, and of judging a contemporary art project through the lens of a revisionary take on an academic discipline. Here we find a critical difference demarcated in relation to the usual parameters for assessing the biennial as an exhibitionary mode.

Until 1998, no reflection on the formation of Brazilian culture had been considered worthy of such explicit engagement by the Fundação Bienal. An elite bastion of São Paulo's high society, the Fundação had been founded by Francisco 'Ciccillo' Matarazzo Sobrinho, a Brazilian businessman of Italian descent who was behind several major cultural institutions established in Brazil between 1940 and 1960.[8] Oscar Landmann was Ciccillo Matarazzo's first successor as president of the Fundação, and his son Julio Landmann held the position at the time of the 1998 Bienal. The profile of the Fundação – privately run, but also public in the sense that in more recent years its funding has depended on tax breaks for its sponsors – can be understood in light of Sérgio Buarque de Holanda's classic account of national societal norms, *Raízes do Brasil* (*Roots of Brazil*, 1936), and specifically in terms of the rise and power of the so-called 'cordial man'.[9] Even today, the management of the Fundação holds to 'gentlemen's agreements', with curators chosen on the basis of 'their' president's particular interests, and with internal teams dedicated to production, archiving, communication and education. To date, the institution consists of an honorary board of former presidents, both living and deceased; lifelong and non-life members; a management board; and a supervisory board, over which Matarazzo continues to rule in posterity as its 'perpetual president'.[10] In all his cultural ventures, from the founding of the Museu de Arte Moderna de São Paulo in 1948 onwards,

—

where noted, texts originally in Portuguese have been translated for this volume.

[8] Matarazzo (1898–1977) founded the Museu de Arte Moderna de São Paulo (MAM SP) in 1948 and the first São Paulo Biennial in 1951. Indirectly, he was responsible for the creation of the Museu de Arte Contemporânea da Universidade de São Paulo (MAC USP) in 1963, which he endowed with artworks and his personal film collection dating from 1949. This film library ultimately led to the creation of the Cinemateca Brasileira. Matarazzo helped found a theatre, Teatro Brasileiro de Comédia (TBC), in 1948, and supported the contruction of studios for a film production company, Companhia Cinematográfica Vera Cruz, in 1949.

[9] Sérgio Buarque de Holanda, *Raízes do Brasil*, São Paulo: Companhia das Letras, 2001, pp.139–51.

[10] As he is listed in the Bienal catalogues, for instance.

Matarazzo demanded the upholding of so-called international standards.[11] The political and economic alliance forged between Brazil and the United States in particular – given the former's modernising project of the 1940s to 60s and its concomitant fascination with the latter's new products and hegemonic centres – forms the ideological context through which to understand this internationalism.

In light of this brief institutional summary, a biennial articulated around the 'Manifesto antropófago' (1928) of modernist poet Oswald de Andrade was sure to have shock value.[12] The choice of this text as a historical anchor proposed no less than a paradigm shift in relation to the birth of modernism in Brazil, specifically diverting attention away from the Semana de Arte Moderna (Week of Modern Art) held at São Paulo's opera house in 1922 – an international assembly that was conventionally hailed as responsible for the spread of European avant-garde Cubism, Dada and Surrealism to Brazil. The notion of Brazil having to catch up culturally with Europe was, of course, troublesome, but it was long assumed inevitable. In the words of Benedito Nunes, referring to the concept of anthropophagy in relation to the literary avant-garde: 'European currents intervening in the development of our modernism were seen as a necessary evil, or as a kind of rite of passage that Brazilian literature had to go through before reaching the normality of adult life.'[13] Making the 'Manifesto' definitive for Brazilian art at the expense of the Week of Modern Art represented a dramatic historicising manoeuvre on the part of Herkenhoff. As he later reiterated, the early 1920s had little to offer the idea of modern art in Brazil breaking away from the art of the past: 'The most curious paradox is that in the year of the Week of Modern Art, there was not a single modern artist in São Paulo who was worthy of being included in the classification of "modern", that is, within the framework of the Week of Modern Art.'[14]

The subtitle for the 'Núcleo Histórico', 'Antropofagia e Histórias de Canibalismos', requires an additional understanding of the distinction that Andrade made between *anthropophagy* and *cannibalism*, words which are

—

[11] See Mario Cesar Carvalho, 'Bye-bye, província', *Folha de S. Paulo*, 20 May 2001, available at http://www1.folha.uol.com.br/folha/especial/bienal50anos/fj2005200101.htm (last accessed on 4 March 2015).

[12] Although the choice of this text coincided with its seventieth anniversary, none of Herkenhoff's declarations hinted that he was proposing a celebration around the date.

[13] Benedito Nunes, 'Antropofagia e vanguarda: Acerca do canibalismo literário', in *Oswald Canibal*, São Paulo: Perspectiva, 1979, p.8.

[14] Paulo Herkenhoff, '1922, um ano sem arte moderna', in *Arte Brasileira na coleção Fadel: Da inquietação do moderno à autonomia da linguagem*, Rio de Janeiro: Andréa Jakobsson Estúdio, 2002, p.194. Herkenhoff relocates the emancipatory idea of Brazilian art from Tarsila do Amaral's anthrophagistic painting to the writings of Andrade and Raul Bopp. See also P. Herkenhoff, 'Bienal 1998: princípios e processos', in *marcelina*, vol.1, 2008, p.29. The magazine featured an edited version of a seminar given by Herkenhoff at Faculdade Santa Marcelina, São Paulo, 12 March 2008, organised by the author. Some parts of this essay contain excerpts from the unpublished transcript.

widely considered interchangeable. In short, anthropophagy refers to the ritualised translation of a worldview through the act of ingestion, whereas cannibalism opposes this spiritual understanding, describing instead the 'materialistic and immoral interpretation of it by the Jesuits and colonisers'.[15] As he further clarifies, cannibalism may be 'anthropophagy due to gluttony or anthropophagy due to hunger, as found in reports from besieged cities and lost travellers'.[16] Andrade's interest in the indigenous practice of anthropophagy refers to its rule of selectiveness: not everything is eaten, only that which is lacking for the constitution of an ideal identity. Myth accounts for a transfer of values from the one deceased, with refinements that recall the Greeks choosing different words to describe ways of dying.[17] In his curatorial take on anthropophagy, Herkenhoff attempted to present intersections between approaches to the idea, crossing the lived understanding of indigenous peoples, as studied and analysed by anthropologists, and the allegorical sense found in Andrade's artistic manifesto, not based on fieldwork.

Included as part of the 'Núcleo Histórico' were texts, presented in display cases, offering a carefully selected syllabus on anthropophagy. Eduardo Viveiros de Castro's experiences with the Araweté people and his idea of 'Amerindian perspectivism' was represented in *Araweté: os deuses canibais* (1986; its title literally translates as 'Araweté: The Cannibalistic Gods', though it was published in English in 1992 as *From the Enemy's Point of View: Humanity and Divinity in an Amazonian Society*.) There were literary works by Andrade's contemporary Mário de Andrade (no relation), as well as *Feuilles de Route* (1924) by the Swiss-born writer Blaise Cendrars, whose name is traditionally inseparable from Brazilian modernism. Also on display were: one of only eight copies of the first edition of Michel de Montaigne's *Essais* (1580–95); Jean de Léry's *Histoire d'un voyage fait en la terre du Brésil* (*History of a Voyage to the Land of Brazil*, 1578); the *Encyclopaedia Acephalica*, which compiled texts from the 1940s onwards by Georges Bataille and his contemporaries; and a first edition, from 1955, of Claude Lévi-Strauss's *Tristes Tropiques* along with three of his anthropological works. The bibliography then reached into the 1990s with titles by Frank Lestringant and Emmanuel Ménard.

pp.*114–73*

fig.55–57

The curatorial agenda for the 24th Bienal proposed a symmetrical relation between patriarchal norms in Brazilian society and the adoption of a Eurocentric view of art history. Herkenhoff would later reflect that the 'colonial process was a war between cannibalisms', and further:

> *The full logic of the colonial regime appears to be represented throughout the process of the religious missions as an ideological preparation for*

—

[15] O. Andrade, 'A crise da filosofia messiânica', in *A utopia antropofágica*: *Obras completas de Oswald de Andrade*, São Paulo: Globo, Secretaria de Estado da Cultura, 1990, pp.101–55.

[16] *Ibid.*, p.101.

[17] See Jean-Pierre Vernant, *L'individu, la mort, l'amour: Soi-même et l'autre en Grèce ancienne*, Paris: Gallimard, 1989.

submission. […] Redemption signified rescuing the Indians from extreme 'barbarism' – cannibalism – through their conversion to Christianity; in exchange, they were offered the Eucharist as consumption of the transubstantiated body of Christ per the doctrine of the Fourth Council of the Lateran.[18]

A vision such as this could only come punctuated with violence to convey the murder scene's digestive terminology and moral brutality, and so it did in the Bienal, by way of juxtaposing heterogeneous imagery that disrupted artistic and museological norms. In the development of his approach, Herkenhoff revealed a profound familiarity with Andrade's writings, from the exaltation of native primitivism in his 'Pau-Brasil' poetry and his 1924 manifesto announcing this literary practice, to 'A crise da filosofia messiânica' ('The Crisis of Messianic Philosophy', 1950), the poet's renowned thesis, which, incidentally, was rejected in the process of a competition for the chair of philosophy at the Universidade de São Paulo (USP).[19] The development of Andrade's thought in this direction reflected his view that the 'civilised' patriarchal system, transmitted by European culture, would not allow for alterity and produced 'false utopias'; whereas matriarchy – identifiable with aspects of Brazilian culture such as hospitality, generosity and solidarity – beckoned a form of civility far from the coercive system of European organisation.[20]

In 1950, the same year that he was denied the professorship in São Paulo, the poet drew on two key ideas in Buarque de Holanda's aforementioned study, *Raízes do Brasil*, in order to elaborate his definition of otherness in terms of 'dread of living with oneself' and 'living in others'.[21] Expanding on

—

[18] P. Herkenhoff, 'Missions', in P. Herkenhoff (ed.), *Amazonia: Ciclos da Modernidade* (exh. cat.), Rio de Janeiro: Centro Cultural Banco do Brasil, 2012, p.160. Both Herkenhoff and Régis Michel, curator of the section of the 'Núcleo Histórico' on nineteenth-century art, understood Christian communion as a stage (the 'highest', for Michel) of Western cannibalism. According to Herkenhoff, Brazil's cultural modernisation project (its Enlightenment and its emancipatory character) 'came in through the Amazon region, Rio de Janeiro and Minas Gerais' (*ibid.*, p.163). He would dismiss the importance of the 1922 Week of Modern Art in São Paulo: 'Sometimes we need to forget about the Modern Art Week. After all, it couldn't bring itself to embrace Ismael Nery from Pará' (*ibid.*, p.183). For the exhibition 'Amazonia', it is evident that the curator revisited and developed the strategies of the 'Núcleo Histórico'.

[19] Herkenhoff's familiarity was demonstrated through his extensive quotation of different interpretations of Andrade's work and Brazilian modernism in his curatorial texts and in his many public statements to the press as well as in the guided visits he gave during the exhibition.

[20] On the question of 'false utopias', Nunes notes that Andrade's singular approach borrows from Nietzsche and Freud to criticise orthodox Marxism. See B. Nunes, 'Antropofagia ao alcance de todos', in O. Andrade, *A utopia antropofágica, op. cit.*, p.37.

[21] S. Buarque de Holanda, *Raízes do Brasil, op. cit.*, pp.141–51; and O. Andrade, 'Um aspecto antropofágico da cultura brasileira: o homem cordial', *Anais do Primeiro Congresso Brasileiro de Filosofia*, vol.1, March 1950, pp.229–31.

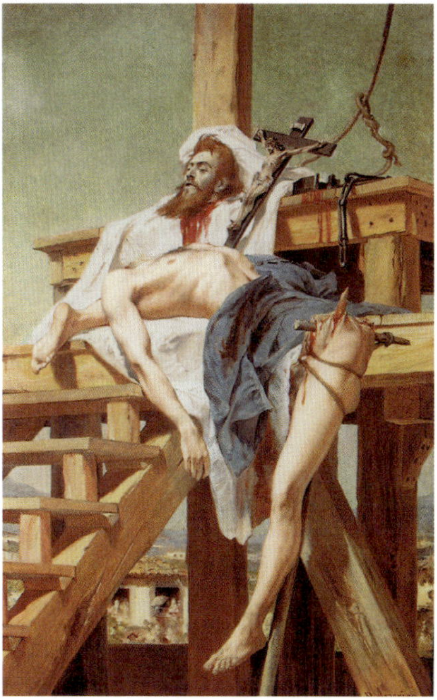

Pedro Américo, *Tiradentes esquartejado* (*Tiradentes Dismembered*), 1893, oil on canvas, 270 × 165 cm: Collection of Museu Mariano Procópio, Juiz de Fora

the idea of anthropophagy in the 'cordial man', Andrade argued: 'It all relates to the existence of two cultural hemispheres dividing history into Matriarchy and Patriarchy. The former was the world of primitive man. The latter, of civilised man. One produced an anthropophagous culture, the other, a messianic one.'[22] The critical valency of the 24th Bienal, dubbed the 'Anthropophagy Biennial', was heightened by the realisation that the ideological legacy of the colonial era had yet to disappear, and that it continued to exert a sly influence on social relations. At its close, Andrade's 'Manifesto antropófago' addresses this sharply, in the author's characteristically playful yet challenging manner: 'Our independence has not yet been proclaimed.'[23] It was not by chance, then, that the exhibition set aside a prominent place for Tiradentes, the martyr of Brazil's struggle for independence,[24] portrayed in Pedro Américo's canvas *Tiradentes esquartejado* (*Tiradentes Dismembered*, 1893), which shows his decapitated body drawn and quartered, a crucifix set next to his severed head. This violence signifies a precise and savage human reckoning that galvanised the logic of the curatorial design for the whole of the 'Núcleo Histórico': 'This *Tiradentes* ended up being a kind of symbolic

fig.58

pp.*114–73*

—

[22] *Ibid.*, p.102.

[23] O. Andrade, 'Manifesto antropófago', *op. cit.*, p.537.

[24] Tiradentes (Joaquim José da Silva Xavier, 1746–92) was hanged for his role in plotting an uprising to bring in a republican regime and gain independence from Portugal, an episode known as the Minas Gerais Conspiracy (*Inconfidência mineira*).

provision for a society emerging from colonialism, resorting to a keen metaphor of colonisation as a cannibalising process – hence its crucial significance for this exhibition.'[25]

At the 24th Bienal, the display of museum artefacts itself became a cannibalistic device, eliminating notions of evolution and influence typical of the natural sciences without dispensing with historicising narratives. On the contrary, the curator assumed such narratives as the exhibition's horizon by writing about 'histories', 'stories' and 'cannibalisms', in the plural – hence, the tangible meaning conveyed by the flows mapped in the diagram Herkenhoff produced for his installation plan, which was then posted on walls within the exhibition. Since the assumption was that colonisation could not be ended merely by declaring the country's independence, Américo's painting functioned to integrate and activate a whole constellation of mythic, real, programmatic and psychological images of cannibalism and enslavement. For Herkenhoff, the Law of the Father (Andrade's patriarchal society) could be summarised as a multitude of repressive impulses issuing, for example, from the Catholic Church, colonisation, the State and Sigmund Freud's reality principle in psychoanalysis. Herkenhoff proposed a theory of art articulated along three axes – interrogative, dialogic and erotic – while referring to the exhibition as an 'inventive and poetic interpretation of art'[26] and finding its avowal in the following line from Andrade's 'Manifesto': 'The spirit refuses to conceive the spirit without body.'[27] As such it becomes evident that, in terms of hermeneutics, the curatorial strategy was to be scrupulously justified art historically, in its choice of works, while also allowing for extravagance. In this context, Jacques Lacan's words from *The Four Fundamental Concepts of Psychoanalysis* (1973) not only provide an epigraph for the curatorial design – opening the curatorial essay in the catalogue – they also expose the inevitability of the exhibition's sensory component: 'What value has my desire for you?'[28]

1. A Dialogic Conception of History and the 'Núcleo Histórico': Transversalities and Contaminations

pp.*114–73* Upon entering the 'Núcleo Histórico', visitors were met with an introductory text, in the customary manner for a museum display. One would think that a quote from Benedito Nunes, a celebrated interpreter of Andrade's works, would be the obvious choice to provide authoritative guidance. Readers of

—

[25] Document signed by the curatorial team for the 24th Bienal, Arquivo Histórico Wanda Svevo / Fundação Bienal de São Paulo.

[26] P. Herkenhoff, 'Introdução geral' / 'General introduction' (trans. V. Cordeiro), in *XXIV Bienal de São Paulo: Núcleo Histórico: Antropofagia e Histórias de Canibalismos*, *op. cit.*, p.37.

[27] O. Andrade, 'Manifesto antropófago', *op. cit.*, p.537.

[28] Jacques Lacan, *The Four Fundamental Concepts of Psychoanalysis* (1973, trans. Alan Sheridan), London: Hogarth Press and The Institute of Psychoanalysis, 1977, p.192; quoted in P. Herkenhoff 'Introdução geral' / 'General introduction', *op. cit.*, p.22.

his small masterpiece *Oswald Canibal* (1979) would spot several of its referents featured in Herkenhoff's curatorial selection and catalogue texts: Tristan Tzara's Dada manifestos; Surrealism and the pataphysical wisdom of Alfred Jarry's *Ubu Roi* (1896); Freud's *Totem and Taboo* (1913); and the writings of the Marquis de Sade. However, to introduce anthropophagy at the section entrance, the curator instead used text drawn from the writings of Mikhail Bakhtin:

> *The excess of my seeing is the bud in which slumbers form* [...]. *But in order that this bud should really unfold into the blossom of consummating form, the excess of my seeing must 'fill in' the horizon of the other human being* [...] *without at the same time forfeiting his distinctiveness. I must empathise or project myself into this other human being,* see his world axiologically from within *as he sees his world; I must put myself in his place and then, after returning to my own place, 'fill in' his horizon through that excess of seeing which opens out from this, my own, place outside him.* I must enframe him, create a consummating environment for him out of this excess of my own seeing, knowing, desiring and feeling.[29]

Why Bakhtin, a thinker still little studied in Brazil? One would have expected the voice of a Brazilian specialist to take up the issues of modernism and anthropophagy. However, the pertinence of this choice transcended Bakhtin's 'foreign' position. Bakhtin is not only the Russian literary critic who developed a dialogue between sign systems, but also and in particular he was early to take up the subject of dialogical relations based on otherness, an essential concept for Herkenhoff's programme.

For Bakhtin, a dialogic relation entails 'not a dialogue in the narrative sense, nor in the abstract sense; rather it is a dialogue between points of view, each with its own concrete language that cannot be translated into the other'.[30] Or, to put it in terms even closer to the display strategies of the 'Núcleo Histórico' via Michael Holquist's gloss on the centrality of dialogue and its various processes to Bakhtin's theory: 'A word, discourse, language or culture undergoes "dialogisation" when it becomes relativised, de-privileged, aware of competing definitions for the same things.'[31]

—

[29] Mikhail M. Bakhtin, 'Author and Hero in Aesthetic Activity' (c.1920–23), in *Art and Answerability: Early Philosophical Essays by M. M. Bakhtin* (ed. Michael Holquist and Vadim Liapunov, trans. V. Liapunov), Austin: University of Texas Press, 1990, pp.24–25. Emphasis mine. Bakhtin's ideas were first published in Brazil in the 1960s thanks to the professor and Russian translator Boris Schnaiderman at the Universidade de São Paulo (USP). However, the regime installed by the 1964 military coup abruptly halted the circulation of Russian authors in Brazil.

[30] M.M. Bakhtin, 'From the Prehistory of Novelistic Discourse' (1975), in *The Dialogic Imagination: Four Essays* (ed. Michael Holquist, trans. Caryl Emerson and M. Holquist), Austin: University of Texas Press, 1981, p.76.

[31] M. Holquist, 'Glossary', in *ibid.*, p.427.

pp.114–73 The 'Núcleo Histórico' abandoned the closed framing structure of 'special exhibitions' that previous editions of the Bienal invariably organised to separate historical from contemporary sections. A primary aim for this core element of the 1998 exhibition project was to deconstruct hierarchical relations between genres, dates, techniques and locations (systems of classification seen to be indebted to an Enlightenment conception of the world) and to bring elements from the past into the *here and now*. Herkenhoff spread an iconically powerful selection of works across the museological top-floor space to establish a tissue of dialogues, or what we might call 'transversalities' – developing a structure that recalled Aby Warburg's strategies for his unfinished *Mnemosyne Atlas* (begun in 1924). In the top corner of a wall in the 'Dada and Surrealism' display, for instance, Herkenhoff brazenly
fig.70 hung Vik Muniz's work *Sigmund*, from his 1997 series of 'chocolate portraits', rather like an epigraph, or a few words isolated in the corner of a page.[32] Somewhat similarly, other works were placed at ground level, on the edge of dividing screens: for example, Artur Barrio's *T.E. (trouxas ensangüentadas)* (*T.E. (bloody bundles),* 1969) acted as marginalia for the Francis Bacon display. Such dialogues between historical and contemporary works, and between Western art and Brazilian culture, were viewed by some visitors as purely arbitrary and authoritarian curatorial interventions. And it was precisely the originality of the 'Núcleo Histórico' that drew some of the 24th Bienal's severest criticisms.[33]

The scope of the 'Núcleo Histórico' also revealed the Brazilian curator's knowledge of the diagrams of Alfred H. Barr, Jr, in particular his chart for the exhibition 'Cubism and Abstract Art', held at the Museum of Modern Art in New York in 1936.[34] In contrast to this influential US model for the history of modern painting, there are transversal lines in Herkenhoff's aforementioned graphic chart – part installation plan, part conceptual mapping – and these afford a survey of a diversity of cultures posed by the
fig.38 anthropophagous agenda. For his diagram he brought together such names as Montaigne, Staden, Léry, Thévet, de Bry, Eckhout, Aleijadinho and the Cuzco artistic tradition; all placed in the top-central rectangle, between Cildo Meireles to the left and Vincent van Gogh and Paul Gauguin to the right (a Gauguin-dedicated area within the exhibition ultimately failed to materialise). Tarsila do Amaral appeared in the centre, with lines linking out to a left column listing Cildo Meireles, Alfredo Volpi and Hélio Oiticica, among others.

—

[32] P. Herkenhoff uses the expression 'revisionist vomit' to explain Muniz's chocolate image, see 'Introdução geral' / 'General introduction', *op. cit.*, p.43.

[33] See, for instance, the critical comments in Ricardo Fabbrini, 'As utopias e o canibal', *Folha de S. Paulo*, *Jornal de Resenhas*, 12 December 1998, available at http://www1.folha.uol.com.br/fsp/resenha/rs12129805.htm (last accessed on 4 March 2015). *Jornal de Resenhas* was a monthly insert in the daily newpaper *Folha de S. Paulo* between 1995 and 2004, an initiative of the faculty of philosophy and the human sciences at the USP, which tended to echo 'scholarly' opinion.

[34] 'Cubism and Abstract Art', Museum of Modern Art (MoMA), New York, 2 March to 19 April 1936, curated by Alfred H. Barr, Jr.

In keeping with the open and collective approach that Herkenhoff was hoping to achieve at the 24th Bienal, sub-curation was a feature of the 'Núcleo Histórico', with each artist or historical section assigned to a p.116 particular curator. The selection process highlighted certain Brazilian artists through contributions from curators specially commissioned on the strength of their academic standing; for example, the room for Tarsila was organised by Sônia Salzstein, and Volpi's room by Aracy Amaral – both showing a fig.83-91 generous selection of works in the manner of museum retrospectives. In the diagram, Oiticica was linked downwards to the section titled 'Monocromos' (with Piero Manzoni, Robert Ryman, Lucio Fontana, Yayoi Kusama, Yves Klein and Oiticica again), which was linked downwards in turn to Venezuelan painter Armando Reverón, whose box reconnected with Tarsila's central position. A line also extended from Tarsila towards van Gogh and Gauguin (whose names, in the top right of the diagram, would coincide with the position of the sun in Tarsila's painting *Antropofagia* (1929)). p.257 Another central rectangle just above Tarsila contained Oswald de Andrade's 'Manifesto antropófago' (Tarsila was Andrade's wife at the time of his writing the 'Manifesto'), Mário de Andrade and Raul Bopp; from its top the Dada and Surrealism section emerged: Picabia, Dalí, Masson, Freud, Bataille and Caillois. Above that was a group including Goya, Géricault, Moreau and Américo, linked from the aforementioned group headed by Montaigne.

The uncanny character of the 'Núcleo Histórico' was further accentuated by the fact that, despite uniting many canonical works of art in a heritage-listed building, this section of the exhibition was not held in a museum.[35] To reinforce its undermining of established systems of museological display, a strategy of 'contamination' was employed throughout the exhibition. Herkenhoff and Adriano Pedrosa have described how 'contamination is connected to cannibalism, to its affliction insofar as human flesh contaminated human flesh. When a person doesn't follow the rules as regards consumption of the human body, he or she immediately becomes a diseased person.'[36] This approach opposed chronological histories of genres, and deliberately spread anachronisms across the show like a virus taking over a weakened body. A point to bear in mind here is that, by the mid-1990s, paranoia relating to the AIDS epidemic was at its peak in Brazil, so the term 'contamination' added a further set of moral and political implications. While inventing a particular system of display to reflect an alternative historical narrative – anthropophagy – Herkenhoff conducted a practical test of a

—

[35] On opening night, the Matarazzo Pavilion was struck by a hailstorm that caused leaks in the air-conditioned section. Press coverage of the incident queried the state of the artworks on show and voiced fears of the institution's international image being affected. The museologist Margaret de Moraes ensured the integrity of the works and the exhibition was closed to the public during the four days of emergency repair work.

[36] P. Herkenhoff and A. Pedrosa, 'The Brazilian Curator Private / The Carioca Curator', *TRANS>*, no.6, 1999, pp.6–15, available at http://transmag.org/nuevo_transmag/contents/vols.php?vista=issue&tipoproy=Cultural%20Conditioning&proyeccion=10 (last accessed on 4 March 2015).

theory of art based on a porous process of dialogue / contamination between works, a theory meant to replace Hegel's philosophy of (art) history as universal truth or Kant's rigid aesthetic categories.

fig.54 A fine example of such contamination – and one that most scandalised patrolling modernist historians – was Tunga's sculpture *TaCaPe* (1986–97), leaning against the wall next to one of Eckhout's five seventeenth-century paintings of Amazonian indigenous peoples. This curatorial gesture prompted protest on the grounds that there seemed to be an illustrative reflection between the represented utilitarian object – the weapon depicted in the painting – and the object formalised in Tunga's sculpture. Yet, granted that these pieces all belong to the symbolic register of art, how could this be an illustrative reflection, if the 'authentic' object – the artefact/weapon itself – was not in the exhibition room?

The juxtaposition of artworks highlighted aspects of nudity for Tupi and Tarairiu Indian women; historical painted images of these women, presented together with the phallic form of a contemporary sculpture, suggested a link between sexuality and violence, as Herkenhoff has since explained:

> *One woman is dressed. On her head, she carries produce she has gathered and her finely crafted basket is a sign of material culture. Her dress defines a morality while the child at her breast shows that nudity is motherhood. The other woman carries a basket of human body parts and her nudity indicates a sexual availability, a certain amorality; there is a dog instead of a child beside her and the Indians seen between her legs are going to war. Neither demeaning nor usurping the place of the Indian, it enabled correlation and indirectly evoked the cultural relativity noted by Michel de Montaigne's comparison of cannibalism in Brazil to torture perpetrated by European armies.*[37]

Equally important for the curators was the fact that they would expose acts of pillage without 'benefitting' from them: 'The contamination of the contemporary by the historical, or vice versa, allows us to act in another way. For this Bienal – where the anthropological and historical questions were so fundamental for the present time – we never wanted to (and in fact never did) exhibit ethnographic pieces that had been removed from a living culture.'[38]

This point brings to mind the looting of cultural heritages that characterised colonial 'civilising' processes and enriched museum holdings, and bears comparison to more recent exhibition initiatives as diverse as 'Brazil: Body

—

[37] P. Herkenhoff, unpublished transcript of seminar at Faculdade Santa Marcelina, 12 March 2008; a summary of his presentation and the subsequent discussion was published in *marcelina* as 'Bienal 1998: princípios e processos', *op. cit.* This style of interpreting works prevailed during training tours that Herkenhoff led with art educators.

[38] P. Herkenhoff and A. Pedrosa, 'The Brazilian Curator Private / The Carioca Curator', *op. cit.*

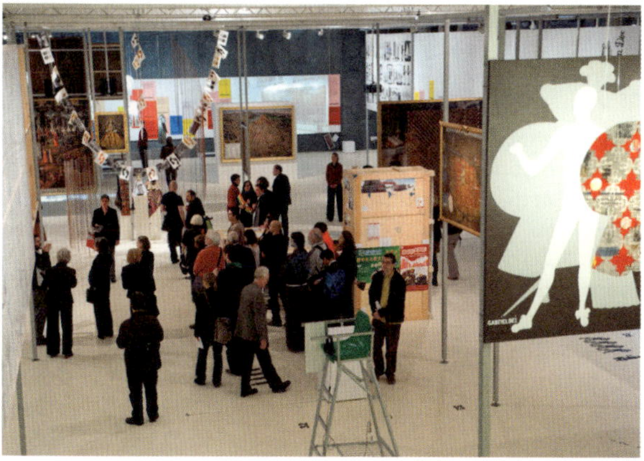

Installation view, 'Princípio Potosí' ('The Potosí Principle'), Haus der Kulturen der Welt, Berlin, 2010. Photography: Sebastian Bolesch/HKW

and Soul' (2001–02), coordinated by BrasilConnects for the Guggenheim museums in New York and Bilbao,[39] and 'Princípio Potosí' ('The Potosí Principle', 2010–11), curated by Alice Creischer, Max Jorge Hinderer Cruz and Andreas Siekmann for the Museo Nacional Centro de Arte Reina Sofía (MNCARS) in Madrid, Haus der Kulturen der Welt in Berlin, and the Museo Nacional de Etnografía y Folklore (MUSEF) and Museo Nacional de Arte (MNA) in La Paz.[40] Irrespective of their differing ideological approaches, both these later exhibitions raised ethical issues relating to the circulation of their products and icons. In the case of 'Brazil: Body and Soul', it could actually be argued that shipping an altar from the Basílica de São Bento de Olinda to New York replicated the historical process of colonial violence and command of the means of production. Thus, by showing Adriana Varejão's painting *Proposta para uma catequese* (*Proposal for a Catechism,* 1993) – a work which indicated colonialism as a form of (destructive) cannibalism and utilised the forms of religious painting without importing actual historical artefacts – and Tunga's *TaCaPe,* Herkenhoff was deftly avoiding controversial issues over cultural property.

fig.56

fig.54

As well as recasting cultural histories in a Brazilian mould, the 'Núcleo Histórico' sought to complicate notions of 'Brazilian-ness'.[41] Exemplary in

—

[39] 'Brazil: Body and Soul', Solomon R. Guggenheim Museum, New York, 12 October 2001 to 27 January 2002, and Guggenheim Museum Bilbao, 24 March to 27 September 2002. The curatorial design was articulated between Guggenheim staff members, headed by Thomas Krens and curators Lisa Dennison and Germano Celant, and the Brazilians Nelson Aguilar, Emanoel Araújo and Mari Marino; Edward J. Sullivan led the curatorial team.

[40] 'Princípio Potosí', MNCARS, Madrid, 12 May to 6 September 2010; HKW Berlin, 7 October 2010 to 2 January 2011; MUSEF and MNA, La Paz, 22 February to 30 April 2011.

[41] The 24th Bienal was accompanied by a film programme on issues of identity, and not just relating to Brazilian identity, curated by Catherine David. Some films

fig.49–51 this regard was the subsection titled 'A Cor no Modernismo Brasileiro' ('Colour in Brazilian Modernism'), which showed contradictions within the national culture, using examples from Anita Malfatti, Vicente do Rêgo Monteiro, Oswaldo Goeldi, Lasar Segall, Flávio de Carvalho, Di Cavalcanti and Alberto da Veiga Guignard. This might sound like an academic approach that prioritised a formalistic interpretation, but it raised pigment to the status of a national project (much as skin pigmentation refers to Brazil's ethnic miscegenation) and made an important connection to the work of Brazilian
fig.83–98 artists elsewhere in the 'Núcleo Histórico', notably Tarsila, Volpi, Oiticica and Meireles (the latter reassembled his *Desvio para o vermelho* (*Red Shift*, 1967–84)). This was part of another strategic calculation: knowing that the symbolism of colour was so dear to German Romanticism,[42] the curators posed the question of whether Brazilian modernism would be able to free itself from a tropical vision. Herkenhoff explained in the accompanying publication: 'We'd like to stress that if for Hegel the jungle was a space outside of history, for Brazilian artists it was the only way to stress an autochthonous history, prior to colonisation, in their modern political project of cultural emancipation.'[43]

Concerning Tarsila's work, Herkenhoff highlighted the local colour of its rustic, wild, earthy, melancholy, silent and strident expressions; in Volpi's, the chromatic significance of the vernacular. There was consistency, but no commitment to uniformity. Forces were joined to discuss the idea of 'a single colour system' in Brazilian art production. Far from being conventional or equally laudatory for all, this reflection enabled Herkenhoff to follow these artists in their constant shuttling back and forth between European and Brazilian geographies and influences.[44] The force of this curatorial proposal was especially sharp in Herkenhoff's placement of Goeldi's woodcuts on an equal footing with European paintings: 'In spite of his affinities with

—

were ethnographic classics that dealt directly with cannibalism, others concerned more distant and yet related subjects such as terrorism and apartheid. The exhibition installation designed by Paulo Mendes da Rocha had video monitors on which footage articulated 'attunements' or 'counterpoints' with works on the building's middle floor.

[42] The German heritage in Brazilian culture was problematised in an ironic line from musician-writer Caetano Veloso's song 'Língua' on his album *Velô* (1984): 'What does this language want / What can it do? If you have an incredible idea you better write a song / It is well known that you can only philosophise in German.' The writer Antônio Cícero notes the disguised presence of Heidegger in another line from the song – 'Gosto de ser e de estar' – as a 'poetic-philosophical privilege not shared by the German language'. Herkenhoff's commentary adds Hegel and Kant to this list. See A. Cícero, 'A filosofia e a língua alemã', *Folha de S. Paulo*, 'Ilustrada' section, 5 May 2007, available at http://www1.folha.uol.com.br/fsp/ilustrad/fq0505200726.htm (last accessed on 4 March 2015).

[43] P. Herkenhoff, 'A cor no modernismo brasileiro – a navegação com muitas bússolas' / 'Color in Brazilian modernism – navigating with many compasses' (trans. Odile Cisneros), in *XXIV Bienal de São Paulo. Núcleo Histórico: Antropofagia e Histórias de Canibalismos, op. cit.*, p.348. Translation revised for this volume.

[44] Tarsila travelled extensively in Europe and Russia and settled in São Paulo late in life; Volpi was born in Italy but spent most of his life in São Paulo.

German expressionism, Goeldi could never be mistaken for a European artist. Neither [Edvard] Munch nor any [...] German expressionist ever developed a method of colour construction that could compare to his.'[45]

Within this phenomenological problematisation of colour, and taking light as an inherent condition, curator Luis Pérez-Oramas presented a set of around twenty near-white landscapes by the Venezuelan painter Armando Reverón. Produced between 1925 and 1942, these oil paintings on canvas would subsequently impress a certain number of São Paulo painters in the latter half of the century who were still clinging to the Greenbergian model.[46] Local critics and artists showed their enthusiasm for the brushwork in these paintings, but were not lured by the adventure of undermining the notion of formalist 'influence'. Yet they showed interest in creating nuances within the model of modernity, with equatorial America posing its own issues for historical revisionism, just as Andrade's 'Manifesto' had put in question the centre-periphery interrelation ('Without us Europe would not even have its poor declaration of the rights of man') and claims to precedence ('We already had communism. We already had the surrealist language. The golden age.').[47] Seen in this light, did Reverón's paintings point to a belated (almost anachronistic) impressionism, since he had, in Herkenhoff's words, 'come back from Paris to live in the jungle'? Or did these paintings augur the monochromatic journey that would nourish generations of minimalists and post-minimalists? fig.64

Adjacent to the Reverón display was 'Monocromos' – a section entirely devoted to monochromatic works – which prompted the curatorial team to take another leap in their historicising trajectory. Extrapolating from the internationalism that had been part of the Bienal since its inception in 1951, Herkenhoff would later suggest that 'art history no longer has an absolute centre';[48] at the 24th Bienal, the 'Monocromos' prompted him to spell out a curatorial policy for working with this 'de-centred world', requiring a robust sense of context even when presenting works bereft of representation: fig.64–68

> *There was the political intention of making history by giving people the very finest of Brazilian art, as Oswald de Andrade had suggested.* [...] *taking anthropophagy as a negotiating process on the one hand, and a strategy for autonomous production on the other. Thus the white monochromes were*

—

[45] P. Herkenhoff, 'A cor no modernismo brasileiro – a navegação com muitas bússolas' / 'Color in Brazilian modernism – navigating with many compasses', *op. cit.*, p.352.

[46] The best known example would be Paulo Pasta, an artist whose trajectory paralled the 1980s 'return to painting' and who avowed his debt to Reverón's work in his own attempts to 'paint the light'. See Sylvia R. Fernandes, 'À luz da criação: Sublimação e processo criativo', *Percurso*, no.44, June 2010, available at http://revistapercurso.uol.com.br/index.php?apg=artigo_view&ida=100&id_tema=56 (last accessed on 4 March 2015).

[47] O. Andrade, 'Manifesto antropófago', *op. cit.*, p.537.

[48] P. Herkenhoff, 'Introdução geral' / 'General Introduction', *op. cit.*, p.40.

seen as this stage of autonomy based on a de-centred matrix. Malevich was an eccentric working in Russia during the Soviet period under the initial revolutionary impulse. For me, this is producing history – history in the sense of developing a discourse on a social process.[49]

Although aware of misgivings about the applicability of the 'Manifesto' in this context, Herkenhoff did not retreat – even faced with the reluctance of his associate curator. Pedrosa argued that the 'Monocromos' section was 'a very fine exhibition, but also the Achilles heel' of the 'Núcleo Histórico', fig.64 that 'despite its keen beauty and its articulating force (with Reverón and fig.65 Oiticica)', this section had only a 'tenuous connection' with anthropophagy and histories of cannibalism.[50]

The resonances of the 'Manifesto' become stronger on revisiting Freud's *Totem and Taboo*, which condenses the history of civilisation and its transition from natural state to society, from nature to culture, in connection to the prohibition of incest (a process of internalisation). To substantiate Andrade's call for 'the permanent transformation of taboo into totem',[51] fig.58-61 Régis Michel, curator of 'Século XIX', the nineteenth-century art section, unveiled a selection of works notable for their ferocity: while conjoining the Enlightenment crisis with cannibalism, Michel ushered in a crowd of monsters and executioners. He also encouraged the breakdown of the Law of the Father (the Eucharistic rite) and the way in which this Father's defeat led to chronological inversions. Thus, Michel was presenting a Goya that had read Freud, a Rodin who was unknowingly a 'manifest expert in the fig.58 theatre of *drives*'.[52] His three-step 'Modo de usar' ('User's Guide'), which provided the titles for the three sections of 'Século XIX', was used as wall text: '1. Taboo: the father eats the son'; '2. Transgression: the sons eat the father'; '3. Totem: society eats its children.'[53] As Herkenhoff explained:

—

[49] P. Herkenhoff, unpublished transcript of seminar at Faculdade Santa Marcelina, 12 March 2008, *op. cit.*

[50] Letter from A. Pedrosa to P. Herkenhoff, 5 March 1998, Arquivo Histórico Wanda Svevo / Fundação Bienal de São Paulo. In Pedrosa's view, commissioning a text for each artist in the 'Monocromos' section, based on the notion of the biennial as a group show, would amount to excessive emphasis on individual artists. He also argued for the inclusion of a Felix Gonzalez-Torres drawing and Derek Jarman's film *Blue* (1993) to impart 'latent and urgent content – body, disease' to a historical room.

[51] O. Andrade, 'Manifesto antropófago', *op. cit.*, p.537.

[52] Régis Michel, 'A síndrome de Saturno ou a Lei do Pai: máquinas canibais da modernidade' / 'The Saturn syndrome or the Law of the Father: cannibal machines of modernity', in *XXIV Bienal de São Paulo: Núcleo Histórico: Antropofagia e Histórias de Canibalismos, op. cit.*, p.138. Translation revised for this volume. The last sentences of the essay read: 'Neither totem nor taboo. The desire (of the other) always ends up by exceeding the law (of the father). Thus – at last – breaks the chain of *metaphors*: the desire alone is cannibal…' (p.133). Notable terms elsewhere in the essay include: 'schizophrenic machine', 'phallic woman', 'body without organs'.

[53] See *ibid.*, pp.120–47. For his analysis of cannibalism, Michel referenced Moreau, Géricault, Goya, Munch, Rodin, William Blake, Jean-Baptiste Carpeaux,

[The curatorial design] *for this room is focused around the gathering of mythological cannibalism (Gustave Moreau), eventual cannibalism among Europeans (Géricault) and cannibalism by the other. If real cannibalism in America no longer caused the same impact, nonetheless Goya represents it among the Iroquois. Régis Michel guides the display toward the issues of totem and taboo, the transgression and devourment of the sons by their fathers and vice versa. He expands the spectrum to include Desprez, Füssli, Blake or Munch. His analysis indicates the origining of the sources of Freud's psychoanalytic theory. European art readopts Dante's literature with the figure of Ugolino, the father who devours his children. Inscribed by Rodin on the Door of Hell* [*La Porte de l'Enfer*, 1880–1917)], *the theme was explored by artists such as Carpeaux and Géricault.*[54]

Wall texts in Michel's section reflected upon practices relating to patricide and totemic meals, presenting them as key to realising the notion of otherness. However, by this point in the visitor's itinerary, references to Andrade's original text were moving in several opposing directions; for example, in contrast to Michel's approach there was Pedrosa's exploration of anthropophagy as amorous fusion in his subsection of 'Arte Contemporânea Brasileira' titled 'Um e Outro'. As Pedrosa explains in the catalogue, this reading of anthropophagy was 'psychoanalytic and subjective', focused on sexuality and the desire of lovers to fuse with or ingest one another, 'articulated with the double, symmetry, the mirror, the body in pieces and the pieces of the body, flesh, skin, the scar, birth, invagination, shelter, the ship, the surroundings.'[55] Still, let us bear in mind that in cannibalism there is no consensus between parties.

fig.20–26

Under the sign of 'Manifesto antropófago', a multiplicity of body-related issues spread across the entire exhibition. A key example was the extensive presentation of paintings by Francis Bacon at the physical centre of the 'Núcleo Histórico'. In Herkenhoff's words, Bacon synthesised 'painting of the human condition', and Dawn Ades, who curated this section, avoided the terms 'quotation' and 'appropriation' in referring to the repertoire of reworked images, revealing an explicit effort to incorporate his work within the 'Brazilian' register: 'Many crucial aspects of Bacon's painting can be related to [the theme of anthropophagy]: the physical fact of the human body, the reality of the flesh and the violence of sensation, which he continually reworks through paint; fragmentation of the body, the fusion of bodies in desire, their tension in the extremity of sensations, bodies revealed through X-ray and stripped for sacrifice (as in the *Oresteia* triptych [1981]).'[56]

fig.58, 62 and 73–74

—

Louis-Jean Desprez and Johann Heinrich Fuseli.

[54] P. Herkenhoff, 'Introdução geral' / 'General introduction', *op. cit.*, p.41.

[55] A. Pedrosa, 'Um e Outro' / 'One and Other', in *XXIV Bienal de São Paulo: Arte Contemporânea Brasileira: Um e/entre Outro/s* (exh. cat.), São Paulo: Fundação Bienal, 1998, p.100.

[56] Dawn Ades, 'Francis Bacon: As fronteiras do corpo' / 'Boundaries of the body' (trans. Claudio Frederico da Silva Ramos), in *XXIV Bienal de São Paulo: Núcleo Histórico: Antropofagia e Histórias de Canibalismos*, *op. cit.*, p.416.

fig.40, 46–48, p.131 and p.156

A selection of works by Maria Martins, Lygia Clark and Louise Bourgeois were shown on the same floor of the Matarazzo Pavilion, at the entrance to the air-conditioned section of the 'Núcleo Histórico'; the works were all charged with violence (in this case, the violence of cannibalistic voracity), from Martins's *O Impossível* (*Impossible*, 1945) to Bourgeois's *The Destruction of the Father* (1974), which relates to family gatherings at the dining table. The presentation of Clark's works was essential to actualise the psychoanalytic dimension of the 'Manifesto', particularly her proposition of 'anthropophagic drool' in *Baba antropofágica* (*Anthropophagic drool*, 1973). Into this scenario, in which the mouth and orality exerted full power over the visitor's experience, Herkenhoff was able to add, nearby, Bruce Nauman's *Anthro/Socio* (1992), with its refrain 'feed me ... eat me ... anthropology'.[57]

In short, arguing for the historical core as the high point of the 24th Bienal requires endorsing anthropophagy as strategy, theory and cultural critique – indeed as a philosophical system for life, or, as Viveiros de Castro would put it, a *cosmovisão* (worldview).[58]

The attempt to turn a concept into a critical operation can be seen in another exhibition more or less contemporaneous with the 24th Bienal. In 1996, Yve-Alain Bois and Rosalind Krauss employed a notion from Bataille to organise 'L'Informe: mode d'emploi' ('Formless: A User's Guide') at the Centre Georges Pompidou in Paris, thus broadening their understanding of modernist art practices.[59] The rotating signs at the 24th Bienal and 'L'Informe' belong to the same historical period and evince converging interests: 'Manifesto antropófago' was issued in 1928 and 'L'Informe' appeared in 1929 (as part of the 'critical dictionary' that Bataille published in the journal *Documents*, which he ran between 1929 and 1930). As it transpired, the re-fertilising of these sources would provide narrative solutions to formalist interpretations of modernism.[60] The two muses, Andrade and Bataille, shared other concerns, including political engagement with unorthodox Marxism and a taste for art permeated by ethnology and psychoanalysis.

—

[57] 'Nauman explores the real human condition, from sex to our permanent need to manifest ourselves. [...] His installation *Anthro/Socio* indicates that this Bienal introduces five "ethnographies": Jean de Léry, whose book Lévi-Strauss denominated "ethnography breviary", the "Manifesto antropófago", Siqueiros's "Ethnography" and the figure of Lévi-Strauss, among others. "Help-me/Hurt-me, Sociology. Feed-me/Eat-me, Anthropology" cries out once in the void.' P. Herkenhoff, 'Introdução geral' / 'General introduction', *op. cit.*, p.47.

[58] For Eduardo Viveiros de Castro, anthropology must be made into an ongoing exercise of decolonisation of thought. See his *Métaphysiques cannibales: Lignes d'anthropologie post-structurale*, Paris: Presses Universitaires de France, 2009.

[59] 'L'Informe: mode d'emploi', Centre Georges Pompidou, Paris, 22 May to 26 August 1996.

[60] Yve-Alain Bois, 'The Use Value of "Formless"', in Y.-A. Bois and Rosalind Krauss (ed.), *Formless: A User's Guide*, Cambridge, MA: The MIT Press, 1997, p.13. Krauss's text 'The Destiny of the *Informe*' mentions that this presentation was scheduled while another institution was preparing a similar show, 'From Formless to Abject', which was subsequently cancelled (*ibid.*, p.235).

In these two exhibitions, the curatorial approach took certain terminological precautions. Both exhibitions eschewed thematisation in order to safeguard against literal or poor metaphors. In 'L'Informe', a particular aim was to stand against the fetishisation of the abject that was in vogue in the US at the time. In addition to a system of 'porous classification' to replace aesthetic categories, Bois invoked 'ease in relation to style' as well as to chronology.[61] Similar characteristics governed the 'Núcleo Histórico', not to mention that 'a user's guide' – the subtitle for 'L'Informe' – also appeared in the wall text in Michel's 'Século XIX' room – perhaps coincidentally, or merely anticipating fig.58–61 a difficult reception (the expression had already gained literary recognition in Georges Perec's 1978 novel *La Vie mode d'emploi* (*Life: A User's Manual*)). Nevertheless, it is interesting to note the heterology of formlessness and anthropophagy with regard to life – as well as the parallel importation of these concepts, from avant-garde histories, to be used as critical tools for exhibition-making. (Although similarities with the work of the editors of *October* end here.)

During the process of reflection prior to his appointment, Herkenhoff considered and ruled out some other possible concepts as themes, such as 'baroque', 'Neoconcrete' and 'unruly counterculture', before arriving at anthropophagy and Andrade's 'Manifesto'. At the time it was often argued that curators, particularly those from the southern hemisphere, were using the term 'anthropophagy' to designate the recycling of European languages; however, in such readings the term was never given the multiplicity of meanings that Herkenhoff sought to impart. The open and collective approach to curatorial design led to dozens of interlocutors being asked to update the modernist manifesto, and a list of 165 definitions was produced for the catalogue.[62] This list – deliberately open-ended, as stated in the catalogue – produced a polysemy of concepts and took anthropophagy in countless contradictory directions.

Had the scope of anthropophagy perhaps prompted excessive use of metaphors and slipped toward an entropic loss of meaning? An inevitable question arises from the speculative exercise that launched anthropophagy toward multiple meanings beyond those Andrade had anticipated: how might polyphony and dilution be combined? While polyphony brought some less-than-persuasive resonances for the 'Manifesto' (such as 'evil eye' or 'connectivity'),[63] some curatorial proposals for the exhibition were, in fact, rejected for the sake of precision and rigour. Among several such cases,

—

[61] See Y.-A. Bois, 'The Use Value of "Formless"', *op. cit.*, pp.16–21. Bois also uses a very interesting expression to qualify their curatorial methodology based on Bataille: 'taxinomie volatile'.

[62] See '165, entre 1000, formas de antropofagia e canibalismo (um pequeno exercício crítico, interpretativo, poético e especulativo)' / '165, among 1000, forms of *antropofagia* and cannibalism (a small, critical, interpretative, poetic, and speculative exercise)', in *XXIV Bienal de São Paulo: Núcleo Histórico: Antropofagia e Histórias de Canibalismos, op. cit.*, inside covers.

[63] To quote just two of the 165 selections in *ibid.*

Herkenhoff's letter to Alanna Heiss, the executive director of P.S.1 in Queens, New York, rejecting the project 'Flaming Creature: The Art and Times of Jack Smith', curated by Edward Leffingwell, deserves special mention: 'We are dealing with very specific issues here at the 24th Biennial concerning *antropofagia*, and the presence of the artists selected is extremely punctual and has been thought out in a tightly articulated way.'[64] As previously noted, this 'tight articulation' was not necessarily evident to visitors of the Bienal. The curatorial approach was a 'process of temporarily projecting senses and meanings on the work, its contextualisation. One of the projection modes would be *defamiliarisation*', in Herkenhoff's description. 'Curatorial practice therefore involves submitting an artwork to a *hermeneutic hypothesis* that is at the same time problematising.'[65] This would be one of the basic distinctions between anthropophagy as concept and as theme: working in a thematic way would imply a narrower selection of works, those easily identifiable with reference to anthropophagy, in a straightforward correspondence between the 'theme' of the exhibition and its manifest content. Herkenhoff argued that curatorial designs should not denote any kind of convenience, otherwise they might lead to works' instrumentalisation (as mere illustrations of anthropophagy, for example); instead, he emphasised that the curator's and visitor's 'criterion of truth' must be in the eye alone, following Jean-François Lyotard: 'Reading is hearing [understanding], not seeing.'[66] Employing anthropophagy as a concept required that the visual character of the exhibition should supervene on any secondary conceptualisations or thematisations. Or, in the words of André Breton, there was a need to invest in the eye in its wild state ('l'oeil à l'état sauvage') [67] as a way of invoking the plasticity of a desire that the tongue, or language, never attains.

An important guiding principle for the Bienal's curatorial team was 'the thickness of the gaze', a notion derived from Lyotard's account of *épaisseur*, of thickness or density,[68] to designate a quality more than a concept; in Lyotard's *Discourse, Figure*, the term is used in relation to features of the world neither linguistic nor discursive but nonetheless meaningful, conveying what he describes at one point as 'silent meaning'.[69] *Discourse, Figure*

—

[64] Letter from P. Herkenhoff to Alanna Heiss, date unknown, Arquivo Histórico Wanda Svevo / Fundação Bienal de São Paulo.

[65] P. Herkenhoff, unpublished transcript of seminar at Faculdade Santa Marcelina, 12 March 2008, *op. cit.* Exemplary cases of 'defamiliarisation' were spread around the exhibition layout, thus boosting its 'contamination' strategy. It was a 'dialogic gesture, like placing an impressive piece by a Brazilian artist in the room of a European or US artist'; this gesture 'has the function of showing historicity, such as Lygia Clark and Mira Schendel facing Eva Hesse and Louise Bourgeois, brought together in the same venue, for the first time.' *Ibid.*, p.36.

[66] Jean-François Lyotard, *Discourse, Figure* (1971, trans. Antony Hudek), Minneapolis: University of Minnesota Press, 2011, p.211.

[67] Noting that vision precedes language, André Breton's *Surrealism and Painting* (1928) begins: 'The eye exists in its savage state.' See A. Breton, *Surrealism and Painting*, Boston: Museum of Fine Arts Boston Publications, 2002, p.1.

[68] P. Herkenhoff, 'Introdução geral' / 'General introduction', *op. cit.*, p.35.

[69] J.-F. Lyotard, *Discourse, Figure, op. cit.*, p.103.

influenced Herkenhoff in developing the Bienal's educational programme and in particular its emphasis on visual engagement and the artistic experience of images. Herkenhoff and the Bienal team also adopted Lyotard's *épaisseur* in an expanded sense, to evoke an accumulation of meaning – historical, cultural, visual, iconographic – explaining that they were pursuing a 'dense' period in the history of art in Brazil to build their programme, and that anthropophagy represented this 'occurrence of extreme density'.[70]

In 1998, a turn towards Lyotard risked appearing anachronistic. Establishing a transversal dialogue between Andrade's anthropophagic devouring and Lyotard's philosophical writings – for instance, his well-known *The Postmodern Condition: A Report on Knowledge* (1979) – meant returning to the quarrel between moderns and postmoderns, between supporters of a desirable but incomplete Enlightenment project and the proponents of 'postmodernism', in both its philosophical and more popularised forms. Hence, adopting Lyotard implicitly raised questions around a 'new subjectivity' expressed in art and architecture (especially by the eclectic or hybrid style that led to the cynicism of 'citationism') as well as in 1980s appropriationism, the 'return to painting' of the Italian Transvanguardia artists and German Neo-Expressionism, as represented at the 1985 Bienal curated by Sheila Leirner. Why, then, embrace the French author mercilessly criticised in the philosophical battle waged by Jürgen Habermas in *The Philosophical Discourse of Modernity: Twelve Lectures* (1985)?[71] What place would there be for Lyotard at a Bienal reaffirming its Brazilian national identity?

Yet Lyotard's vision of postmodernism – in its critique of the 'grand narratives' of European modernity such as those given by Hegel and Kant, for example – can also be read as a manifestation of the crisis of the Eurocentric perspective. Let us return to the 'Manifesto' of 1928, wherein Andrade posed an idea that was more complex than the forms of hybridity or acculturation discussed by postmodernists. And let us return to a work in the 'Núcleo Histórico' that amplifies this idea: Tarsila's painting *A Negra* fig.83
(*The Negress*, 1923). This classic example of the Brazilian ingestion of codes learned from the Europeans Fernand Léger, André Lhote and Albert Gleizes shows a flair for synthesis – the body's metabolic and psychic processes for working through issues – as translated by Andrade: 'I am interested only in what is not mine. Law of man. Law of the anthropophagite.'[72]

—

[70] See *XXIV Bienal de São Paulo: Núcleo Histórico: Antropofagia e Histórias de Canibalismos*, *op. cit.*, inside cover. Herkenhoff would later reflect that 'the Bienal would be examining an issue related to Brazilian art that awaited historical reflection and an assessment of its impact on contemporary culture.' P. Herkenhoff, 'Bienal 1998: princípios e processos', *op. cit.*, p.27.
[71] The attempt to reconstruct the philosophical discourse of modernity was made after Lyotard's *La Condition postmoderne* and the reception of French neo-structuralism in Germany. In addition to Hegel's concept of modernity, the Habermas lectures examine the views of Nietzsche, Horkheimer and Adorno, Heidegger, Derrida, Bataille and Foucault.
[72] O. Andrade, 'Manifesto antropófago', *op. cit.*, p.536.

More than rejecting Eurocentrism, the 'Manifesto' condemns both ethnocentrism and logocentrism. As curator of the 24th Bienal, Herkenhoff was not pursuing philosophical or anthropological recognition, but taking up a position '*vis-à-vis* the discipline of art history'.[73] *Thickness* and *density* are assessed by the eye, and not by reading, a proposition which resounded in
pp.114–73 the visual stimulus provided by the teeming imagery of the 'Núcleo Histórico'. From this perspective, we may say that the curator's strategy worked, for the memory of the 24th Bienal remains tied to one single component of the show as a whole: to quote Andrade, it is the 'proof of the pudding' of its legacy.[74]

2. Latin American and Brazilian Narratives in the Bienal de São Paulo and Exhibitions Beyond

The Bienal de São Paulo was conceived to foster artistic contacts between countries, taking into account a global economic system polarised between so-called developed nations and those described as underdeveloped or developing. Although its organisers did not say so explicitly, the first Bienal in 1951 showed an understanding of the relationship between modernity and industrial modernisation and therefore sought to be receptive to US capital. In the face of ideological conflict pitting the rival models of capitalism and state socialism against each other, São Paulo's economic vigour showed that the city had the potential to play a strategic role (with its witch-hunting campaigns to spot communist agents 'infiltrating' the cultural world). Both the structure of national delegations and the internationalist approach, as present in the origins of the Bienal de São Paulo, reflected the foreign policy of a country with an eye on association with Europe and the United States.

Brazil's drive towards internationalisation was already discernible in the foreign policy of Getúlio Vargas's first presidential administration (1930–45), and became still more so in his second term of office (from 1951–54), which coincided with the inauguration of the Bienal. The Tenth Inter-American Conference, in 1954, led to a sharpening of discords between Brazil and its neighbouring countries. Guatemala's elected government was about to initiate a new social process by expropriating some 255,000 acres owned by the United Fruit Company, a US-based multinational company in operation from 1899 to 1970 and the largest planter of tropical fruit for export in Colombia, Costa Rica, Jamaica, Nicaragua and Panama, among other countries. The Guatemalan measure sought to divide the bigger land holdings. However, Brazil had signed a military aid agreement with the US in 1952; bound to Washington by this, the Inter-American Treaty of Reciprocal Assistance, and other international agreements that obliged the country to 'act jointly in the common defense and maintenance of peace and security of the Western Hemisphere',[75] Brazil additionally ratified the

—

[73] P. Herkenhoff, 'Introdução geral' / 'General introduction', *op. cit.*, p.35.
[74] O. Andrade, 'Manifesto antropófago', *op. cit.*, p.536.

Caracas Declaration of 1954 and rejected changes underway in Guatemala on the grounds of their instigating land reform and leading the country towards communism. A few months later, the CIA orchestrated the overthrow of the Guatemalan government in support of the brazenly pro-US administration of Carlos Castillo Armas.[76]

Problematic international relations have played a role well beyond the first three editions of the Bienal, and indeed throughout its history. Episodes like this prompted much-needed political reassessment of the underlying logic of countries sending delegations to São Paulo biennials, which persisted until the 27th event, in 2006.[77] While some nations acted in an amateurish manner, sending friends or family members as representatives, others placed delegations at the service of foreign policy. The symbolic role assigned to Latin American countries as part of an ambitious plan to hold a regular art exhibition in São Paulo along the lines of the Venice Biennale is a history that deserves further investigation. From its earliest years, the mission of the Bienal de São Paulo, particularly in light of the political and economic interests of Ciccillo Matarazzo, resembled that of the Expositions Universelles, in terms of pursuing industrial and developmental aims. Indeed, certain clauses in official cooperation agreements between participating countries throw into relief the stated aim that the Bienal constitute a 'permanent body for artistic and cultural exchange between the continents'.[78]

—

[75] 'Military Assistance Agreement Between the United States of America and the Republic of the United States of Brazil, 15 March 1952', in *United States Treaties and Other International Agreements*, vol.4, part 1, Washington DC: US Government Printing Office, 1955, pp.170–83, Portuguese version available at http://www.cnen.gov.br/Doc/pdf/Tratados/ACOR0021.pdf (last accessed on 4 March 2015).

[76] I am indebted to the collection of research articles on Brazil during the second administration of Getúlio Vargas assembled by the Centro de Pesquisa e Documentação de História Contemporânea do Brasil (CPDOC) for this account. See http://cpdoc.fgv.br/producao/dossies/AEraVargas2/artigos (last accessed on 4 March 2015); see also 'Tenth Inter-American Conference', *The American Journal of International Law*, vol.48, no.3, Supplement: Official Documents (July 1954), pp.123–32, and 'Latin America and United States Military Assistance' (20 June 1960), available at http://www.dod.mil/pubs/foi/International_security_affairs/latinAmerica/613.pdf (last accessed on 4 March 2015).

[77] Prior to 2006, Venice had dictated the dates and the Bienal de São Paulo had been held alternately on even- and odd-number years. There was a financial side to the argument: the international agencies charged with fostering cultural development got their budgetary allocations in alternate years to fund the 'Western' world's 'only' two 'international' exhibitions based on delegations from the different countries. For the 2006 edition – directed by myself – the Bienal had requested, for the first time in its history, that an international board (Aracy Amaral, Manuel Borja-Villel, João Fernandes, Paulo Herkenhoff and Lynn Zelevansky) appoint the head curator. The cessation of national delegations happened in 2006 solely due to the fact that it was one of the premises of the curatorial project.

[78] *Bienal de São Paulo 50 anos, 1951–2001 / 50 years of the São Paulo Biennial, op. cit.*, p.264.

In the discourse of São Paulo's elite and leading post-War intellectuals, international cultural exchange was supported as a means of freeing the country from provincialism.[79] Their ambition was for a Brazil updated with established Western canons, as if these values were beyond scrutiny. Thus, instead of the explosive identity issues posed by the law of anthropophagy, the drive to be modern was oriented to the so-called universal values of civil society. Confined to the domain of the literary avant-garde, the programmatic content of Andrade's theses was neutralised. Seen as a mere flight of fancy coming from a writer, its power remained latent for nearly forty years, until the rise of Tropicalismo in the late 1960s, which made a claim for the rescue of anthropophagite consciousness.[80]

Nevertheless, Andrade had noted that Brazil's subjection dated back to its colonisation: 'Our independence has not yet been proclaimed.'[81] The Brazilian reality was a gradually maturing and necessarily controversial process because of its aspirations towards internationalisation. A summary by critic and curator Aracy Amaral identifies certain key actors and precursors in Parisian institutions such as the Maison de l'Amérique Latine, which was founded in 1923, and the Musée Galliéra, founded in 1924.[82] (Paris drew modernists who wanted both an artistic education and to engage with its avant-garde effervescence.)

The inaugural Bienal de São Paulo is remembered for contributions by Max Bill, including *Tripartite Unity* (1948–49), which won the sculpture prize, and Le Corbusier, who was awarded the international grand prize for

—

[79] For a summary of precursors for Brazilian cultural internationalism, see Aracy Amaral, 'Brasil: Commemorative Exhibitions – or, Notes on the Presence of Brazilian Modernists in International Exhibitions', paper given at the conference 'Grand Expositions: Iberian and Latin American Modernisms in the Museum', Yale University, New Haven, 26 to 27 October 2001, available at http://www.lehman.cuny.edu/ciberletras/v08/amaral.html (last accessed on 4 March 2015).

[80] This neo-anthrophagism arose in the creative process of a significant set of artists, such as musicians and composers Caetano Veloso and Gilberto Gil and dramatist José Celso Martinez. With Tropicalismo, the anthropophagic interplay between national roots and cultural importation was given new life, which saw the audacity and values of the 'Manifesto' amplified by the culture industry. Again, a conflict erupted, opposing the left-wing messages of the Brazilian intelligentsia and the mainstream acceptance of a movement without any real project or promise – worst of all, Tropicalismo declared that it endorsed mass media penetration. Celso Favaretto's important study *tropicália alegoria alegria* (1976) explains how elements such as 'the grotesque, erotic, obscene and ridiculous' fueled both cultural movements. See C. Favaretto, *tropicália alegoria alegria,* São Paulo: ateliê editorial, 1996, pp.48–49.

[81] O. Andrade, 'Manifesto antropófago', *op. cit.*, p.539.

[82] See A. Amaral, 'Brasil: Commemorative Exhibitions or: Notes on the presence of Brazilian Modernists in International Exhibitions', *op. cit.* This brief report also lists the anthological exhibition 'Art of Latin America since Independence' at Yale University Art Gallery, New Haven from 27 January to 13 March 1966, curated by Terence Grieder and Stanton Catlin; it travelled to University of Texas Art Museum, Austin, San Francisco Museum of Art, La Jolla Museum of Art, San Diego and Isaac Delgado Museum of Art, New Orleans.

architecture. The reception of works by these participants indicated that local artists identified with the geometric lines and constructivism of the Ulm School of Design as the successor to the Bauhaus, and with the architectural rationalism of modernist urban planning in Europe. The award to Le Corbusier consolidated the impact of his travels and lectures in Brazil in 1929 and 1936, and further endorsed his influence on the design of the Ministry of Education and Health Building (now renamed Palácio Gustavo Capanema) in downtown Rio de Janeiro. This building, viewed as an icon of modern architecture in Brazil, was designed in the 1930s by a team of young architects that included Oscar Niemeyer working under Lúcio Costa. Niemeyer would work with Costa again in the design and construction of the capital city of Brasília, commissioned by President Juscelino Kubitschek.[83]

Aracy Amaral has noted the significance of the first Bienal on the basis of the special room it dedicated to the thought and legacy of Uruguayan artist Joaquín Torres-García (1874–1949). Torres-García spent 43 years in Europe, with a brief stay in the US, before returning to his homeland to devise a utopian theory of 'constructive universalism' specifically designed for South America. According to Amaral:

> *Since that time, in Brazil, Concrete art and constructivism have signified an integration with the developed* [world], *an aspiration to identify with the most advanced industrialisation, and this implies a desire for self-affirmation in terms of identity by fiercely rejecting the troubled reality that has always shaped our socio-economic or cultural environment.* [...] *This line has invariably been followed since the 50s by a large part of so-called experimental art in the major centres such as Rio de Janeiro and São Paulo, in a conflict opposing conceptual and constructive artists on the one hand, and figurative and magical ones on the other.*[84]

Alexander Calder is another key figure in the development of abstract art in Brazil: he visited in 1948 and his work was a highlight of the second Bienal,[85] an event still remembered for having brought in Picasso's *Guernica.* Organised p.58
as part of São Paulo's fourth-centennial celebrations, the Bienal of 1953 was held in two pavilions in Ibirapuera Park, to which it drew no fewer than 717 foreign artists from 33 countries, including 189 from Brazil.

—

[83] Designed by urban planner Costa and architect Niemeyer, the new capital was inaugurated in 1960. Settling the central area of Brazil's vast territory had been a long-standing ambition since the colonial period.

[84] A. Amaral, 'Modernidade e identidade: as duas Américas Latinas ou três, fora do tempo', in Ana Maria Belluzzo (ed.), *Modernidade: vanguardas artísticas na América Latina*, São Paulo: Unesp, 1990, p.181.

[85] Calder visited Brazil in 1948, 1959 and 1960, and had a special room at the second Bienal de São Paulo in 1953. The critic Mário Pedrosa, who had been following Calder's output since 1948, wrote several pieces on his work, see for instance, M. Pedrosa, 'Calder and Brasília', *Jornal do Brasil*, Rio de Janeiro, 9 March 1960.

The characteristics of a Brazilian art practice that 'devoured' and metabolised foreign influences showed no signs of a collective articulation until the emergence of Concrete art in Brazil in the 1950s. In 1955, the third Bienal featured Concrete works by Milton Dacosta, Franz Weissmann and Ivan Serpa, whilst one particular room showcased prints by the Mexican muralists José Clemente Orozco, Diego Rivera, Rufino Tamayo and David Alfaro Siqueiros. Siqueiros was to return for the Anthropophagy Biennial, with a selection curated by Mari Carmen Ramírez. His 'political project for cultural emancipation', to quote Herkenhoff on the work of contemporaneous Brazilian artists,[86] may be related to the contradictions and irreverence to be found in Andrade's 'Manifesto'.

Meanwhile, far from these South American developments, the first documenta exhibition was being held in Kassel, Germany at the initiative of artist, curator and professor Arnold Bode, to rehabilitate the modernism of artists banned by the Nazi regime.[87] In 1959, documenta 2 drew on more recent art while still emphasising chronological and aesthetic continuity.[88] In the same year, *Jornal do Brasil*'s Sunday supplement published the 'Manifesto Neoconcreto' ('Neoconcrete Manifesto'), taking its stand against art being driven to 'a dangerously rationalist exacerbation'.[89]

In the US at this time, the CIA was using its influence to consolidate an international modern art movement, harnessing the reputation of a generation of US abstract painters for European consumption, particularly German.[90] During the 1940s, Nelson A. Rockefeller simultaneously held positions as president of the board of trustees for New York's MoMA and as head of the Office of the Coordinator of Inter-American Affairs (OCIAA), responsible for promoting the Good Neighbor Policy (US foreign policy towards Latin America at the time). An interest in Brazilian culture was evident in the 1943 MoMA exhibition 'Brazil Builds', which helped establish the international prestige of Brazilian modernist architecture.[91] Here it is worth reiterating

—

[86] P. Herkenhoff, 'A cor no modernismo brasileiro – a navegação com muitas bússolas' / 'Color in Brazilian modernism – navigating with many compasses', *op. cit.*, p.348.

[87] Documenta, curated by Arnold Bode, took place at the Museum Fridericianum, Kassel, 16 July to 18 September 1955.

[88] See essays by Roland Nachtigäller, Philipp Gutbrod and others in Michael Glasmeier and Karin Stengel (ed.), *50 Jahre / Years documenta: Archive in Motion*, Göttingen: Documenta, Museum Fridericianum Veranstaltungs GmbH and Steidl Verlag, 2005.

[89] Amílcar de Castro, Lygia Clark, Ferreira Gullar, Reynaldo Jardim, Lygia Pape, Theon Spanúdis and Franz Weissmann, 'Manifesto Neoconcreto', *Jornal do Brasil*, 23 March 1959. See A. Amaral (ed.), *Arte construtiva no Brasil: Coleção Adolpho Leirner / Constructive Art in Brazil: Adolpho Leirner Collection*, São Paulo: DBA, 1998, p.270.

[90] See Frances Stonor Saunders, *Who Paid the Piper? The CIA and the Cultural Cold War,* London: Granta Books, 2000.

[91] 'Brazil Builds', a project by Philip L. Goodwin with the collaboration of photographer and architect G.E. Kidder Smith and Alice Carson, took place at MoMA,

the ideological context of post-War international relations, and specifically Brazil's reputation for being a future trading ally of the United States, which had committed to integration with the southern continent, claiming to promote a modern style in order to consolidate the culture of the Western bloc. Based on an agenda of major exhibitions – MoMA also hosted 'Portinari of Brazil' in 1940 and 'Latin American Architecture since 1945' in 1955[92] – this discourse in favour of closer relations would actually pave the way for subsequent US hegemony.[93]

The 1960s took on a different hue. As a businessman, Ciccillo Matarazzo was at this time facing financial difficulties. Not wanting to lose the benefits of remaining in circles of international influence, he took the strategic decision to restructure the management system of the Bienal de São Paulo, maintaining his overall control but reorganising it as a foundation eligible for state and municipal funding.[94] In 1963, he put an end to the activities of the São Paulo Museu de Arte Moderna (MAM SP), the museum he had founded in 1948, gifting the holdings, as acquired through exhibition awards, and also his personal art collection, to the Universidade de São Paulo.[95] This episode points towards a problematic cultural lack of appreciation for tradition: sacrificing an institution responsible for what have been described as 'more permanent and profound' activities,[96] namely the MAM SP, and leaving its collection to an uncertain fate in order to focus energies on a temporary event to be held every two years.

But then the 1964 military coup plunged Brazil into a period of authoritarianism and changed its course. A mass rally held on 3 March 1963 at Central do Brasil, a large square in Rio de Janeiro, mobilised over 200,000

—

New York from 13 January to 28 February 1943. It ran in parallel with another show at MoMA with the same national focus: 'Faces and Places in Brazil: Photographs by Genevieve Naylor'. Naylor had been sent to Brazil in 1940 by Rockfeller's agency to provide photographs that would support its needs for propaganda.

[92] 'Portinari of Brazil' was held from 9 October to 17 November 1940 and 'Latin American Architecture since 1945', curated by Henry-Russell Hitchcock, from 23 November 1955 to 19 February 1956, both at MoMA, New York.

[93] See Patricio del Real, 'Building a Continent: The Idea of Latin American Architecture in the Early Postwar', unpublished doctoral thesis, New York: Columbia University, 2012. Contrary to established interpretations of these exhibitions as creating national narratives, del Real investigates the strategic role played by Nelson Rockefeller as he shaped a certain style to be imposed from outside.

[94] See '6ª Bienal de São Paulo', in *Bienal 50 anos, 1951–2001 / 50 years of the São Paulo Biennial*, *op. cit.*, p.112.

[95] There is extensive literature on Ciccillo Matarazzo's endowment of his personal collection to the USP, which used it to set up its Museu de Arte Contemporânea (MAC-USP) in 1963. See, for example, Annateresa Fabris, 'Um "fogo de palha aceso": considerações sobre o primeiro momento do Museu de Arte Moderna de São Paulo' / 'A "a flash in the pan that is really gold": considerations on the inception of the Museu de Arte Moderna de São Paulo', in *MAM 60* (exh. cat.), São Paulo: Museu de Arte Moderna de São Paulo, 2008.

[96] M. Pedrosa, 'Depoimento sobre o MAM', in Otília Arantes (ed.), *Política das artes*, São Paulo: Editora da Universidade de São Paulo, Textos Escolhidos I, 1995.

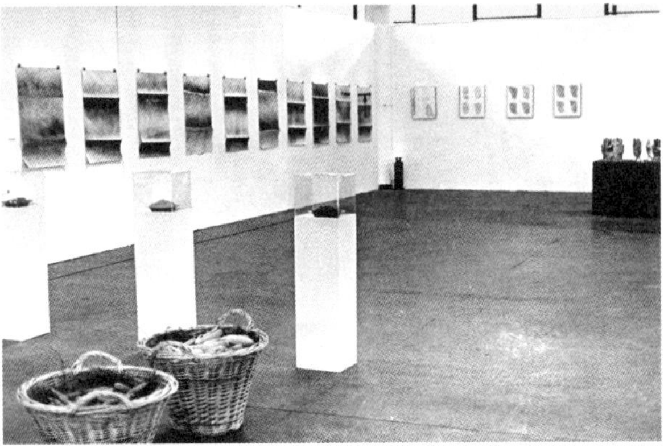

Installation view, 'Mitos e Magia' ('Myths and Magic'), I Bienal Latino-Americana de São Paulo, Pavilhão Engenheiro Armando Arruda Pereira, 1978, with work by Colorindo Testa and Jorge González Mir, Grupo de los Trece and Vicente Marotta
© the artists; Arquivo Histórico Wanda Svevo / Fundação Bienal São Paulo

people. At the rally, President João Goulart thanked the trade unions for turning out and advocated agrarian reform against private monopolies. The speech hastened his deposition and triggered a series of tragic events: on assuming power following the coup, Marshal Castelo Branco imposed censorship restrictions and suspended direct elections and existing political parties. In 1968, Congress was shut down and the military regime promulgated Institutional Act Number 5 (AI–5) to revoke political rights and persecute trade unions and universities. The tenth Bienal, in 1969, known as the 'boycott Bienal', was held at the same time as a new, political police force was organised; the government meanwhile prohibited a section of Brazilian artists at the sixth Paris Biennale that year. After that, the quality of the Bienal de São Paulo became uneven, showing both a lack of unity and a dependence on funding from Brazil's Ministry of Foreign Affairs to get delegations from abroad to attend.

Throughout the early period of the Bienal de São Paulo, the art of South America was given only minor status. Yet there were later moves by the Fundação Bienal to address this through cultivating a new forum:[97] in 1978 Aracy Amaral collaborated on the first Bienal Latino-Americana in São Paulo with Juan Acha, a Peruvian-born art theorist then based in Mexico, among others. Amaral was proposing a substitute to the idea of national

—

[97] As articulated in the exhibition catalogue for the first Bienal Latino-Americana of 1978: 'With the creation of Latin American biennial exhibitions, the Fundação Bienal de São Paulo aims to provide artists and intellectuals from Latin America with a meeting point and a chance to jointly research, discuss and, if possible, determine what may be called Latin American art.' *I Bienal Latino-Americana de São Paulo,* São Paulo: Fundação Bienal, 1978, p.19. The foundation's vice-president Oscar Landmann decisively influenced arrangements for this exhibition. See http://www.unicamp.br/chaa/eha/atas/2012/Gabriela%20Lodo.pdf (last accessed on 4 March 2015). Only one edition of the Bienal Latino-Americana happened, and while Ciccillo Matarazzo was still alive, titled 'Mitos e Magia' ('Myths and Magic'), at the Pavilhão Engenheiro Armando Arruda Pereira, 3 November to 17 December 1978.

biennials – such as the 1970 I Bienal Nacional São Paulo – whose purpose was to present a national selection for the next international event.[98] She later reflected:

> *We Latin Americans were there* [at the Bienal de São Paulo] *as 'hangers on', so to speak ... We were constantly looking at what was going on in Europe, and then in the United States, never seeing ourselves as possible points of departure or critical revision of* [art in] *the metropolis.* [...] *In the early 1970s,* [...] *the complaints we frequently heard in Latin America were to the effect that the Bienal de São Paulo was subserviently bound to European critics and unaware of Latin American art; it was betraying its vocation that ought to have been – due to its own location – disseminating and studying the art of countries in our continent, and projecting them internationally.*[99]

Amaral's project to establish a Latin American biennial in São Paulo, bringing together critics from the entire continent for ongoing meetings, ultimately failed. There would be no subsequent editions.

In the 1980s, after a decade in which the Bienal de São Paulo's international prestige dropped, Fundação Bienal President Luiz Diederichsen Villares engaged the assistance of historian Walter Zanini, since 1963 the first director of the Museu de Arte Contemporânea da Universidade de São Paulo (MAC USP). Zanini curated the sixteen and seventeenth editions of the Bienal, in p.38 1981 and 1983, and attempted to mitigate the policy of national delegations through the installation plan for the sixteenth edition. His strategy, which was met with local resistance, consisted of distributing works around the notion of 'language relations and analogies'[100] – in other words, on the basis of visual or conceptual affinity – instead of by nationality.

Those in the Brazilian artistic milieu were eager for their work to be appreciated regardless of narratives involving national or regional identities, which were thought to be based on misplaced premises. Exemplary in their minds was the curator Kynaston McShine's exhibition 'Information' (1970), for MoMA in New York, which provided an international overview of Conceptual art and included four Brazilian artists: Oiticica, Meireles, Barrio and Guilherme Vaz.[101] Its curatorial framework suited their need to be acknowledged beyond their homeland in a highly visible context; bypassing the absence of an established art circuit in Brazil, they could show experimental works. Establishing relations with Conceptual art and bolstering its attempt to set

—

[98] The I Bienal Nacional de São Paulo was also known as Pré-Bienal. Its last edition happened in 1976, before being substituted in 1978 by the I Bienal Latino-Americana.

[99] A. Amaral, *Arte e meio artístico: entre a feijoada e o x-burguer (1961–1981)*, São Paulo: Nobel, 1983, pp.297 and 299.

[100] W. Zanini, 'Introduction', in *Catálogo da 16ª Bienal de São Paulo* (exh. cat.), São Paulo: Fundação Bienal, 1981, p.21.

[101] 'Information', MoMA, New York, 2 July to 20 September 1970.

Installation view, 16th Bienal de São Paulo, Ciccillo Matarazzo Pavilion, 1981
© Agência Estado

Installation view, 17th Bienal de São Paulo, Ciccillo Matarazzo Pavilion, 1983, section on Fluxus International & Co.
© Arquivo Histórico Wanda Svevo / Fundação Bienal São Paulo

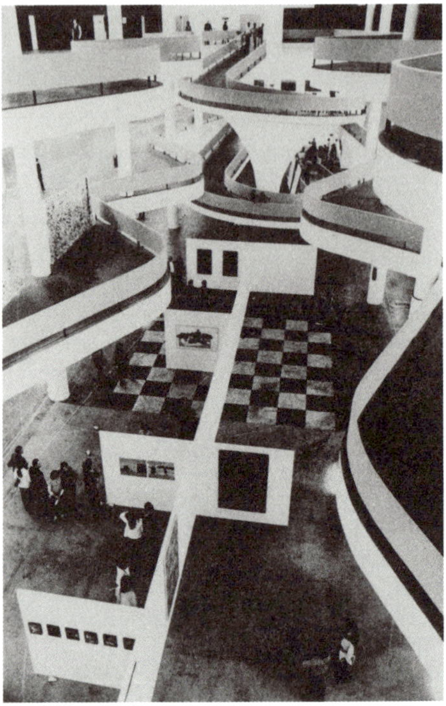

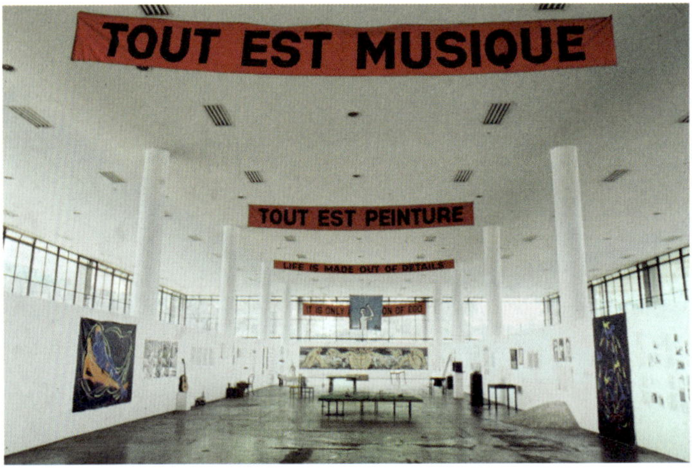

a world standard – a system and rationality anchored in the US – did not at first present problems of principle.[102] On the contrary, it made sense: the theoretical scope of Conceptualism legitimised a nobler vision than the 'national identity' claimed by the military regime since 1964.

Conceptual art's internationalism allowed for an apolitical and ambiguous diversity absent from the art of neighbouring countries such as Chile and Argentina. It neither attached importance to a specific context nor made concessions to the institutionalised and stigmatised Hispanic American ghetto in the US.[103] Its strictness – its objectivity, so to speak – authorised artistic production to disconnect from local idiosyncrasies. For the sake of a rigorous formal organisation, intellectuals and artists strained to get rid of ideological signifiers. They made claims for an intelligence which would later slide into formalist appreciation of the intrinsic issues raised by artistic practice. McShine's exhibition allowed Brazilian artists safe conduct to exhibit abroad freely, without risk of being manipulated by political interests from within Brazil. Both Oiticica and Meireles insisted on decoupling their participation from their nationality, as clearly expressed by the former in the exhibition catalogue for 'Information': 'I am not here representing Brazil; or representing anything else: the ideas of representing-representation-etc. are over.'[104]

The retrospective interpretations of this historical moment that have been developed by Latin American curators prove more concerned with the differing contexts of art's production. In particular, Mari Carmen Ramírez, as curator and director of the International Center for the Arts of the Americas at the Museum of Fine Arts in Houston, has advocated for the study of Conceptualism under Latin America's authoritarian regimes, leading to discussion of a 'political conceptualism.'[105]

It is notable how few artists attained international visibility during the 1970s and 80s, when military dictatorships prevailed on the South American continent. The English art critic Guy Brett, closely associated with Signals Gallery in London and with a background interest in kinetic art,

—

[102] It is worth noting that Oiticica rejected both the production of art objects to be displayed in commercial galleries and the 'Conceptual art' designation.

[103] The Guggenheim study grant that took Oiticica to New York in 1970 is awarded on the basis of two separate competitions, one for the US and Canada and the other for residents of Latin America and the Caribbean. Mexico was first to enter the competition, in 1930, followed by Argentina, Chile, Cuba and Puerto Rico; Brazil joined in 1940.

[104] Quoted in *Information* (exh. cat.), New York: MoMA, 1970, p.105. And compare Meireles's comment in the same publication: 'I am here, in this exhibition, to defend neither a career nor any nationality' (p.85).

[105] Mari Carmen Ramírez, 'Tactics for Thriving on Adversity: Conceptualism in Latin America 1960–1980', in M.C. Ramírez, Héctor Olea et al., *Inverted Utopias: Avant-Garde Art in Latin America*, New Haven and Houston: Yale University Press and The Museum of Fine Arts, 2004, pp.425–36.

organised the first solo exhibitions outside of Brazil for Clark and Oiticica, among others.[106] The 1980s accelerated a neocolonial process of cannibalisation in reverse, once travel became easier and more affordable.[107] Although aware of the often-problematic framing of their work, artists typically found themselves unable to resist the siren call to show on an international platform. An emblematic example is 'Magiciens de la Terre', at the Centre Georges Pompidou and the Grande Halle de La Villette in Paris in 1989, for which curator Jean-Hubert Martin selected Meireles, Ronaldo Pereira Rego and Mestre Didi from Brazil as 'magicians' or 'wizards' rather than artists.[108] Another exhibition that stood out in this context was 'Art in Latin America', at London's Hayward Gallery in the same year, curated by Dawn Ades.[109]
fig.70-72 Later asked to address the 'anthropophagic dimensions of Dada and Surrealism' for the 24th Bienal's 'Núcleo Histórico',[110] Ades acknowledged 'Latin America' as being 'clearly a cultural and political designation, as opposed to a neutrally geographical one'.[111] Yet for the Hayward show, despite her awareness of the 'unreal unity' of a 'continental approach', Ades called upon identity factors as a common denominator rather than exploiting the specificities of each country or region. Similarly, the catalogue asserted a 'Latin American aesthetic',[112] with special emphasis on the Mexican artists Manuel Álvarez Bravo, Frida Kahlo, José Clemente Orozco, Diego Rivera and Joaquín Torres-García.

In 1992, to coincide with the anniversary of 'the discovery of America', the Royal Museum of Fine Arts in Antwerp staged 'America: Bride of the Sun, 500 Years Latin America and the Low Countries'; arguably, the most audacious

—

[106] Guy Brett, 'A Radical Leap', in D. Ades (ed.), *Art in Latin America: The Modern Era, 1820–1980*, New Haven and London: Yale University Press and South Bank Centre, 1989, pp.253–83. Brett raised some relevant issues in relation to the terminology used ('Latin American') and introduced the following artists: Lucio Fontana, Alejandro Otero, Jesús Soto, Carlos Cruz-Diez, Lygia Clark, Hélio Oiticica, Lygia Pape, Sergio Camargo, Mira Schendel and Mathias Goeritz.

[107] The story is familiar: weary of its own mythologies, Western civilisation ventured to far-off lands (hence the etymological origin of *exotic*) to draw on fresh images. The European cannibal embodies the reversal of anthropophagy and originates in this journey to a place outside itself.

[108] 'Magiciens de la Terre', Centre Georges Pompidou and the Grande Halle de La Villette, Paris, 18 May to 14 August 1989. For more on this fraught exhibition, see Lucy Steeds et al., *Making Art Global (Part 2): 'Magiciens de la Terre' 1989*, London: Afterall Books, 2013.

[109] 'Art in Latin America: The Modern Era, 1820–1980', Hayward Gallery, London, 18 May to 6 August 1989.

[110] D. Ades 'As dimensões antropofágicas do dadá e do surrealismo' / 'The anthropophagic dimensions of dada and surrealism', in *XXIV Bienal de São Paulo: Núcleo Histórico: Antropofagia e Histórias de Canibalismos, op. cit.*, pp.235–45.

[111] 'It originated in the context of French foreign policy of the 1850s, to cover both those lands that were former Spanish and Portuguese colonies from the Rio Grande in North America south to Cape Horn, and the French- and Spanish-speaking Caribbean.' D. Ades, 'Introduction', in D. Ades (ed.), *Art in Latin America: The Modern Era, 1820–1980, op. cit.*, pp.1–2.

[112] D. Ades, 'Foreword', in *ibid.*, p.ix.

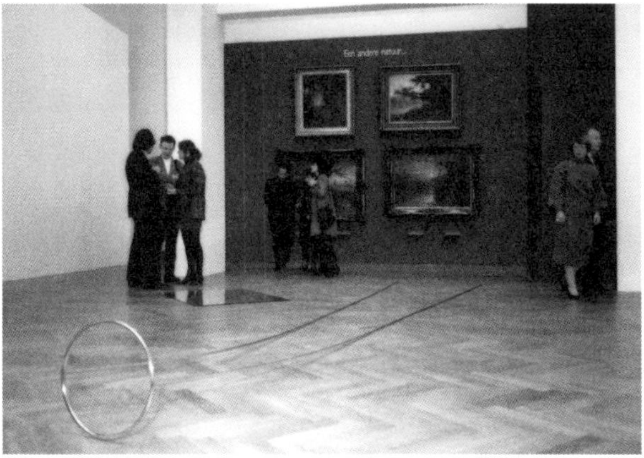

Installation view, 'America, Bride of the Sun: 500 Years Latin America and the Low Countries', Royal Museum of Fine Art, Antwerp, 1992. In foreground: work by Waltercio Caldas © the artist; Archives Royal Museum of Fine Arts Antwerp

exhibition of Latin American art held until that time.[113] In anticipation of the inevitable clichés, an essay by the show's organiser, Paul Vandenbroeck, began with an epigraph in Quechuan, then set out to deconstruct prevailing historical narratives, from the alleged 'discovery' of the Americas by Spanish conquistadores to the use of imagery to propagate an exoticism based on human and territorial geography.

The difficulties and implications of the processes of the institutionalisation of Latin American art were the subject of 'Cartographies', a project started p.42
by Ivo Mesquita in 1989.[114] In discursive terms, he questioned the assumption of continental integration and engaged with Marta Traba's classification of Latin American art according to 'open areas', 'closed areas' and 'islands', further positing additional subdivisions within these categories.[115] Mesquita's proposal was based on his observations as a traveller, relating to topography, climatic conditions and behaviour:

> *Latin America does not exist under a single identity. Generally speaking, there are at least six different cultural areas: the Amazon and the Caribbean area (Venezuela, Northern Brazil, Eastern Colombia,* [the Guianas] *and*

—

[113] 'America: Bride of the Sun, 500 Years Latin America and the Low Countries', Royal Museum of Fine Arts, Antwerp, 1 February to 31 May 1992.

[114] The exhibition 'Cartographies' was held at Winnipeg Art Gallery, 19 March to 6 June 1993. It travelled to Museo de Artes Visuales Alejandro Otero, Caracas, 12 August to 19 September 1993; Biblioteca Luis Angel Arango, Bogotá, 21 October to 12 December 1993; the National Gallery of Canada, Ottawa, 18 February to 1 May 1994; and The Bronx Museum of the Arts, New York, 10 June 1994 to 22 January 1995. See Ivo Mesquita, P. Herkenhoff and Justo Pastor Mellado (ed.), *Cartographies* (exh. cat.), Winnipeg: Winnipeg Art Gallery, 1993.

[115] Marta Traba, 'La década de la entrega: 1960–1970', in *Dos décadas vulnerables en las artes plásticas latinoamericanas, 1950–1970*, Buenos Aires and Mexico City: Siglo Veintiuno Editores, 2005, pp.141–204.

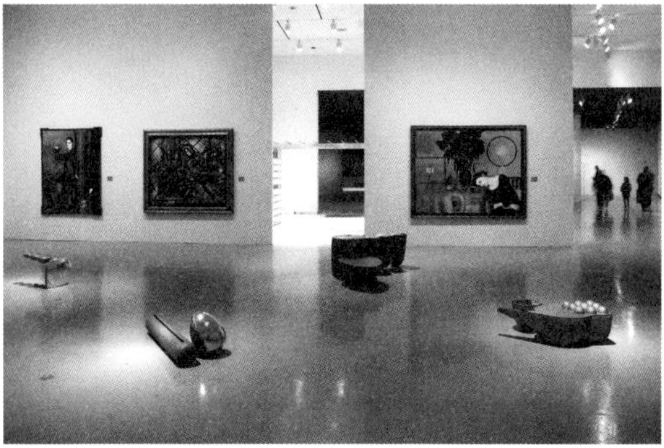

Installation view, 'Cartographies', Winnipeg Art Gallery, 1993.
From left to right: Julio Galán: *Niño posando como Egipcio*, 1984, *Secreto Eterno*, 1987, *Retrato de Luisa*, 1990. On the floor: Germán Botero: *Alqumia*, 1992, *Maguare*, 1988, *Crisol*, 1992, *Piel Plana*, 1989

Courtesy Winnipeg Art Gallery

> *the Caribbean); the Southern Cone (Chile, Argentina, Uruguay, Paraguay and Southern Brazil); the Andean Group (Bolivia, Peru, Ecuador and Colombia); Mexico; Central America; and Northeast Brazil.*[116]

The author presented a rapid summary of the modernity-postmodernity debate, reducing Western thought to a pursuit of 'truth' and claiming a 'postmodern' perspective in order to propose an alternative cartography open to other 'systems of perception'.[117] Mesquita's association of a curatorial strategy with its ability to produce 'imaginary maps' feeds the belief in travelling as a transformative experience, as if the traveller's eye could suspend his or her systems of reference:

> *Thus, the concept of cartography serves the need for a working method that involves the curator gazing over the artistic production of the present, preserving a sensitive eye to the internal confrontations that art sets up for itself in an effort to constitute a contemporary visuality. This is why the curator does not follow any sort of set protocol or any a priori definition, for his work is born from the observation of transformations he perceives in the territories he traverses.*[118]

Catherine de Zegher, who selected twentieth-century works for 'America: p.41 Bride of the Sun', admitted that being unable to produce an egalitarian discourse is an inseparable part of the survey travel method: 'Only the fact of visiting as a curator from the "centre" to the "periphery" and already by merely praising their work, you are involuntarily showing the "undeclared notion of the European superiority".'[119] Her response illuminates the hierarchy

—

[116] I. Mesquita, 'Cartographies', in *Cartographies*, *op. cit.*, p.31.
[117] *Ibid.*, p.23.
[118] *Ibid.*, p.21.
[119] Benjamin Buchloh & Catherine de Zegher, 'Ver America: A written exchange', in *America: Bride of the Sun, 500 Years Latin America and the Low Countries* (exh. cat), Antwerp and Ghent: Royal Museum of Fine Arts and Imschoot Books, 1991, p.232.

into which the curator is placed by globalisation, regardless of their nationality. In other words, the act of deciding what deserves 'to be on the global map' constitutes the real power relationship.

The catalogue for 'Cartographies' contains a large network of terms by Herkenhoff under the title 'Incomplete Glossary of Sources of Latin American Art'.[120] These short but dense notes deploy quotations and characters to deconstruct prevailing clichés; not only to dismantle an established discourse but to erect something in its place, since Brazil's social-cultural reality remained sequestered within a European and US historiography based on reiterating the canon.[121] However, for a South American curator, moving beyond national borders was synonymous with political exile or joining the diaspora, at least until the military dictatorship ended and democracy was reintroduced in the mid-1980s. At that time, very few critics succeeded in combining a regional institutional influence with connections on a continental scale, two notable exceptions being Amaral and Traba. Indeed, Rina Carvajal, the Venezuelan curator selected by Herkenhoff for the 'Latin American' section of 'Roteiros...', was actually living in New York at the time of the 24th Bienal.

The point here is to ask how the 24th Bienal could avoid being confounded with a certain fad for 'margins', triggered by 'Magiciens de la Terre', without getting caught up in nationalistic snares. It is significant, in this regard, that for the main exhibition Herkenhoff sought to address two further predicates: ethnography and modernity.[122] In the same way as 'America: Bride of the Sun', the 'Núcleo Histórico' showed landscapes and ethnic portraits by European travellers, colonial 'caste paintings' and allegorical imagery from different continents.[123] Herkenhoff called on Ana Maria Belluzzo, of USP, to curate the Eckhout display, and on the French historian Jean-François Chougnet for the section devoted to art from the sixteenth to the eighteenth centuries. The 'Núcleo Histórico' distinguished itself, and in comparison to 'America: Bride of the Sun', through the legitimacy afforded by its context:

p.*41*
pp.*114–73*
fig.52–55
fig.55–57

—

[120] P. Herkenhoff, 'Incomplete Glossary of Sources of Latin American Art', in *Cartographies*, *op. cit.*, pp.7–85 and 169–91, and this volume, pp.230–47.
[121] '... the *Cartographies* exhibition has two objectives: first, to present a sample of the production of contemporary Latin American art and participate in the current debate about this alleged category of art; second, to propose a curatorial methodology capable of approaching the production of contemporary art, critically standing up to institutionalised tradition and preserving the specificity of the plastic discourses.' I. Mesquita, 'Cartographies', *op. cit*, p.13.
[122] The 'Núcleo Histórico' lost a room that would have been devoted to anthropology when sponsors withdrew at the last minute. Herkenhoff had asked anthropologist Manuela Carneiro da Cunha to curate the room.
[123] Soon after the 24th Bienal, two of its curators, Ivo Mesquita and Adriano Pedrosa, organized 'F[r]icciones' (2000–01) at the Museo Nacional Centro de Arte Reina Sofía (MNCARS), Madrid, the same institution that would host 'Princípio Potosí' a decade later, in 2010. Both exhibitions took on the laborious task of gathering religious paintings and sculptures from the colonial period to contextualise contemporary output from South America.

the ideological ballast of its narrative could be interwoven with the historical conditions of the host institution and its place of origin.

The phenomenon of Western exhibitions commemorating the anniversaries of the discovery and the independence of the continent was also significant in that it triggered shared feelings for artists. Many aspired to exhibit at so-called 'first-world' museums and knew it was a strategic step toward internationalisation. In this respect, being selected for the celebrated if controversial exhibition 'Magiciens de la Terre' was acknowledged as a beneficial process towards greater visibility. Curatorial criteria mattered less than the prestige of showing work at Centre Pompidou.

Although uncomfortable, the exotic notion of a 'Latin American' aesthetic has very seldom stopped artists from accepting invitations to show abroad. The struggle to break out of such a framing reached a new turning point in 1996, when Gerardo Mosquera, a key member of the curatorial team for the first three Bienales de La Habana, stated that Latin America and Africa were 'colonial inventions to be reinvented'.[124] After 1989, other critics preferred to use the expression 'art *coming* from South America', as a new attempt to bypass ill-considered notions of cultural identity; this expression not only includes the alterity of the foreigner but is also intended to voice the reality of several migrations.[125] In 1997, the year before the 24th Bienal, the first edition of the Mercosul Biennial was held in Porto Alegre to strengthen a free-trade agreement between five South American countries: Argentina, Brazil, Paraguay, Uruguay and Venezuela. (Although, in this case, signing an economic protocol was hardly likely to foster a channel of communication capable of working with the region's identity issues.)[126]

The fact that art departments at Brazilian universities still align the 24th Bienal with multicultural studies rather than, say, postcolonial studies indicates that the debate is still immature. Theses and dissertations referencing the 24th Bienal often demonstrate some prejudice in relation to the curator's intellectual stance, ignoring that Herkenhoff had specifically rejected 'the ideology of multiculturalism, with its system of ethnic classification developed by North American society',[127] and failing to acknowledge that he

—

[124] G. Mosquera, 'El arte latinoamericano deja de serlo', in *ARCO Latino* (exh. cat.), Madrid: ARCO, 1996, pp.7–10. A reader of Lévi-Strauss, the Cuban curator posed diffuse lines of disagreement with Herkenhoff's interpretive model.

[125] See, for instance, Jesús Fuenmayor, *Arte da América do Sul: Ponto de viragem 1989*, Porto: Fundação de Serralves / Jornal Público, Colecção de Arte Contemporânea, 2006. Still, the fall of the Berlin Wall remains ground zero for a contemporary reality yet to be deciphered.

[126] In this biennial's more recent iterations, its initial role has been reshaped: it has become yet another international forum discussing the circulation of art in the age of globalisation.

[127] P. Herkenhoff, 'Ir e vir' / 'To come and go' (trans. V. Cordeiro), in *XXIV Bienal de São Paulo: Roteiros. Roteiros. Roteiros. Roteiros. Roteiros. Roteiros. Roteiros.*, *op. cit.*, p.27.

located the nub of the problem in Brazil's colonial legacy. It is an over-simplification to interpret the international reputation of the 24th Bienal based solely on the fact that the concept of anthropophagy was adaptable to global agendas.

In rounding off this narrative, a decision made in 1998 should be mentioned: the removal of the letter *I*, for 'International', from the Bienal's formal title, thus altering the Portuguese acronym from BISP to BSP. Normally this would suggest a more local perspective, yet it was a very different gesture from Amaral's attempt, in the late 1970s, to give visibility to Latin American countries. In 1998, the act of abolishing *I* was more ambitious, since it operated from the status of the institution to 'correct' the stream of the canon of art history – the idea being that *international* revealed an unsolved inferiority complex in relation to the hegemonic centres.[128] Thus, the removal of the letter should be seen together with other organisational measures to turn the Bienal de São Paulo into a regular art event unhindered by the machinations of foreign powers. The curator accomplished this same process of asserting independence, but within the context of art history. The power of the turnaround resided precisely in the attempt to expand artistic internationalism beyond hegemonic parameters.[129]

3. Beyond the 'Núcleo Histórico' in 1998

Paulo Herkenhoff was commissioned to curate the 24th Bienal early in 1997. As already noted, Bienal curators are appointed each time by the president of the Fundação Bienal, a precedent that resulted in a valuable alliance for the 24th edition between Herkenhoff and then-president Julio Landmann; the two men's ideas and principles were well attuned. The two Bienals preceding the 1998 iteration had been headed by Edemar Cid Ferreira, as president, with overall strategic planning by chief curator Nelson Aguilar, an art historian and professor at the Universidade Estadual de Campinas (UNICAMP). More even than a structure, Landmann and Herkenhoff were left with the legacy of a widespread mentality among Fundação Bienal board members, to repeat the same formula as previous editions. The expectation was that they would continue working along the same lines: 'According to its new formalised goals, the Bienal was supposed to invite the largest number of countries possible while also bringing artists of renown, besides presenting a heavyweight histori-cal module. Composed as much as possible by names known to the general public and, therefore, able to attract the public to the event and,

—

[128] Adriano Pedrosa notes that 'the curatorship found it unnecessary, and in fact rather provincial, to name a feature which the exhibition and the city so eloquently affirm'. A. Pedrosa, 'Editor's Note', in *XXIV Bienal de São Paulo: Núcleo Histórico: Antropofagia e Histórias de Canibalismos, op. cit.*, p.551.

[129] See V. Spricigo, 'Contribuições para uma reflexão crítica sobre a Bienal de São Paulo no contexto da globalização cultural', available at http://www.forumpermanente.org/revista/numero-1/discussao-bissexta/vinicius-spricigo/contribuicoes-para-uma-reflexao-critica-sobre-a-bienal-de-sao-paulo-no-contexto-da-globalizacao-cultural (last accessed on 4 March 2015).

indirectly, to contemporary art.'[130] Ferreira's 'bigger is better' motto also sought to justify a project for building a permanent museum space in the Bienal pavilion: 'This was the only way through which the Brazilian public would really perceive the importance of the link between precursors and renewers and would have the rare opportunity to ascertain that art does not mean fashion, but intuition of the unique instant only grasped by real creators.'[131] Fabio Cypriano, art critic for the newspaper *Folha de S. Paulo*, characterised the era of Ferreira as privileging 'an event-based culture to the detriment of its heritage; a concern to ensure massive visitation; lending the exhibitions a spectacular air; using art as entertainment; Brazil's engagement in the global art system; the notion of art as a business; an approach based on personal influence or charisma; leveraging the fragile nature of art institutions in Brazil'.[132] Ferreira exerted his power and influence over board members even when removed from his duties, talking of investment in the millions to back a Brazilian national narrative. Hence his investing in pharaonic set designs rather than museological criteria when showing art historical heritage pieces.[133]

To make matters worse, Ferreira's reputation migrated from the cultural sections of the press to the crime pages when his business, Banco Santos, went bankrupt and faced money laundering charges. Whereas Ciccillo Matarazzo's personal fortune helped build a public art collection, Ferreira's financial activities were denounced as benefitting his private collection of an estimated 9,000 works. Criminal charges snowballed and led to his personal property being confiscated;[134] ironically, today much of the former Banco Santos Cid Ferreira Collection is held in escrow by several institutions in

—

[130] *Bienal de São Paulo 50 anos, 1951–2001 / 50 years of the São Paulo Biennial*, *op. cit.*, p.240. The figures were always impressive under Ferreira's leadership: the 22nd Biennial had 27 special rooms, and 87 countries were represented at the 23rd.

[131] E.C. Ferreira, 'A 22ª Bienal Internacional de São Paulo: Honrar e renovar a tradição' / 'The 22nd Bienal Internacional de São Paulo: Honoring and renewing tradition', in *22ª Bienal de São Paulo - Salas Especiais I* (exh. cat.), São Paulo: Fundação Bienal, 1994, p.22.

[132] F. Cypriano, 'A era Edemar Cid Ferreira em quatro movimentos', lesson plan for class at Escola São Paulo, 2013.

[133] To stage ambitious exhibitions commemorating 'the discovery of America', Ferreira, alleging a need to fill a gap in academic literature, commissioned illustrious individuals to draw up a temporal arc stretching from prehistory to the contemporary period. He then created a dissident wing of the Fundação Bienal, called BrasilConnects, and an association named Brasil 500 Anos (Brazil 500 Years). Thus, Ibirapuera Park became the epicentre of the 'discovery' of Brazil. An operation on this scale could not ignore the coveted showcase in Venice. The exhibition 'Brazil in Venice' (2001), on the occasion of the 49th Venice Biennale, sought to rewrite history by using icons replete with powerful exotic appeal.

[134] See, for instance, the account by Brazil's Superior Court of Justice, available at http://stj.jus.br/portal_stj/publicacao/engine.wsp?tmp.area=398&tmp.texto=91950 (last accessed on 4 March 2015). See also 'StAR – Stolen Asset Recovery Initiative – Corruption Cases – Edemar Cid Ferreira / Banco Santos, S.A. Art Repatriation Case', available at http://star.worldbank.org/corruption-cases/node/18495 (last accessed on 4 March 2015).

São Paulo, including the Museu de Arte Sacra and the Museu de Arqueologia e Etnologia and Museu de Arte Contemporânea at USP.[135]

Soon after taking over in 1997, Herkenhoff asked Adriano Pedrosa to join him as associate curator, and after that both took all decisions concerning their edition of the Bienal.[136] Herkenhoff defined his curatorial strategy in opposition to the divisions he had seen in the previous edition curated by Aguilar: national delegations, a section called 'Universalis' (divided into seven geographical regions with six representatives each) and individual rooms showing special exhibitions. As stated in an internal memo circulated at the time: 'In all segments we are planning a more integrated exhibition and thus discouraging curators and artists to think in terms of closed-off "rooms".'[137]

But how would the Bienal's guiding principle of *density* be preserved at the scale of a biennial exhibition that covered more than 30,000 square metres? Together with Pedrosa and the ten curators invited to work on 'Roteiros...', pp.*100–13* Herkenhoff refined his exhibition strategy, asking them to collaborate regarding their guest artists by doing away with individual rooms and pursuing 'articulations and juxtapositions in the context of a collective exhibition'.[138] The mission of translating the curatorial concept into spatial terms was entrusted to the architect Paulo Mendes da Rocha, a standout figure of the 'São Paulo school' of modernist architecture. Mendes da Rocha, who had also worked on the previous Bienal, was given the task of providing open and transparent areas without demarcating territories or building walls. The curators explained their *démarche* as follows:

> *Most of our public come just once to the Bienal, thus the challenge is to make an exhibition which is conceptually complex and spatially light.* [...] *Of course we understand specific needs for rooms and walls, silence and isolation, yet we would like to limit those, as we are doing in other segments of the XXIV Bienal, to instances when it is strictly necessary. In short we would like to reverse the assumption that one nation = one artist = one room.*[139]

—

[135] To understand the many lawsuits brought against the banker and businessman, and his 21-year prison sentence for leaving behind a R$2.2 billion shortfall (more than US$1 billion at the current exchange rate), see Mario Cesar Carvalho's reports for the newspaper *Folha de S. Paulo*, 'Ilustrada' section, available at http://www1.folha.uol.com.br/fsp/mercado/me2701201114.htm (last accessed on 4 March 2015). In May 2015 a mistrial was declared due to a procedural error – at the time of writing, the case continues.

[136] During the aforementioned presentation given at Faculdade Santa Marcelina on the 12 March 2008, Herkenhoff mentioned an exhibition curated by Pedrosa he had seen and that had been decisive in his selection of the associate curator: 'Pequenas Mãos', Paço Imperial, Rio de Janeiro, 1996.

[137] 'Newsletter: To all curators and institutions responsible for National Representations', 9 January 1998, Arquivo Histórico Wanda Svevo / Fundação Bienal de São Paulo.

[138] Fax from A. Pedrosa to P. Herkenhoff, 5 March 1998, Arquivo Histórico Wanda Svevo / Fundação Bienal de São Paulo.

[139] 'Newsletter: To all curators and institutions responsible for National Representations', *op. cit.*

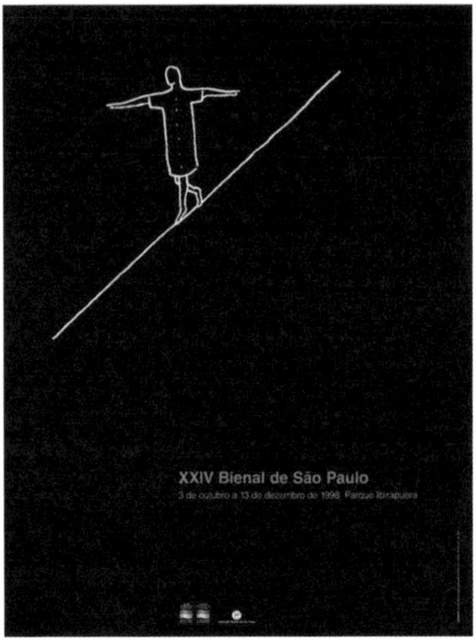

Raul Loureiro and Rodrigo Cerviño Lopez, poster for the 24th Bienal de São Paulo, 1998, inspired by a work by Leonilson
© Raul Loureiro and Rodrigo Cerviño Lopez

Compared to the 'great disputes' of previous editions, Herkenhoff had a different approach to this 'central' space on the ground floor of the pavilion: 'In the past, the space has been used to exhibit works by Anish Kapoor, Richard Long and Joseph Beuys. It is a very marked space, charged with an intense architectural drama. I did not want to significantly exercise power over it.'[140] In terms of the 'public front' of the Bienal, on the north-east façade of the fig.1-3 Bienal pavilion Regina Silveira presented her *Tropel* (*Throng*, 1998), which showed the paw prints of various animal species. The exhibition's iconic poster featured a Leonilson drawing, a figure with open arms stepping along a tightrope. Although this showed no obvious relationship with anthropophagy, the image can be seen to reflect the difficulty of finding an upright position and a measure for balance – challenging harmony and stability – whilst also suggesting the plurality of history: Herkenhoff has repeatedly noted Leonilson as an artist whose work questions the notion of univocal truth.[141] The design of the 24th Bienal de São Paulo logo was also inspired by one of Leonilson's works,[142] acting as a tribute to this Brazilian artist who died as a result of AIDS in 1993.

—

[140] See P. Herkenhoff and A. Pedrosa, 'The Brazilian Curator Private' / 'The Carioca Curator', *op. cit.*

[141] See my *Leonilson: São tantas as verdades*, São Paulo: Projeto Leonilson, SESI, 1995.

[142] 'A fragment of his sculpture was selected for the logo because the globe represents the international character of the Bienal de São Paulo. What is more, the work was featured at the nineteenth Bienal, in 1987. The choice then rescues a fragment of this Foundation's memory (and history) to make it contemporary and meaningful.' Document signed by Raul Loureiro (designer) and A. Pedrosa, Arquivo Histórico Wanda Svevo / Fundação Bienal de São Paulo, date unknown.

The emphatic presence of Brazilian artists in every section of the 24th Bienal far exceeded the space initially allocated for their 'national representation' and strengthened Herkenhoff's proposed Brazilian narrative. Compared to the previous edition, which featured the smallest proportion of Brazilian artists in the Bienal's history, the numbers for the 1998 edition were significant: 271 artists showed work, of whom 71 were Brazilian.[143] In addition to some thirty names in the section 'Arte Contemporânea Brasileira: Um e/entre Outro/s', other Brazilian artists were scattered around the 'Núcleo Histórico', for example in the so-called 'colour axis' and 'Monochromos', as well as the Latin American segment of 'Roteiros...'. Thanks to the device of 'contamination', Herkenhoff was able to place specific artists, very often Brazilian, in various curators' rooms, preventing the consolidation of individualism and clear national identities. Thus, Oiticica's *B33 Bólide Caixa 18, poema caixa 02 'Homenagem a Cara de Cavalo'* (*B33 Box Bolide 18, Box Poem 02 'Homage to Horse Face'*, 1965–66) was moved around during the exhibition (included within 'Monochromos' and the David Alfaro Siqueiros space, for example) and the two performers of a work by Laura Lima, *Untitled* (1998), constantly moved throughout the floors.[144] Alongside the concept of contamination, Herkenhoff proposed that single works could function with a certain 'magnetic' force, producing fields of interaction within the space, in order to annul the premise that an artist has to be represented by a great number of works.[145] For example, a single piece such as Barrio's *T.E. (trouxas ensangüentadas)*, which was inserted into Bacon's room had, according to this logic, the power to unleash a debate about the 'nature of painting'.[146] In the curator's words: 'Take, for example, the notion of "magnetised space". [Waltercio] Caldas wanted to magnetise the entire biennial, he explained that there should be no space where things were hidden, all places were worthy of attention, ideas which are also present in the conception of Lygia Pape's work.'[147]

pp.*78–99*
fig.83–98 and 64–68
fig.28 and 36
fig.76–77
fig.75–76
fig.20, 25 and 43
fig.74

—

[143] For the 23rd edition, 135 artists were featured, of whom only 11 were Brazilian. With a few exceptions, the percentage of Brazilian artists at each Bienal has tended to be around twenty to thirty per cent. See *Bienal de São Paulo 50 anos, 1951–2001 / 50 years of the São Paulo Biennial, op. cit.*

[144] In addition, Herkenhoff introduced Anna Bella Geiger into 'Colour in Brazilian Modernism'; Barrio's *T.E. (trouxas ensangüentadas)* was placed beside the Bacon display and his *Livro de carne* (*Book of meat*, 1979/1998) in the 'Literature' section; Meireles was combined with van Gogh; Ernesto Neto and Vik Muniz were inserted into the 'Surrealism and Dada' space; a Mira Schendel *Droguinha* was placed next to works by Eva Hesse and Robert Smithson; Tunga's work appeared in both 'Colour in Brazilian Modernism' and the Eckhout room; the work by Laura Lima (*Untitled*, 1998) constantly moved through the floors; the display of Alberto Giacometti's and Maria Martins's sculptures in close proximity had unprecedented visual impact; and Adriana Varejão made a strong appearance across the entire exhibition, in the 'Núcleo Histórico' as a point of articulation for various exhibits, with her painting *Mapa de Lopo Homem* (1992) in dialogue with the 'Roteiros...' section, and her graphic project *Luta de guerreiro nus* (*Nude warriors' fight*, 1998), which was published in the catalogue.

[145] P. Herkenhoff, 'Bienal 1998: princípios e processos', *op. cit.*, p.36.

[146] *Ibid.*

[147] P. Herkenhoff and A. Pedrosa, 'The Brazilian Curator Private / The Carioca Curator', *op. cit.*

Contamination through magnetism, contact, contagion and porosity – this curatorial tool was used beyond its specific meaning in the 'Manifesto' to work around the problem of putting together a cohesive exhibition when the Fundação Bienal's regulations still delegated the selection of foreign artists to their respective embassies, consulates and international cultural agencies.[148] According to Julio Landmann, national delegations were part of a political mechanism that seemed insurmountable for the Fundação Bienal in view of its historical relations with the Ministry of Foreign Affairs: 'Itamaraty [the foreign ministry] is the oldest official partner of the Bienal, offering a secure support in our institution's lifetime of almost half a century.'[149] Lengthy customs procedures for temporary imports meant that in many instances the Fundação Bienal had to open exhibitions before works from foreign countries could be installed. Historically, the curator of the Bienal had little leeway to turn down international referrals based on the argument that the show would not enjoy financial health without official support from those countries responding to the call for participation. Yet the experience of the 26th edition proved that disadvantaged countries were unable to sponsor their artists, leaving them reliant on the minimal means offered at the venue (basic installation, labels and lighting) whereas rich countries would even send their own technical teams to ensure the high standard of their displays. With the way these huge differences in display budget were managed by the Bienal, the pavilion often had dreary areas reflecting the power of hegemonic centres. Given this context, how to establish a parity between centre and periphery?

In his public statements, Herkenhoff has mentioned several attempts to circumvent a design subordinated to the 'festival of nations' (66 countries were represented in the 24th Bienal overall).[150] First of all, the theoretical
pp.*114–73*
foundation of the 'Núcleo Histórico' allowed juxtapositions of works irrespective of geopolitical criteria. But what about the countries that were still being asked to participate on an official basis? According to the rules established in 1996, national representation had been limited to one artist per country, a measure to increase direct requests from the Brazilian curators.

—

[148] This worked in reverse, too, when foreign embassies or consulates asked the Fundação Bienal for names of Brazilian artists to show at other international events – and not only in the Venice Biennale but also, for instance, in the second Johannesburg Biennale of 1997 (as confirmed in a letter written by Peter Tjabbes, 10 July 1997, Arquivo Histórico Wanda Svevo / Fundação Bienal de São Paulo). It should be noted that from the 1970s onwards the curator of the Bienal was able to make a few direct invitations to artists from outside of Brazil. See, for instance, all those from Germany who were additionally involved over the years, beyond those nationally nominated, as meticulously recorded in Ulrike Groos and Sebastian Preuss, *German Art in São Paulo*, Ostfildern-Ruit: Hatje Cantz, 2013.

[149] J. Landmann, 'Apresentação do Presidente da Fundação Bienal de São Paulo' / 'Fundação Bienal de São Paulo President's Foreword' (trans. V. Cordeiro), in *XXIV Bienal de São Paulo: Representações Nacionais*, São Paulo: Fundação Bienal, 1998, p.18.

[150] See *Bienal de São Paulo 50 anos, 1951–2001 / 50 years of the São Paulo Biennial*, *op. cit.*, p.258.

Nonetheless, as with Venice, the general concept of the biennial was typically treated very loosely by the curators assigned to represent their respective countries. In 1998, even though an effort was made to spread the 'Manifesto' amongst them, these curators had fewer chances to get committed to the general concept, and thus the least interesting part of the 24th Bienal was still to be found in the 'Representações Nacionais'. pp.68–77

With one exception: in a unique event in the history of the Fundação Bienal, the Central American and Caribbean countries were given special attention. Based on his previous contacts in the region, Herkenhoff asked Virginia Pérez-Ratton, then with Museo de Arte y Diseño Contemporáneo de Costa Rica (MADC), 'to travel to the area's countries in order to coordinate curatorial decisions when choosing country representatives, thus aiming for joint participation by following certain conceptual parameters. However, the 24th Bienal was set to heighten the visibility of the event as a whole in the exhibition space and book. Far from being ghettoised, this grouping arrangement was the articulated sum of symbolic production in the region.'[151]

The relationships developed with Central America and the Caribbean were extended within the 'Roteiros…' section, which was intended to send anthropophagy beyond Brazilian territory. pp.100–13 Although 'Roteiros…' was equivalent to the 'Universalis' section of the 23rd Bienal, the difference in tone was palpable. The team of ten curators from various countries, assembled by Herkenhoff and Pedrosa, actively examined Andrade's 'Manifesto' before arguing for their selections of artists.[152] After all, with the Cold War and the old dichotomy between East and West at an end, the international situation seemed favourable for the 24th Bienal to make the 'periphery' stand out.[153]

An extract from Marco Polo's thirteenth-century travelogue was selected to open up the 'Roteiros…' catalogue, under the aegis of postcolonial debate. In his foreword, Herkenhoff states that the strategy of displacing hegemonic centres began with the commission of two curators – one Belgian, Bart de Baere, and one Finnish, Maaretta Jaukkuri – to reflect a different Europe.[154] Without a doubt, a more traditional configuration would have invested in

—

[151] J. Landmann, 'Apresentação do Presidente da Fundação Bienal de São Paulo' / 'Fundação Bienal de São Paulo President's Foreword', *op. cit.*, p.19. Landmann added: 'This project was presented by Herkenhoff and Pérez-Ratton to the assembly at the seventeenth meeting of the Central-American Cultural and Educational Coordination in San José, in 1998, with the presence of representatives from Costa Rica, El Salvador, Guatemala, Honduras, Nicaragua, Panama [and the] Dominican Republic, who praised the Bienal's initiative.'
[152] Symptomatic of the increasing use of the internet within professional networks, Pedrosa coordinated an online chat platform for the contributing curators.
[153] It is worth mentioning that the Bienal de La Habana, which had similar aims, was by that time facing internal and international difficulties as globalisation accelerated. Meanwhile, the collapse of the Communist bloc leveraged the creation of Manifesta as a roving biennial focusing on European issues, within Europe but not restricted to European artists.
[154] P. Herkenhoff, 'Ir e vir' / 'To come and go', *op. cit.*, p.26.

those countries that usually had the 'best' rooms as result of their cultural (read 'diplomatic') relations with Brazil – in particular, Germany, France and Britain. Whereas in the 'Manifesto' the notion of otherness signifies the devouring of foreign references, the curatorial strategy was to complicate and disrupt hegemonic alliances and relations (the 'capitalist modus vivendi', in Andrade's words). Here, again, the term most often used to define the
pp.*100–13*
curatorial design in the 'Roteiros...' was 'cartography', with curators who specialised in breaking down borders, from Africa (Lorna Ferguson and Awa Meité), Latin America (Carvajal), Asia (Apinan Poshyananda), Canada and the US (Mesquita), Oceania (Louise Neri), Europe (Baere and Jaukkuri) and the Middle East (Ami Steinitz and Vasif Kortun).[155]

For Canada and the US, the change in procedure reached a radical pitch, since the designated curator of the region was from Brazil rather than North America. Moreover, Mesquita opted not to group his selection within a specific area, instead spreading his artists throughout the pavilion. His contribution might be remembered as the most significant of the 'Roteiros...', as a compelling reflection on end-of-millennium disillusionment. Mesquita brought to
fig.34
fig.17–18 and 63
Brazil impressive works by Andrea Fraser, General Idea (AA Bronson, Felix Partz and Jorge Zontal), Janet Cardiff, Jeff Wall, Michael Asher and Sherrie Levine. The 'Roteiros...' section devoted to Africa featured the most artists, thirteen, compared to Europe's ten. Latin America, too, was represented by ten artists – an unprecedented development in view of the distance that Brazil was keeping from its southern neighbours on the continent at the time.[156]

—

The role played by the 24th Bienal publications and their singularity in comparison with previous editions also deserves close attention. Catalogues for the Bienal de São Paulo were usually plain affairs consisting of a bare institutional report, a curatorial statement, installation plans and humdrum information on the artists and works involved – useful only as basic sources of reference. These publications were designed to supply a bibliography to the local art communities, since tax incentives and other subsidies made it possible for the Fundação Bienal to set affordable prices on the volumes and to distribute them free to libraries across Brazil.[157]

—

[155] In the case of 'the Arab world', the combination of Israeli and Turkish curators gave rise to some conflict; regarding the 'Roteiros...' selection overall, Herkenhoff wrote: 'For fear or indignation to work with curators from the "enemy's side", some artists preferred not to participate in these Roteiros.' P. Herkenhoff, 'Ir e vir' / 'To come and go', *op. cit.*, p.29.

[156] For full details on the 'Roteiros...' section, see pp.100–13. 'Roteiros...' was also designed to include a web art segment for the first time at a biennial, with contributions from Ricardo Ribenboim and Ricardo Anderáos. Curators' fees for the 'Roteiros...' were US$4,000–10,000.

[157] The Fundação Bienal had a long-standing commitment to displaying the works submitted by different nations and featuring them in the exhibition catalogue. Even so, national representatives often produced leaflets and sometimes even hardcover books to publicise their official guests, regardless of the institution's lack of financial resources.

In many ways, the 24th Bienal denoted a paradigm shift for the Fundação Bienal's publishing concepts. Pedrosa devised the editorial approach, and each component of the exhibition was given its own dedicated volume. From the outset, there was clearly an aim for this iteration of the Bienal to be appreciated as a rewriting of history. In other words, its publications, as discursive instruments that would outlast the biennial, took on an academic rigour far beyond the standard documentary function of an exhibition catalogue. The release of these accompanying volumes introduced an entirely new perspective for the Bienal, producing literature without having to observe the tradition of mirroring the works shown. As Pedrosa commented: 'There are works in the exhibition that do not appear in the books, as there are artists who develop specific projects for the publications, yet are not in the pavilion.'[158] fig.99–102

In addition to requesting the usual institutional and curatorial texts, the editors commissioned more academic essays and reprinted extracts from historical works. These excerpts wove a transversality of reference points well beyond the specific boundaries of art theory. Their horizon was encyclopaedic, with the 'Núcleo Histórico' volume alone running to 560 pages.[159] That book begins with an excerpt from François Rabelais's *Pantagruel* (c.1532) and ends with a few lines from Roland Barthes: 'Union. Dream of total union with the loved being.'[160] Throughout, the publication features extracts from a multitude of voices, including Freud, Bakhtin, Bataille, Lacan, Jorge Luis Borges, Pierre Fédida, Sara Maitland and Tennessee Williams. In turn, the 336-page *Roteiros...* includes excerpts from Italo Calvino, Manthia Diawara, Jamaica Kincaid, Marco Polo and Borges again. Texts were printed in Portuguese and English, with the exception of Carvajal's 'Roteiros América Latina' essay, which appeared in English and Spanish, 'acknowledging the primacy of [Spanish] on the subcontinent'.[161]

However, the abundant Western references in the catalogues stand out against the relative absence of Brazilian authors.[162] The catalogue's privileging of Western rather than Brazilian modernities seems in direct contradiction with

—

[158] A. Pedrosa, 'Editor's Note', in *XXIV Bienal de São Paulo: Núcleo Histórico: Antropofagia e Histórias de Canibalismos, op. cit.*, pp.550–51. The note was printed at the back of each of the four volumes. In this volume, two double spreads were devoted to Varejão's *Luta de guerreiros nus*. In *Roteiros...*, one double spread features Olafur Eliasson's work and three double spreads featured Rosangela Rennó's work.

[159] As Pedrosa explained to Herkenhoff in a fax, 'this historic tome is now quite voluminous, encyclopedic' (5 March 1998, Arquivo Histórico Wanda Svevo / Fundação Bienal de São Paulo).

[160] Roland Barthes, *A Lover's Discourse: Fragments* (trans. Richard Howard), New York: Farrar, Straus and Girard, 2001, p.226.

[161] A. Pedrosa, 'Editor's Note', in *XXIV Bienal de São Paulo: Núcleo Histórico: Antropofagia e Histórias de Canibalismos, op. cit.*, p.551.

[162] Herkenhoff's bibliographical orientation changes in the catalogue for another exhibition he curated, 'Amazonia: Cycles of Modernity', in the context of the conference 'Rio+20', 20 to 22 June 2012, across ten locations, including the Museu de Arte Moderna, Rio de Janeiro. In this project, Western authors made way for the voices of Brazilian novelists Mário de Andrade, Milton Hatoum and Dalcídio Jurandir, and his conception of the Enlightenment becomes clearer with excerpts from Antonio Vieira's 'Sermão do Espírito Santo' (Sermon of the Holy Spirit).

Herkenhoff's ambition for an exhibition that would mark the Bienal's 'coming of age', a Kantian reference to evoke a 'modern political project of cultural emancipation'.[163] Herkenhoff meticulously associated the choice of Andrade's 'Manifesto' with a curatorial strategy of greater reach than the mere expectation of a list of artists: the ambition was to engender the Bienal's ability to have the courage to think for itself as an institution, and to confront the influence of Western 'paternalism'. So, when the curator announced the urgency of this 'coming of age', the talk of anthropophagy established a correspondence with the intellectual autonomy that Kant discussed in his essay asking 'What is Enlightenment?'. The curatorial strategy imparted to Andrade a timbre from Kant – that one should think for oneself, without being led by others. Hence, it is striking that in the case of the catalogues the Western canon remains so present.

fig.102 The publication for 'Arte Contemporânea Brasileira: Um e/entre Outro/s' was postponed in order to be able to document and highlight the spatial relations established in the exhibition space. In addition to in situ images of works, other devices were introduced, in particular the use of footnote-style smaller images, since the list of technical data for the works would not reflect the dialogues provided by their display. In short, there were graphic and editorial measures to ensure that future appreciation of the Bienal would grasp its dialogic value.[164]

As already mentioned, the majority of the wall texts were overloaded with concepts derived from Marxism and psychoanalysis.[165] As a kind of counter-balance, the curatorial rhetoric frequently expressed its investment in public education, consistent with the Bienal's long-standing commitments and complemented by Herkenhoff's understanding of the curator's social role. The 'Núcleo Educação', the educational programme of the Bienal developed by Evelyn Ioschpe, can be understood as the third strand of the 24th Bienal, alongside the exhibition and the publications.[166] The programme produced content that was distributed to 15,000 classrooms to help train 1,000 teachers,

—

[163] Immanuel Kant, 'Beantwortung der Frage: Was ist Aufklärung?' ('An Answer to the Question: What is Enlightenment?'), 1784.

[164] Raul Loureiro and Rodrigo Cerviño Lopez did the graphic design for the publications.

[165] This is how Herkenhoff defended Régis Michel's theoretically complex curatorial approach, for example: 'The room organised by Régis Michel offered a matrix that in some ways ran parallel to the development of Marxism and preceded the emergence of psychoanalysis. He was criticised for his having "too many texts on the walls", for instance, but this was part of Michel's curatorial method. Eight years later, he was asked to lead a seminar for a USP graduate program … Imagine if they had recognised his erudition to discuss the Goyas, Géricaults and Rodins at the biennial. […] Ten years later, masters and doctoral students have written more theses on the 24th Bienal than there are analytical texts produced in the city.' P. Herkenhoff, 'Bienal 1998: princípios e processos', *op. cit.*, p.34.

[166] For more on the educational programme, see Carmen Mörsch and Catrin Seefranz, 'Out of the *cantinho* – Art Education at the 24th Bienal de São Paulo', in this volume, pp.188–204.

who were grouped by their specific training (most had no artistic background). Herkenhoff then arranged to lead sessions for each teacher group, followed by questions and discussion.[167]

A key issue in producing the educational materials offered by the exhibition was to ensure the lasting effect of its content, to aim for its continued circulation in schools even after the exhibition had ended. These materials, in addition to the catalogues, not only released visitors from any obligation to follow a fixed itinerary, but stood its ground in the absence of the event itself. The project of the 'Núcleo Educação' was to encompass 'all segments of the public education system, not just those teaching art' – not least because teaching visual art and culture through images was a relatively recent practice in the Brazilian curriculum.[168]

The dialectical relationship between 'modern art' and art production from outside industrialised centres could no longer be overlooked. Herkenhoff's curatorial tactic focused on formulating general questions rather than providing answers; and alongside images reproduced in the educational charts, blunt questions were posed: What is photography? What is racism? What is anthropophagy at the social level?[169] Conceptual though this may seem, Herkenhoff sought to focus on 'interpreting works of art' – a gap he had spotted in Brazil's education system. His use of Lyotard's concept of *épaisseur*, of density or thickness, was not restricted to a discursive report, nor to a formal debate, but applied to the very act of seeing – hence a curatorial selection based on strong visual analysis was developed especially to stimulate students' learning about the key works in the 24th Bienal. Seth Siegelaub's motto brings an irreplaceable truth: 'Figures don't lie...'[170]

—

[167] According to Herkenhoff, 200,000 elementary school students, in the state sector, visited the exhibition. The *Núcleo Educação* report submitted to the Wanda Svevo Archive at the Fundação Bienal specifies that people 'came from 231 cities located in 18 states in Brazil, and from 14 other countries'. Producing educational content on this scale is now part of the São Paulo Bienal's institutional programme: each iteration distributes specific educational material free of charge for Brazil's schools and libraries, besides offering teacher-training programmes. Shortcomings in children's art education in Brazil have historical roots; few major initiatives or authors have focused on this type of learning. In this context, critic Mário Pedrosa would emphasise Ivan Serpa's 'little school' and children's art exhibitions at Rio de Janeiro's Museu de Arte Moderna, as well as the occupational therapy section developed by Dr Nise da Silveira at the Engenho de Dentro Psychiatric Centre. Pedrosa himself wrote several pieces on two 'new' worlds that emerged almost simultaneously in the social sciences. As well as warning against the 'notion of white superiority over other peoples from the economic and cultural periphery', his understanding of the place of a child's imagination in the perspective of a freer society includes Freud's 'discovery' of the unconscious world that was 'neglected or ignored by the intellectualist rationalist prejudices of this same bourgeois culture.' See M. Pedrosa, 'A Bienal de cá para lá', in O.B.F. Arantes (ed.), *Política das Artes,* São Paulo: Edusp, 1995, p.286.
[168] *Núcleo Educação* report submitted to the Wanda Svevo Archive, *op. cit.*
[169] From P. Herkenhoff, unpublished transcript of seminar at Faculdade Santa Marcelina, 12 March 2008, *op. cit.*
[170] See Seth Siegelaub, 'On Exhibitions and the World at Large: In Conversation with

Paradoxically, the 24th Bienal has become important for its ability to not only put forward Andrade's 'Manifesto' but also to transcend it. Its logic was so intrinsically derived from the exhibition that it cannot be used as a model.[171] It remains unique in its genre because it was oriented toward the comprehension of an 'international present'.[172] Of course, it would be an odd comparison to link Andrade with a transnational discourse. Nonetheless, it is true that the Bienal broke new ground in terms of understanding the perspective of the South (the adage of many curators, less or more relevant, after 1998) and marked a distinction among previous editions. The Bienal de São Paulo successfully broke out of its peripheral position in its 24th edition by reassessing the type of modernity introduced by Western narratives. By combining past and future, this emancipatory struggle fused with the educational project. As in Ciccillo Matarazzo's lifetime, it was a tour de force to raise quality to first-world standards and to develop institutional diplomacy; except that, this time, Western civilisation and related issues of modernity gained a critical framing. Today, Herkenhoff's curatorial selection of high-powered iconic works continues to fuel a powerful imaginary for new generations of curators.

4. The Anthropophagy Biennial in the Brazilian Art System Today

To bring out São Paulo's strategic position in relation to the biennial model one has to go back to the 1950s, when Venice and Kassel alone vied within Europe for prestige among contemporary art specialists, quite unlike the current situation. The art traveller's route is now extended to take in, for example, Sydney (which avoided national delegations from the start, in 1973), Havana (since 1984), Istanbul (since 1987) and numerous others – notably Lyon, Gwangju, Dakar, Berlin, Mercosul, Shanghai and Taipei in the 1990s – clearly showing that the advance of the biennial model will not be deterred by territorial or ideological limits. Despite periodic claims that they are founded on civil uprisings or social interventions, all these events bear an uncomfortable resemblance to art fairs. This can be understood as a result of recent factors, for example the emergence of a professionalised network of curatorial agents not directly working in the art market (commercial galleries) but helping to set criteria for collecting, primarily for corporate groups rather than museums, foundations or cultural centres.

Given late capitalism's cultural logic, the dizzying numbers of new venues are marketed so astutely that artists and visitors are still presented as the principal beneficiaries of the staging of biennials. Each city is potentially a headquarters, even at the 'end of the world' (The End of the World Biennial was created in 2007 in Ushuaia, capital of Argentina's Tierra del Fuego Province). Since the

—

Charles Harrison, 1969', in L. Steeds (ed.), *Exhibition: Documents of Contemporary Art*, London and Cambridge, MA: Whitechapel Gallery and The MIT Press, 2014, p.36. The full sentence is: 'Figures don't lie; accountants do.'

[171] See Maria Helena Carvalhaes, 'Dez anos depois: um debate com Paulo Herkenhoff', *marcelina*, vol.1, 2008, p.41.

[172] L. Steeds, 'Introduction // Contemporary Exhibitions: Art at Large in the World' in L. Steeds (ed.), *Exhibition: Documents of Contemporary Art*, *op. cit.*, p.13.

1990s, 'biennial culture' has become widespread enough to prompt an interest in historicising its own growth. The scale of this complexity led to a forum held at the 2009 Bergen Biennial Conference that endorsed 'biennialogy' (a history of biennials) and coined the verb 'biennialise'.[173]

All these details take on a new relevance when we assess the customary historical rooms that give the Bienal de São Paulo its local reputation. The problem is that the Bienal continues to emphasise the goal of public education, ignoring that São Paulo's reality has dramatically changed – and understandings of the Bienal's 'public' with it – and that the city has now to address its own periphery. How to encourage the integration of a population that does not even have the right to mobility, having to deal every day with the urban chaos of public transport? Behind a calculated blindness, there obviously remains a 'civilising' mission, conveying an ideal, 'universal' canon (the wealthy industrialised countries' culture and democracy) intended to 'enlighten' a context that, paradoxically, has other cultural priorities. The arrival of Picasso's *Guernica* at the second Bienal in 1953 is a cultural 'myth' that has yet to be surpassed – most of all by the Fundação's board of directors. p.58

For a biennial that was originally attached to a modern art museum,[174] success cannot be equated with that of other, later, global exhibitions. To be attached to a modern art museum reflected the aim of interweaving a promising collection with an educational programme built on the premise of escorting the megalopolis to it. But the mid- or long-term rationale – that this model is necessary to structure an art circuit in connection with schools, cultural centres, galleries and collectors – is a stage that has already been reached.This parallels Herkenhoff's more-or-less modernist goal that an 'art exhibition means building citizenship, in which education is fundamental and the curator is an agent of this process'.[175]

In Brazil, São Paulo is not only the dominant city of Brazilian academia[176] and of art history, but also a challenge for urban anthropology, Herkenhoff

—

[173] The call for contributions from critics was headed: 'To biennial or not to biennial?'. Bergen Kunsthall organised an international conference in 2009 to compile a critical review of the biennial model before moving forward with plans to design its 'Scandinavia's key-city' image. See Elena Filipovic, Marieke van Hal and Solveig Øvstebø (ed.), *The Biennial Reader: An Anthology on Large-Scale Perennial Exhibitions of Contemporary Art,* Bergen: Hatje Cantz & Bergen Kunsthall, 2010.

[174] As part of the slow but sure institutionalisation process, Wanda Svevo established contemporary art archives in 1955 at MAM-SP, which hosted the first five editions of the Bienal. By classifying and archiving documents (press clippings, photographs, letters and so forth) pertaining to the institution's activities, the event's organisers were quick to show their grasp of its vocation for the next generation of art researchers.

[175] M.H. Carvalhaes, 'Dez anos depois: um debate com Paulo Herkenhoff', *op. cit.*, p.39.

[176] The Universidade de São Paulo – USP has been hailed as South America's best public university by at least one ranking system. See *Times Higher Education* university rankings 2013–14, available at http://www.timeshighereducation.co.uk/world-university-rankings/2013-14/world-ranking/region/south-america (last accessed on 4 March 2015).

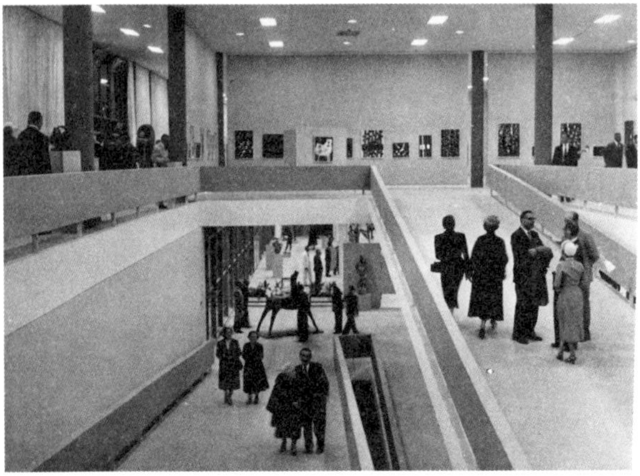

Installation view, II Bienal do Museu de Arte Moderna, Pavilhão das Nações, 1953–54. © Arquivo Histórico Wanda Svevo / Fundação Bienal São Paulo

has affirmed.[177] The city is an accumulation of superlatives: the world's fourth-largest urban agglomeration; South America's most influential financial centre, hosting seventeen of the world's twenty largest banks; socially, a melting pot of Japanese, Italian, Bolivian, Korean, north-eastern Brazilian, Jewish, Arab and other immigrant communities; and with high levels of social inequality and crime. Its social and economic configuration has always and inevitably challenged each Bienal curator's logic, but Herkenhoff pondered São Paulo in comparison with two very different cities that periodically host major exhibitions, Kassel and Venice:

> *Kassel retains its position as an event for reflection. This status is not reached by showing artists A, B or C, Richard Serra or Anselm Kiefer. A potentially more interesting difference between São Paulo, Venice and Kassel is that the Bienal de São Paulo has a lively and productive metropolis backing it; Kassel is a small town and Venice, a heritage-listed tourist monument. What I proposed to do was move São Paulo away from Venice and closer to Kassel. In other words, switch from Venice's political model to Kassel's intellectual one. I did so secretively to avoid alarming Ciccillo Matarazzo's heirs.*[178]

Yet this intellectual character had to be compatible with targeting a wider audience, rather than São Paulo professionals alone. Different agreements were articulated in an arrangement of balance and diplomacy: Herkenhoff's outline for an event that cost over US$15 million kept one foot in each camp as it successfully mastered the dialectic of international relations and local sovereignty,[179] in a process of fine-tuning identity issues with an understanding

—

[177] See P. Herkenhoff, 'Bienal 1998: princípios e processos', *op. cit.*, pp.26–27.
[178] *Ibid.*, p.22. The São Paulo population, numbering 2.5 million at the time of its first biennial, had grown to nearly 20 million by 2014.
[179] On its opening date, the press reported a total budget of R$15 million. At that time, the Brazilian currency was on a par with the US dollar. Sponsoring the

of how Brazil's image would be projected internationally. In eschewing the belief that the Week of Modern Art in 1922 had established a 'foundational myth', the curator showed his talent as a strategist.[180] As earlier detailed, the 'Núcleo Histórico' had a complicated, almost paradoxical status as a 'museum' within a temporary exhibition format. Biennials lack a permanent collection of their own for interchanges with other institutions, making the value of establishing relationships for institutional loans comparable to that of the works themselves. The 24th Bienal spared no effort in arranging the logistics (packing, transport, insurance) required to ship works from 110 museums around the world. A brief glance of a single item of correspondence – picked at random from the archives – suffices to gauge the scale of this operation: the list of Régis Michel's requests alone shows unprecedented complexity in terms of the usual models for contemporary art biennials.[181] Each step taken by the curatorial team was orchestrated for institutional purposes, to ensure repercussions with the international community while boosting the Fundação Bienal's image internationally. Developing closer relations for the Bienal de São Paulo to tap international cooperation inevitably brings to mind Ciccillo Matarazzo's diplomatic manoeuvres of the 1950s;[182] the extensive negotiations undertaken by Herkenhoff and the curatorial team were part of a remarkable vision to establish a network for the future.

—

Francis Bacon room alone cost R$500,000. The estimated budget for the 31st Bienal was R$22 million (approximately US$8.1 million).

[180] Philosopher Marilena Chauí has written an excellent study on how several Brazilian myths have validated authoritarian processes. See M. Chauí, *Brasil: Mito fundador e sociedade autoritária*, São Paulo: Fundação Perseu Abramo, 2000.

[181] The list mentioned four Carpeaux drawings, a Chassériau, a de Chevanard, two Delacroix, a Goya, a Luc-Olivier Merson and a Raffet from the Louvre's graphic arts department. It also included two of Géricault's sketches for *The Raft of the Medusa* (1818–19) from the Louvre's painting department, which had also been requested by another exhibition due to open at the same time. Herkenhoff's 'Solomonic solution' had each event receiving one of the sketches. The Musée d'Orsay in Paris was asked to lend two Jean-Louis-Ernest Meissonier oil paintings (or, alternatively, a watercolour); Musée Rodin, eleven drawings; Musée Gustave Moreau, two watercolours and three drawings; École Nationale Supérieure des Beaux-Arts, three drawings by Carpeaux and one by Géricault; Bibliothèque Nationale, four Desprez prints; Besançon's Musée des Beaux-Arts, a Géricault drawing and two Goya paintings on wood; Marseilles's Musée des Beaux-Arts, three Bernard Valere prints; Musée d'Art et d'Histoire of Metz, a Moreau painting; Musée Fabre of Montpellier, a Géricault painting and a Chevanard; and Musée des Beaux-Arts of Rouen, four Géricault drawings and a Moreau painting. In addition to works from several French provinces, Michel listed other European cities to complete his selection: Hamburg, Leipzig, Neuss, Weimar, Oxford, Cambridge, Linz, Brussels, Amsterdam, Oslo and Stockholm.

[182] Note the major change in terms of the person currently filling this role: the curator, rather than the Fundação Bienal president. Historically, the São Paulo Bienal's curator has had limited independence and has been subject to interference from Fundação Bienal officers and directors when selecting artists and rooms. Herkenhoff's review of the 24th Bienial lists seven principles or practices that must be met with a '*no*': interference, accomplished facts, opportunism, failing to submit records, letting things go on until somebody gives up, 'democratism' and yielding to pressure. See P. Herkenhoff, 'Bienal 1998: princípios e processos', *op. cit.*, pp.26–27.

The project overall sought to reverse the flow of interpretations that had previously placed Brazil in a minor position. Perhaps more ambitiously still, it set out to steer around the trap of multiculturalism. This task was even thornier in consideration of another of Herkenhoff's curatorial aims, thus defined: 'The exhibition was to be aimed at the Brazilian public.'[183] After visiting the 'empty' Johannesburg Biennale in 1997, Herkenhoff realised that 'the biennial must not be made for the international scene. [...] Rather than something curators do for themselves and their professional project, a biennial is clearly a collective social project.'[184]

Herkenhoff's appointment, given his status as a curator from Rio, may well have hurt the local pride of certain people in São Paulo. After all, the Modern Art Week preceding Oswald de Andrade's 'Manifesto' was itself launched in São Paulo's municipal theatre! A comparison of the modernist poet's letters with the reception that art critics subsequently afforded the exhibition may show minor sentimental coincidences between Andrade and Herkenhoff, as if the latter personified the controversy between the former and the intelligentsia of his day.[185] Both men showed confidence in the revolutionary power of ideas. Andrade wrote: 'The masses, dear fellow, will have to rise to the level of the finest quality material, which is what I make. [...] To doubt the masses' ability to understand is to doubt revolutionary progress itself.'[186] Likewise, Herkenhoff always insisted on upholding the complexity of his own project, rather than diluting it for the perceived requirements of a mass audience.[187] Yet there was also a distinct lack of understanding in the 24th Bienal's critical and intellectual reception, as Herkenhoff would reflect ten years later: 'Paradoxically, at the Anthropophagy Biennial an antithetical reaction was observed – an absolute refusal to discuss the art on show. According to Claude Lévi-Strauss, anthropoemic culture, unlike anthropophagy, is one that does not assimilate any exchange with the other, ultimately it involves vomit.'[188]

—

An institutional crisis was to grip the Fundação Bienal after the 24th edition due to reports of financial irregularities under the chairmanship of the architect Carlos Bratke, Landmann's appointed successor. Alfons Hug curated the 25th and 26th editions, in 2002 and 2004. Through a manoeuvre by the

—

[183] Herkenhoff had statistics showing that '40% of the public were visiting the exhibition for the first time', which meant that 'certain physical barriers symbolising social exclusion' had to be tackled. See *ibid.*, p.27.

[184] P. Herkenhoff, unpublished transcript of seminar at Faculdade Santa Marcelina, 12 March 2008, *op. cit.*

[185] Andrade and Herkenhoff also resemble each other in their repeated attacks on academic circles, within which their work has been disparaged as inadequate by academic standards.

[186] O. Andrade, 'Carta a Afrânio Zuccolotto', *Ritmo*, November 1935.

[187] Herkenhoff has also refuted the pertinence of the term 'blockbuster' to describe any edition of the Bienal, since the admission tickets could never cover the budget of producing the exhibition. See P. Herkenhoff, 'Bienal 1998: princípios e processos', *op. cit.*, p.21.

[188] *Ibid.*, p.34.

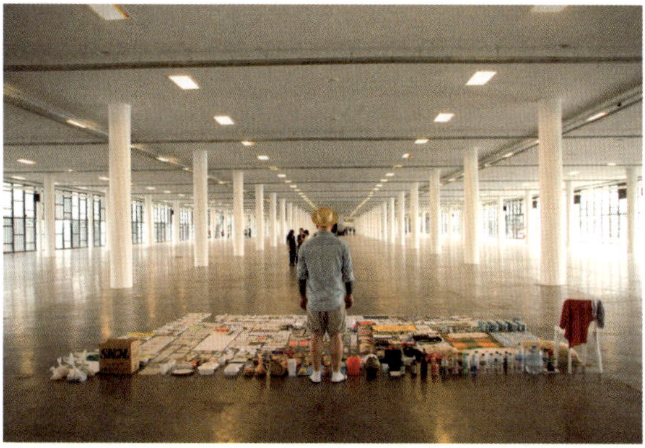

Installation view, 28th Bienal de São Paulo, Ciccillo Matarazzo Pavilion, 2008.
In foreground: Maurício Ianês, *Untitled (The Kindness of Strangers)*, 2008
© the artist; Amilcar Packer

subsequent president Manoel Pires da Costa, who was elected in 2002,[189] Edemar Cid Ferreira was reinstated to the board despite having been charged with fraudulent activities. The news of his renewed position revealed an ethical crisis on top of the financial one, and prompted Cildo Meireles to withdraw from participating as an artist in the 27th Bienal.[190] Financial accounts submitted during Pires da Costa's mandate were rejected, thus exacerbating the institutional crisis and revealing a lack of administrative transparency. With debts building up,[191] and time running short to organise the 28th Bienal, curator Ivo Mesquita and associate curator Ana Paula Cohen decide to leave the pavilion's middle floor dramatically empty as a basis for re-examining the biennial model.

In this dystopian scenario, the 1998 Bienal stands out as a rare instance of the institution attempting to professionalise its management and, further, to make a break from the cronyism typical of the hereditary captaincies of Brazil's colonial period. The 24th Bienal was inarguably a watershed moment between European and US exhibitions. In an interview given in 2001, curator Catherine David stated it was the best edition of the Bienal de São Paulo's history, and that, compared to the Venice Biennale, the São Paulo institution held much more potential to mirror social and contemporary issues.[192]

—

[189] Manoel Pires da Costa was elected president of the Fundação Bienal after being condemned for irregularities in the financial market during his mandate as president of the BM&F (Futures and Commodities Exchange). See http://www.istoe.com.br/reportagens/30739_TESTEMUNHAS+CHAVE (last accessed on 4 March 2015). Nevertheless, he was appointed by the Board to preside the Fundação for three mandates, despite allegations concerning accounting practices under his management, from 2002 to 2010, in power during the curatorships of Alfons Hug (2004), Lisette Lagnado (2006) and Ivo Mesquita and Ana Paula Cohen (2008).
[190] Ferreira still holds a seat on the Fundação Bienal Board. Despite the incident involving him and Meireles, the latter showed work at the 29th Bienal, curated by Moacir dos Anjos and Agnaldo Farias in 2010.
[191] In 2012, the press reported a shortfall of R$75 million.
[192] Catherine David, interviewed in F. Cypriano, 'Curadora critica Guggenheim

The 'Núcleo Histórico' turned out to be much more than a structural support in Herkenhoff's curatorial design for the 24th Bienal. From the outset, it overshadowed the other sections and was perceived as an attempt to bring together several disciplines in support of a 'cultural strategy', as Andrade would have wished. It is true that official statements emphasised the existence of multiple assumptions and strategies to avoid the event's scale and scope being confused with the identity of a museum. Nevertheless, boundaries or demarcations between excluding territories were often blurred. The very real complexity of the operation lay in devising a different narrative – forming the basis for, in the long term, a different international agenda. Not even the hailstorm that hit the building on the opening night, causing leaks in the top-floor exhibition area where the 'Núcleo Histórico' was located, could detract from the work that had been done.

Well over a decade since the Anthropophagy Biennial, some of the event's successes may be said to lie in its internationalising Brazilian artists (although it did not do this for other Latin American artists to the same extent). Despite more recent biennials joining the region's art circuit – Havana and Mercosul in particular – São Paulo remains relevant for more than its historical precedent within the South American continent, with participation still enjoying a high level of prestige. Whilst São Paulo may have outshone Venice (as the Son kills the Father) and elevated recognition of Brazilian art to a new level, a different order of problems has emerged in connection with its international prestige. The São Paulo event is at an unexpected crossroads: how to cope with higher expectations from the international system than from its local audience? Assessed in terms of critical pedagogy and analysing the gap between an event and its academic reflection, as well as between an event and the masses, we find that the Bienal has yet to imprint an ethical standard for its curatorial strategy that demonstrates its independence from the metropolis or any force that expresses power.[193] Regrettably, even the abolishment of national representations would not constitute the desired horizon of autonomy: today market imperatives threaten to drown contributions, including the most radical works, in ever-murkier waters.

Translated from Portuguese by Izabel Burbridge.

—

no Brasil', *Folha de S. Paulo*, 'Ilustrada' section, 6 February 2001, available at http://www1.folha.uol.com.br/fsp/ilustrad/fq0602200121.htm (last accessed on 4 March 2015). Agnaldo Farias would also declare the 24th Bienal the 'best exhibition of its kind' in *Bienal de São Paulo 50 anos, 1951–2001 / 50 years of the São Paulo Biennial, op. cit.*, p.254.

[193] One cannot forget the growth of the art fair SP Arte, which takes place in the same pavilion as the Bienal and shares the modernist aura of the architecture. This cohabitation represents a compelling challenge ahead if the Bienal really wants to distinguish itself as a different category of art show.

The 24th Bienal de São Paulo 1998

The 24th Bienal de São Paulo
Ciccillo Matarazzo Pavilion, Ibirapuera Park, São Paulo
3 October–13 December 1998

'Representações Nacionais' ('National Representations')
Ground floor (across two levels connected by a ramp)

'Arte Contemporânea Brasileira: Um e/entre Outro/s'
('Brazilian Contemporary Art: One and/among Other/s')
Primarily on the first floor (north-east side)

'Roteiros. Roteiros. Roteiros. Roteiros. Roteiros.
Roteiros. Roteiros.' ('Routes. Routes. Routes. Routes.
Routes. Routes. Routes.')
Primarily on the first floor (south-west side)

'Núcleo Histórico: Antropofagia e Histórias de Canibalismos'
('Historical Nucleus: Anthropophagy and Histories
of Cannibalisms')
Second (top) floor

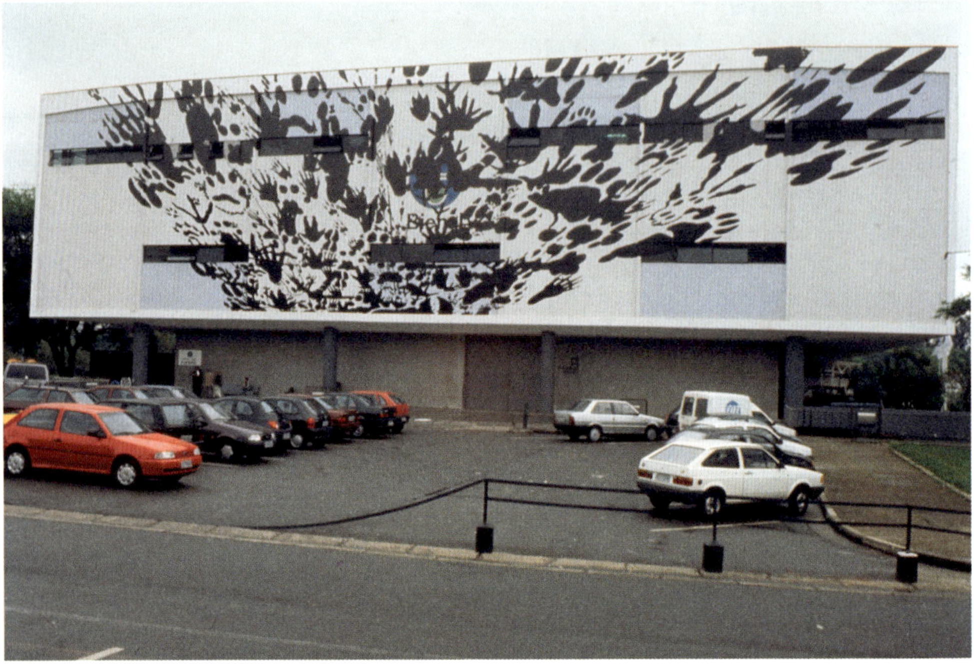

fig.1

Outside the Bienal building, Regina Silveira's vinyl *Tropel* (*Throng*, 1998), part of the 'Arte Contemporânea Brasileira' section curated by Paulo Herkenhoff and Adriano Pedrosa, appeared on the façade of the Ciccillo Matarazzo Pavilion in Ibirapuera Park, alongside Bienal billboards stating 'Só a antropofagia nos une' ('Only antropophagia unites us'), a phrase taken from Oswald de Andrade's 'Manifesto antropófago'.

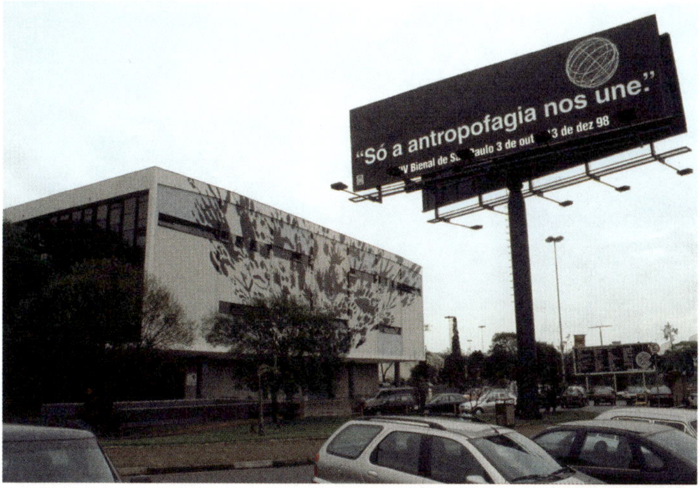

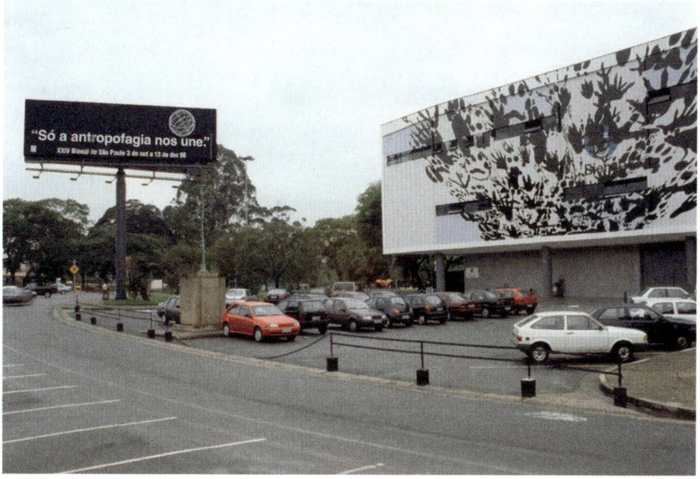

fig.2 and 3

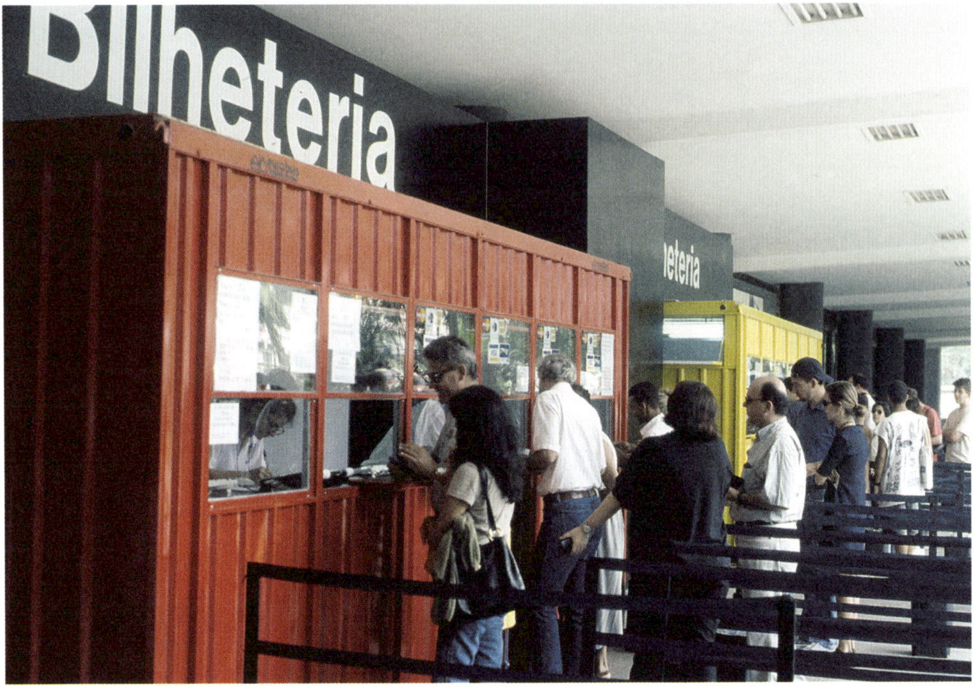

fig.4

The exhibition box office was located outside the Pavilion.

The entrance to the Bienal, via the Rua de Serviços (Street of Services), housed a number of stands by corporate sponsors, such as Kodak, Sudameris Bank and the financial newspaper *Gazeta Mercantil*, and was the home of the Sala Educação (educational centre), sponsored by HSBC Bank. There was a text on the windowpane that read: 'Teacher, this room is for you! Use this space of the 24th Bienal de São Paulo to search for guided tours and projects'.

The website for the Bienal – accessible at the exhibition at a dedicated 'Web Bienal' station – also made available a range of teaching materials, as well as exhibition maps, interactive documentation and 'Webarte', an online exhibition. According to the catalogue, 'Webarte' was curated by Mark van de Walle, and featured the artists Dennis Balk, Sue de Beer, Erik and Heather ChanSchatz and John Simon, among others; it also included a section titled 'seja antropofágico: webcanibalize!' ('be anthropophagic: cannibalise the web!'), which was curated by Ricardo Ribenboim and Ricardo Anderáos, with projects by Fabiana de Barros (*Vulnerables*, 1998–99), Gisela Domschke and Fabio Itapura (*The Buzzing Diary*, n.d.) and Kiko Goifman and Jurandir Müller (*Valetes em Slow Motion*, 1998).

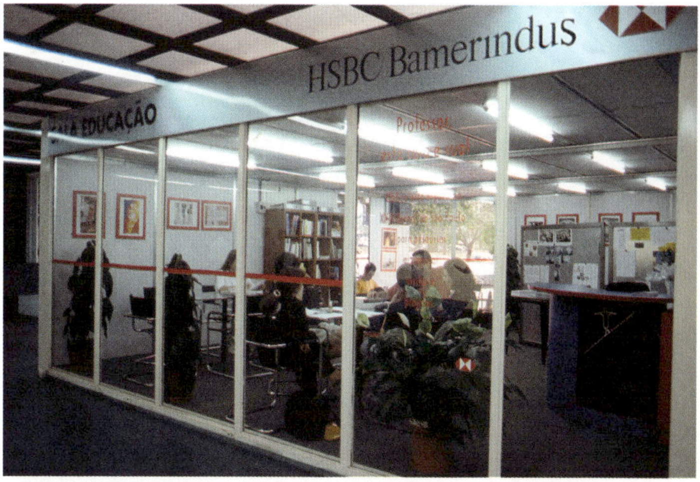

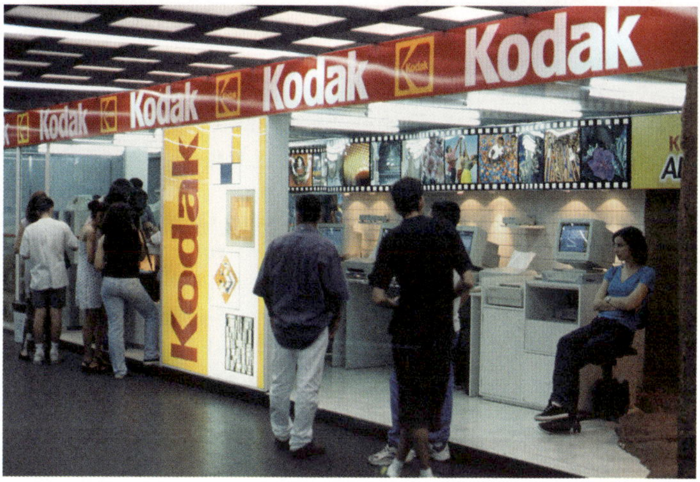

fig.5 and 6

'Representações Nacionais' ('National Representations')

Representações Nacionais

The national representations were installed across the ground floor of the Ciccillo Matarazzo Pavilion, with artists from 54 different countries. A section focusing on Central America and the Caribbean was curated by Virginia Pérez-Ratton.

Mario Abreu (Venezuela, curated by Anita Tapias)
Regina Aguilar (Honduras, curated by Virginia Pérez-Ratton)
Carlos Aguirre (Mexico, curated by Carlos Aranda, Rita Eder and Sylvia Pandolfi Elliman)
Hüseyin Bahri Alptekin (Turkey, curated by Vasif Kortun)
Allora & Calzadilla (Puerto Rico, curated by Virginia Pérez-Ratton)
Fernando Alvim (Angola)
Mirosław Bałka (Poland, curated by Anda Rottenberg)
Moisés Barrios (Guatemala, curated by Virginia Pérez-Ratton)
Mario Benjamin (Haiti, curated by Virginia Pérez-Ratton)
Ernest Breleur (Martinique, curated by Virginia Pérez-Ratton)
Carlos Capelán (Uruguay)
Valia Carvalho (Bolivia, curated by Pedro Querejazu)
Lourdes Castro and Francisco Tropa (Portugal, curated by João Fernandes)
Albert Chong (Jamaica, curated by Virginia Pérez-Ratton)
Nicola Costantino (Argentina, curated by Edward Shaw)
Michael Craig-Martin (Great Britain, curated by Andrea Rose and Clairrie Rudrum)
Arturo Duclos (Chile, curated by Gaspar Galaz and Justo Pastor Mellado)
Sandra Eleta (Panama, curated by Virginia Pérez-Ratton)
Olafur Eliasson (Denmark, curated by Marianne Krogh Jensen)
Sylvie Fleury (Switzerland, curated by Pierre-André Lienhard)
Hilmar Fredriksen (Norway, curated by Velaug Bollingmo)
Carlos Garaicoa (Cuba, curated by Virginia Pérez-Ratton)
Zvi Goldstein (Israel, curated by Sergio Edelsztein)
Pan Gongkai (China, curated by Xu Jiang)
Abigail Hadeed (Republic of Trinidad and Tobago, curated by Virginia Pérez-Ratton)
Elias Helm (Colombia, curated by Miguel L. Rojas-Sotelo)

Kimsooja (South Korea, curated by Young-Ho Kim)
William Kentridge (South Africa, curated by Lorna Ferguson)
Abdoulaye Konaté (Mali, curated by Awa Meité)
Elke Krystufek (Austria, curated by Brigitte Huck)
Mischa Kuball (Germany, curated by Karin Stempel)
Oleg Kulik (Russia, curated by Constantin Bokhorov)
Toshihiro Kuno (Japan, curated by Kazuzo Yamawaki)
Martin López (Dominican Republic, curated by Virginia Pérez-Ratton)
Geoff Lowe (Australia, curated by Louise Neri)
Ken Lum (Canada, curated by Jon Tupper)
Leena Luostarinen (Finland, curated by Kuutti Lavonen)
Brian Maguire (Ireland, curated by Fiach Mac Conghail)
Mark Manders (The Netherlands, curated by Saskia Bos)
Jenny Marketou (Greece, curated by Sania Papa)
Živko Marušič (Slovenia, curated by Lilijana Stepančič)
Maurizio Mochetti (Italy, curated by Anna Mattirolo)
Priscilla Monge (Costa Rica, curated by Virginia Pérez-Ratton)
Johan Muyle (Belgium, curated by Catherine De Croës)
Luis Paredes (Republic of El Salvador, curated by Virginia Pérez-Ratton)
Judy Pfaff (United States, curated by Miranda McClintic)
Raul Quintanilla (Nicaragua, curated by Virginia Pérez-Ratton)
Khalil Rabah (Palestine, curated by Jack Persekian)
Ann-Sofi Sidén (Sweden, curated by Maria Lind)
Antoni Socías (Spain, curated by Santiago B. Olmo)
Pierrick Sorin (France, curated by Hervé Chandès)
Manit Sriwanichpoom (Thailand, curated by Apinan Poshyananda)
Cecilio Thompson (Paraguay, curated by Osvaldo González Real)
Diego Veintimilla (Ecuador)
Moico Yaker (Peru, curated by Gustavo Buntinx)

Countries in brackets are those attributed in the Bienal catalogue. Also on this floor was work by Choi Jeong-Hwa as part of the 'Roteiros Asia' section and Bruce Nauman as part of the 'Núcleo Histórico'.

Artists are identified on the plans by their initials (pp.70–71).

Ciccillo Matarazzo Pavilion, Ibirapuera Park, São Paulo
Ground floor (first floor according to Brazilian convention)

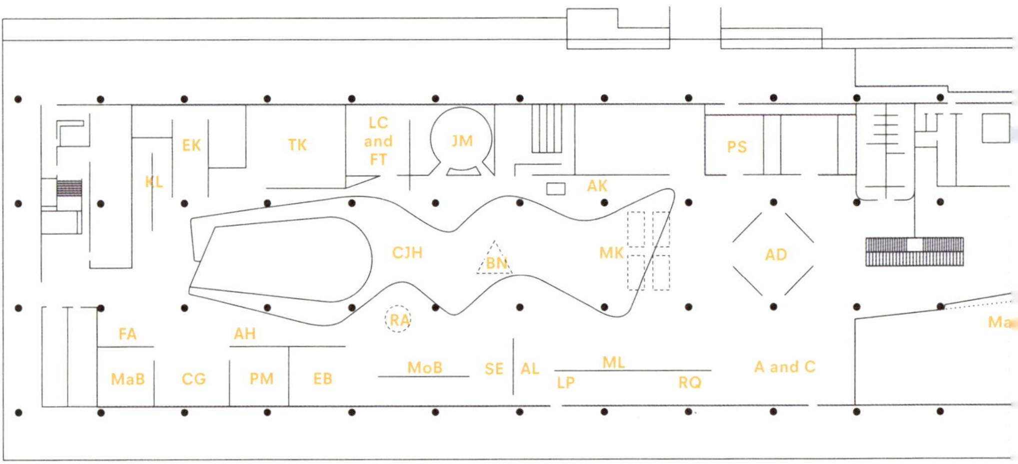

These and following plans are based on floor plans prepared for the 24th Bienal de São Paulo by the exhibition's architecture team: Paulo Mendes da Rocha, Martin Corullon and Joana Fernandes Elito.

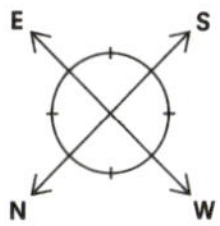
E
S
N
W

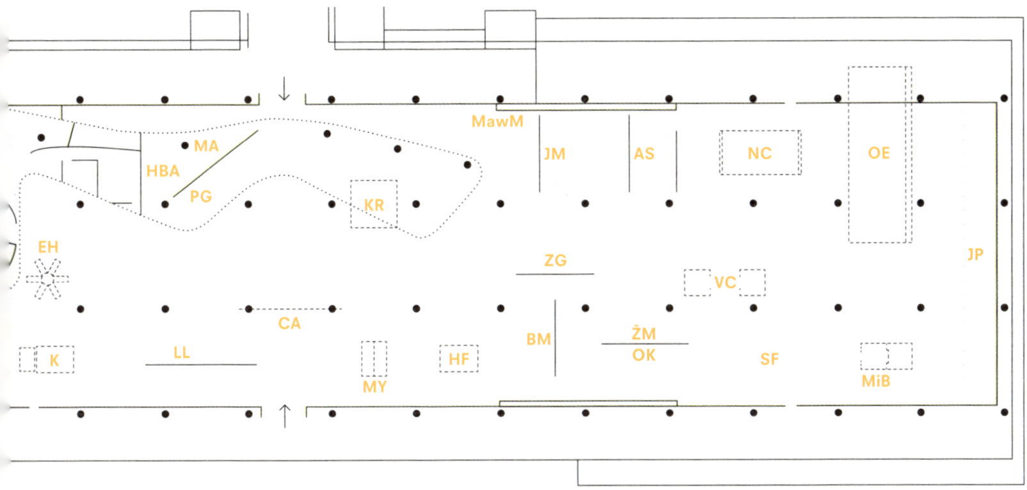
MawM
MA
HBA
PG
JM
AS
NC
OE
KR
EH
ZG
JP
VC
CA
ŽM
OK
BM
LL
K
HF
SF
MY
MiB

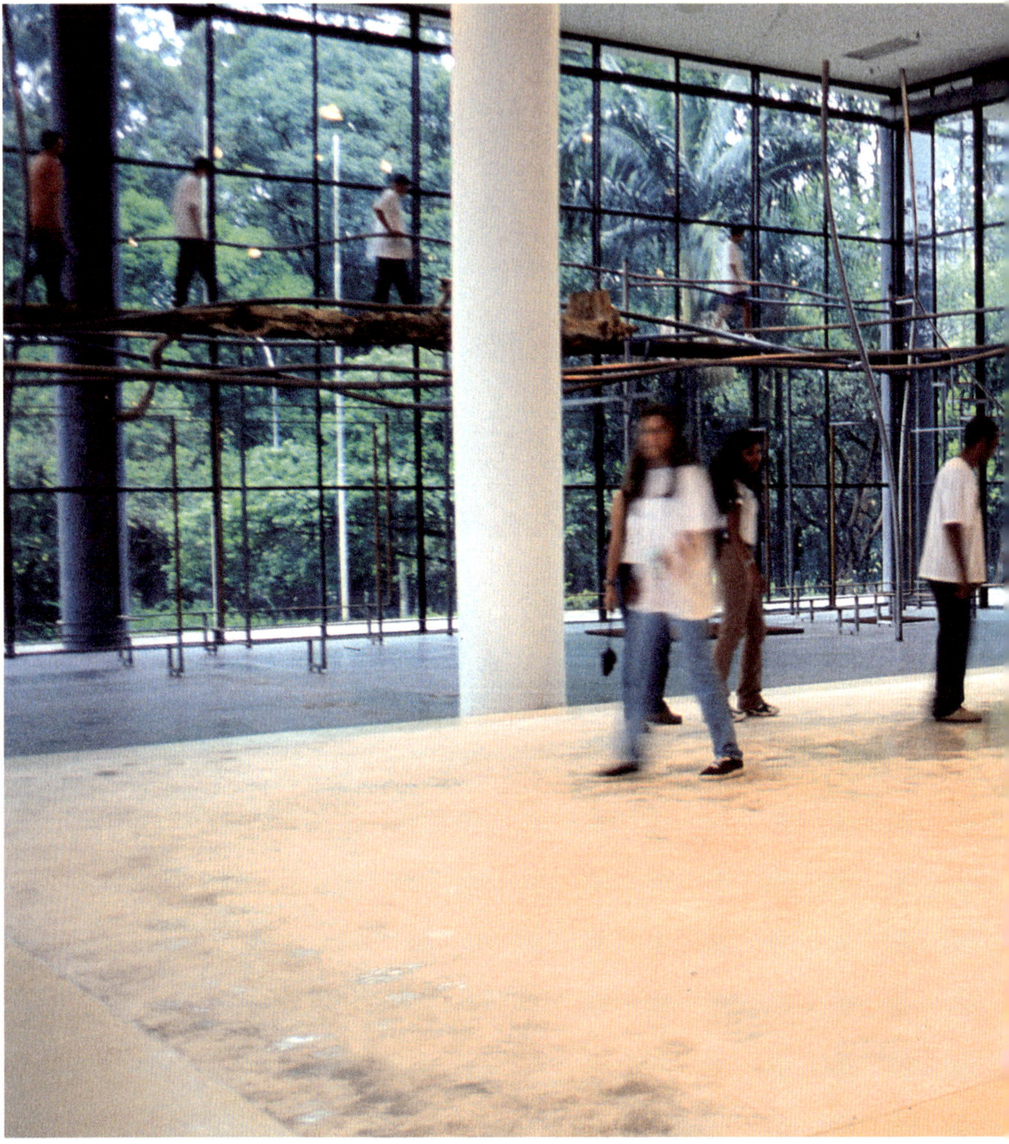

fig.7

Visitors could enter the 'Representações Nacionais' through two possible entrances on the ground floor of the pavilion. Olafur Eliasson's *The Very Large Ice Floor* (1998, representing Denmark) appeared in the south-west corner of the ground floor, as did Judy Pfaff's installation *Coroa De Espinhos* (*Crown of Thorns*, 1998, representing the US), which is seen in the background here, and stretched across the entire width of the building.

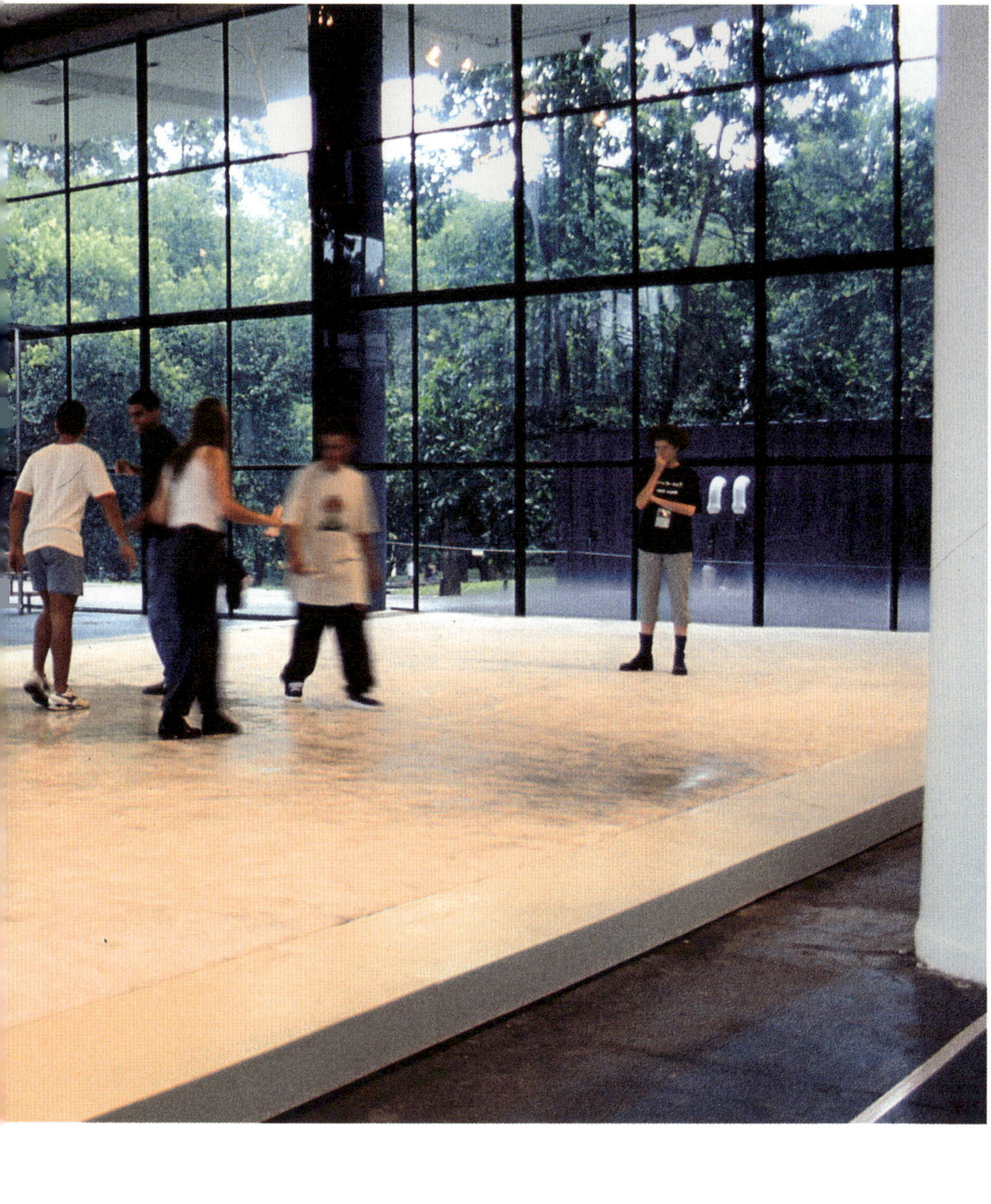

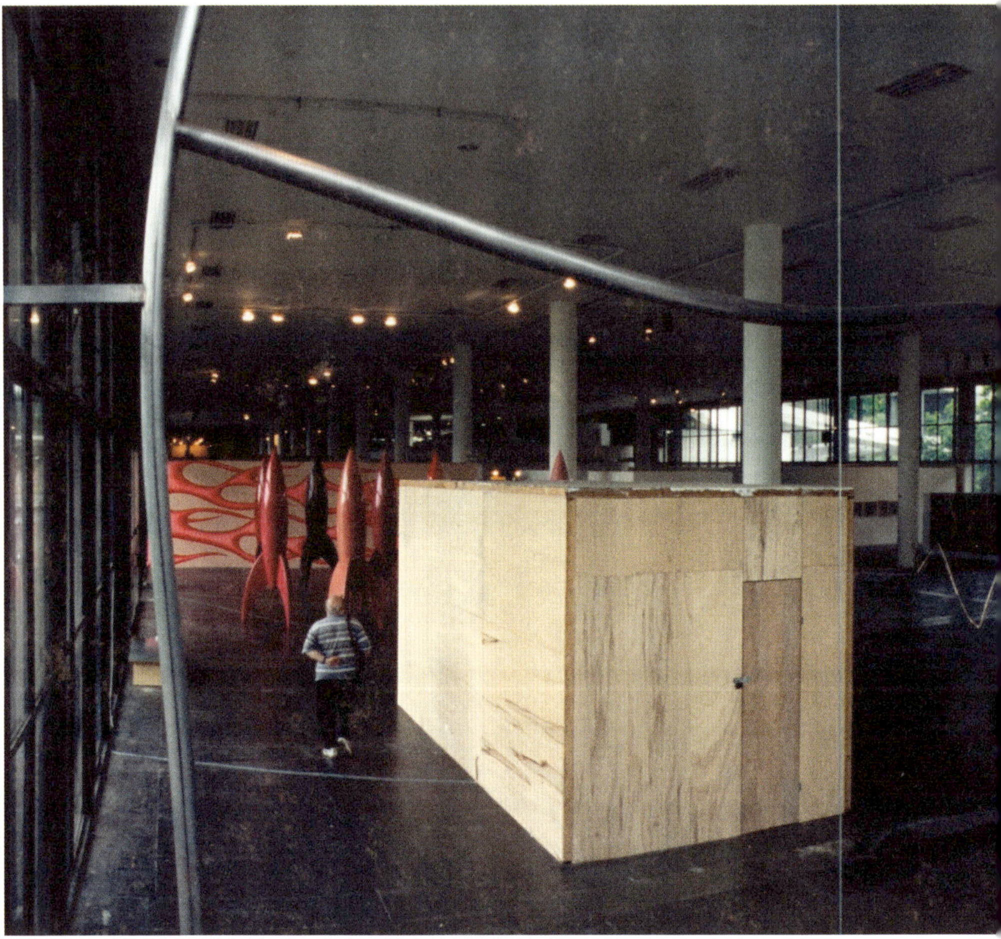

fig.8

View of the west-side corner of the 'Representações Nacionais' segment. From left: a sculpture by Mirosław Bałka titled *a, e, i, o, u* (1997, representing Poland), work by Sylvie Fleury (representing Switzerland) and Judy Pfaff's *Coroa De Espinhos* (1998, representing the US).

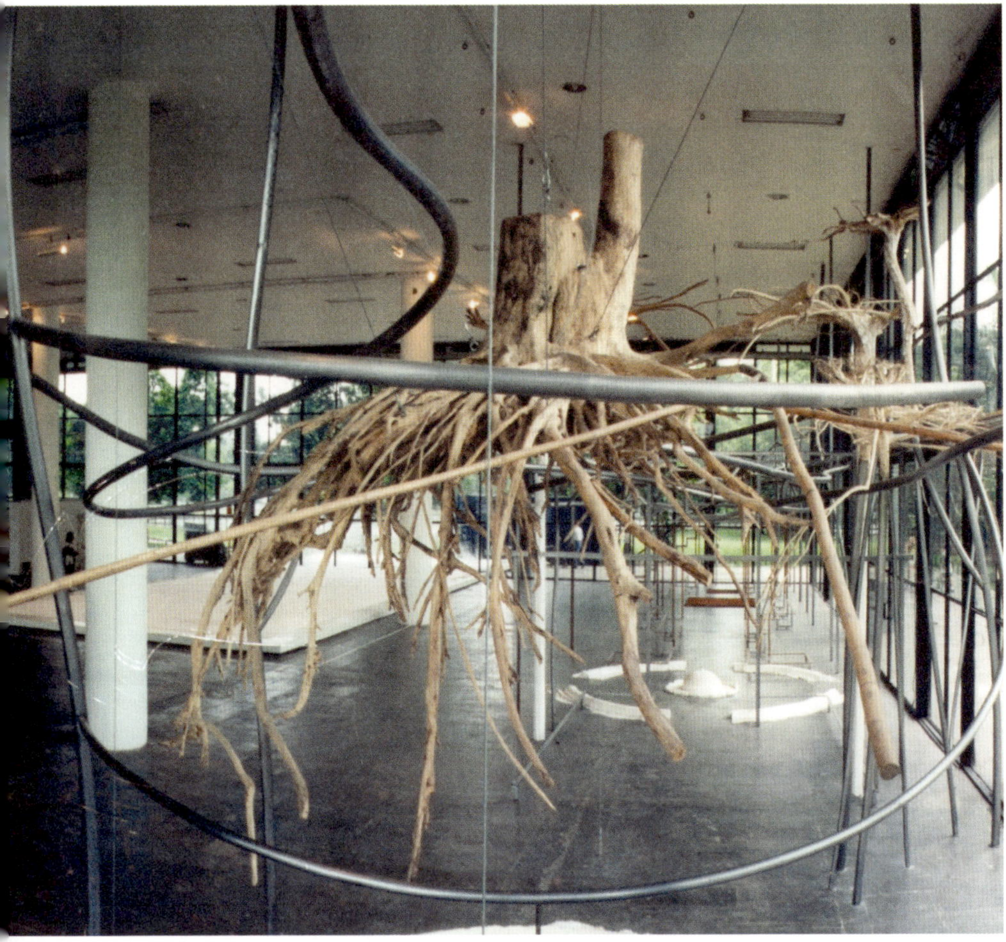

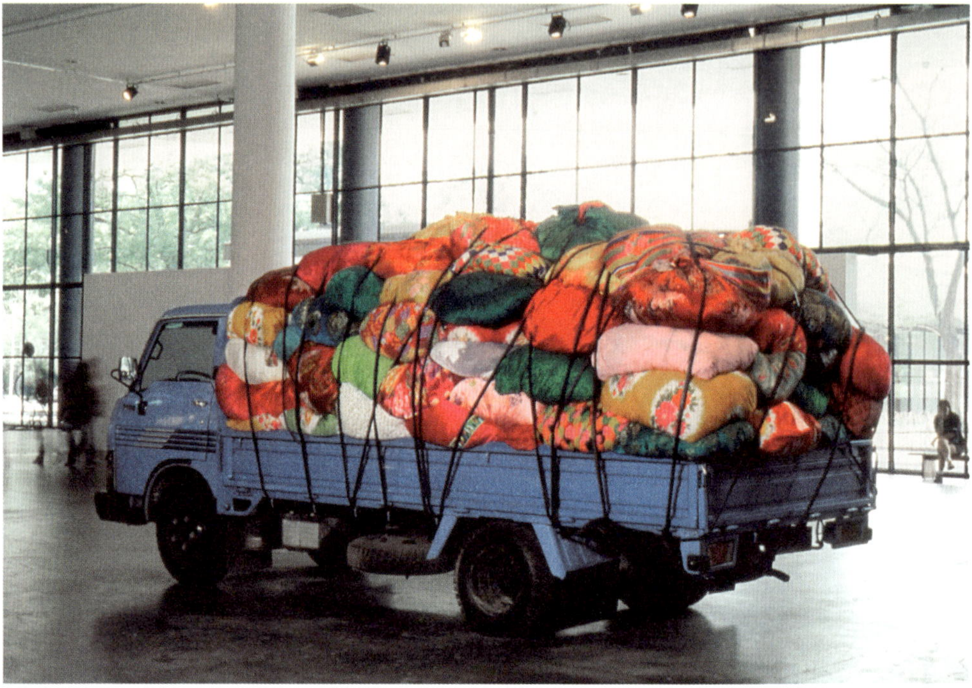

fig.9

At the bottom of the slope connecting the lower half of the ground floor to the upper half was a two-ton truck loaded with bungee cords and *bottaris* (traditional Korean wrapping cloths) that had made its way from Seoul to São Paulo via road and boat – a work by the artist Kimsooja titled *Cities on the Move – 11633 miles Bottari Truck* (1998, representing South Korea).

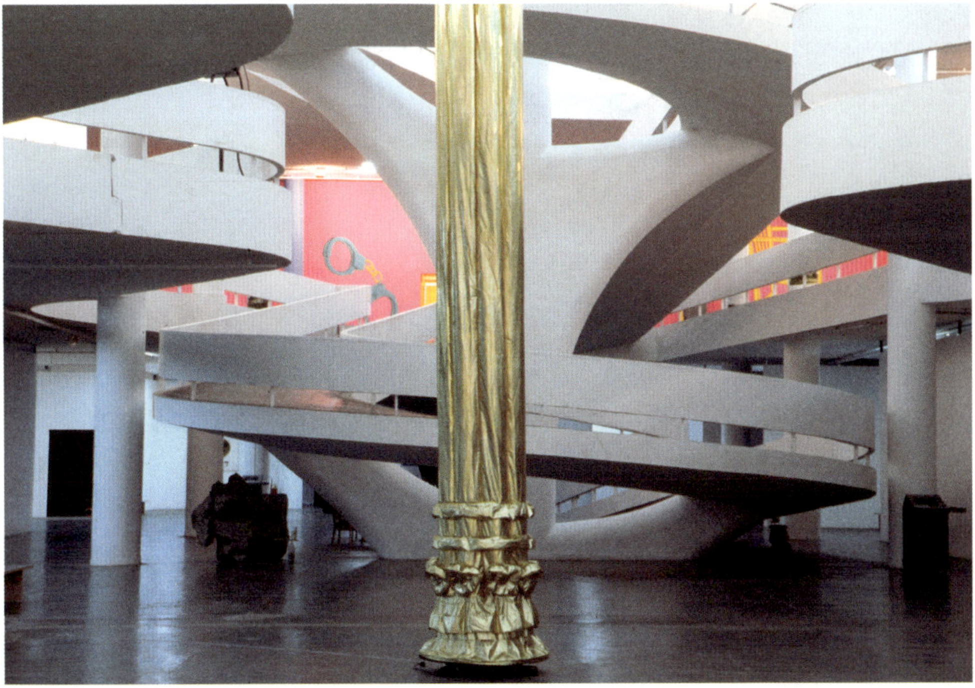

fig.10

Placed in the atrium space next to the building's swirling ramp, Choi Jeong-Hwa's *Encore, Encore, Encore* (1997), part of the 'Roteiros...' section, was an inflated plastic gold column extending upwards through all three floors, with an angel with moving wings at the top. *Making Sense* (1998), a work by Michael Craig-Martin (representating Great Britain), took up the entire background wall on the first floor.

'Arte Contemporânea Brasileira: Um e/entre Outro/s'

'Arte Contemporânea Brasileira: Um e/entre Outro/s'
('Brazilian Contemporary Art: One and/among Other/s')

This section occupied part of the first floor and consisted of two halves that were exhibited in parallel on either side of the atrium: 'Um e Outro' ('One and Other'), curated by Adriano Pedrosa, and 'Um entre Outros' ('One and among Others'), curated by Paulo Herkenhoff.

Claudia Andujar
Artur Barrio
Lenora de Barros
Sandra Cinto
Lygia Clark
Rochelle Costi
Dias & Riedweg (Mauricio Dias and Walter Riedweg)
Iole de Freitas
Edgard de Souza
Anna Bella Geiger
Rubem Grilo
Carmela Gross
Wesley Duke Lee
Leonilson (José Leonilson Bezerra Dias)
Laura Lima
Ivens Machado
Antonio Manuel
Cildo Meireles
Beatriz Milhazes
Vik Muniz
Emmanuel Nassar
Ernesto Neto
Rivane Neuenschwander
Arthur Omar
Nazareth Pacheco
Lygia Pape
Rosângela Rennó
José Resende
Miguel Rio Branco
Daniel Senise
Regina Silveira
Courtney Smith
Valeska Soares
Tunga
Adriana Varejão

This area also featured work by Michael Craig-Martin as part of 'Representações Nacionais' and Michael Asher (with Andrew Freeman) as part of 'Roteiros Canada and US'.

Artists are identified on the plans by their initials (pp.80–81).

Ciccillo Matarazzo Pavilion, Ibirapuera Park, São Paulo
First floor (second floor according to Brazilian convention)

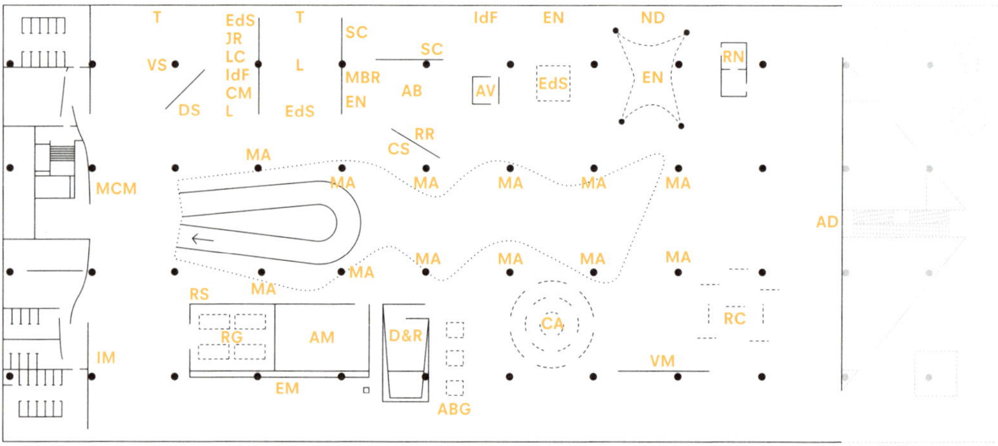

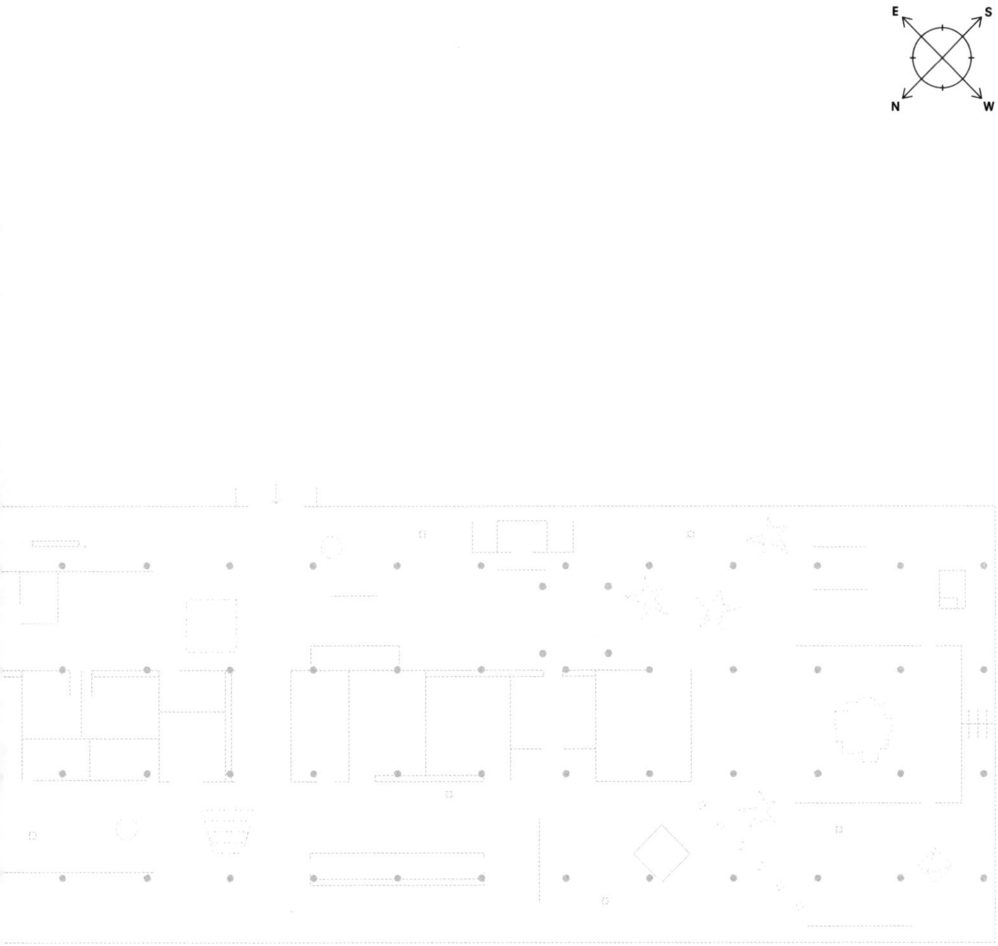
E
S
N
W

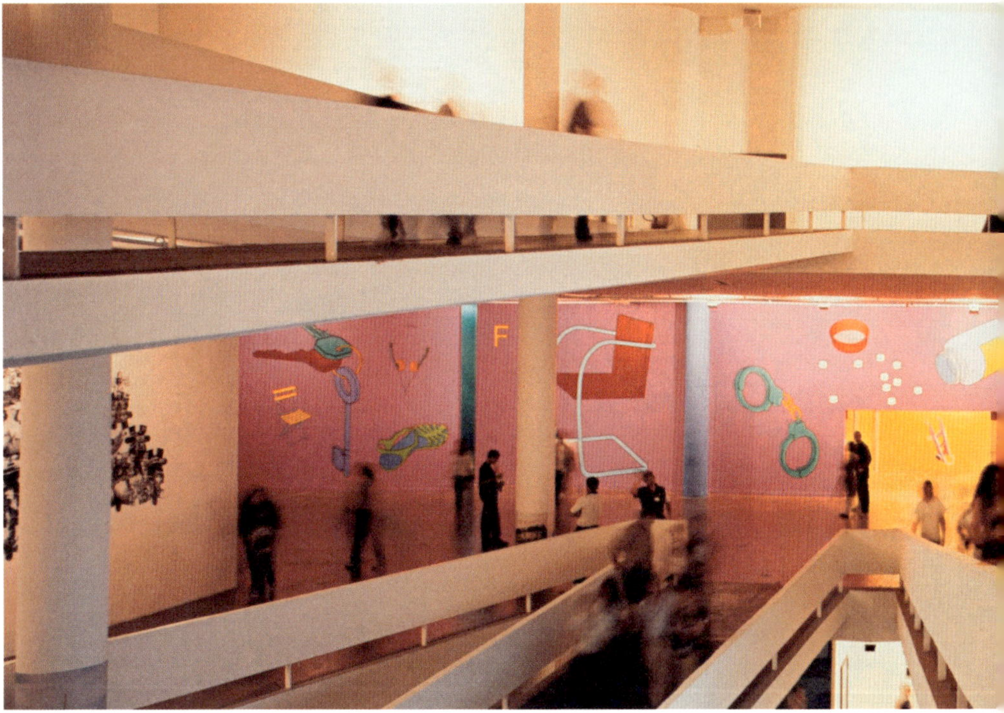

fig.11

Arriving at the first floor via the internal ramp, visitors were met by Michael Craig-Martin's mural *Making Sense* (1998), part of 'Representações Nacionais'. Regina Silveira's *Quebra-cabeça da América Latina* (*Latin American Puzzle*, 1998) is on the left (as part of 'Um entre Outros', the half of the exhibition curated by Paulo Herkenhoff), with Daniel Senise's painting *O Beijo do Elo Perdido* (*We Look at the Kiss of the Missing Link*, 1991) on the right (as part of 'Um e Outro', curated by Adriano Pedrosa). Visible above, on the top floor, is Carmela Gross's *A Negra* (*The Black Woman*, 1997), part of the 'Núcleo Histórico'. Also visible are two photographs from *South Texas Colonias* (1998), a work by Michael Asher (with Andrew Freeman) (fig.18) that was part of Ivo Mesquita's curatorial contribution to 'Roteiros...'.

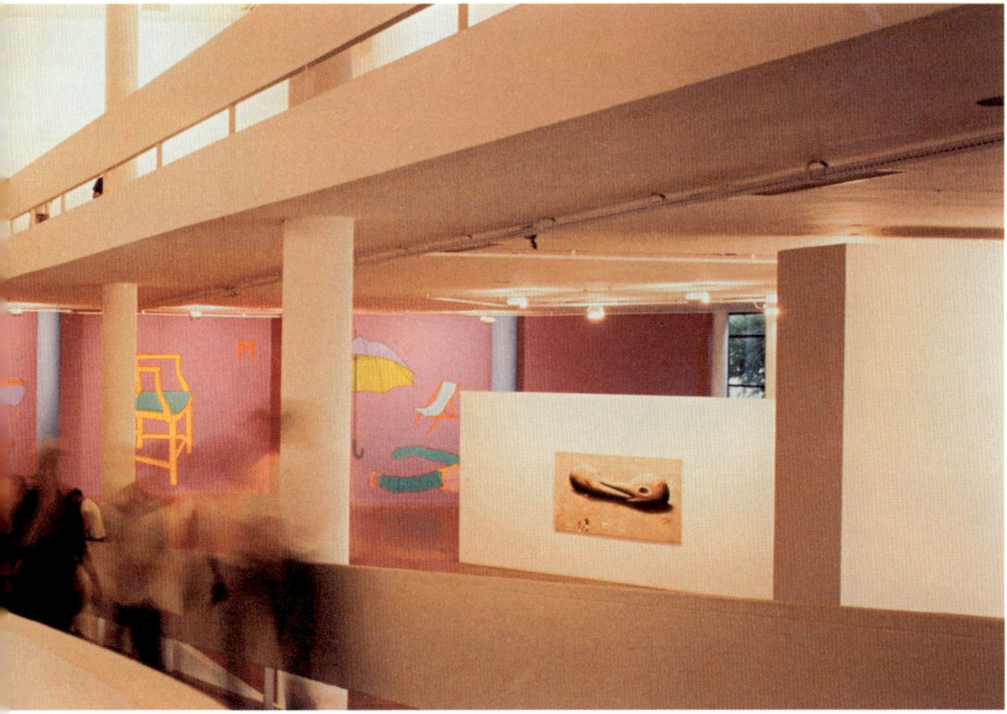

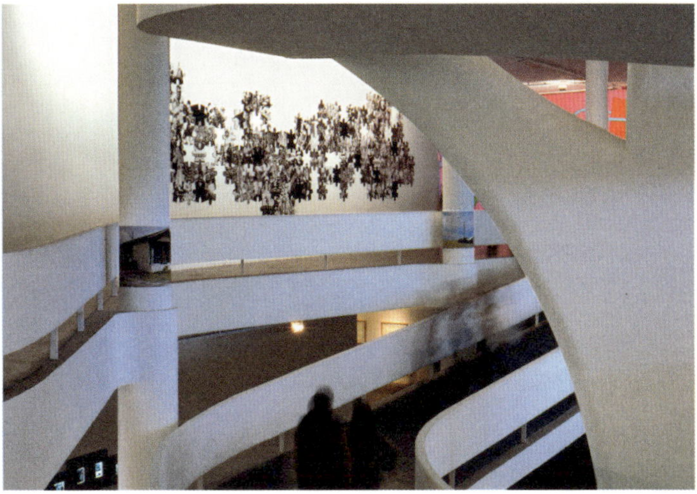

fig.12

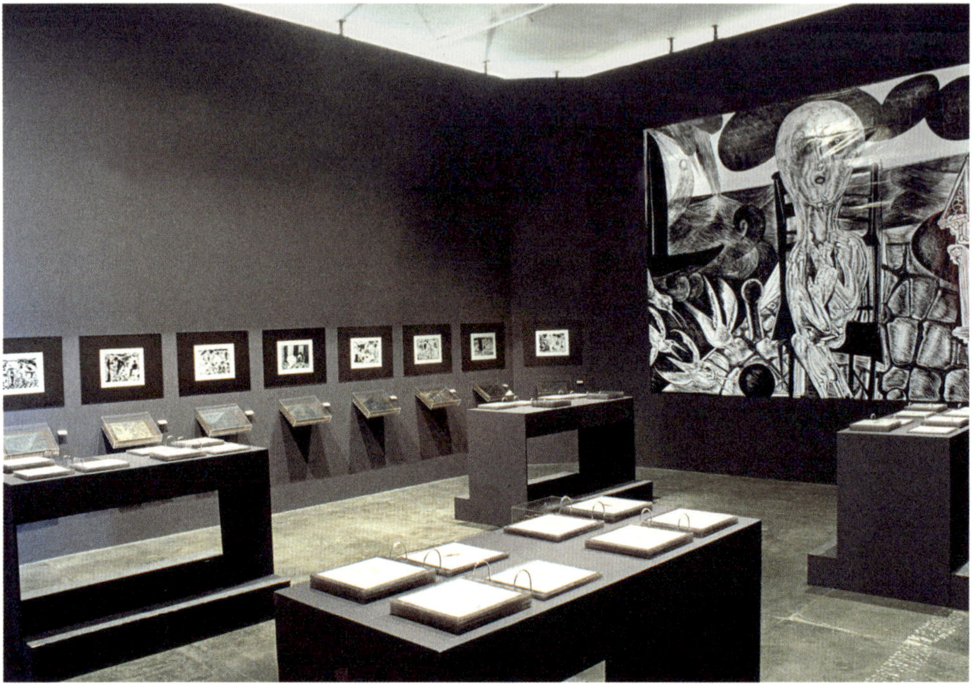

fig.13

Turning left, into the 'Um entre Outros' section, and entering an enclosed space, was a selection of work by Rubem Grilo: 26 woodcuts; 16 notebooks containing miniature sketches, displayed on tables; and the enlarged woodcut print *No cais à espera do barco* (*On the Pier, Waiting for the Boat*, 1998).

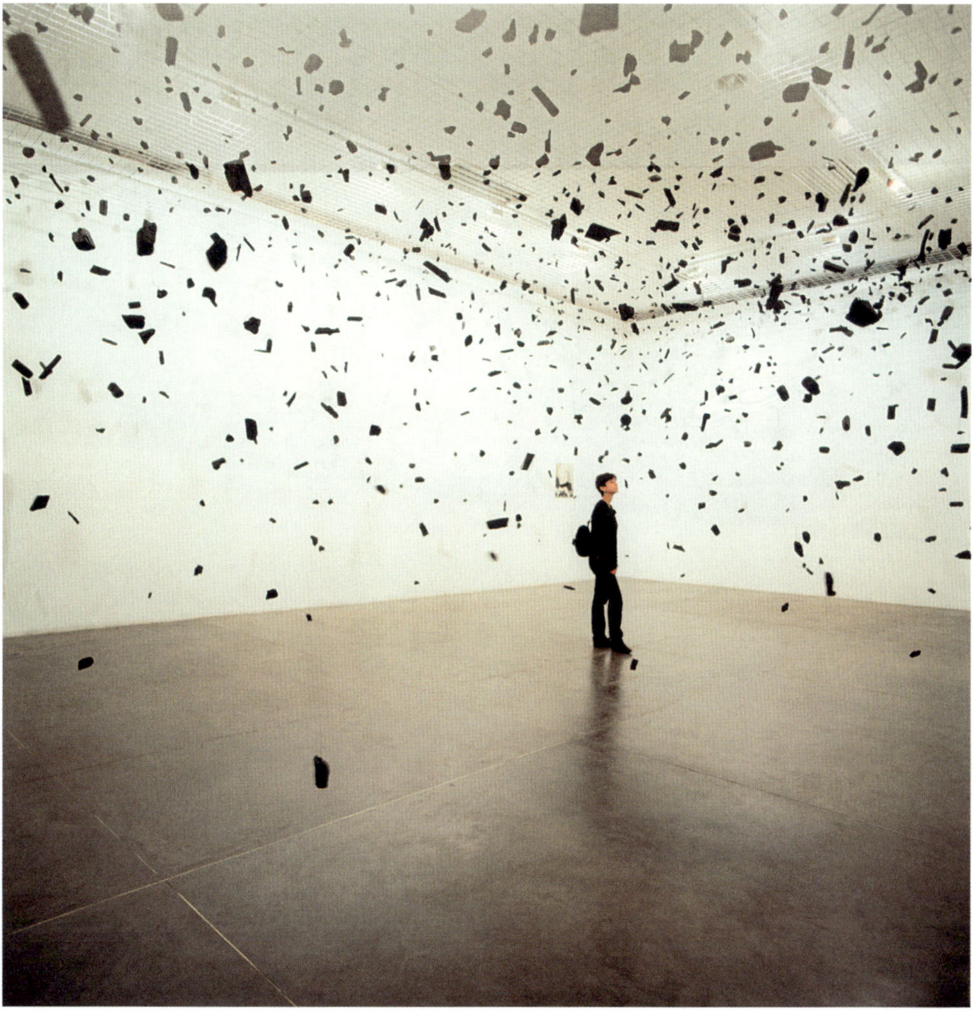

fig.14

In an adjoining room Antonio Manuel's work *Fantasma* (*Phantom,* 1994/98), consisting of coal, thread, flashlight and photograph, was installed.

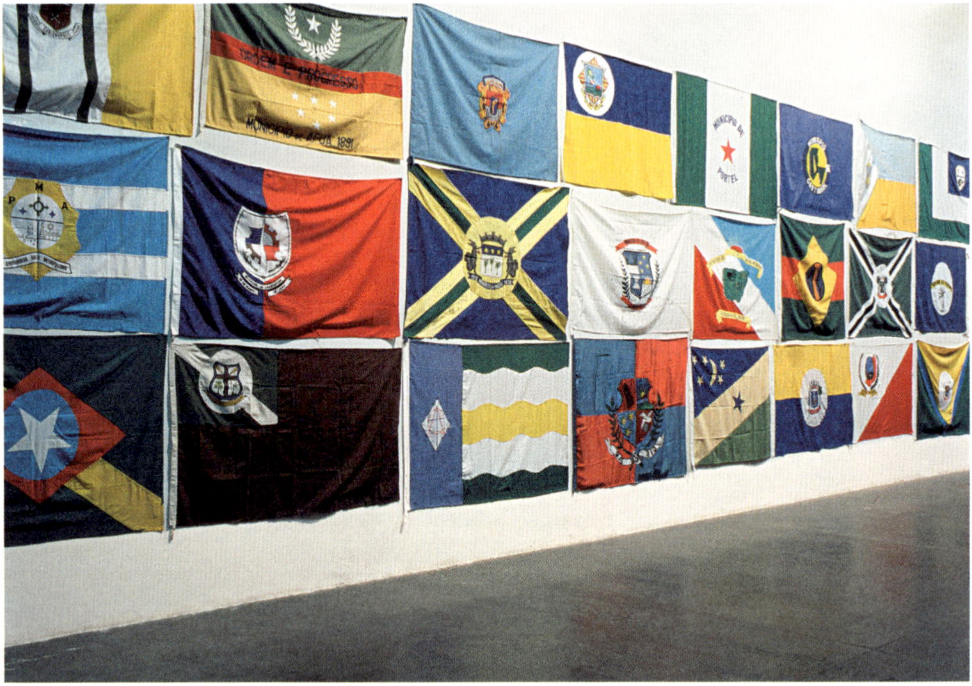

fig.15

On the wall facing the outer windows of the space, Emmanuel Nassar's *Bandeiras* (*Flags*, 1998) hung, composed of flags from the municipalities of the artist's home state Pará, in Northern Brazil. A version of this work was also featured in the catalogue for the 'Representações Nacionais' section.

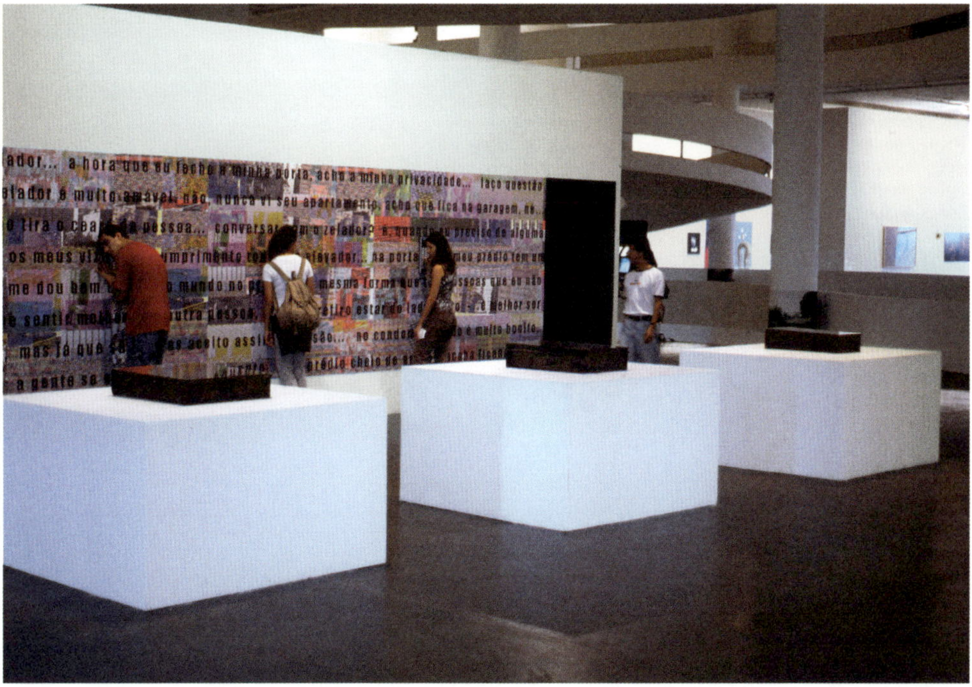

fig.16

This was followed by a stand-alone space for a multimedia work by Dias & Riedweg, *Os Raimundos, os Severinos e os Franciscos* (*The Raimundos, the Severinos and the Franciscos*, 1998), a project produced with doormen from residential buildings in São Paulo (see the interview with the artists in this volume, p.272–79). Visitors can be seen listening to the work's audio component, which played through intercom devices hung on the wall. In front, on white plinths, are three metal file drawers with reconfigured maps by Anna Bella Geiger, from her series *Fronteiriços* (*Borderlines*, 1995–ongoing).

Past an installation of photographs by Claudia Andujar (see fig.27), on a free-standing wall hung photographs from Vik Muniz's *Consequência* (*Aftermath*, 1998), a series of portraits of children formed from dirt and waste that was collected from the streets in Rio de Janeiro. On the far wall, from left, *Consequência* (*Aparecida*), *Consequência* (*Socrates*), *Consequência* (*Angélica*) and *Consequência* (*Madalena*). Muniz's series *Crianças de Açucar* (*Sugar Children*, 1996) was also exhibited (not pictured). On the left, a partial view of the photographic series *Quartos - São Paulo* (*Bedrooms - São Paulo*, 1998) by Rochelle Costi; on the right, wrapped on the column, a photograph from *South Texas Colonias* (1998) by Michael Asher (with Andrew Freeman).

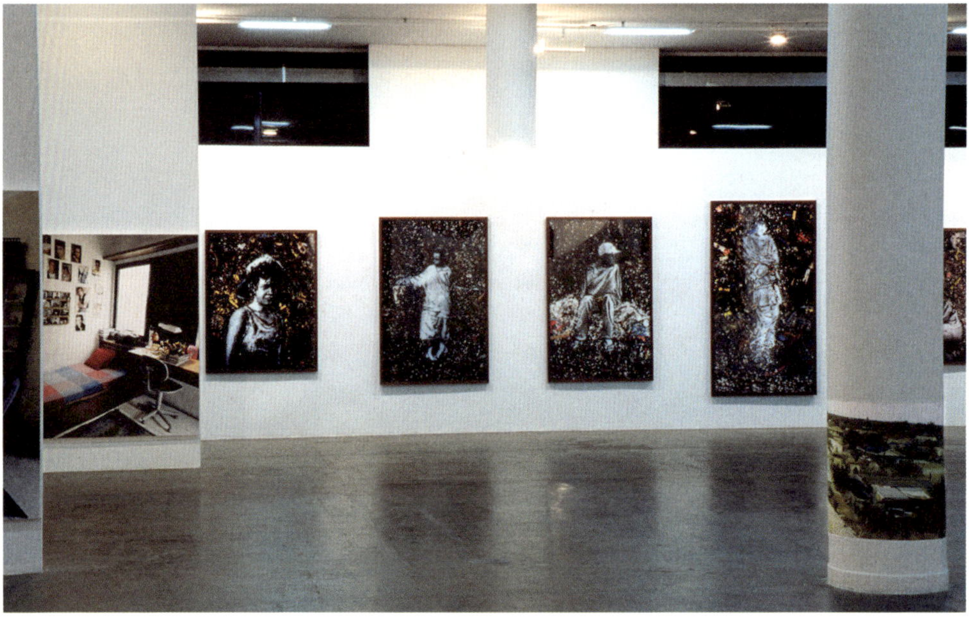

fig.17

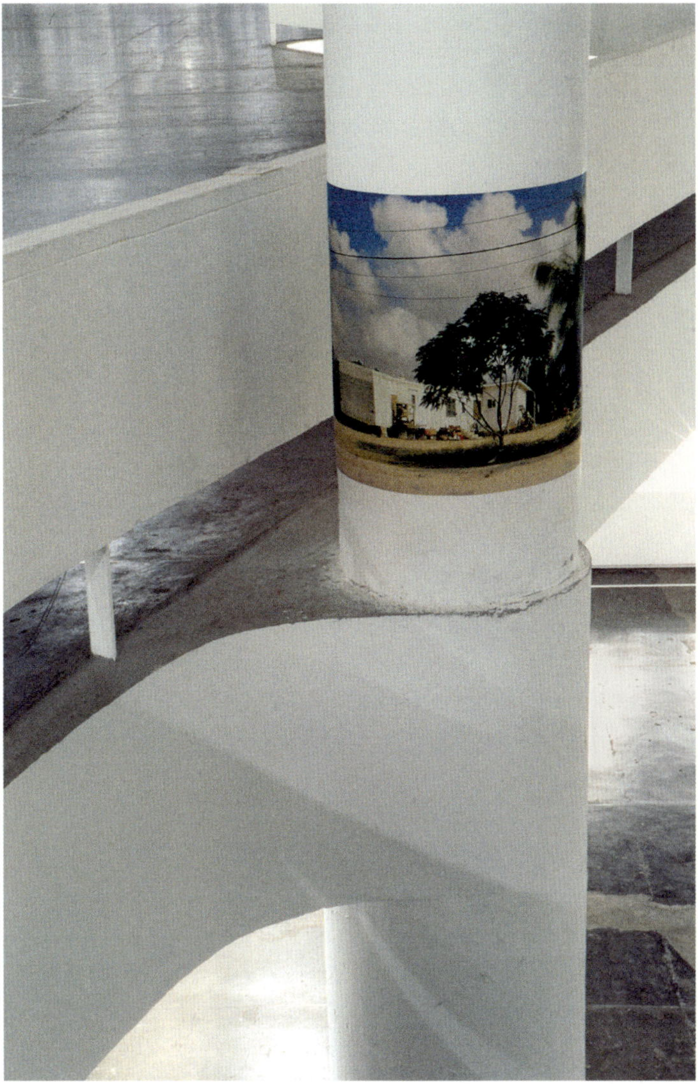

fig.18

South Texas Colonias (1998) by Michael Asher (with Andrew Freeman), a series of fourteen photographs showing makeshift settlements in South Texas, was glued to pillars of the building, with labels describing where each picture was taken. The work formed part of the 'Roteiros Canada and US' section.

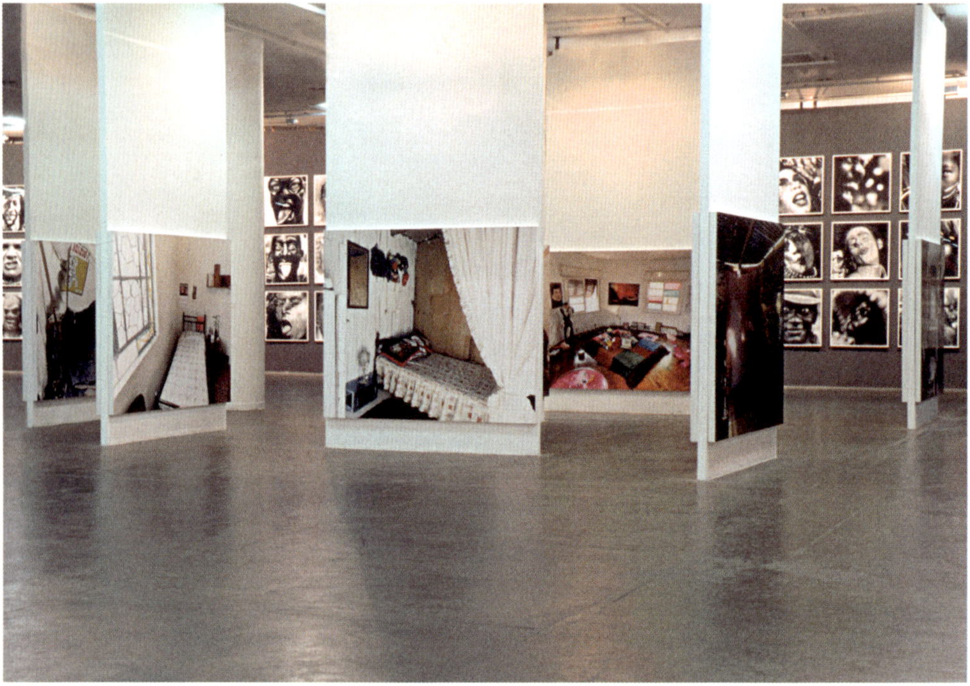

fig.19

Near to Vik Muniz's contribution, Rochelle Costi's *Quartos – São Paulo* (*Bedrooms – São Paulo*, 1998) was on view. On the far wall behind, Arthur Omar's *Antropologia da Face Gloriosa* (*Anthropology of the Glorious Face*, 1973–97), a series of 99 photographs. On the opposite side of the wall from Omar's hanging was the 'Roteiros…' exhibition.

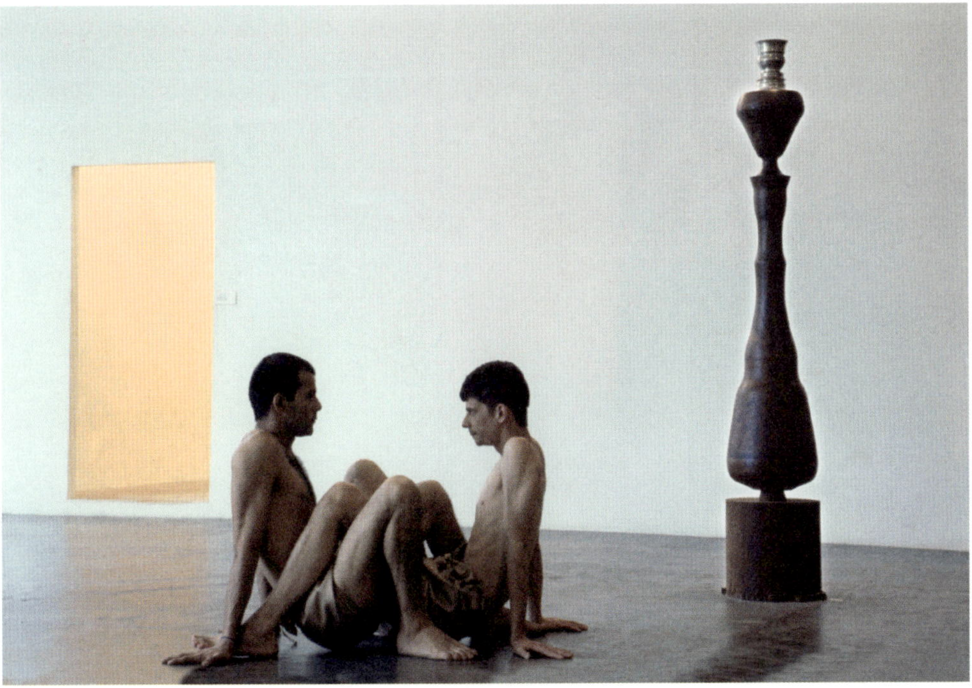

fig.20

Past Arthur Omar's work and going into the 'Um e Outro' half, a small self-contained space held Rivane Neuenschwander's *O trabalho dos dias* (*Work of Days*, 1998), an installation of dust gathered onto squares of adhesive vinyl. In front here, Laura Lima's performative sculpture *Sem título* (*Untitled*, 1997–98), which moved throughout all three floors, is seen alongside Tunga's *Eixo exógeno* (*Exogenous Axis*, 1986).

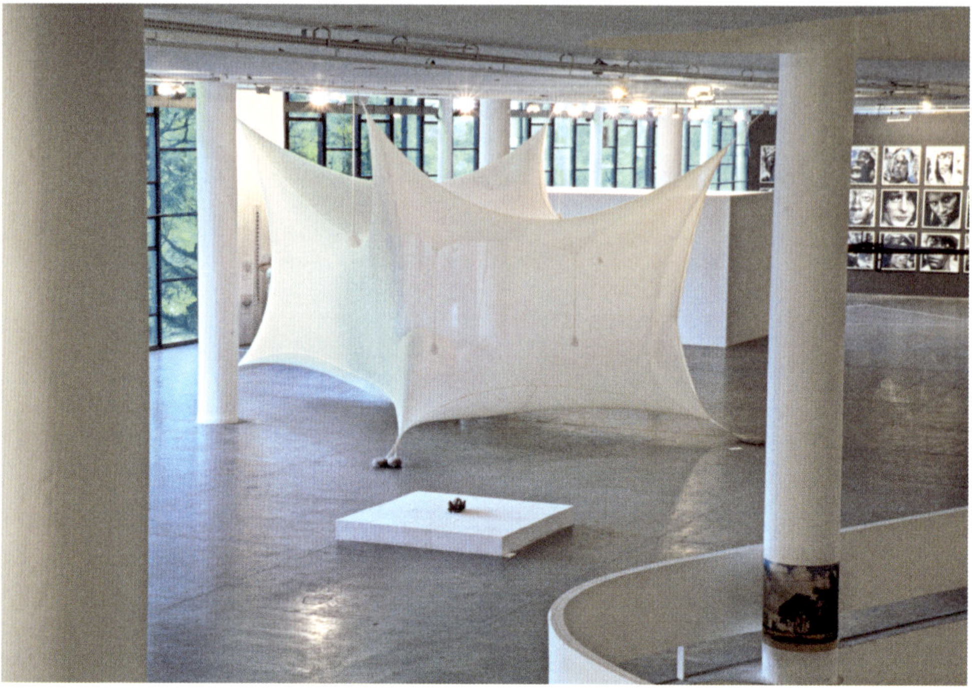

fig.21

'Um e Outro' included several sculptural works and a photograph by Edgard de Souza. From foreground to background: a photograph from the series *South Texas Colonias* (1998) by Michael Asher (with Andrew Freeman); Edgard de Souza's *Sem título* (*Untitled*, 1997); Ernesto Neto's *Nave Deusa* (*Goddess Nave*, 1998); a selection of untitled works by Nazareth Pacheco; the space containing Rivane Neuenschwander's *O trabalho dos dias* (1998) and Arthur Omar's *Antropologia da Face Gloriosa* (1973–97).

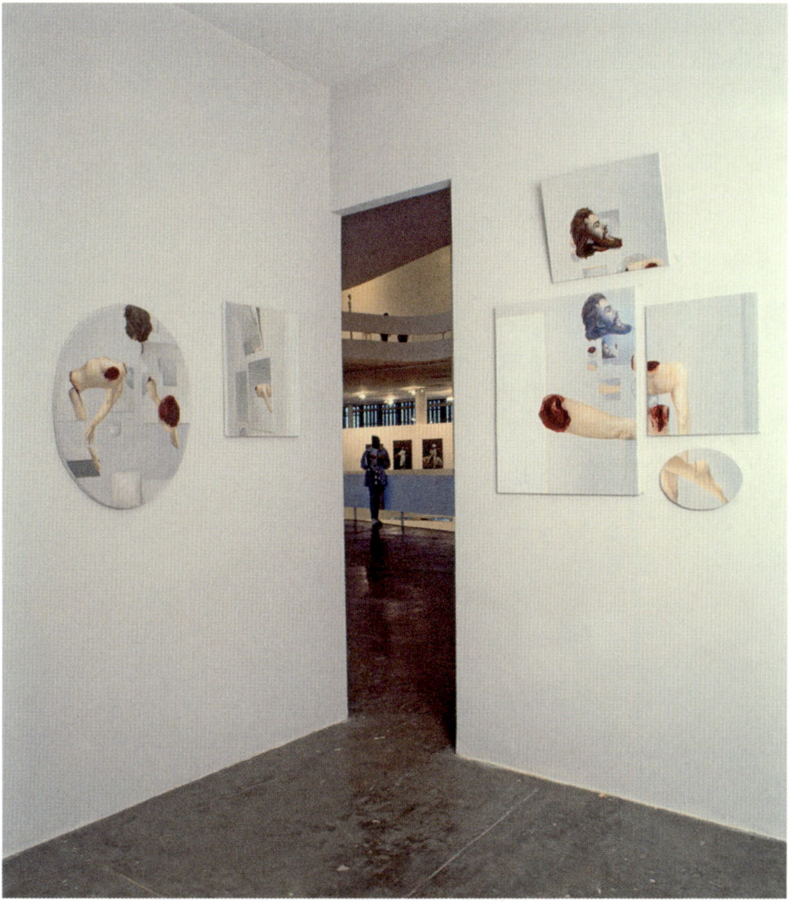

fig.22

Following the works by Ernesto Neto and Edgard de Souza, in a self-contained space, was Adriana Varejão's installation of over twenty oil paintings: *Reflexo de sonhos no sonho de outro espelho* (*Estudo sobre o Tiradentes de Pedro Américo*) (*Reflection of dreams in the dream of another mirror* (*Study after Pedro Américo's Tiradentes*), 1998).

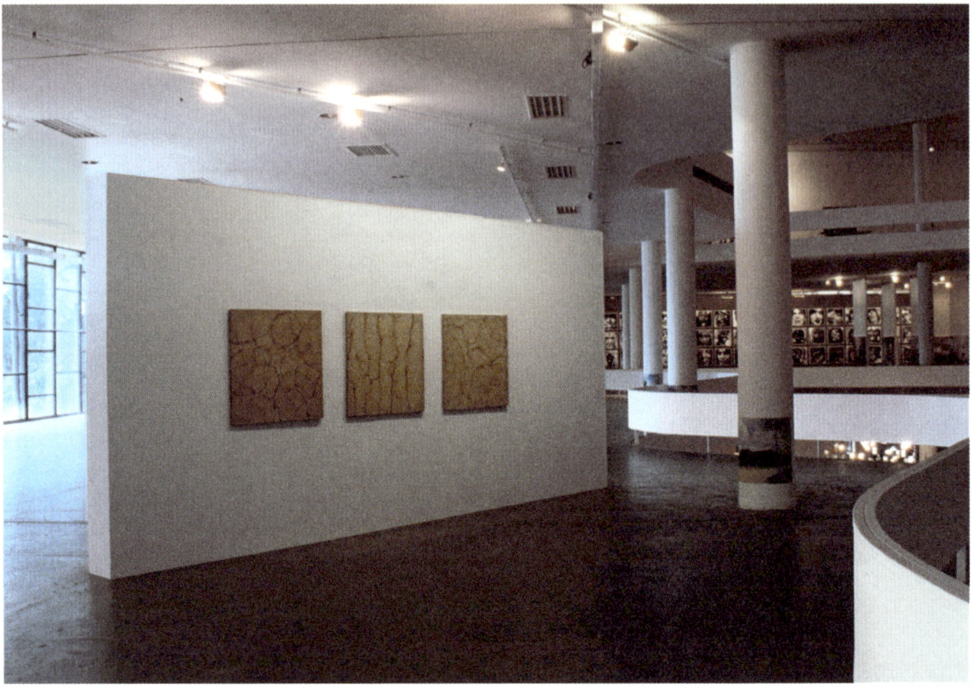

fig.23

Set at an angle parallel to the curved railing of the open space, works from Courtney Smith's series *Cor de Rosa* (*Rose Colour*, 1997); on the columns, photographs from the series *South Texas Colonias* (1998) by Michael Asher (with Andrew Freeman); and in the distance, works by Arthur Omar and Rochelle Costi.

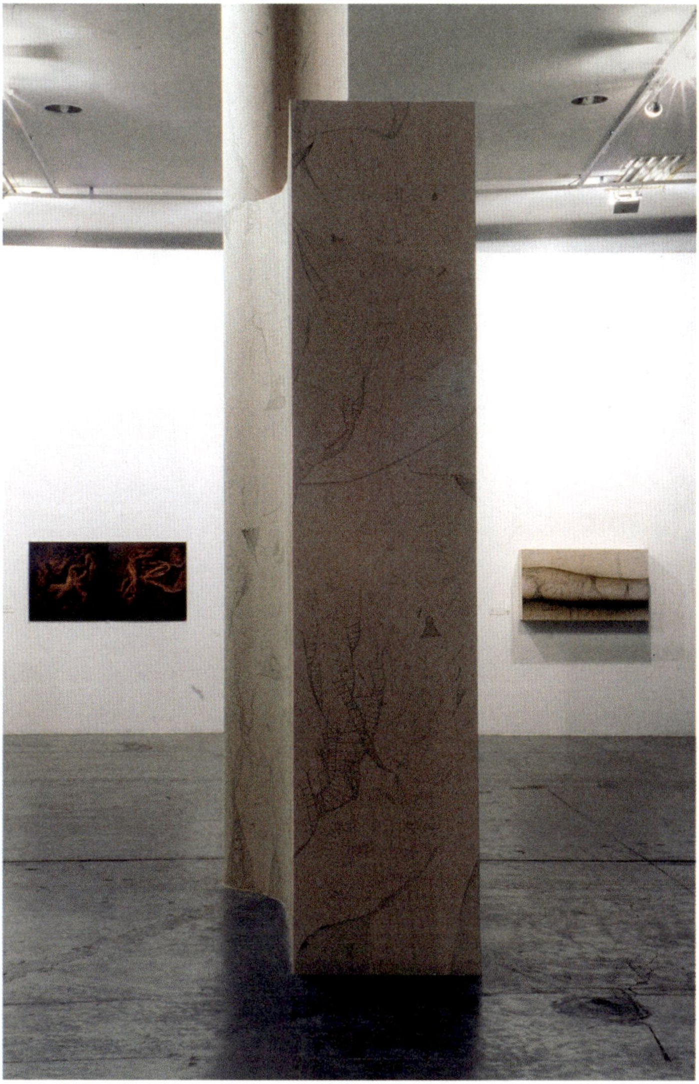

fig.24

Drawings by Sandra Cinto covered an entire free-standing wall, enveloping a column, positioned in parallel with the outer windows of the space. On the wall in the background to the left, a work by Miguel Rio Branco titled *Díptico inferno* (*Hell's Diptych*, 1993–94), and to the right, *Untitled* (1998), a photographic work by Cinto.

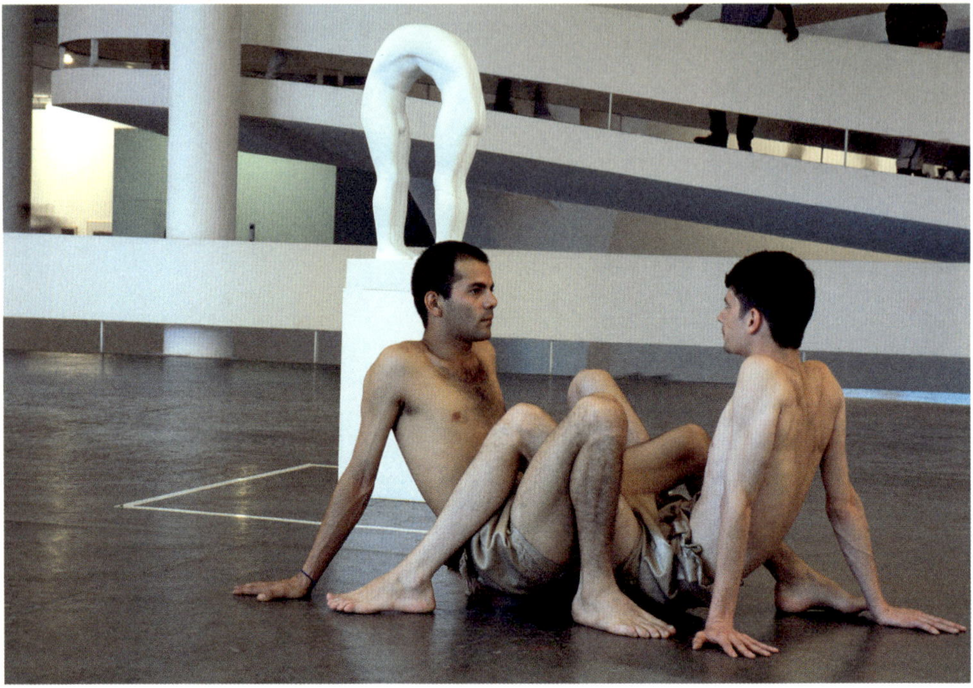

fig.25

Further along, towards the main ramp, was the sculpture *Sem título* (*Dois corpos*) (*Untitled (Two Bodies)*, 1997) by Edgard de Souza, here with the two performers of Laura Lima's *Sem título* (*Untitled*, 1997–98).

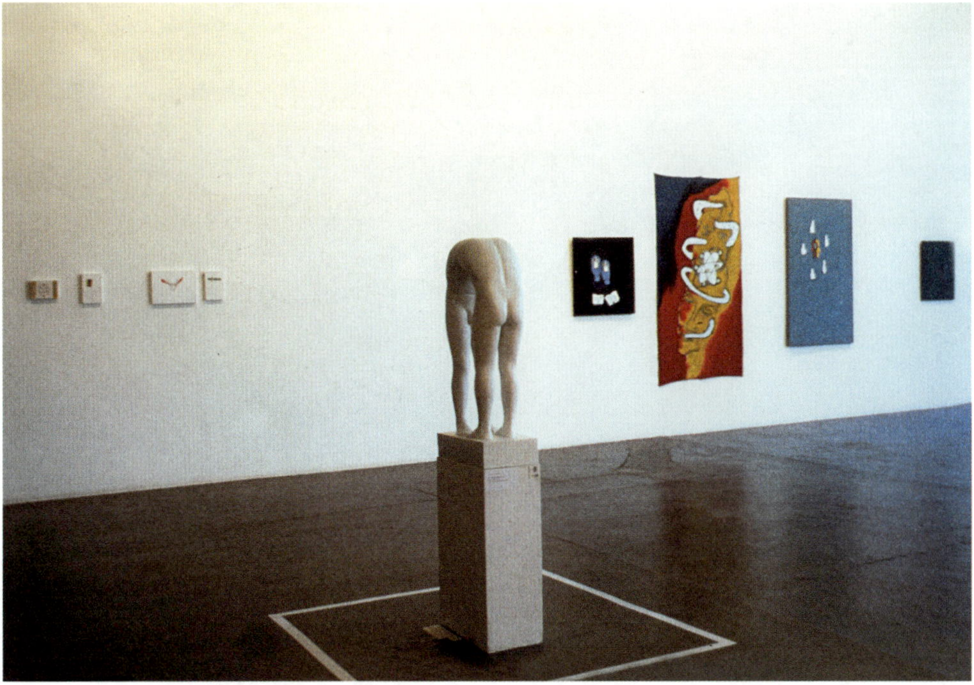

fig.26

Facing the opposite direction, on a wall next to Edgard de Souza's sculpture *Sem título* (*Dois corpos*) (*Untitled* (*Two Bodies*), 1997), hung works by Leonilson, from left to right: four works on paper, *Longo caminho de um rapaz apaixonado* (*Long Way of a Passionate Guy*, 1989), *Extreme Necessity Between Two People* (1990), *Sem título* (*Untitled*, 1985) and *Protected, Crossing Fires* (1990); followed by four works of acrylic on canvas, *Sem título* (*Untitled*, 1990), *Rios De palavras* (*Rivers of Words*, 1987), *Rapaz dividido* (*Divided Guy*, c.1991), *Noite turquesa com números* (*Turquoise night with numbers*, 1988). Returning to Daniel Senise's painting (see fig.11), this corner of 'Um entre Outros' featured works by Iole de Freitas, Leonilson, Cildo Meireles, José Resende and Tunga, relating to the theme of mirroring, and a plinth with Valeska Soares's work *Sem título* (*Untitled*, 1996) (not pictured) from her *dos emaranhados* (*Entanglement*) series.

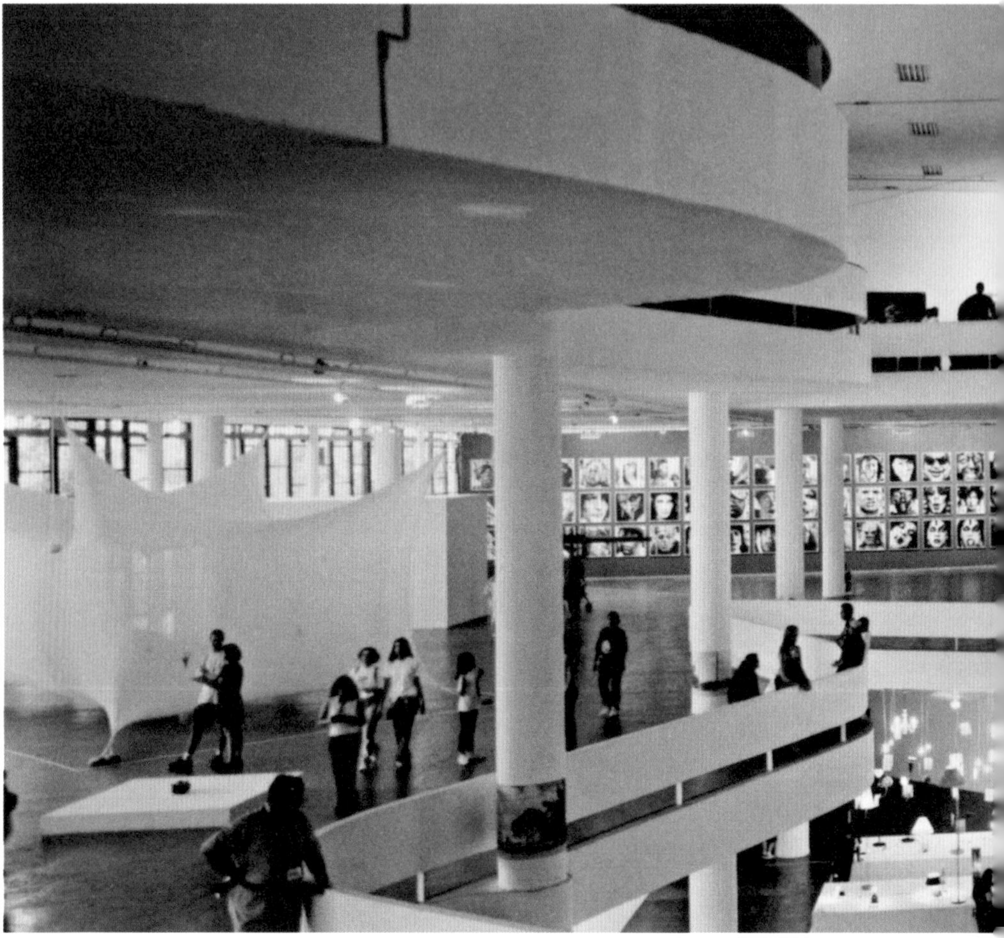

fig.27

View of the 'Arte Contemporânea Brasileira' section, showing, on the right, Claudia Andujar's installation of the photographic work *Yanomami – na sombra das luzes* (*Yanomami – in the Light's Shadow*, 1998), in a circular maze. Clockwise from left, work by Michael Asher (with Andrew Freeman), Edgard de Souza, Ernesto Neto, Rivane Neuenschwander, Arthur Omar, Rochelle Costi, Vik Muniz, Choi Jeong-Hwa and Andujar. Visible on the ground floor, *Private Light/ Public Light* (1998), a work by Mischa Kuball (representing Germany).

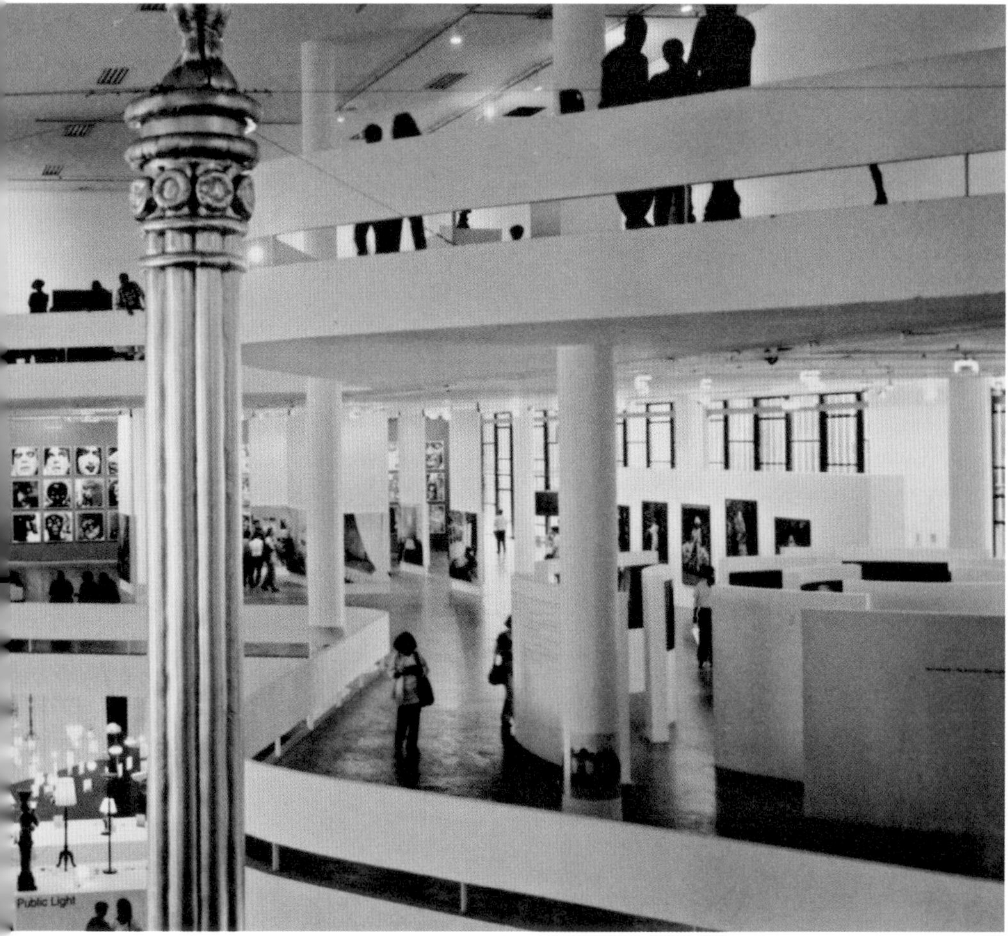
Public Light

'Roteiros. Roteiros. Roteiros. Roteiros. Roteiros. Roteiros. Roteiros.'
('Routes. Routes. Routes. Routes. Routes. Routes. Routes.')

For 'Roteiros...' seven geographic regions (i.e. continent, economic bloc or cultural region) were assigned to ten curators, individually or in pairs, from which to make a 'route'.

Roteiros Africa
(curated by Lorna Ferguson and Awa Meité):
Georges AdéagboFernando Alvim
Candice Breitz
Soly Cissé
Touhami Ennadre
Ahmed Makki Kante
Seydou Keïta
William Kentridge
Abdoulaye Konaté
Joseph Kpobly and Thomas Mulcaire
Moshekwa Langa
Malick Sidibé

Roteiros Asia
(curated by Apinan Poshyananda):
Nobuyoshi Araki
Chien-Jen Chen
Dadang Christanto
Iftikhar and Elizabeth Dadi
Choi Jeong-Hwa
Ing K
Luo Brothers (Luo Wei Bing, Luo Wei Goo and Luo Wei Guo)

Roteiros Canada and US
(curated by Ivo Mesquita):
Michael Asher (with Andrew Freeman)
Janet Cardiff
Andrea Fraser
General Idea (AA Bronson, Felix Partz and Jorge Zontal)
Sherrie Levine
Jeff Wall

Roteiros Oceania
(curated by Louise Neri):
Mark Adams
Mutlu Çerkez
Francis Jupurrurla Kelly

Geoff Lowe
Tracey Moffatt

Roteiros Latin America
(curated by Rina Carvajal):
Francis Alÿs
Juan Dávila
Víctor Grippo
Anna Maria Maiolino
Iñigo Manglano-Ovalle
Gabriel Orozco
Miguel Rio Branco
Doris Salcedo
José Antonio Suárez
Meyer Vaisman

Roteiros Middle East
(curated by Ami Steinitz and Vasif Kortun):
Halil Altındere
Shuka Yehoshua Glotman
Khalil Rabah
Bülent Şangar

Roteiros Europe
(curated by Bart de Baere and Maaretta Jaukkuri):
Rineke Dijkstra
Roza El-Hassan
Honoré d'O
Esko Männikkö
Bjarne Melgaard
Maurice O'Connell
Markus Raetz
Pedro Cabrita Reis
Milica Tomić
Franz West

This area also featured a film and video programme curated by Catherine David as part of the 'Núcleo Histórico', including films by Júlio Bressane, Charles Burnett, Pedro Costa, Adriano Caetano and Bruno Stagnaro, Jorge Furtado, Víctor Gaviria, Johan Grimonprez, Michael Haneke, Kazuo Hara, William Kentridge, Thierry Knauff, Chris Marker, Raoul Peck, Glauber Rocha, Jean Rouch, Elia Suleiman and Zhou Xiaowen.

Artists are identified on the plans by their initials (pp.102–03)

Ciccillo Matarazzo Pavilion, Ibirapuera Park, São Paulo
First floor (second floor according to Brazilian convention)

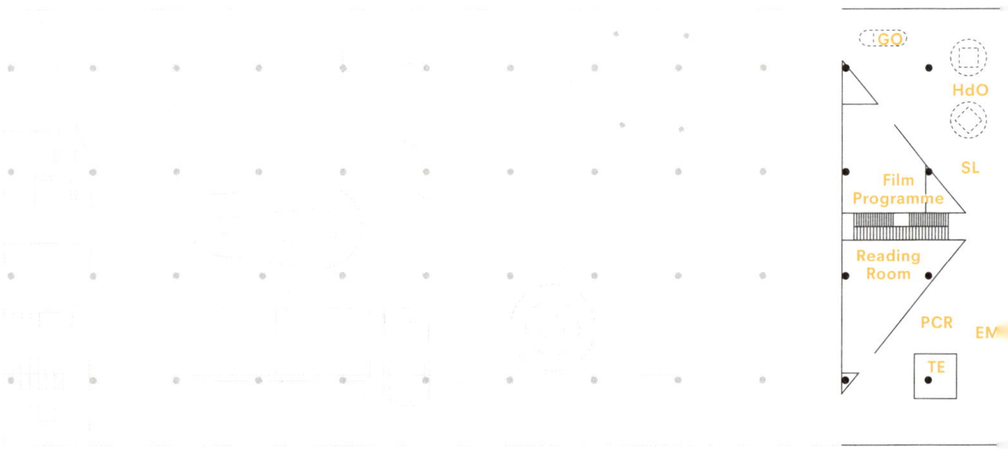

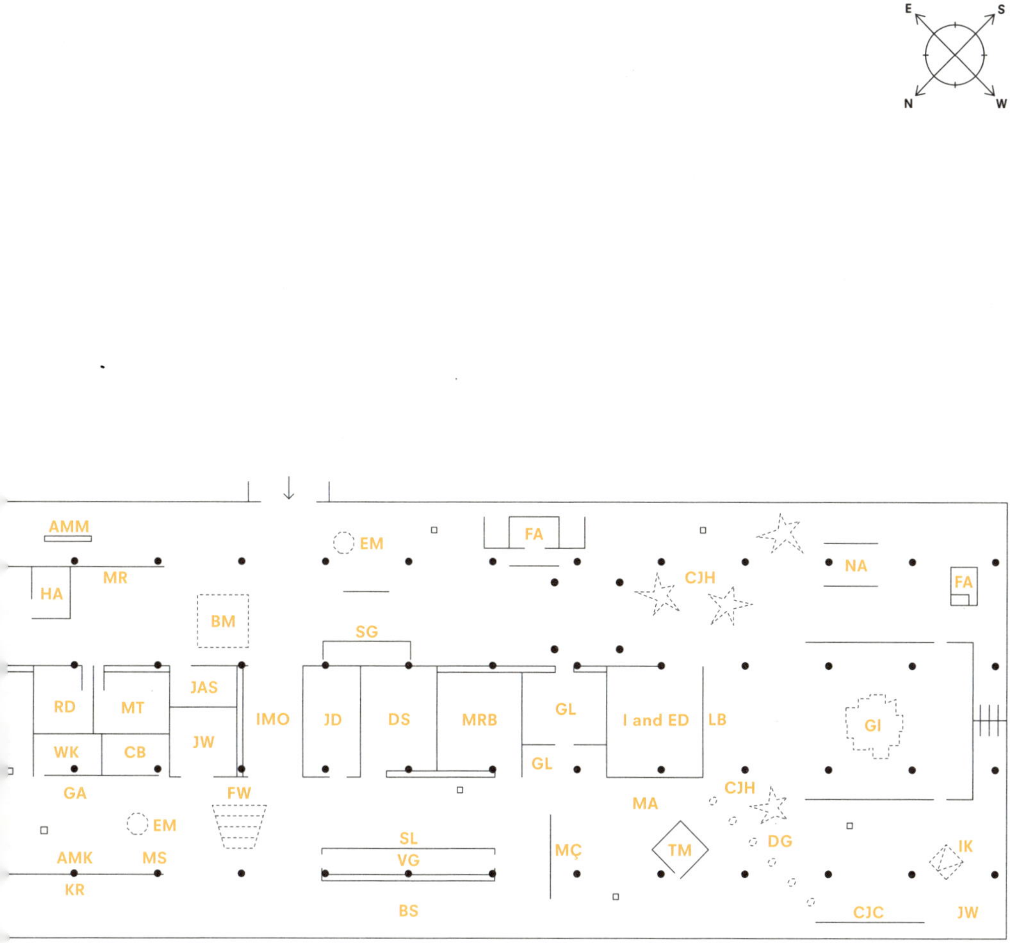
E
S
N
W
AMM
EM
FA
CJH
NA
HA
MR
BM
FA
SG
JAS
RD
MT
IMO
JD
DS
MRB
GL
I and ED
LB
GI
WK
CB
JW
GL
GA
FW
CJH
MA
EM
SL
MÇ
TM
DG
IK
AMK
MS
VG
KR
BS
CJC
JW

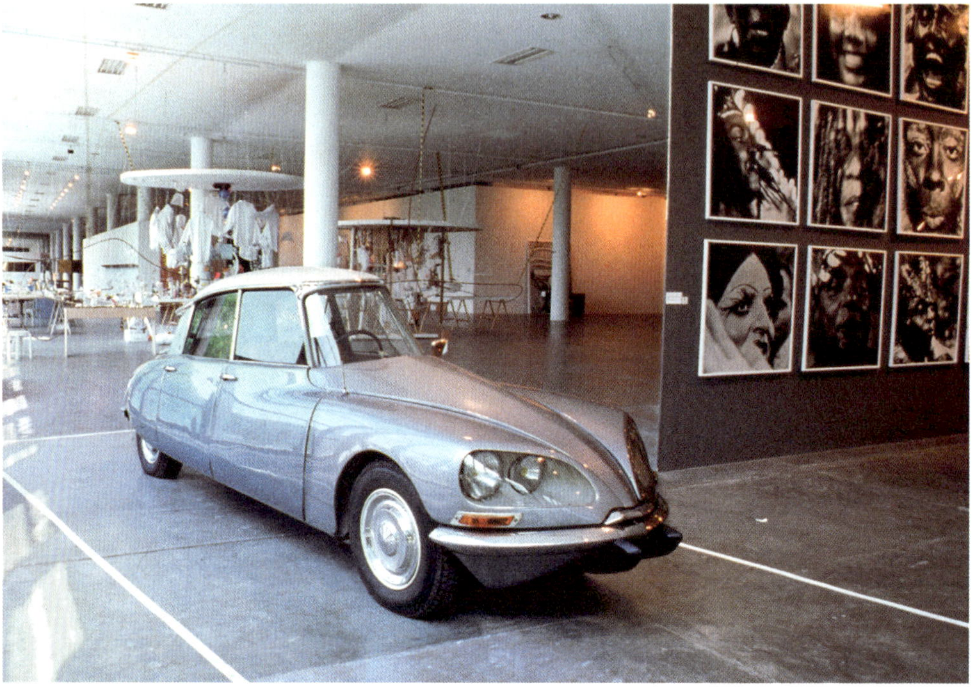

fig.28

Moving past Arthur Omar's *Antropologia da Face Gloriosa* (1973–97) and entering the 'Roteiros...' component of the Bienal, there was Gabriel Orozco's reconfigured car *LA DS* (1993). Partly visible in the background, an installation by Honoré d'O titled *Carousselle Eternelle* (*Eternal Carousel*, 1998) and a work by Roza El-Hassan, *Anasztázia* (*Anastacia*, 1998).

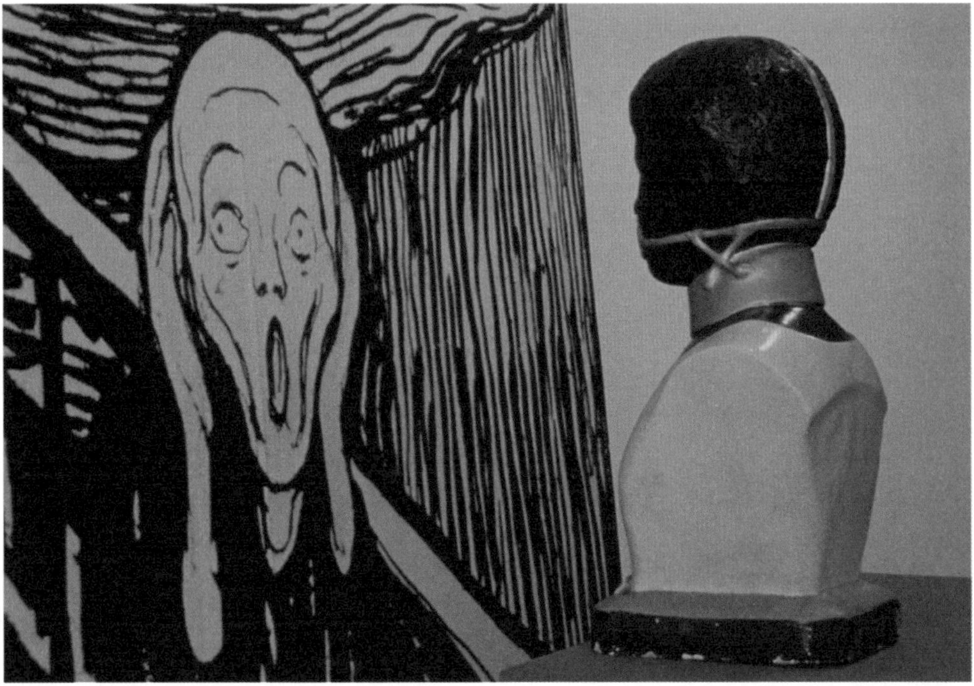

fig.29

In the work *Anasztázia* (*Anastacia*, 1998) by Roza El-Hassan, a plaster cast of Brazilian slave saint Anastacia faces an enlarged print of Edvard Munch's *The Scream*.

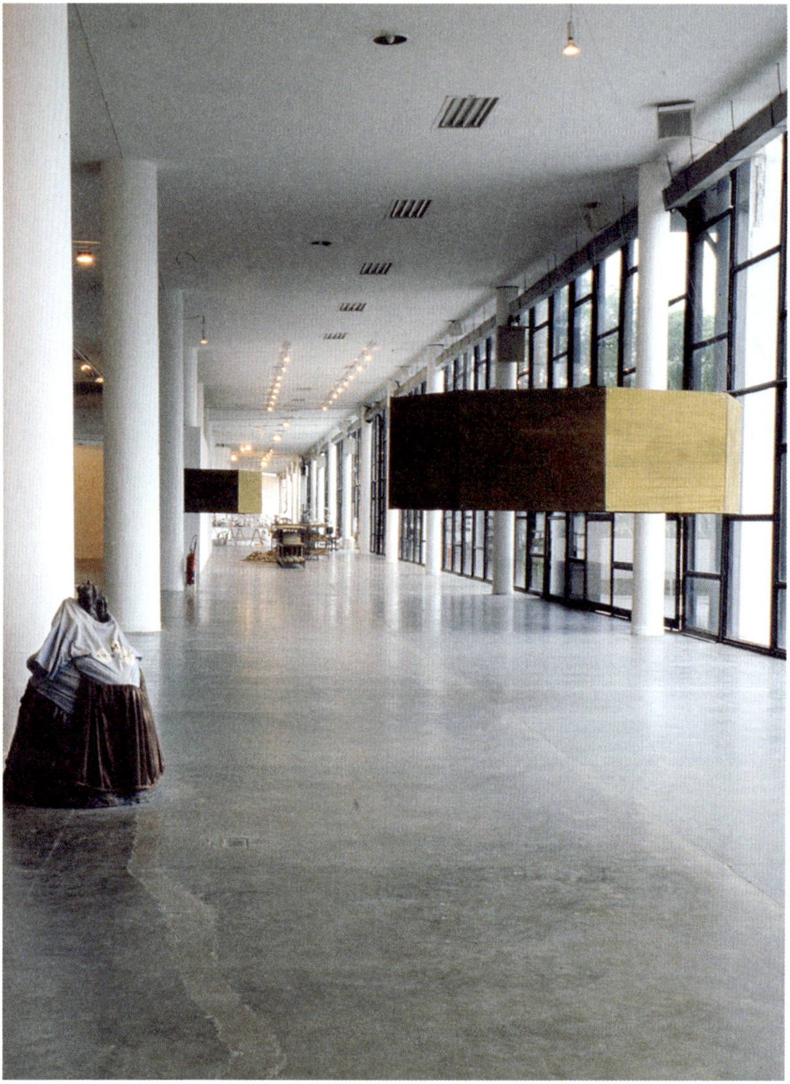

fig.30

Further along in the 'Roteiros...' section (looking back towards Honoré d'O's work), photographic work by Esko Männikkö was installed in several hanging structures.

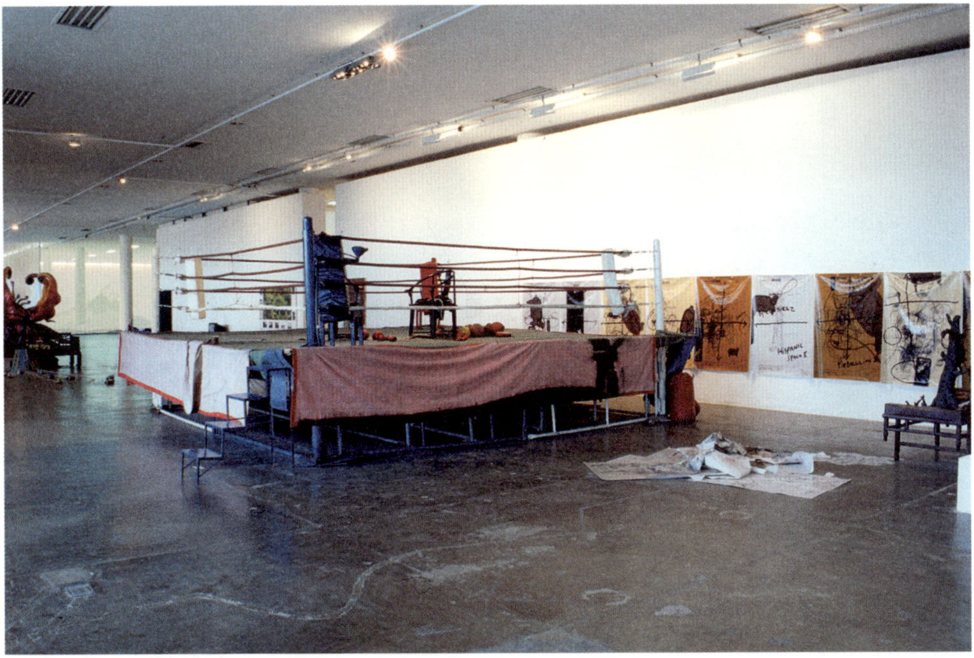

fig.31

In the foreground, the installation *Reinterpretation on Crystal Meth II* (1998) by Bjarne Melgaard; partly visible to the left, Choi Jeong-Hwa's large mechanised sculpture *Dangerous Relationship (Touch Me)* (1998).

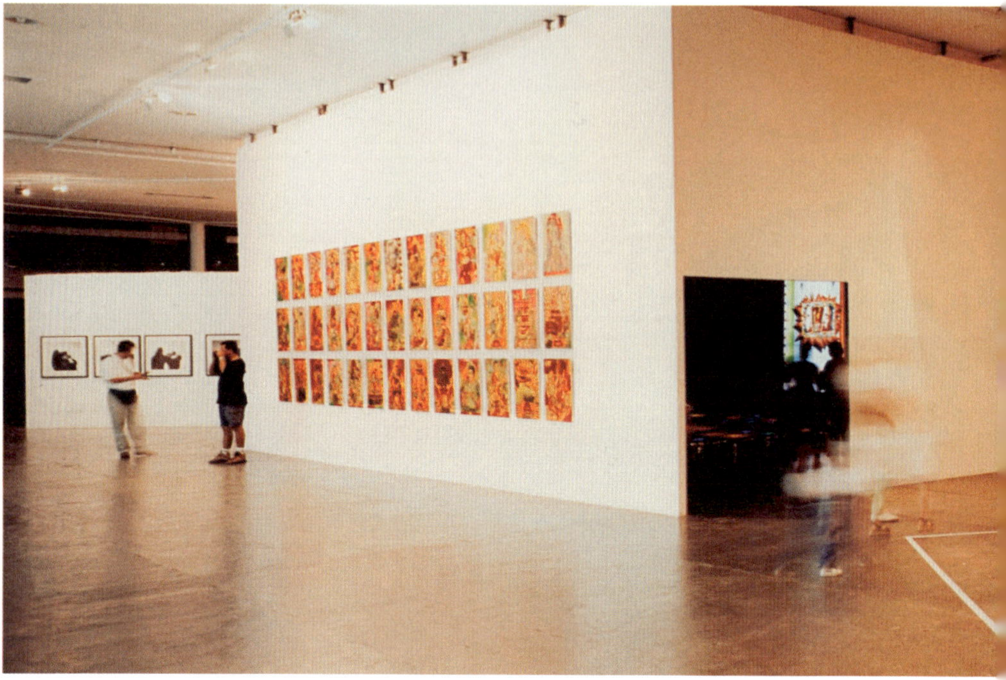

fig.32

From left to right: work by Tracey Moffatt; the Luo Brothers' series of photographs *Welcome to the World's Most Famous Brands* (1997); the entrance to *Power of Love* (1998) by Iftikhar and Elizabeth Dadi; and Choi Jeong-Hwa's sculpture *Dangerous Relationship (Touch Me)* (1998).

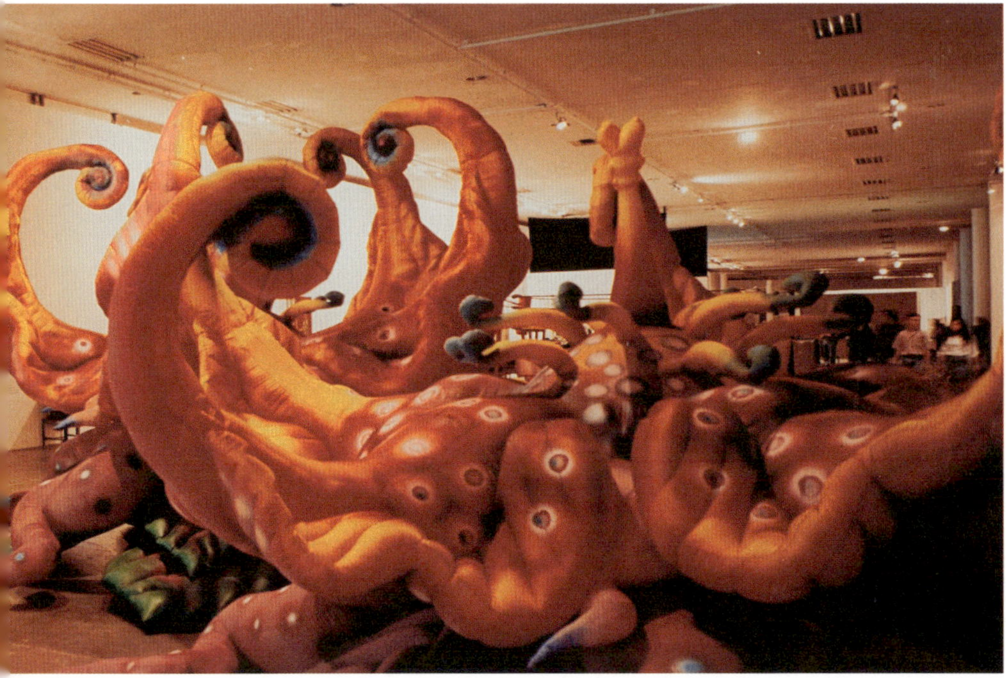

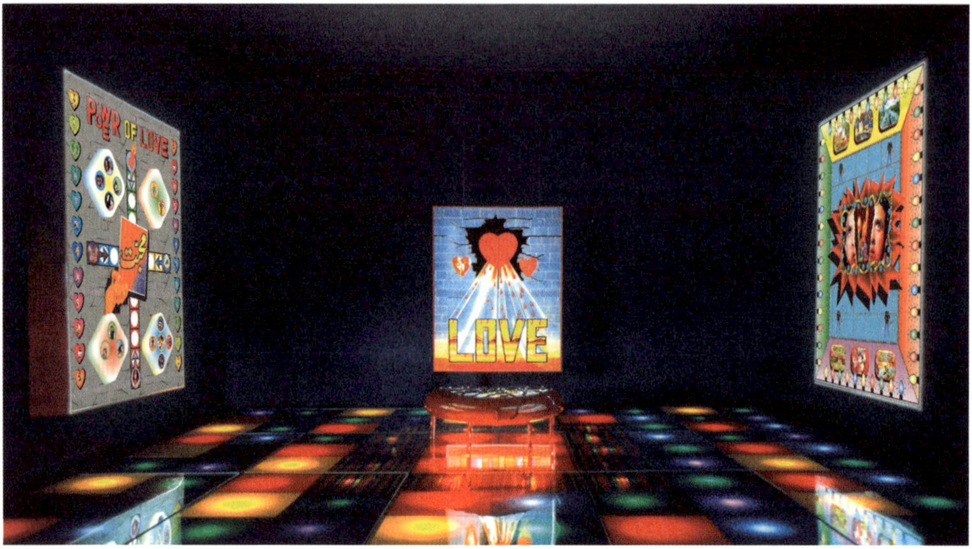

fig.33

Iftikhar and Elizabeth Dadi, *Power of Love*, 1998.

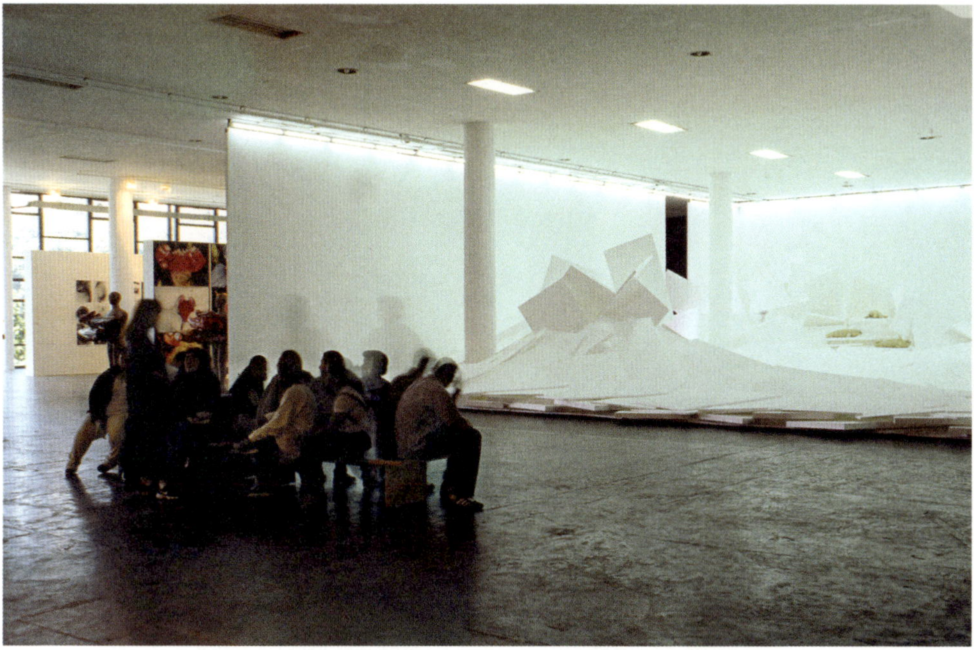

fig.34

To the right, General Idea's installation *Fin de Siècle* (1990), consisting of three stuffed harp seal pups and sheets of polystyrene; in the background, to the left, photographs by Nobuyoshi Araki, including *Erotos* (1993) and *Flower Rondeau* (1997).

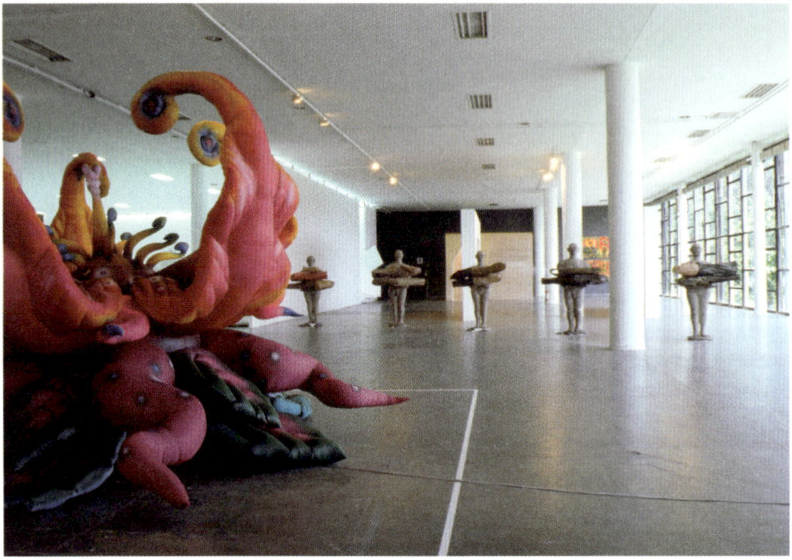

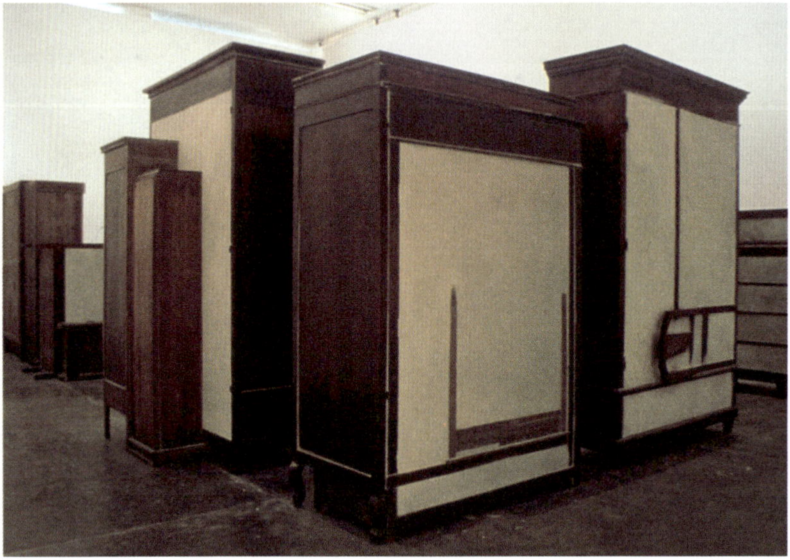

fig.35 and 36

Moving to the other side of the building, Dadang Christanto's *They Give Evidence* (1996–97) formed a diagonal line across the space. Work by Ing K appears in the background, and Choi Jeong-Hwa's *Dangerous Relationship (Touch Me)* is to the left (fig.35). In one of the gallery spaces at the centre of the building was a sculptural installation by Doris Salcedo, part of her *Untitled* series of 1998 (fig.36).

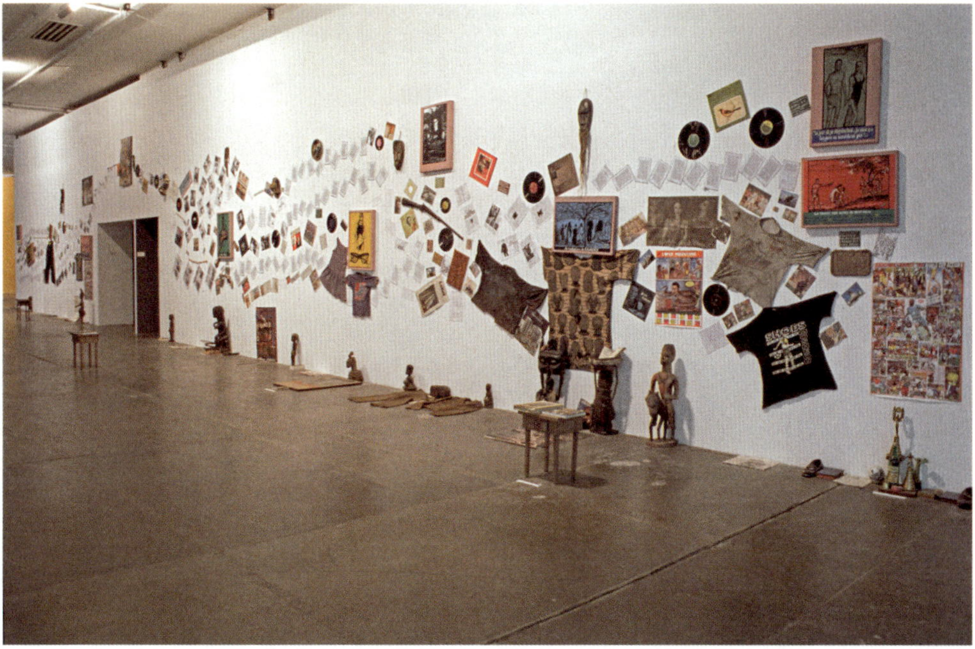

fig.37

Moving back towards the internal ramp and the 'Arte Contemporânea Brasileira' section, an installation by Georges Adéagbo, *Le Cannibalisme* (1998), took up the space alongside the central row of galleries.

Núcleo Histórico: Antropofagia e Histórias de Canibalismos

'Núcleo Histórico: Antropofagia e Histórias de Canibalismos' ('Historical Nucleus: Anthropophagy and Histories of Cannibalisms')

The 'Núcleo Histórico' took up the entirety of the top floor, including the enclosed museum-like structure at its centre. Several of the historical rooms ('Históricos') within the 'Núcleo Histórico' featured 'contaminações'; single works by Brazilian artists strategically inserted to 'contaminate' other displays. Contemporary and modernist works by Brazilian artists were also arranged in a so-called 'Eixo da Cor', or 'Colour Axis', on this floor, as part of the 'Núcleo Histórico'.

Tarsila do Amaral
Francis Bacon
Artur Barrio*
Louise Bourgeois
Waltercio Caldas
Lygia Clark*
CoBrA: Pierre Alechinsky, Karel Appel, Ejler Bille, Eugene Brands, Constant, Corneille, Karl Otto Götz, Egill Jacobsen, Asger Jorn, Carl-Henning Pedersen, Anton Rooskens and Theo Wolvecamp
'A Cor no Modernismo Brasileiro' ('Colour in Brazilian Modernism'): Raul Bopp, Victor Brecheret, Flávio de Carvalho, Blaise Cendrars, Emiliano Di Cavalcanti, Oswaldo Goeldi, Anita Malfatti, Ismael Néry, Hans Nöbauer, Vicente do Rêgo Monteiro, Lasar Segall and Alberto da Veiga Guignard
'Dada e Surrealismo' ('Dada and Surrealism'): Salvador Dalí, Max Ernst, André Masson, Francis Picabia and Wolfgang Paalen
Antonio Dias
Albert Eckhout
Iole de Freitas
Anna Bella Geiger*
Alberto Giacometti
Vincent van Gogh
Carmela Gross
Eva Hesse
Guillermo Kuitca
Wesley Duke Lee*
'Literatura Modernista e Antropologia' ('Modernist Literature and Anthropology')

René Magritte
Maria Martins
Roberto Matta
Cildo Meireles*
Beatriz Milhazes
'Monocromos' ('Monochromes'): Josef Albers, Hans Arp, Hércules Barsotti, Max Bill, Waltercio Caldas, Willys de Castro, Lygia Clark, Antonio Dias, Theo van Doesburg, Lucio Fontana, Mona Hatoum, Yves Klein, Yayoi Kusama, Glenn Ligon, Richard Paul Lohse, Manabu Mabe, Kazimir Malevich, Piero Manzoni, Piet Mondrian, Tomie Ohtake, Hélio Oiticica, Alejandro Otero, Robert Rauschenberg, Robert Ryman, Mira Schendel, Katie van Scherpenberg, Jesús Rafael Soto, Joaquín Torres-García, Nigel Rolfe, Georges Vantongerloo and Friedrich Vordemberge-Gildewart
Vik Muniz*
Bruce Nauman
Ernesto Neto*
Hélio Oiticica*
Dennis Oppenheim
Tony Oursler
Lygia Pape
'Poesia Contemporânea' ('Contemporary Poetry'): Arnaldo Antunes, Lenora de Barros and Walter Silveira
Sigmar Polke
José Resende
Armando Reverón
Gerhard Richter
'Século XIX' ('Nineteenth Century'): Pedro Américo, Valère Bernard, William Blake, Jean-Baptiste Carpeaux, Paul Chenavard, Eugéne Delacroix, Paul Delaroche, Louis-Jean Desprez, Théodore Géricault, Francisco de Goya, Ernest Meissonier, Gustave Moreau, Henry Fuseli, Edvard Munch, Auguste Raffet, Félicien Rops, Auguste Rodin, Pierre Subleyras, Thomas Struth and others
'Séculos XVI–XVIII' ('Sixteenth–Eighteenth Centuries'): Vicente Albán, Aleijadinho (Antônio Francisco Lisboa), Ignácio Maria Barreda, Francisco das Chagas, Manuel Inácio da Costa, Theodore de Bry, José Teófilo de Jesús, Jean de Léry, José Joaquín Magón, Michel de Montaigne, Frans Post, Hans Staden, André Thévet, Ferdinand van Kessel, Jan van Kessel
Mira Schendel*
David Alfaro Siqueiros

Robert Smithson
'Teatro' ('Theatre'): Hélio Eichbauer
Tunga*
Delson Uchôa
Adriana Varejão*
Alfredo Volpi

Curators:
Dawn Ades ('Dada e Surrealismo' and Francis Bacon)
Aracy Amaral (Alfredo Volpi)
Ana Maria Belluzzo (Albert Eckhout and 'Séculos XVI–XVIII')
Yannick Bourguignon (Cildo Meireles)
Daniela Bousso (Dennis Oppenheim and Tony Oursler)
Katia Canton (Maria Martins)
Manuela Carneiro da Cunha (section not realised)
Jean-François Chougnet (Eckhout and 'Séculos XVI–XVIII')
Catherine David (film programme) **
Veit Görner (Sigmar Polke and Gerhard Richter)
Jorge S. Helft (Guillermo Kuitca)
Per Hovdenakk (CoBrA)
Mary Jane Jacob (Eva Hesse and Robert Smithson)
Pedro Corrêa do Lago ('Teatro')
Régis Michel ('Século XIX')
Luis Pérez-Oramas (Armando Reverón)
Didier Ottinger ('Dada e Surrealismo' and René Magritte)
Justo Pastor Mellado (Roberto Matta)
Valéria Piccoli ('Monocromos', co-curated with Paulo Herkenhoff)
Jean-Louis Prat (Alberto Giacometti)
Mari Carmen Ramírez (David Alfaro Siqueiros)
Sônia Salzstein (Tarsila do Amaral)
Robert Storr (Bruce Nauman)
Pieter Tjabbes (Vincent van Gogh)

Also on this floor were works by Franz West as part of 'Roteiros Europe' and Sherrie Levine as part of 'Roteiros Canada and US'.

Artists are identified on the plans by their initials (pp.118–19).

* identified as 'contaminações' (contaminations) in the Bienal catalogue *XXIV Bienal de São Paulo: Arte Contemporânea Brasileira: Um e/entre Outro/s*

** presented on the first floor (pp.80–81)

Ciccillo Matarazzo Pavilion, Ibirapuera Park, São Paulo
Second floor (third floor according to Brazilian convention)

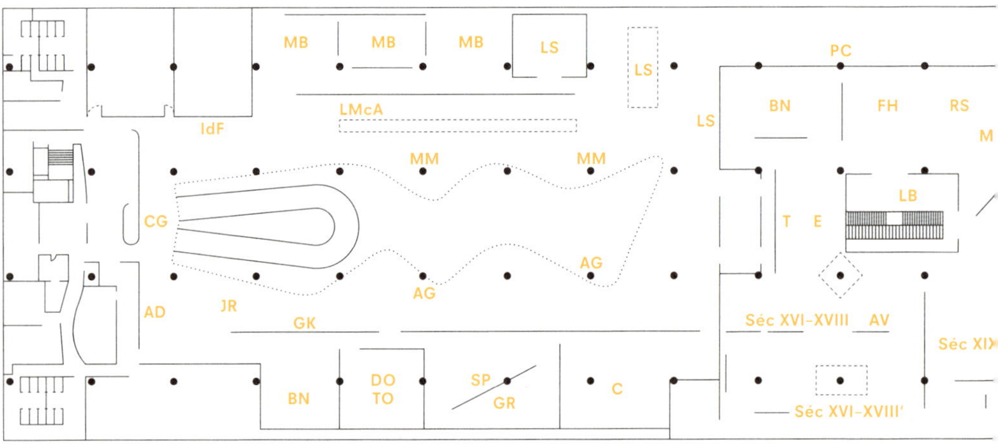

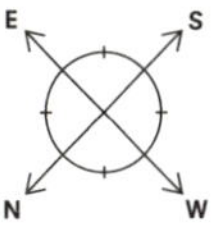
E
S
N
W

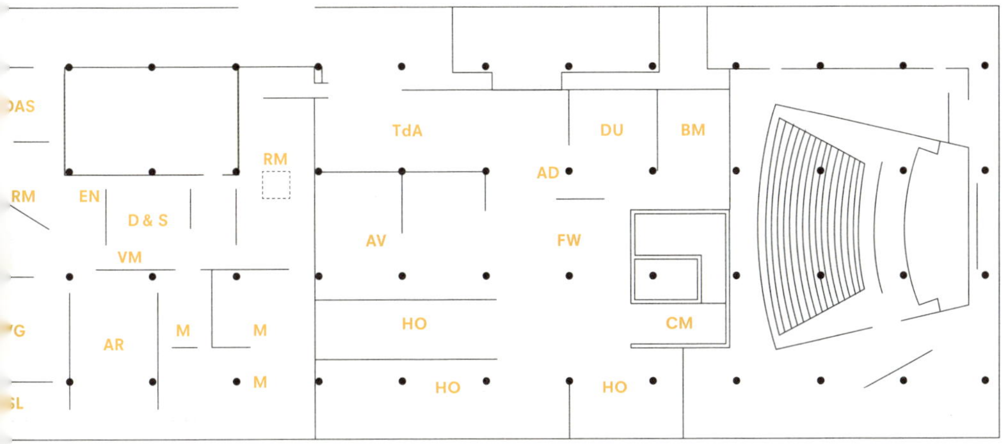
TdA
DU
BM
RM
RM
AD
EN
D & S
AV
FW
VM
HO
CM
AR
M
M
M
HO
HO

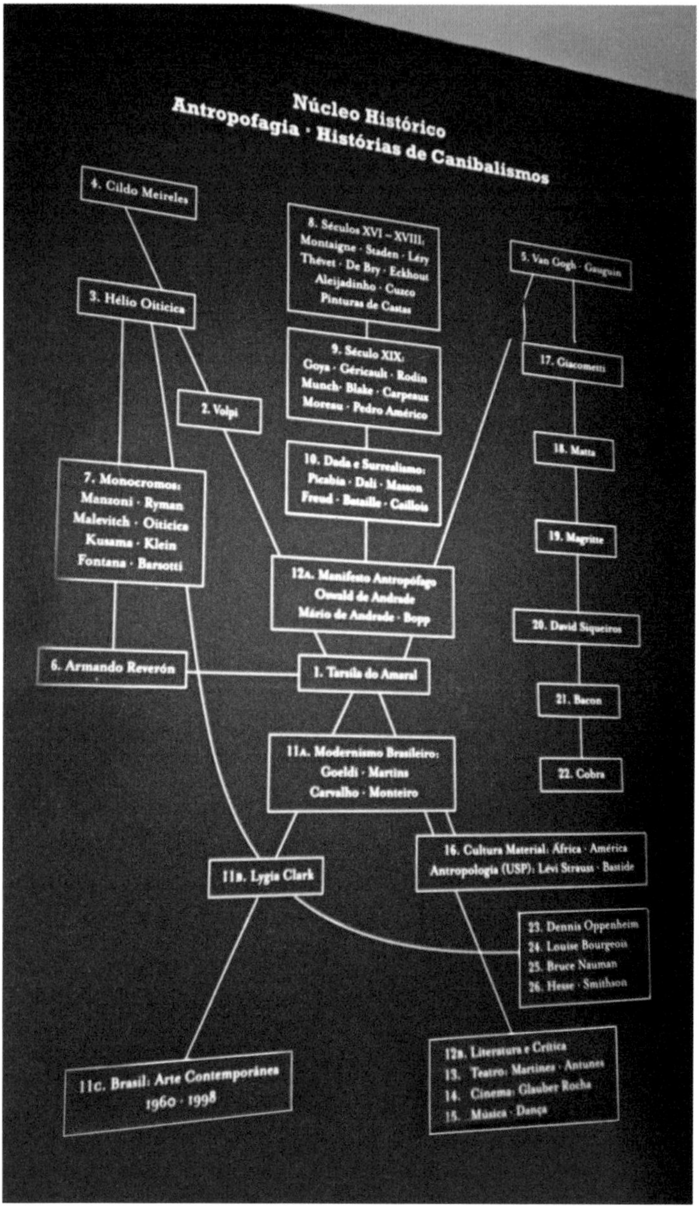

fig.38

Reproduction of the diagram made by Paulo Herkenhoff as part of the conception of the 'Núcleo Histórico', which also informed the installation plan.

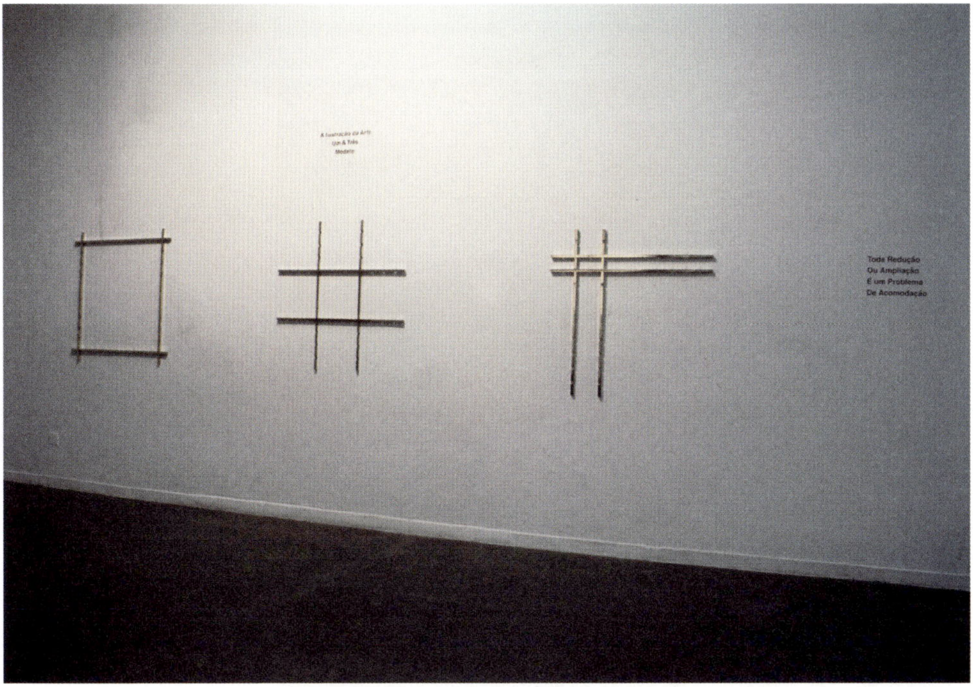

fig.39

Coming up the central ramp to the top floor, visitors were met by Carmela Gross's sculpture *A Negra* (*The Black Woman,* 1997) (not pictured, see fig.11); turning left, Antonio Dias's *The Illustration of Art/One & Three/Stretchers* (1971–74) was displayed on the wall.

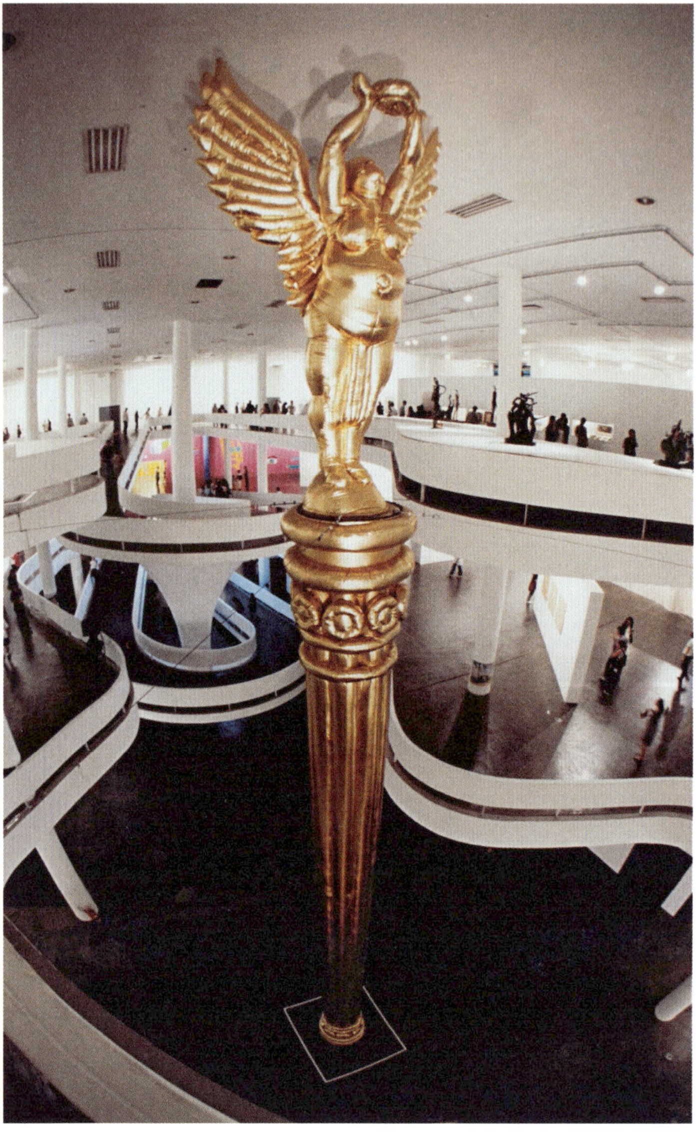

fig.40

View from the top floor of Choi Jeong-Hwa's *Encore, Encore, Encore* (1997), part of the 'Roteiros...' section; in the background, sculptures by Maria Martins also on the top floor (see fig.46), and a series of works by Courtney Smith on the first floor, part of the 'Arte Contemporânea Brasileira' section (see fig.23).

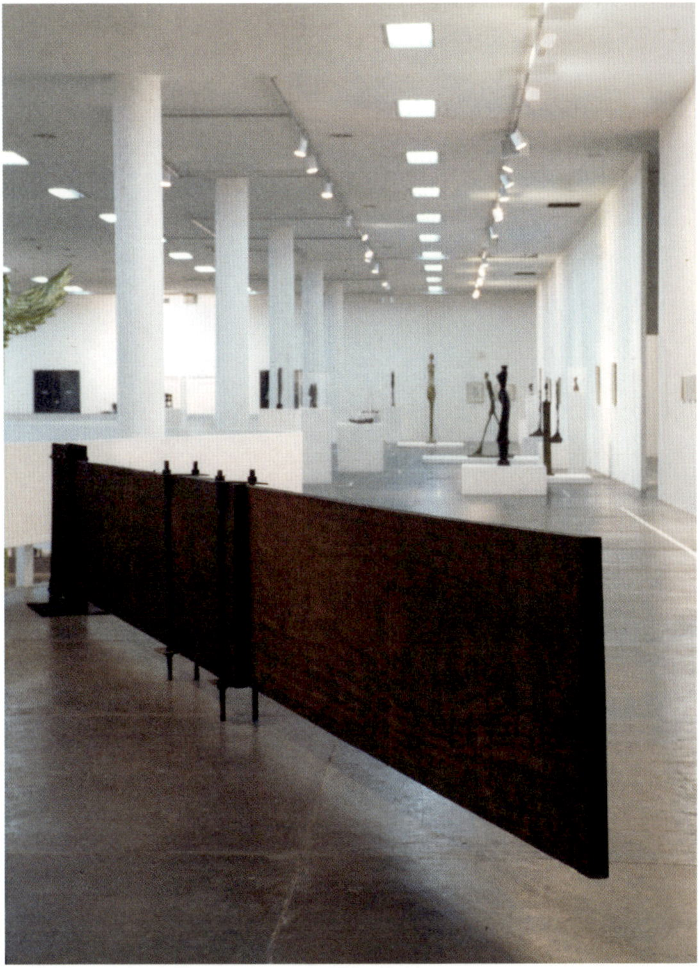

fig.41

Turning to the left, in an open space, an untitled wood-and-steel sculpture (1970–97) by José Resende, with works by Alberto Giacometti behind it, including *Femme de Venise VII* (*Woman from Venice VII*, 1956), *Grande Femme I* (*Tall Woman I*, 1960), *L'Homme qui marche II* (*Walking Man II*, 1960) and *Femme cuillère* (*Spoon Woman*, 1926–27). Visible in the background are the glass doors to the central, enclosed part of the 'Núcleo Histórico'.

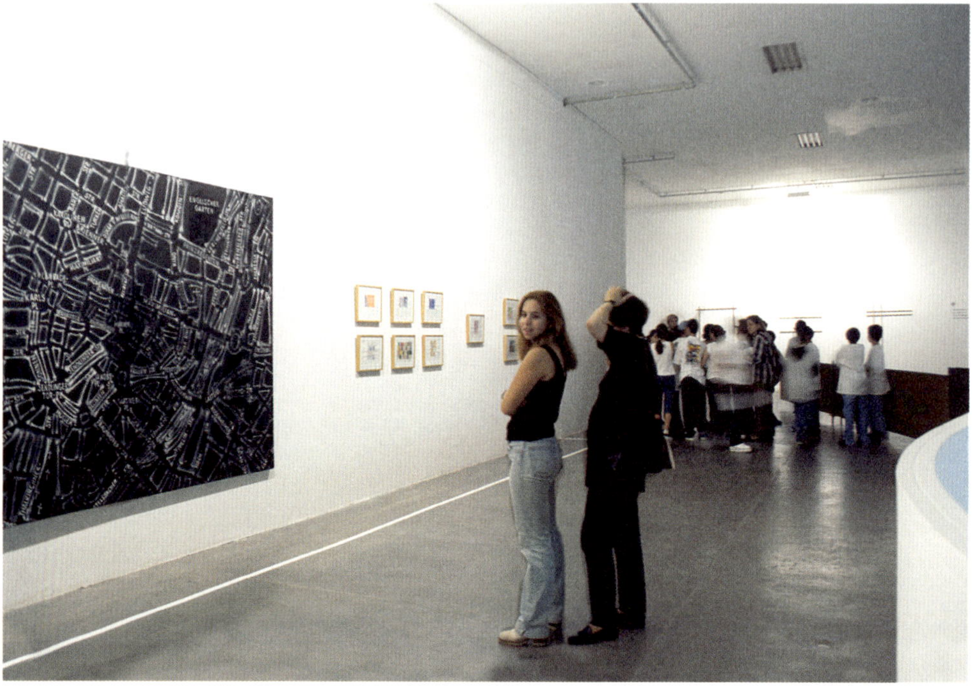

fig.42

Past José Resende's sculpture was work by Guillermo Kuitca, including *Marienplatz* (1991), on the left. Antonio Dias's *The Illustration of Art/One & Three/ Stretchers* (1971) can be seen in the background.

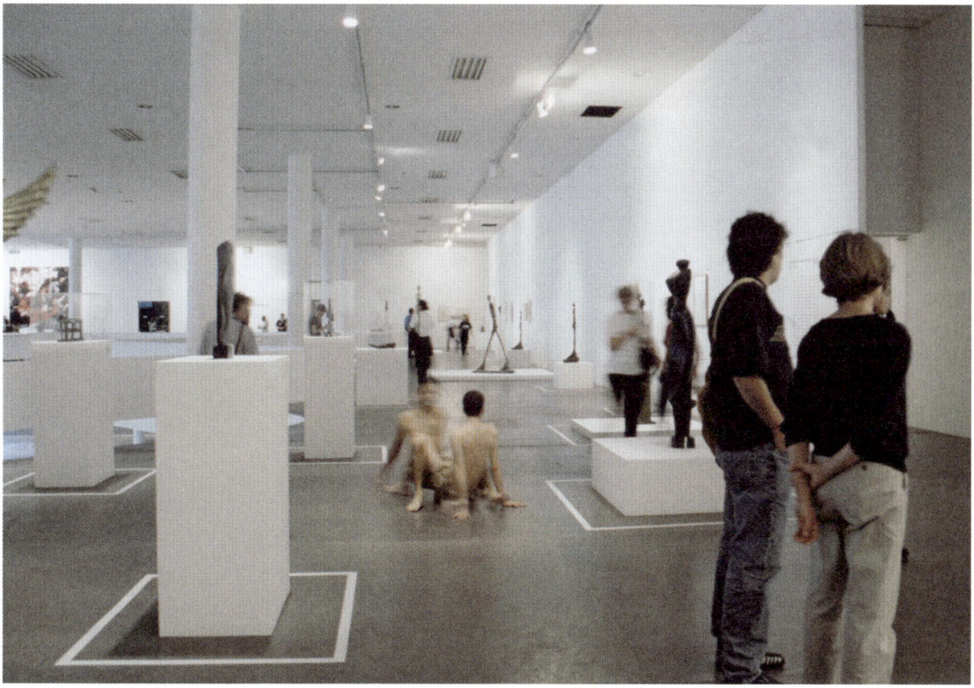

fig.43

Entering the Alberto Giacometti section, curated by Jean-Louis Prat, the top part of Choi Jeong-Hwa's sculpture *Encore, Encore, Encore* (1997), which had moving wings, came into view. Works included Giacometti's *Femme couchée qui rêve* (*Reclining Woman Who Dreams*, 1929), *Objet désagréable à jetér* (*Disagreeable Object to Be Thrown Away*, 1931) and *Femme cuillère* (*Spoon Woman*, 1926–27), seen in the foreground, and *Grande Femme I* (*Tall Woman I*, 1960) and *L'Homme qui marche II* (*Walking Man II*, 1960) further back; in the centre is Laura Lima's performative sculpture *Sem título* (*Untitled*, 1997–98), which moved throughout the exhibition space.

Turning right, the side galleries included a room with works by Bruce Nauman, curated by Robert Storr; a shared space with works by Dennis Oppenheim and Tony Oursler, curated by Daniela Bousso; and one with works by Sigmar Polke and Gerhard Richter, curated by Veit Görner, including Richter's *48 Portraits* (1971–72), pictured here on the right.

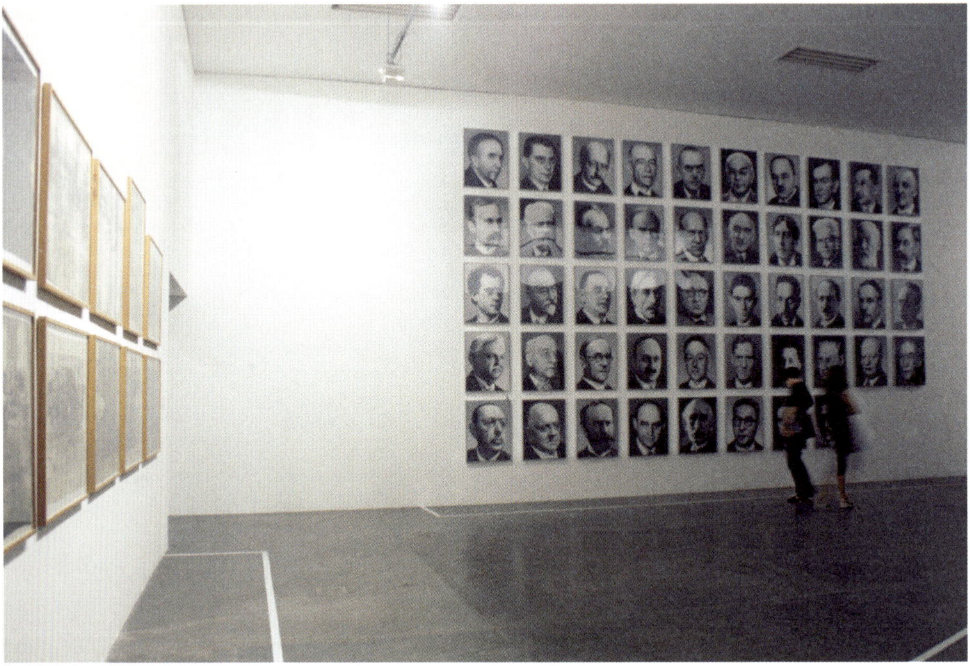

fig.44

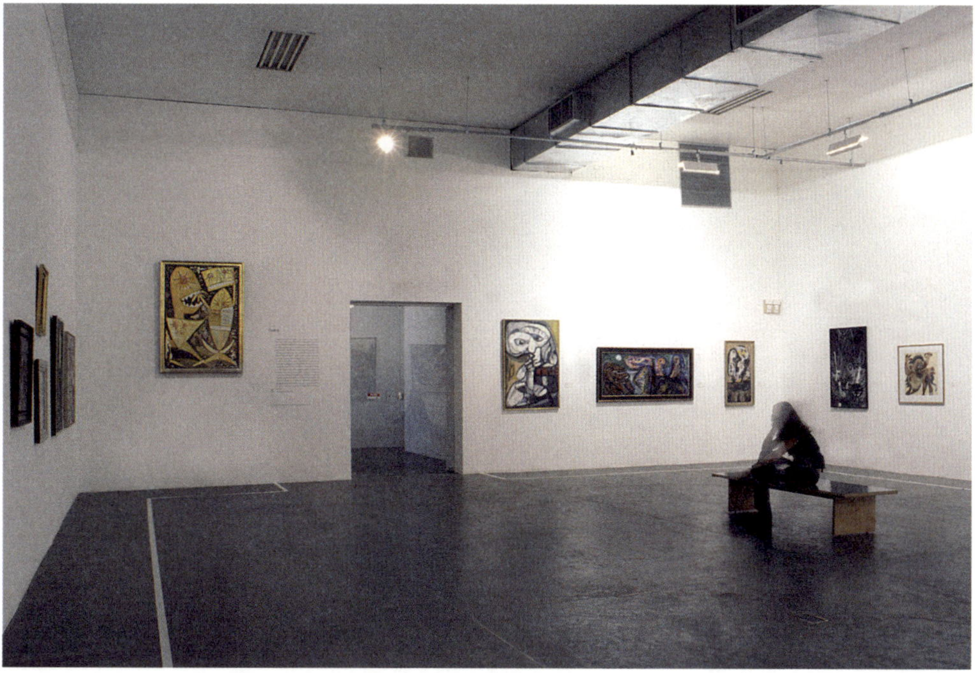

fig.45

A room dedicated to CoBrA paintings and curated by Per Hovdenakk followed. Works included, from left to right: Egill Jacobsen, *Orange objekt II* (*Orange Object II*, 1943); Asger Jorn, *Hvid figur* (*White Figure*, 1954/55), *Studie nr. 4 af opus 2* (*Study no.4 of opus 2*, 1952) and *Havets Guder II* (*Sea Gods II*, 1953); Constant, *Terre brûlée III* (*Scorched Earth III*, 1951); Constant, *Moment érotique* (*Erotic Moment*, 1949); and Corneille, *Vision d'Afrique* (*Vision of Africa*, 1949).

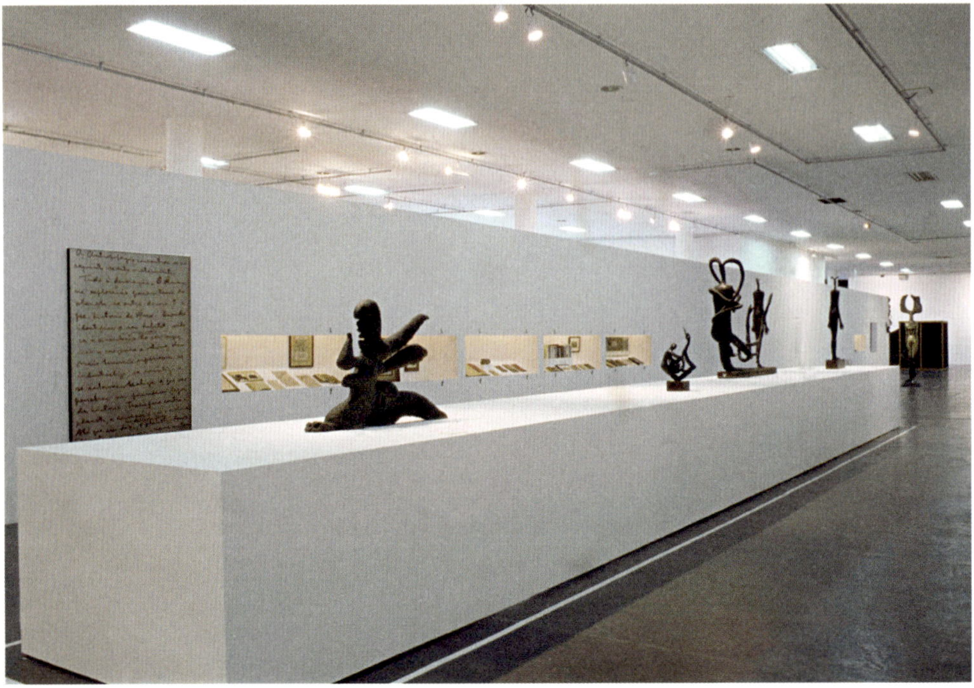

fig.46

Across the open space from Alberto Giacometti's sculptures was a display dedicated to Maria Martins, curated by Katia Canton, with bronze sculptures including *O implacável* (*The Implacable*, 1947), *The Road; The Shadow; Too Long, Too Narrow* (1946) and *La femme a perdu son ombre* (*The Woman Has Lost her Shadow*, 1946) on a central plinth and another placed on the floor farther ahead. In the background, on the left, is an enlarged facsimile of a handwritten manuscript by Oswald de Andrade alongside the display 'Literatura Modernista e Antropologia', a selection of texts, books and images.

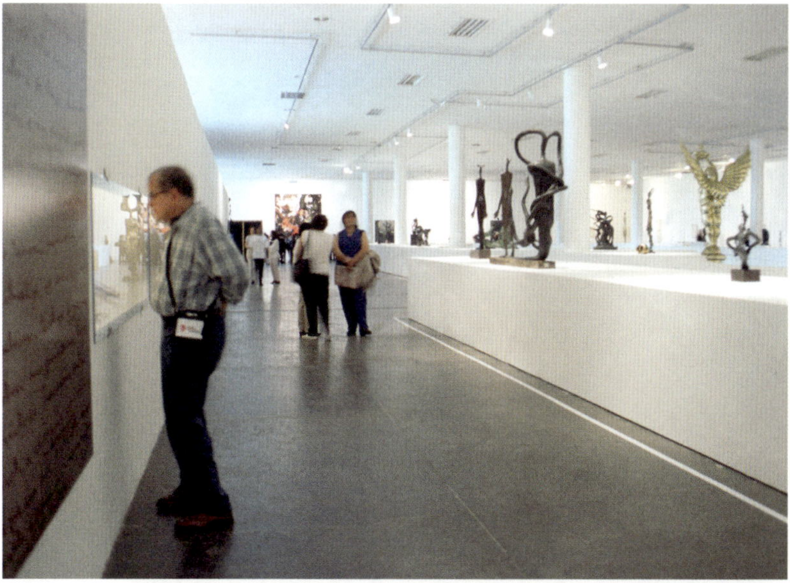

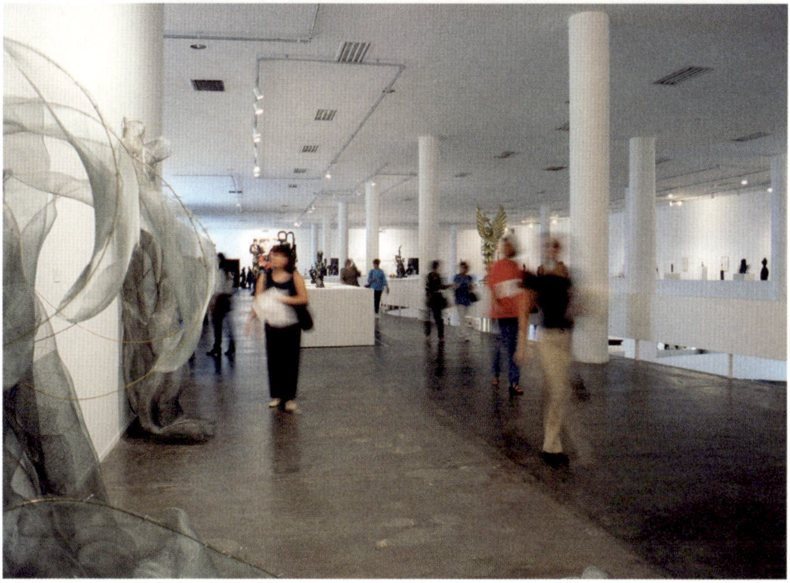

fig.47 and 48

Works by Iole de Freitas and Carmela Gross were juxtaposed to works by Maria Martins. On the left, sculptures from de Freitas's series *Corpo sem órgão* (*Body Without Organs*, 1996) (fig.48), with the Martins display behind.

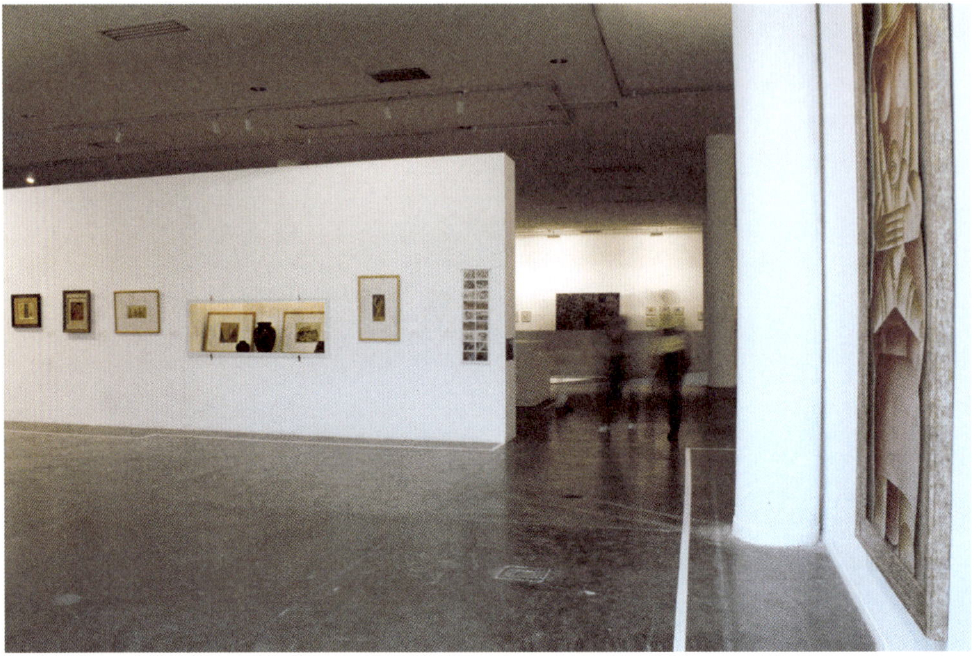

fig.49

In the side galleries behind the Maria Martins section was an exhibition of works dedicated to colour in Brazilian modernism, 'A Cor no Modernismo Brasileiro', which included 'contaminações' (contaminations) by Anna Bella Geiger, in the form of eighteen postcards titled *Brasil nativo, Brasil alienígena* (*Native Brazil, Alien Brazil*, 1976–77), on the wall to the left, and Vicente do Rêgo Monteiro's *Maternidade indígena* (*Indigenous Motherhood*, 1924), on the wall to the right. In the distance, Guillermo Kuitca's *Marienplatz* (1991) can be seen.

Also on view in the same section, Vicente do Rêgo Monteiro's *Menino nu e tartaruga* (*Naked Boy and Turtle*, 1923), on the far left; an anthropomorphic Maracá-phase funerary urn; and Rêgo Monteiro's *O atirador de arco* (*The Arc Sniper*, 1925), on the far right (fig.50). Further along, paintings by Lasar Segall (fig.51): *Banana Plantation* (1927), on the left, and *Red Hill* (1926), on the right. Following the 'A Cor no Modernismo Brasileiro' section, also in the side galleries, a separate and carpeted room (not pictured) held works by Lygia Clark, among them *O eu e o Tu: série roupa-corpo-roupa* (*The I and the You: Clothing-Body-Clothing Series*, 1967), *Obra mole* (*Soft Work*, 1964) and selections from her 1960s *Bichos* (*Beasts*) series.

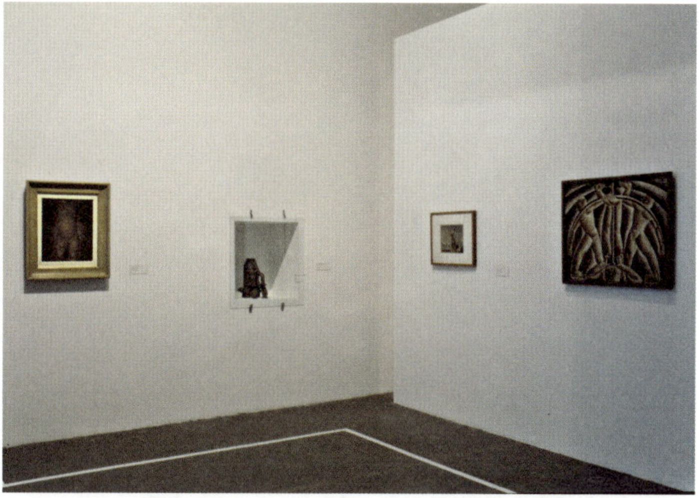

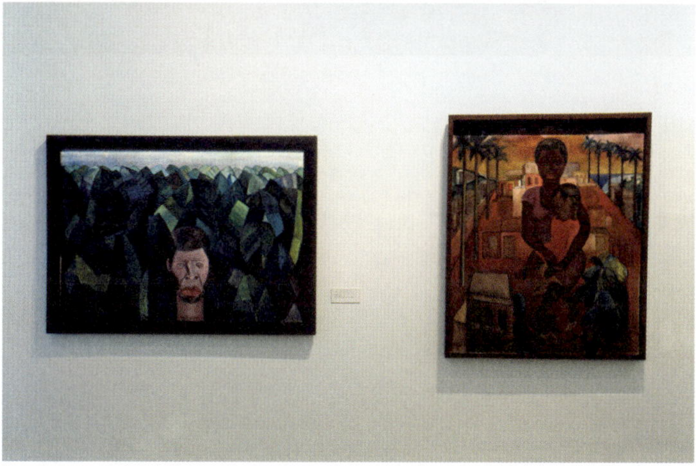

fig.50 and 51

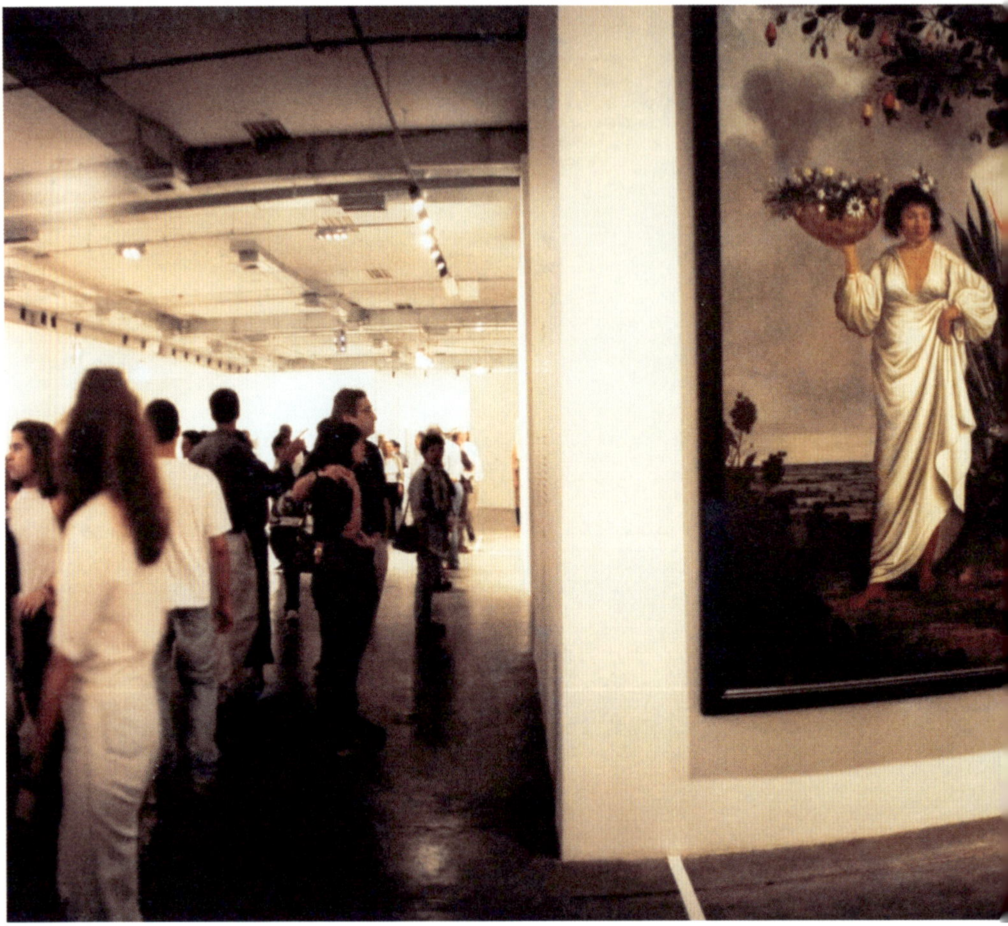

fig.52

Entering the central enclosed space of the 'Núcleo Histórico', the only air-conditioned part of the exhibition, on display was a selection of works by Albert Eckhout, curated by Ana Maria Belluzzo and Jean-François Chougnet. On the wall parallel to the entryway hung four Eckhout paintings from 1641, from left: *Mameluke Woman*, *Tupi Woman*, *African Woman* and *Tarairiu Indian Woman*.

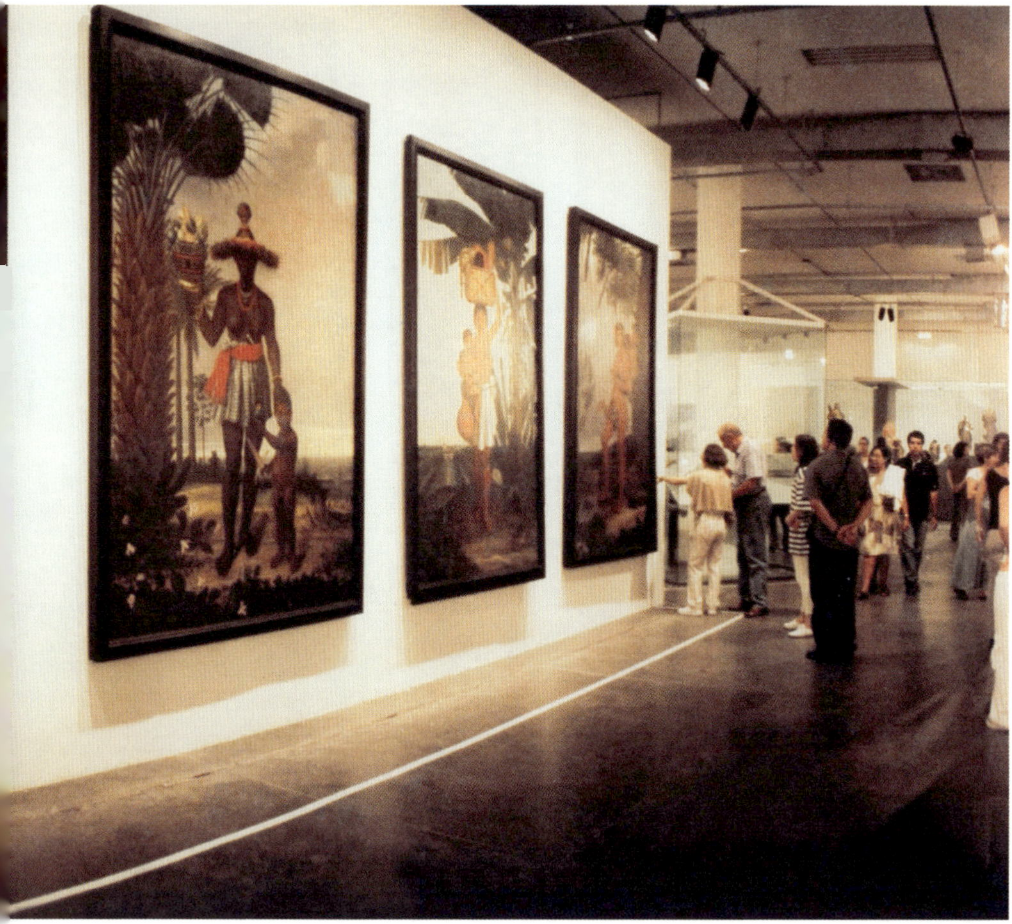

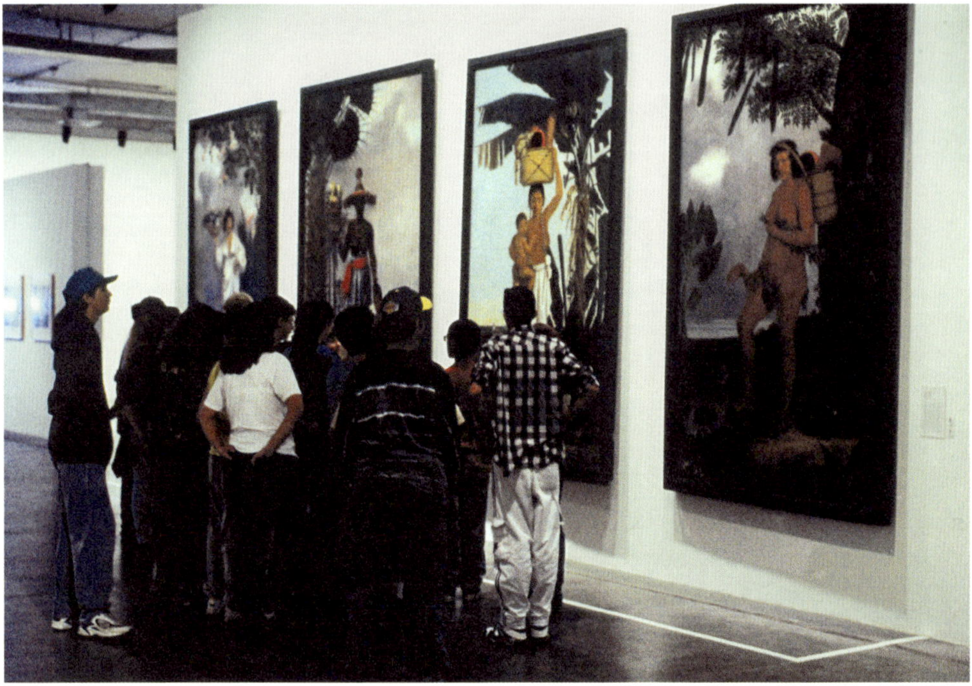

fig.53

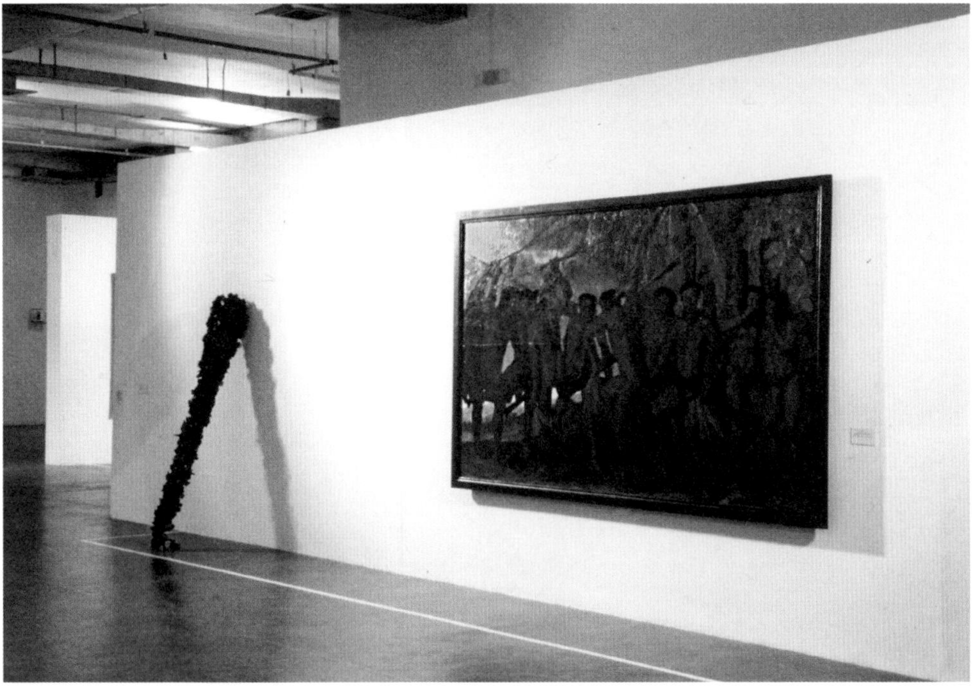

fig.54

Facing these was Albert Eckhout's *Dance of the Tapuyas* (c.1641), with Tunga's *TaCaPe* (1986–97), one of the exhibition's 'contaminações' (contaminations), adjacent, leaning against the wall.

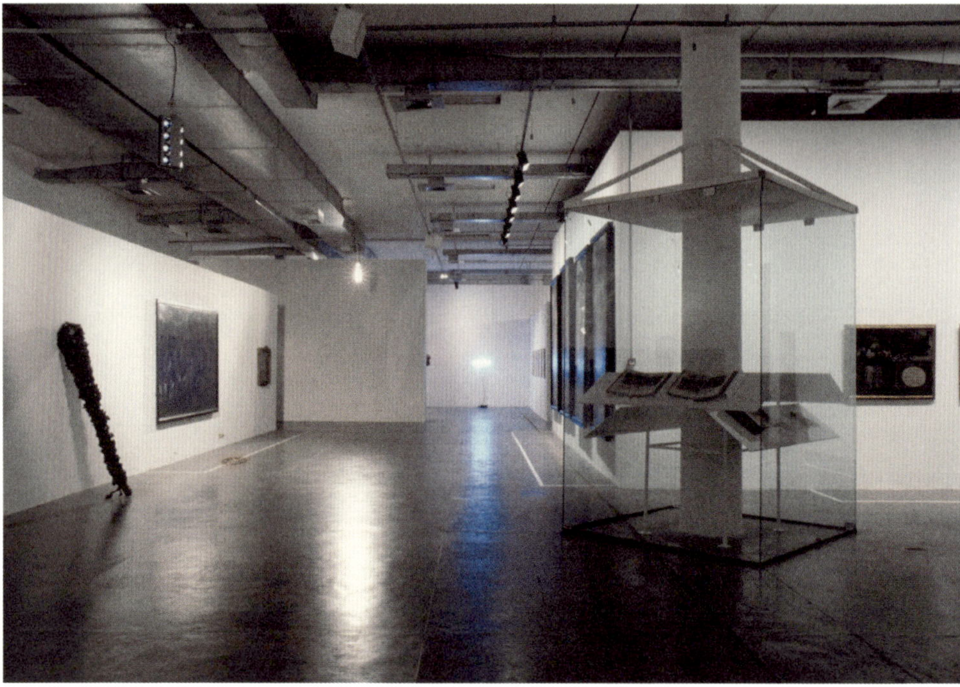

fig.55

To the right of the Eckhout display was the 'Séculos XVI–XVIII' section, also curated by Ana Maria Belluzzo and Jean-François Chougnet. A glass case displayed books, including *Essais* (1580–95) by Michel de Montaigne and *Histoire d'un voyage fait en la terre du Brésil* (*History of a Voyage to the Land of Brazil*, 1578) by Jean de Léry, behind which Vicente Albán's *Indio Principal de Quito con traje de gala* (*The Indian Chief of Quito in Full Dress,* 1783) was hung.

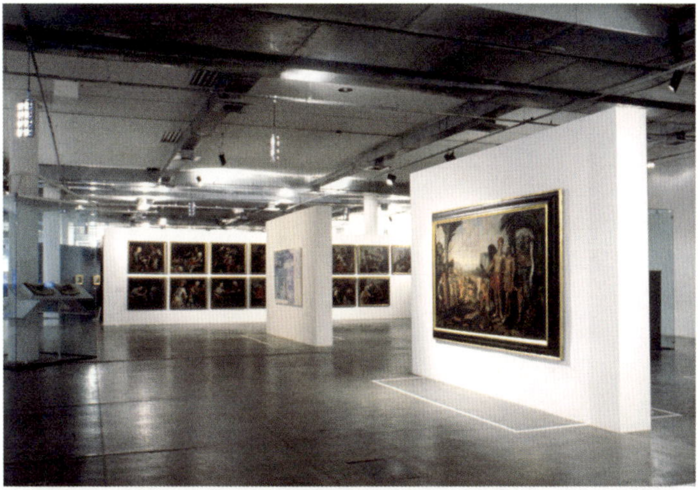

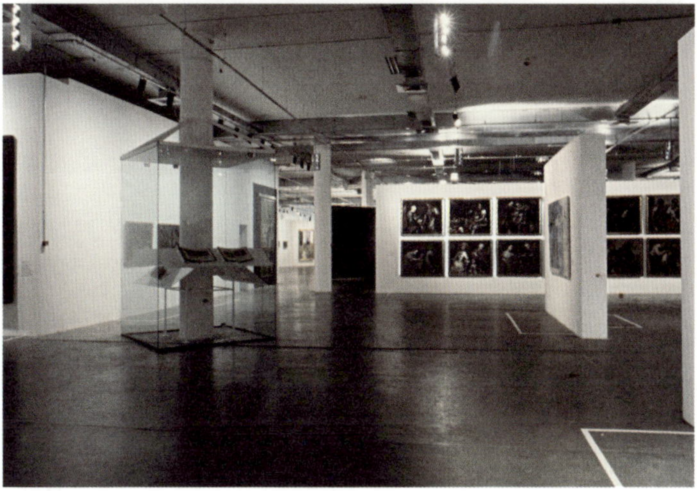

fig.56 and 57

Another view of 'Séculos XVI–XVIII'. A display of José Joachim Magón's eighteenth-century paintings *Las castas mexicanas* (*The Mexican Castes*) is visible on the far wall. On the wall opposite the glass cabinet, at a right angle to the Magón wall, Adriana Varejão's *Proposta para uma Catequese – Parte I Díptico: Morte e Esquartejamento* (*Proposal for a Catechesis – Part I Diptych: Death and Dismemberment*, 1993) was displayed as one of the 'contaminações', with the painting *América* (artist unknown, c.1650) on the next partition along. 'Séculos XVI–XVIII' extended behind the free-standing partitions on the right, where the eighteenth-century polychrome sculpture *Cristo Atado à Coluna*, of Jesus Christ tied to a column, attributed to Francisco das Chagas, was placed.

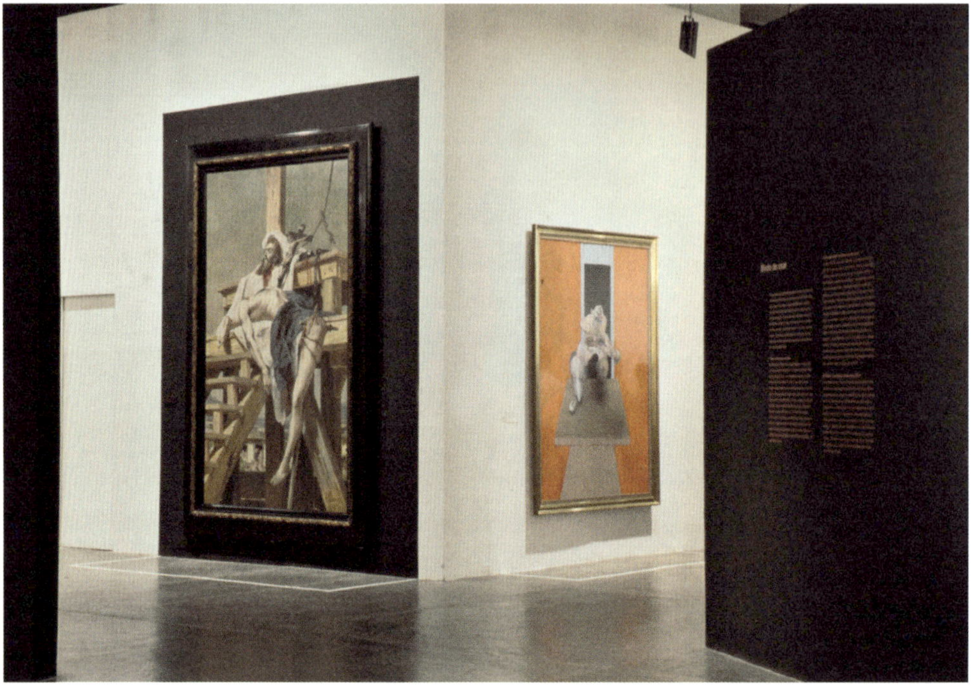

fig.58

The next section, 'Século XIX', dedicated to nineteenth-century art, was curated by Régis Michel, who provided the audience with a 'Modo de Usar' ('Users' Guide'), visible to the right, explaining the division of the section into: '1. Taboo: the father eats the son'; '2. Transgression: the sons eat the father' and '3. Totem: society eats its children'. From left, Pedro Américo's *Tiradentes esquartejado* (*Tiradentes Dismembered*, 1893) and, opening onto the Francis Bacon section, Bacon's *Figure in Movement* (1985).

View of 'Século XIX', with two versions of Auguste Rodin's sculpture *Ugolino* (1882/1906), of the father who devours his sons, on the left, and the severed heads of Théodore Géricault's *Têtes Coupées* (1818–19) painting on the back wall.

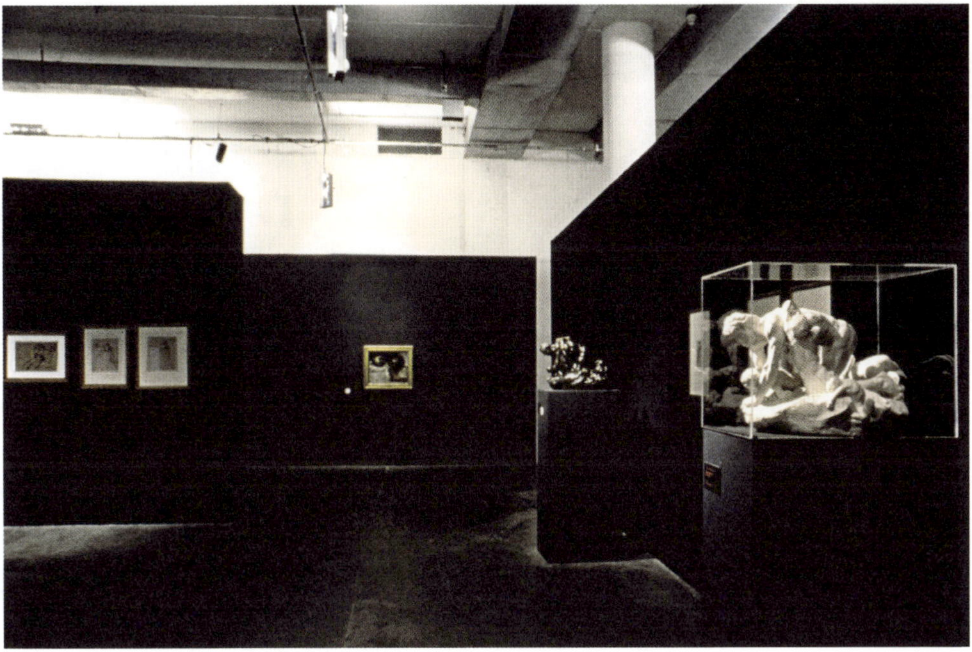

fig.59

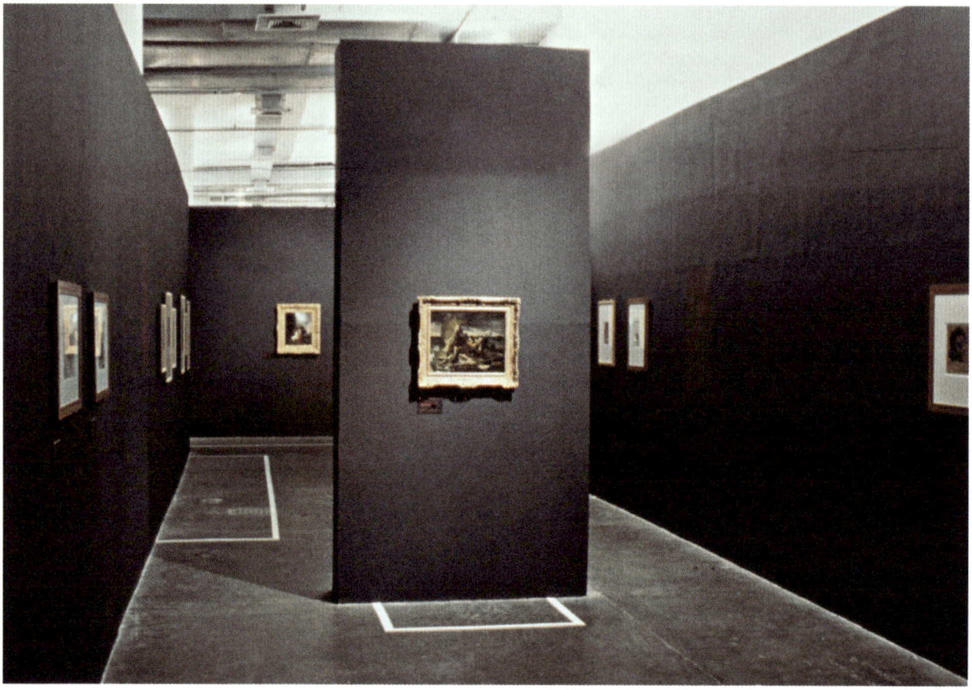

fig.60

View of 'Século XIX', with Théodore Géricault's *Le Radeau de la Méduse - premiére esquisse* (*The Raft of the Medusa - First Sketch*, 1818–19) hung on the central partition and Gustave Moreau's *Diomède dévoré par ses chevaux* (*Diomedes Devoured by His Horses*, 1870) on the wall behind.

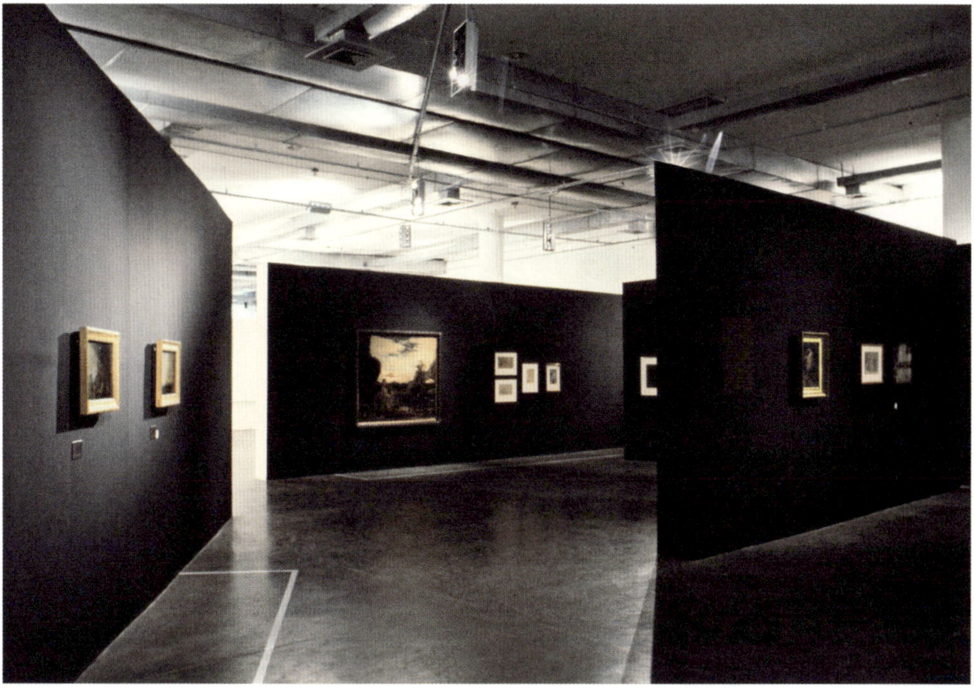

fig.61

Another room in the 'Século XIX' section showed two paintings from Francisco de Goya's *Caníbales* series (c.1798–1800): *Caníbales contemplando restos humanos* and *Caníbales preparando a sus víctimas* (*Cannibals Contemplating Human Remains* and *Cannibals Preparing their Victims*) are visible to the left. On the adjacent wall was Gustave Moreau's *Hercule et l'Hydre de Lerne* (*Hercules and the Hydra from Lerne*, c.1870), and, to the far right on the free-standing partition, William Blake's *Inferno, Canto XXXIII, 13–93, Count Ugolino and his sons in prison* (c.1826).

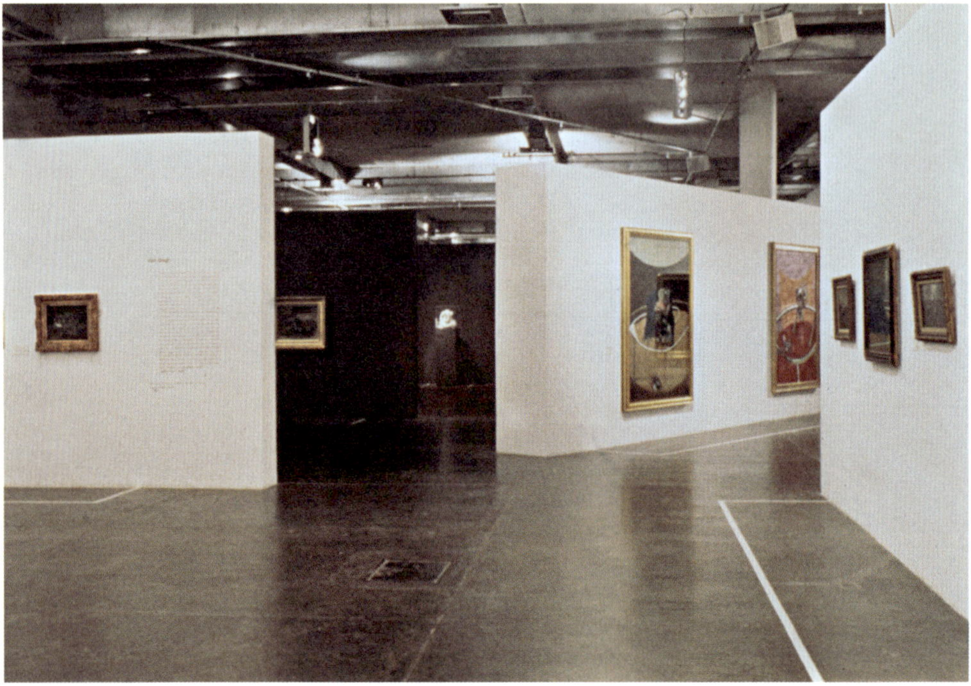

fig.62

In the next section hung works by Vincent van Gogh, curated by Pieter Tjabbes. From left to right: Vincent van Gogh, *Still Life With an Earthen Bowl and Pears* (1885); partial view of 'Século XIX'; Francis Bacon, *Study for Portrait on Folding Bed* (1963) and *The Human Figure in Motion: Woman Emptying a Bowl of Water/Paralytic Child Walking on All Fours* (1965); and three paintings by Vincent van Gogh, including *Farmhouses in Loosduinen Near The Hague at Twilight* (1833).

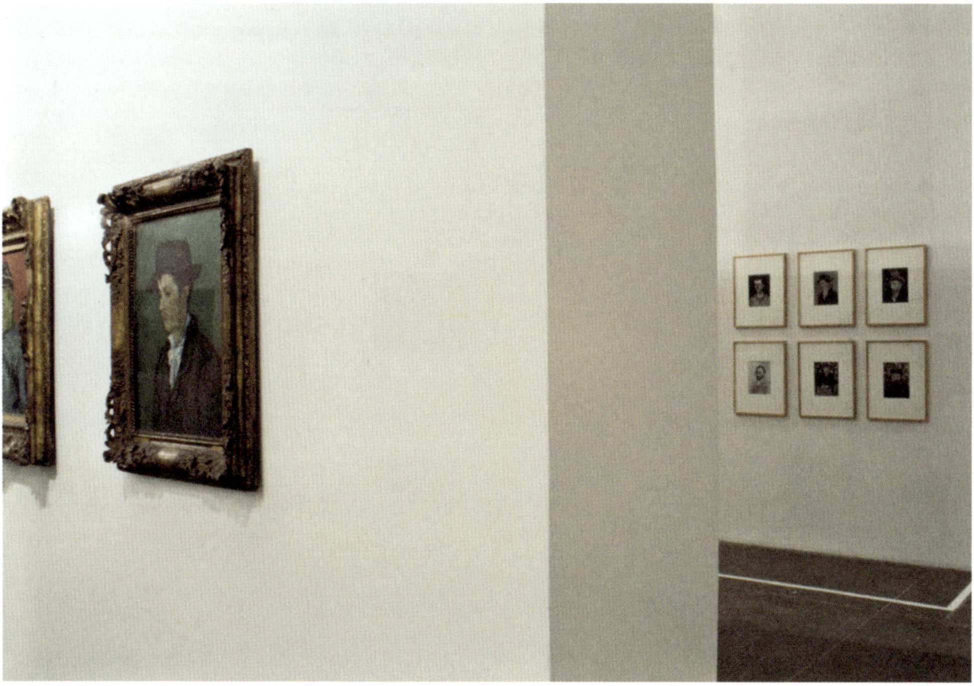

fig.63

Another view of the van Gogh section shows, from left to right: Vincent van Gogh, *The Schoolboy (Camille Roulin)* (1889–90) and *Portrait of Armand Roulin* (1888); Sherrie Levine, *After van Gogh* (1994), as part of 'Roteiros Canada and US'.

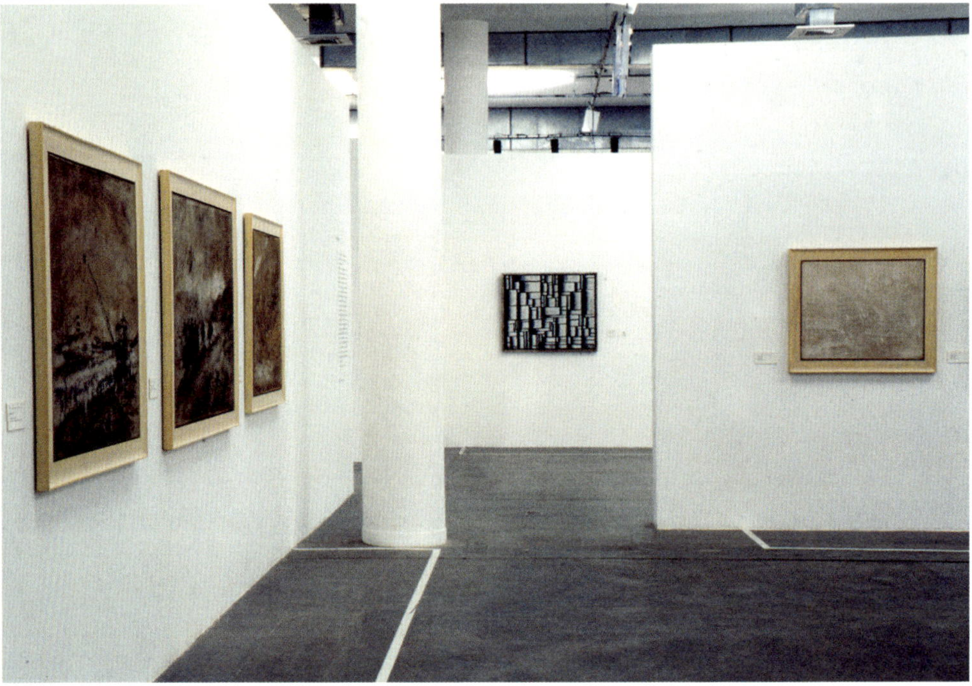

fig.64

Following the van Gogh display was a selection of paintings by Armando Reverón, curated by Luis Pérez-Oramas. His paintings *La grua* (*The Crane*, 1942), *Marina* (*Seascape*, 1944) and *Paisage de Macuto* (*Landscape of Macuto*, 1943) appear on the left; Joaquín Torres-García's *Construcción en blanco y negro* (*Construction in Black and White*, 1938) and Reverón's *El arbol* (*The Tree*, 1931) on the right. Beyond the column was the entrance to the 'Monocromos' section.

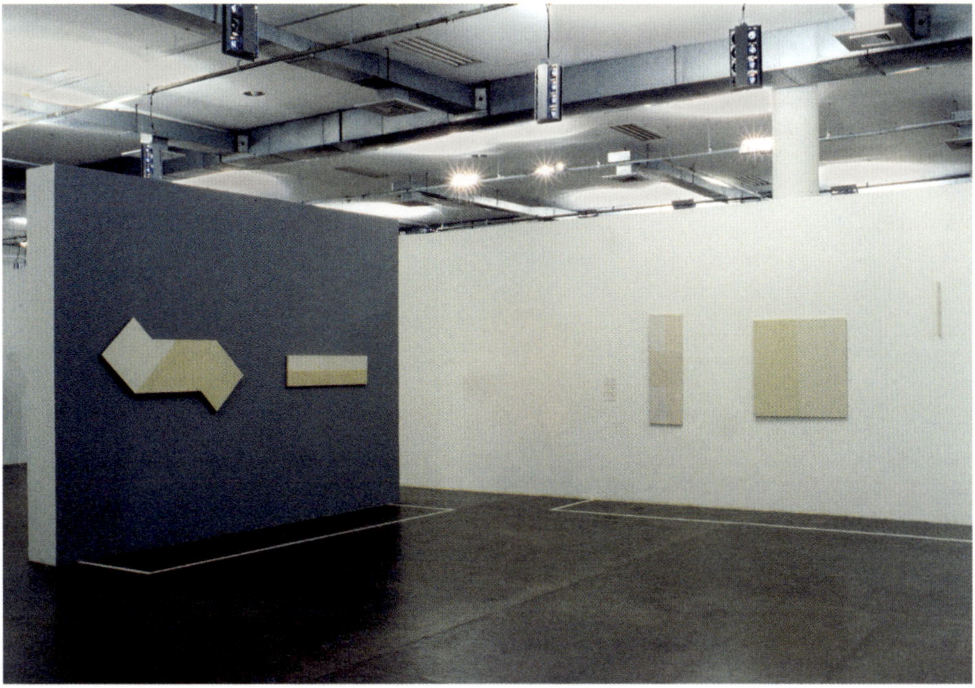

fig.65

The 'Monocromos' section, across three rooms, featured monochromatic works curated by Paulo Herkenhoff with the assistance of Valéria Piccoli. In this room, there were four works from Hélio Oiticica's untitled 'White Series' (all 1959).

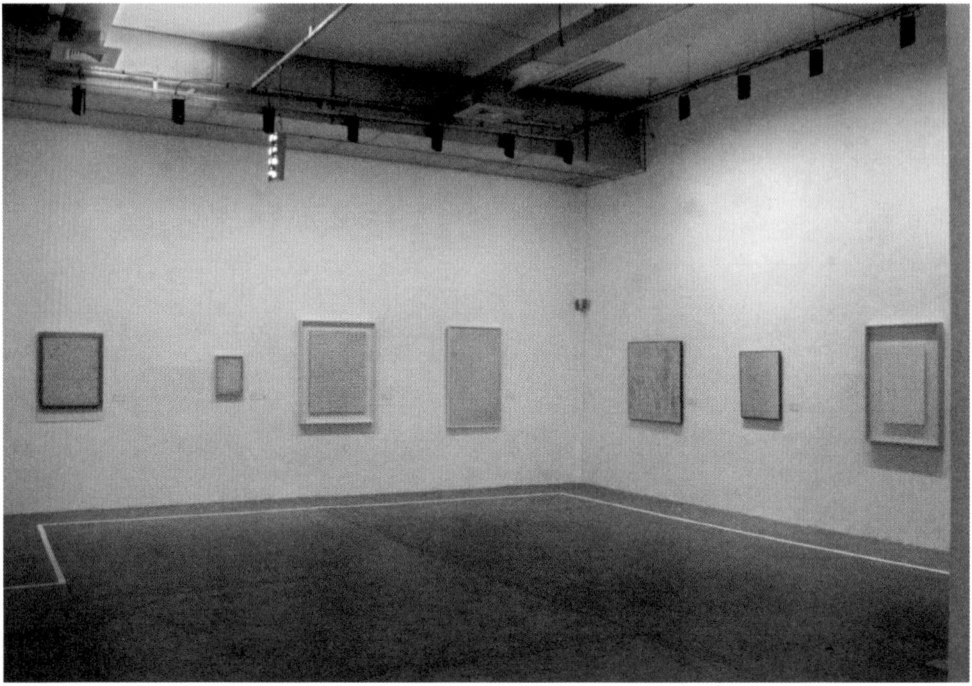

fig.66

The anteroom featured monochromes by Kazimir Malevich, Piet Mondrian, Theo van Doesburg and Georges Vantongerloo, all of whom were reference points for mid-century Brazilian constructivist and concretist artists. 'Monocromos' also featured works by Hércules Barsotti, Antonio Dias, Glenn Ligon, Manabu Mabe and Jesús Rafael Soto, and sections devoted to Lucio Fontana, Yves Klein, Yayoi Kusama (a selection of her *Infinity Net* paintings), Piero Manzoni (the *Achrome* series), Hélio Oiticica, Robert Ryman and Joaquín Torres-García.

View of 'Monocromos' (fig.67), with Jesús Rafael Soto's *Vibración en blanco* (*Vibration in White*, 1960), second from left, and two works by Lucio Fontana, *Concetto spaziale* (*Spatial Concept*, 1950) and *Concetto spaziale/espera* (*Spatial Concept / Waiting*, 1966), third and fourth from left. From left to right (fig.68): Hércules Barsotti, *Branco branco* (*White White*, 1960); Antonio Dias, *Project for an Artistic Attitude* (1970); and Robert Ryman, *Winsor* (1965).

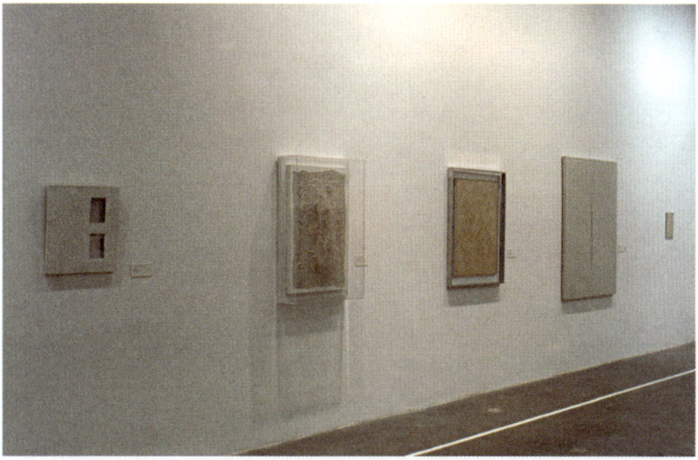

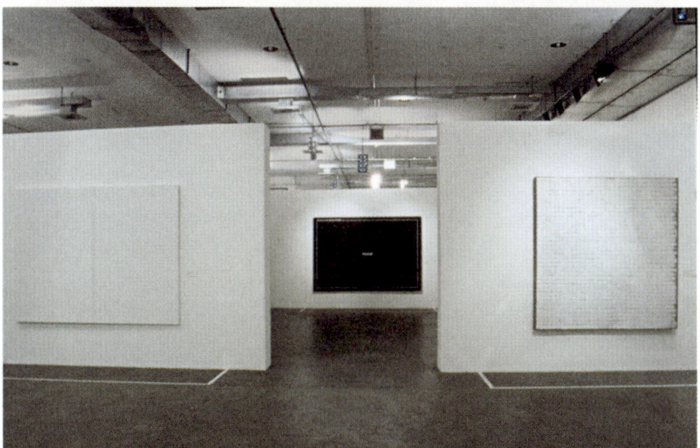

fig.67 and 68

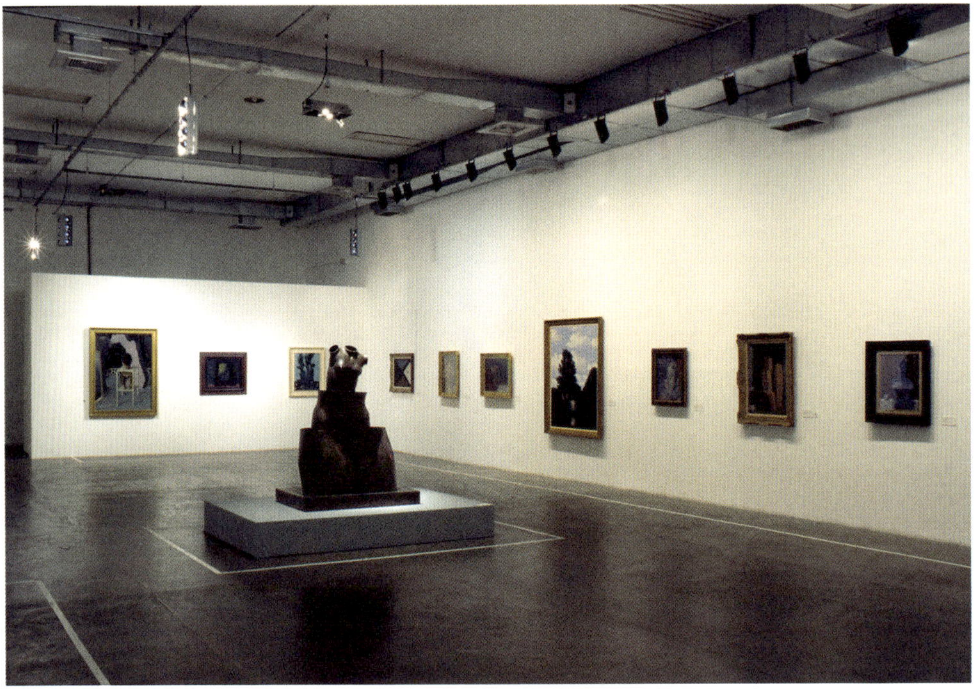

fig.69

The next room, curated by Didier Ottinger, was dedicated to René Magritte and featured paintings such as, from left to right: *Le Mariage du minuit* (*Midnight Marriage*, 1926), *Le Prince des objets* (*Prince of Objects*, 1927), *Campagne II* (*Countryside II*, 1927), *Le sens propre* (*The Literal Meaning*, 1929), *Découverte* (*Discovery*, 1927), *Personnage méditant sur la folie* (*Figure Brooding on Madness*, 1928), *L'Empire des lumières* (*Empire of Light*, 1953–54), *Perspective II: Le balcon de Manet* (*Perspective II: Manet's Balcony*, 1950) and *L'heureux donateur* (*The Happy Donor*, 1966). At the room's centre was his sculpture *La Folie des grandeurs (Megalomania)* (*The Madness of Greatness (Megalomania)*, 1967).

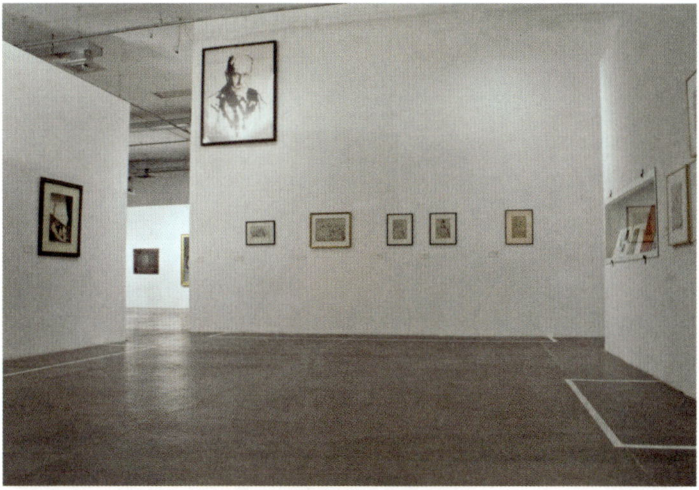

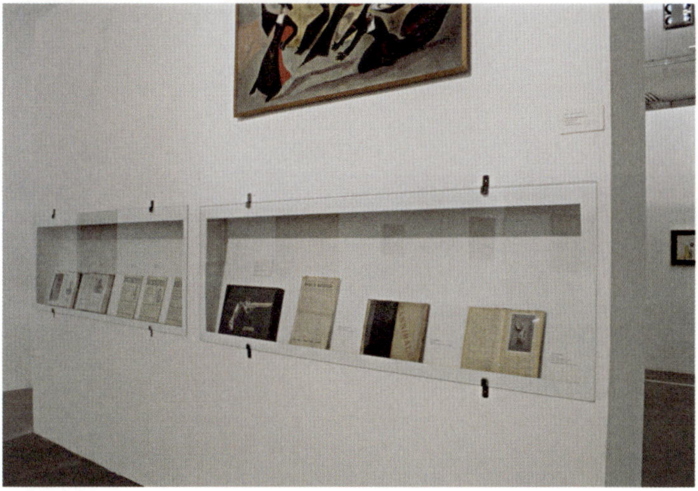

fig.70 and 71

Adjacent to the René Magritte room was a space, curated by Dawn Ades and Didier Ottinger, devoted to Dada and Surrealism and related works. On display was, for example, a selection of drawings by André Masson. Above such works hung one of Paulo Herkenhoff's 'contaminações': a portrait of Sigmund Freud by Vik Muniz, *Sigmund*, from his *Pictures of Chocolate* series (1997) (fig.70). Another view from this section (fig.71) shows a display of publications associated with Dada and Surrealism: *Documents* (1929–30), edited by George Bataille, and *Cannibale* (1920), edited by Francis Picabia. The latter was placed alongside Wolfgang Paalen's bone pistol *Le Génie de l'espèce* (1938).

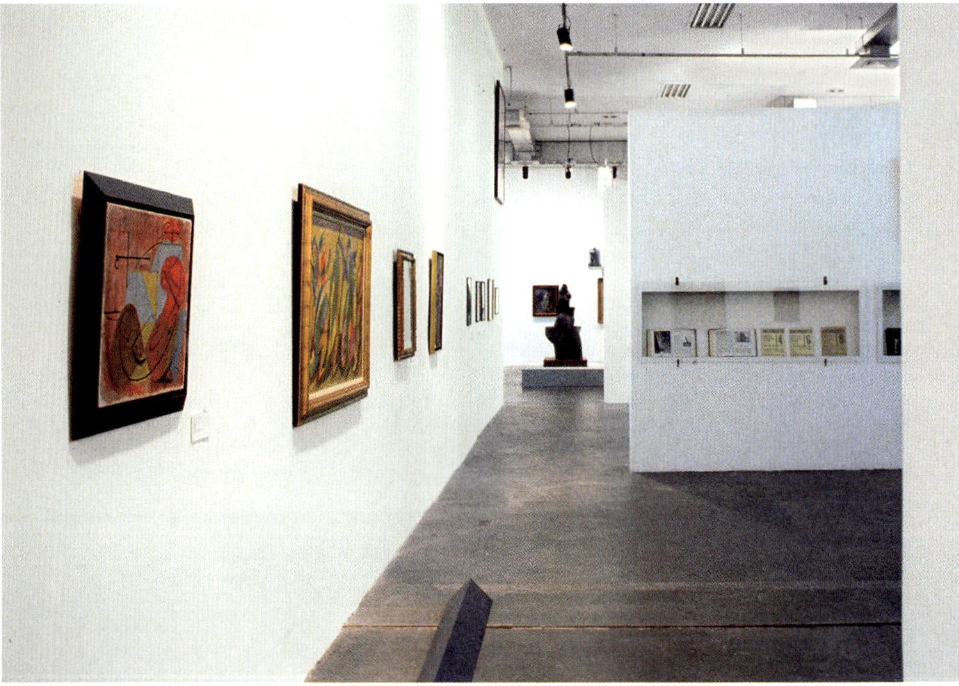

fig.72

On the wall perpendicular to the display of journals hung works such as, second from left, André Masson's *Massacre dans un champ* (*Massacre in a Field*, 1933). René Magritte's sculpture *La Folie des grandeurs (Megalomania)* (1967) is visible in the distance.

The next space presented a range of works by Roberto Matta, curated by Justo Pastor Mellado, and partly visible on the right here. From left to right: the Vincent van Gogh section (*L'Arlésienne* (*Portrait of Madame Ginoux*) (1890), *The Schoolboy* (*Camille Roulin*) (1889–90) and *Portrait of Armand Roulin* (1888)); the Francis Bacon section (*Three Studies for a Portrait of John Edwards* (1984)); and the opening to the Matta section (second, third and fourth from the left: *Composición en tonos verdes* (*Composition in Greens*, 1939); *Boulevard Raspail* (1937); and *Theory of Nature's Strategy (Polypsychology)* (1939).

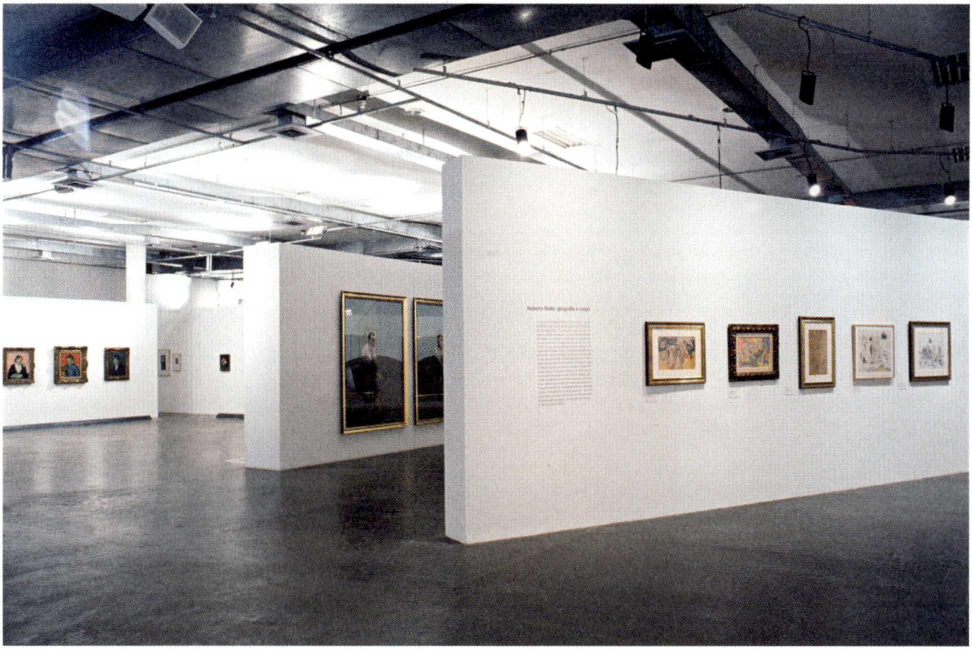

fig.73

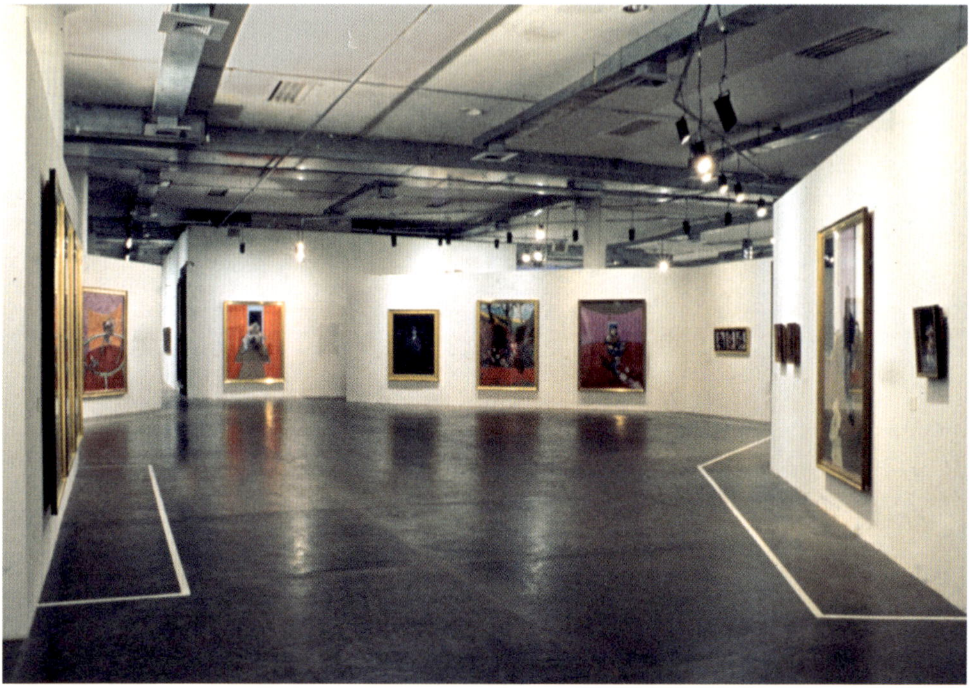

fig.74

The Francis Bacon display formed the centre of this part of the 'Núcleo Histórico'. Curated by Dawn Ades, it included works such as, from left to right: *The Human Figure in Motion: Woman Emptying a Bowl of Water/ Paralytic Child Walking on all Fours* (1965), *Figure in Movement* (1985), *Figure Sitting* (1955), *Study for Portrait of Van Gogh VI* (1957), *Portrait of George Dyer Talking* (1966), *Three Studies of Henrietta Moraes* (1969), *Study for Portrait (Michel Leiris)* (1978), *Portrait of Michel Leiris* (1976), *Self-Portrait* (1973) and *Self-Portrait* (1971). As a 'contaminação' in this section, Artur Barrio's *T.E. (trouxas ensangüentadas)* (*T.E. (bloody bundles)*, 1969) was displayed behind a transparent barrier at ground level.

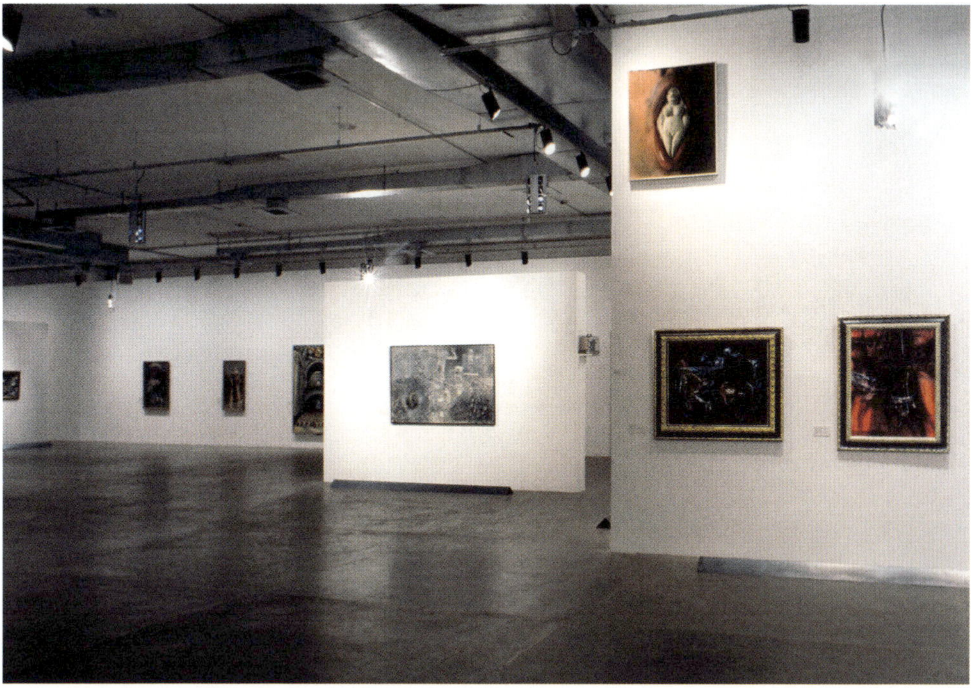

fig.75

Returning to the Roberto Matta section, on the right wall, from left, Ernesto Neto's *O escultor e a deusa* (*The Sculptor and the Goddess*, 1995) was hung above Matta's *Crucifixion* (1938) and *Composition in Magenta: The End of Everything* (1942) as a 'contaminação'. Continuing into the space, there were additional works by Matta, including *Pecador justificado* (*Justified Sinner*, 1952) on the central wall, leading into a room of paintings by David Alfaro Siqueiros, curated by Mari Carmen Ramírez. The Siqueiros room displayed the works, from far left, *Birth of Fascism* (1936), *Ethnography* (1939), *El sollozo* (*The Sob*, 1939) and *El diablo en la iglesia* (*The Devil in the Church*, 1947).

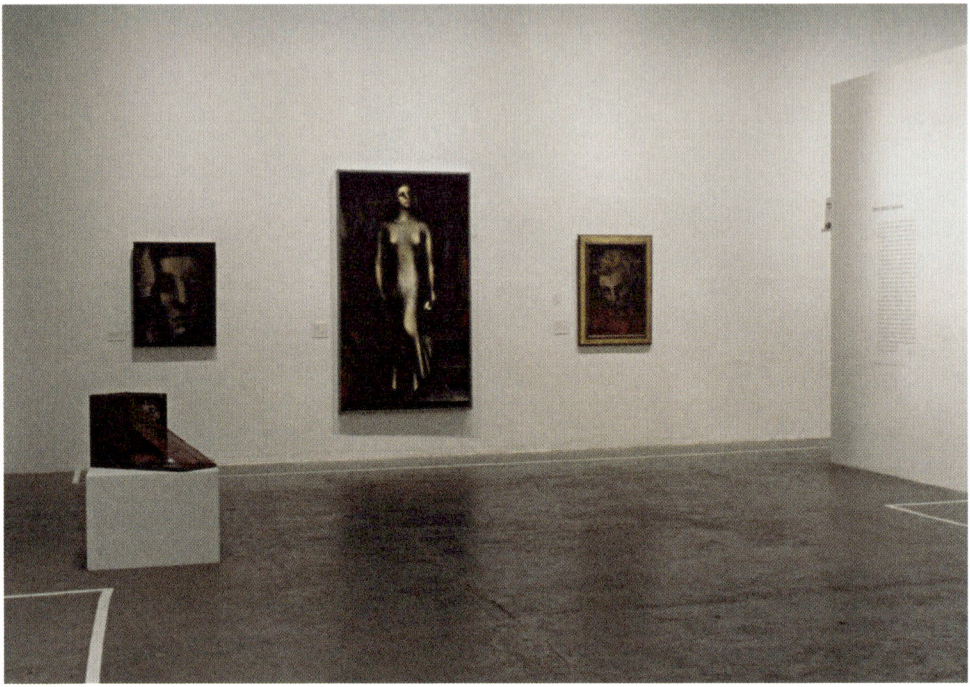

fig.76

Continuing into the David Alfaro Siqueiros display, here appears, on the far left, Hélio Oiticica's *B33 Bólide Caixa 18, poema caixa 02 'Homenagem a Cara de Cavalo' (B33 Box Bolide 18, Box Poem 02 'Homage to Horse Face',* 1965–66), alongside Siqueiros's works on the back wall, from left: *María del Carmen Portela* (1933), *Retrato de María Asúnsolo bajando la escalera* (*Portrait of María Asúnsolo Descending a Staircase*, 1935) and *Ione Robinson* (1931). Oiticica's sculpture was moved around during the period of the exhibition as a 'contaminating element'; it was also included for a time in the 'Monocromos' display, for instance.

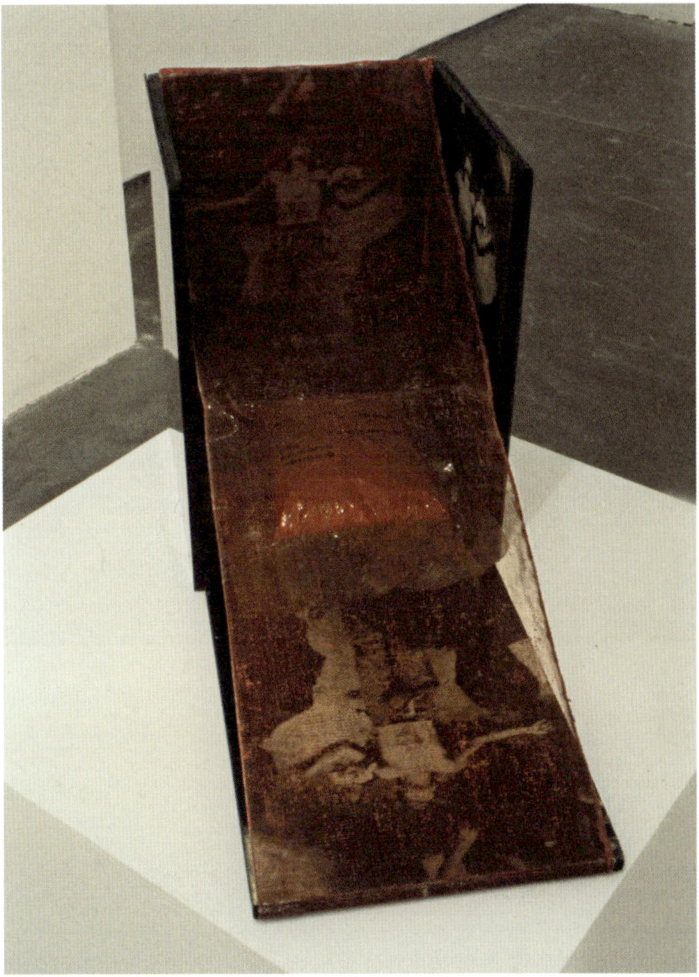

fig.77

Hélio Oiticica, *B33 Bólide Caixa 18, poema caixa 02 'Homenagem a Cara de Cavalo'* (1965–66).

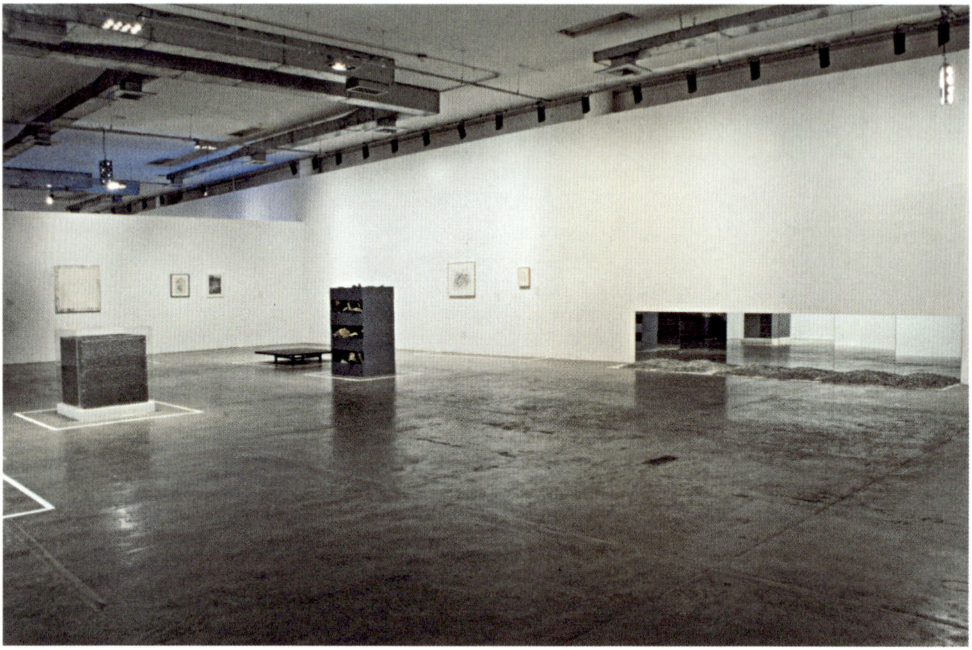

fig.78

The next room featured works by Eva Hesse and Robert Smithson, curated by Mary Jane Jacob. On the floor are, from left: Hesse's *Accession II* (1967) and *Washer Table* (1967); Smithson's *Nonsite (Palisades-Edgewater, New Jersey)* (1968) and *Eight-part piece (Cayuga Salt Mine)* (1969). On the wall, third and fourth from left: Smithson's *Bingham copper mining pit – Utah reclamation project* (1973) and *Island project* (1970). This room opened onto a smaller room displaying work by Louise Bourgeois (not pictured).

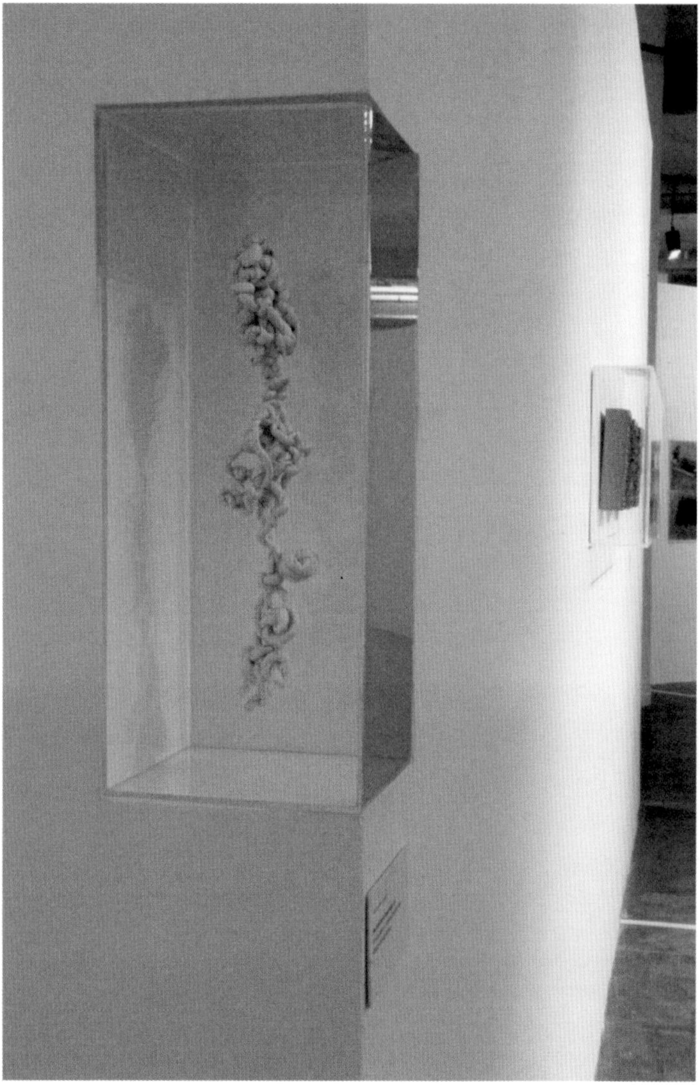

fig.79

In the Eva Hesse and Robert Smithson room, one of the exhibition's 'contaminações', a work by Mira Schendel from her series *Droguinhas* (*Little Nothings*, 1965–66) was inserted in a corner.

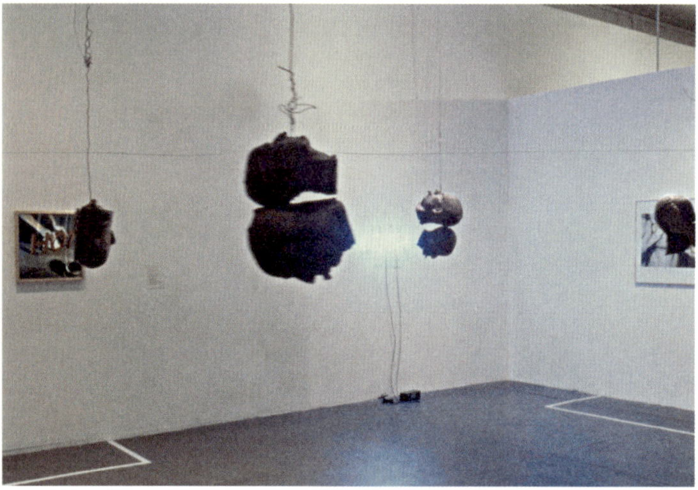

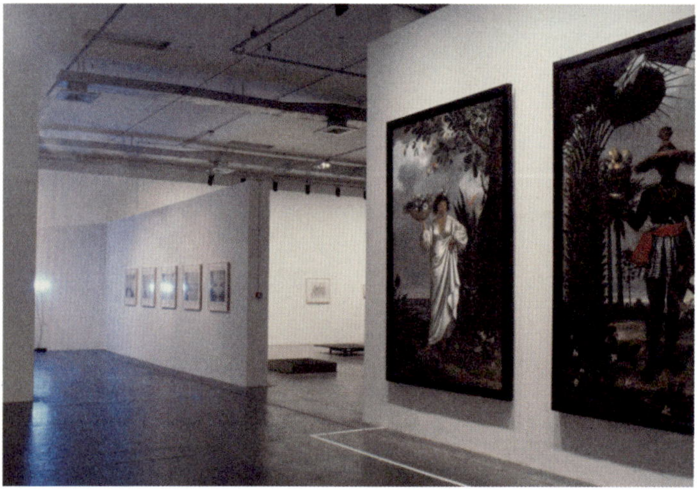

fig.80 and 81

Next to the Eva Hesse and Robert Smithson space was a room dedicated to Bruce Nauman, curated by Robert Storr, which included: *Waxing Hot from Eleven Color Photographs* (1966/70), on the far left; the neon work *EAT/DEATH* (1972); works from *Studies for Holograms (a & b)* (1970), on the far right; and *Four Pairs of Heads* (1991), in the foreground. The Nauman space was adjacent to the display of paintings by Albert Eckhout (fig.81) and the main entrance/exit to the enclosed part of the 'Núcleo Histórico'.

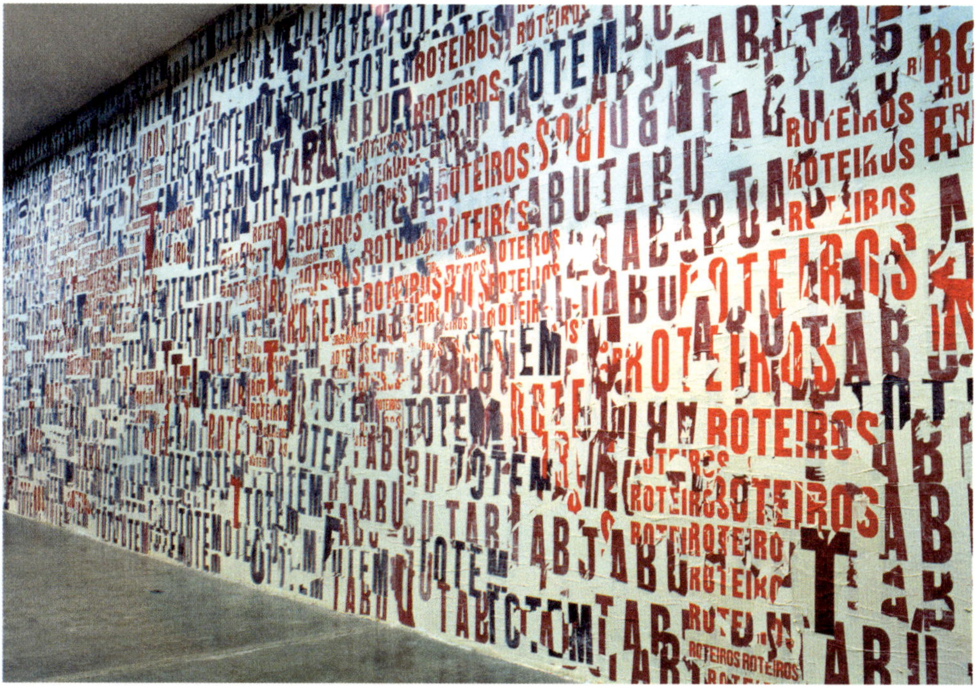

fig.82

Turning right out of the central enclosed space of the 'Núcleo Histórico' and walking around it, visitors passed a section on 'Poesia Contemporânea' ('Contemporary Poetry'), with *Contribuicão multimilionária de todos os erros (Multimillionaire Contribution of All Errors*, 1998), an installation of poetic works by Arnaldo Antunes, Lenora de Barros and Walter Silveira. Pictured is Arnaldo Antunes's *Colagem* (*Collage*, 1998).

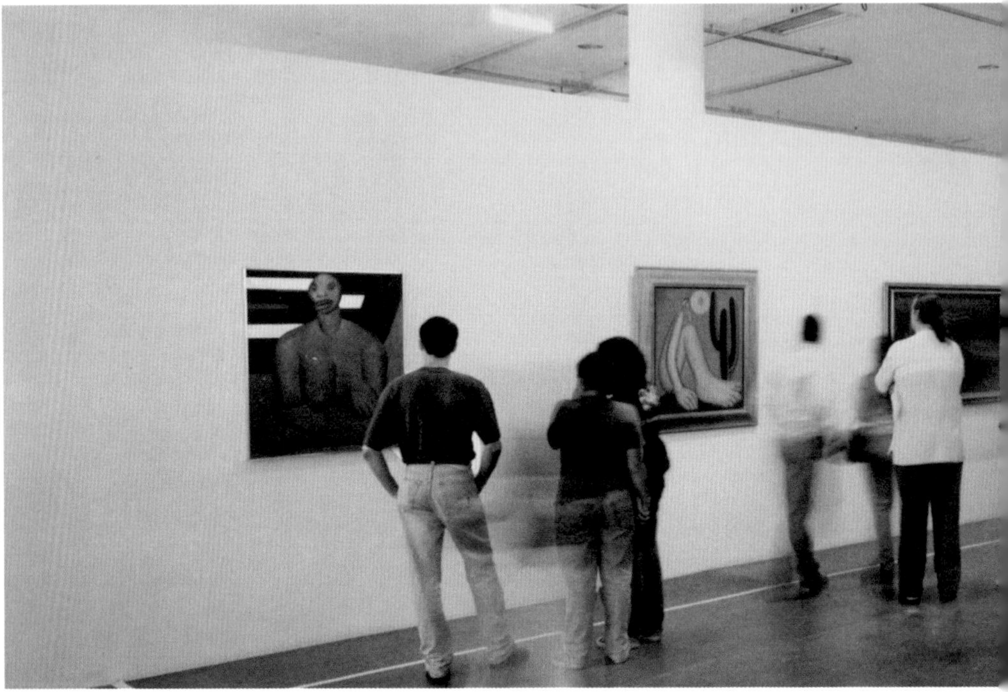

fig.83

This was followed by work by Lygia Pape (not pictured). On the other side of the enclosed museological structure, the space opened onto the so-called 'Eixo da Cor' section, starting with a display of paintings by Tarsila do Amaral, curated by Sônia Salzstein including (on left wall, from left): *A Negra* (*The Negress*, 1923), *Abaporu* (1928) and *Composição* (*Composition*, 1930).

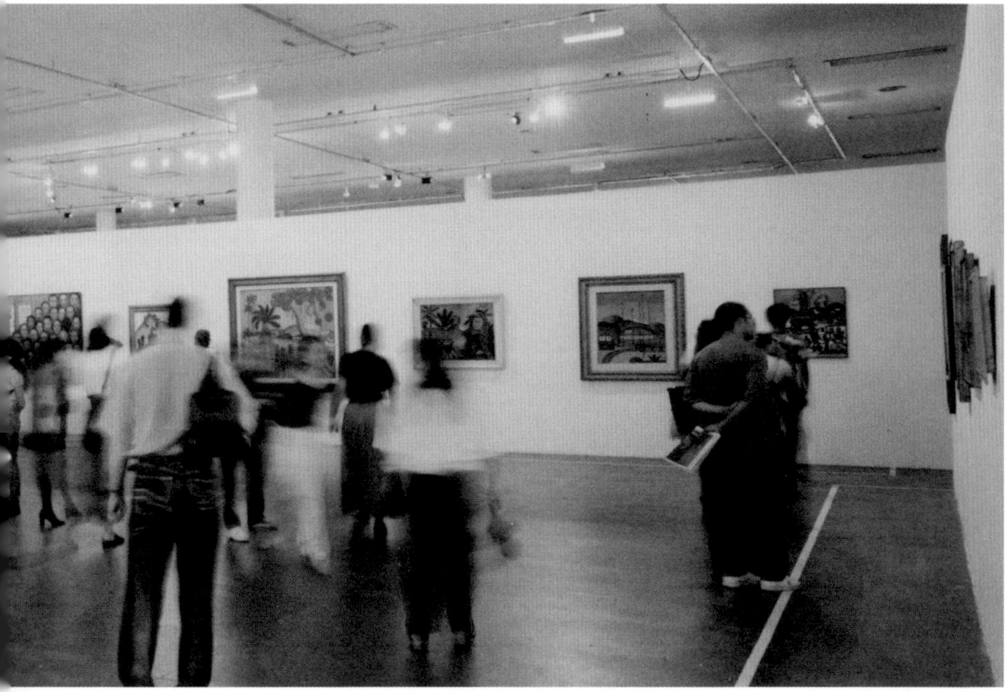

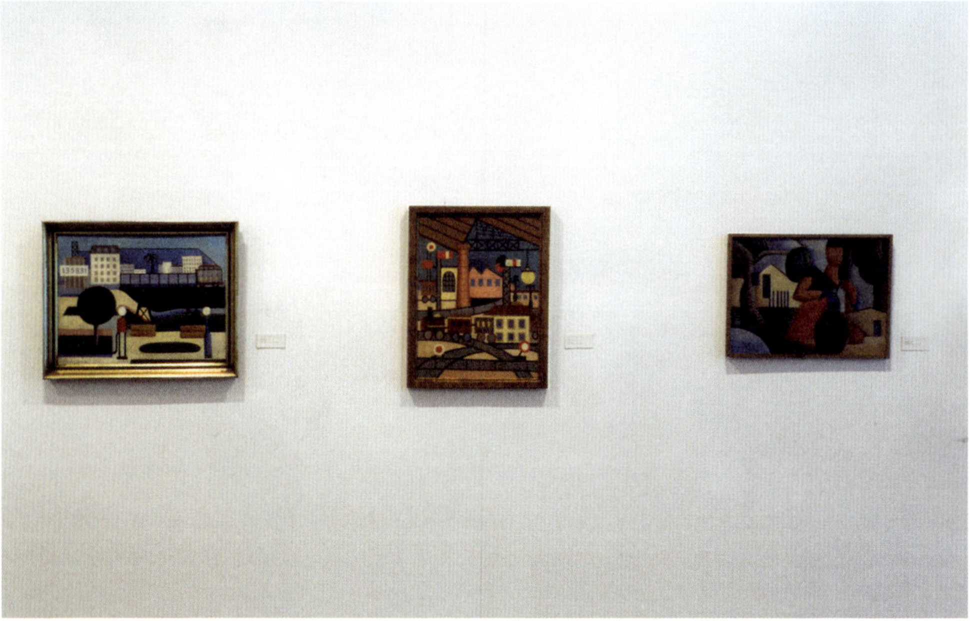

fig.84

On the immediate right-hand wall hung Tarsila do Amaral's paintings, from left to right: *São Paulo* (1924), *A estação* (*The Station*, 1925) and *A caipirinha* (1923).

Within the Tarsila do Amaral display, from left to right: *Operários* (*Workers*, 1933), *Manacá* (1927), *Cartão postal* (*Postcard*, 1928), *O lago* (*The Lake*, 1928), *Paisagem com touro* (*Landscape with Bull*, 1925) and *Carnaval em Madureira* (*Carnival in Madureira*, 1924).

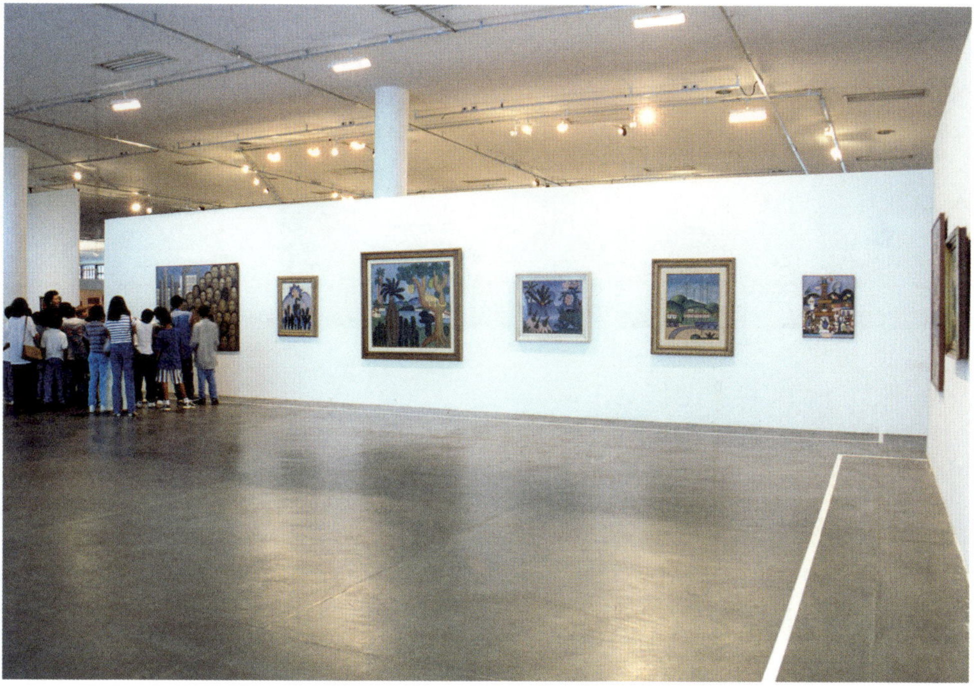

fig.85

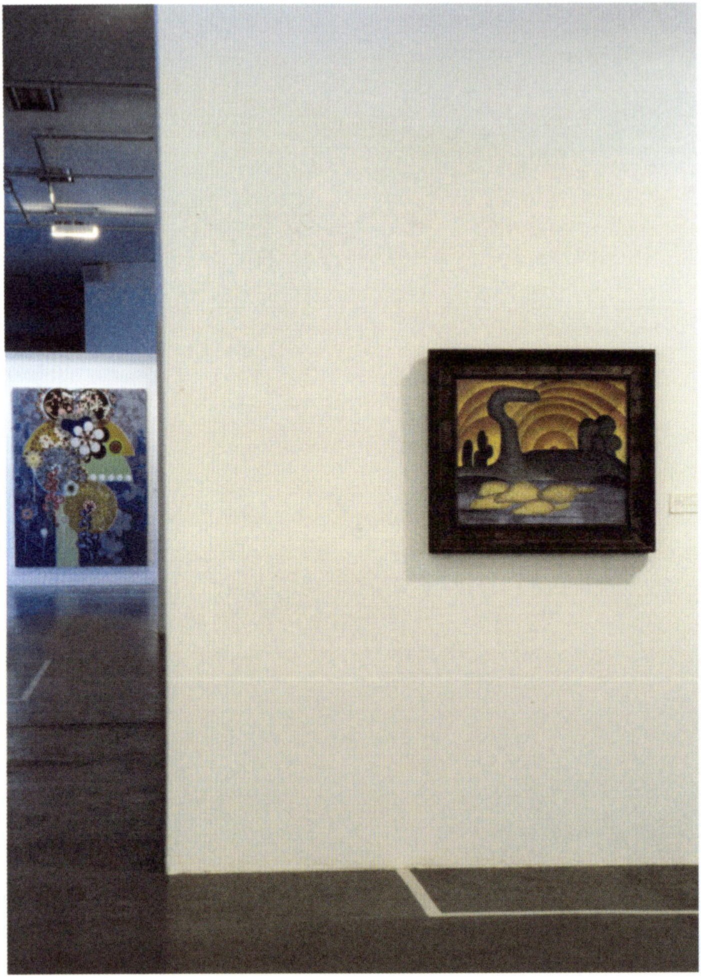

fig.86

Following the display of paintings to the end of the wall, to Tarsila do Amaral's *Sol Poente* (*Setting Sun*, 1929), led to Beatriz Milhazes's work, hung in the space at the far end of the gallery.

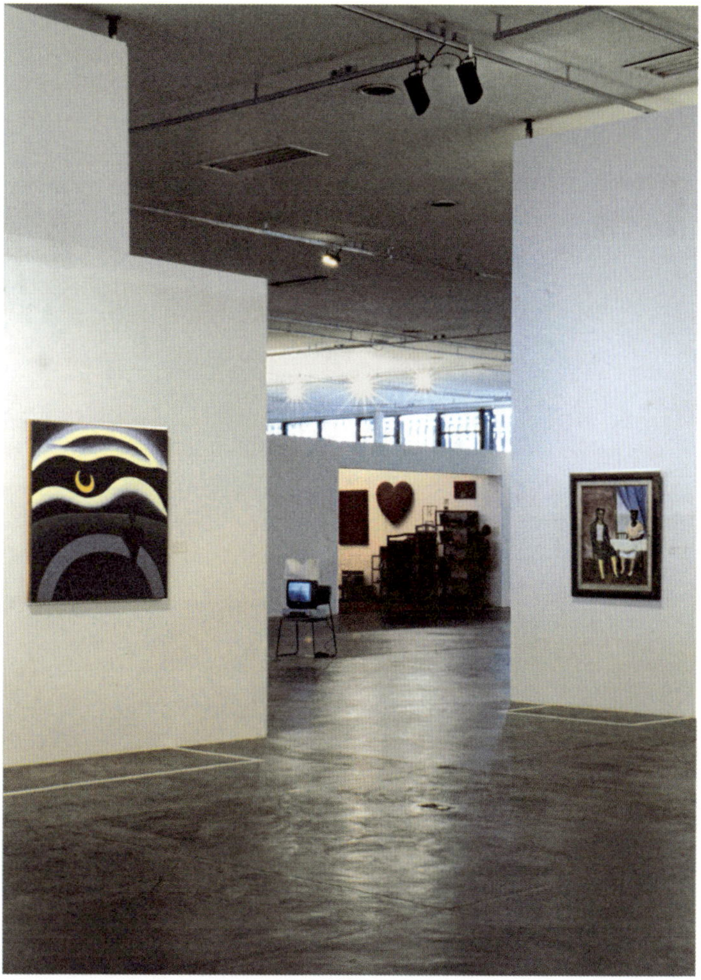

fig.87

Turning right again out of the Tarsila do Amaral display and passing her *A lua* (*The Moon*, 1928) on the left, a partition wall displayed Alfredo Volpi's early painting of two figures *Sem título* (*Untitled*, 1945), with Cildo Meireles's installation *Desvio para o vermelho* (*Red Shift*, 1967–84) and Franz West's video work *Paulo Herkenhoff in his Everyday* (1998), part of 'Roteiros Europe', visible in the next space.

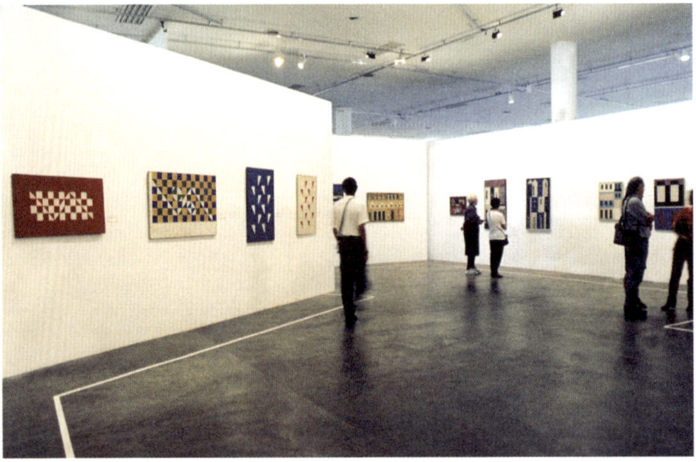

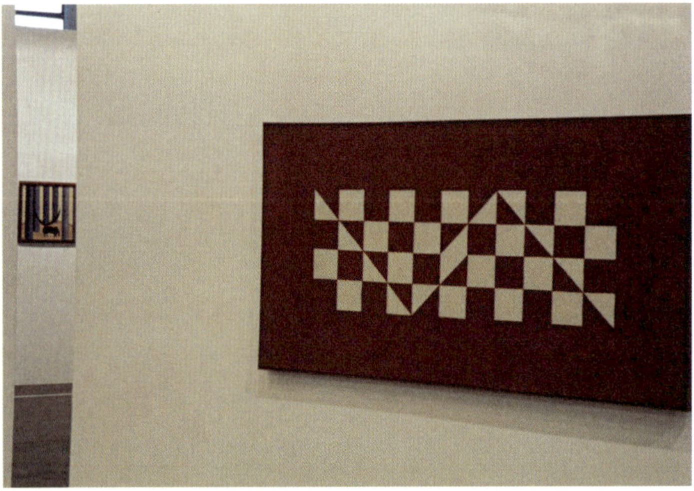

fig.88 and 89

Exiting the Tarsila do Amaral display and turning right, viewers saw a large installation dedicated to the work of Alfredo Volpi, curated by Aracy Amaral. From left: four works from Volpi's *Concretos* (*Concretions*) series and six works from his *Fachada* (*Façades*) series (all mid-1950s). Visible through the partition (fig.89) is Tarsila do Amaral's *Boi na floresta* (*Ox in the Forest*, 1928).

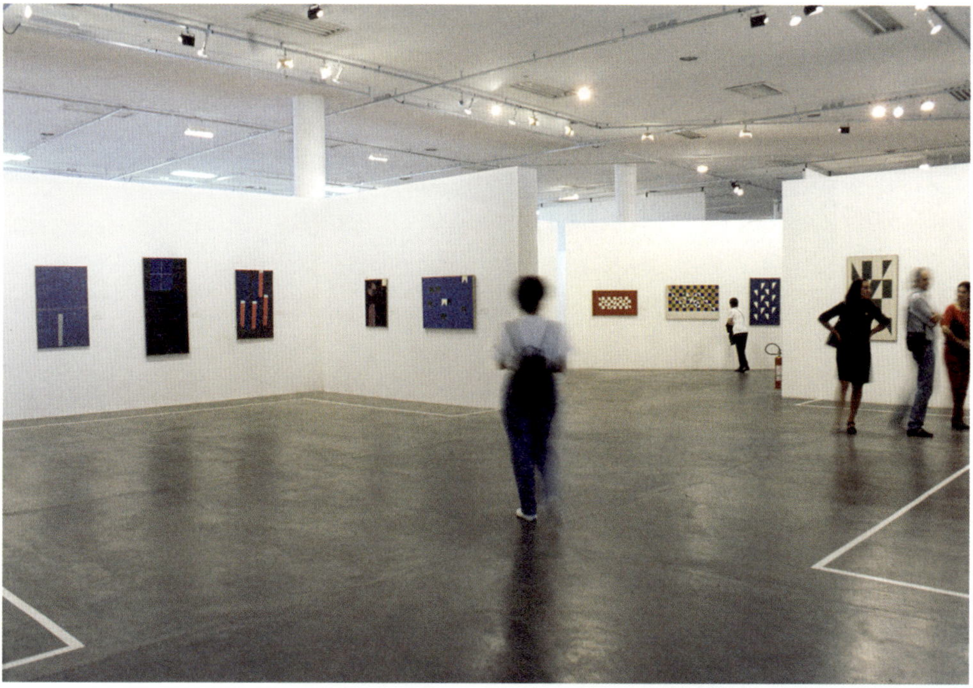

fig.90

Moving into the second area showing Alfredo Volpi's work, on the left wall hung four mid-1960s works from his *Fachada* series and *Bandeirinhas* (*Small Paper Flags*, mid-1960s); on the wall behind and the wall in front to the right, four additional works from his *Concretos* (mid-1950s).

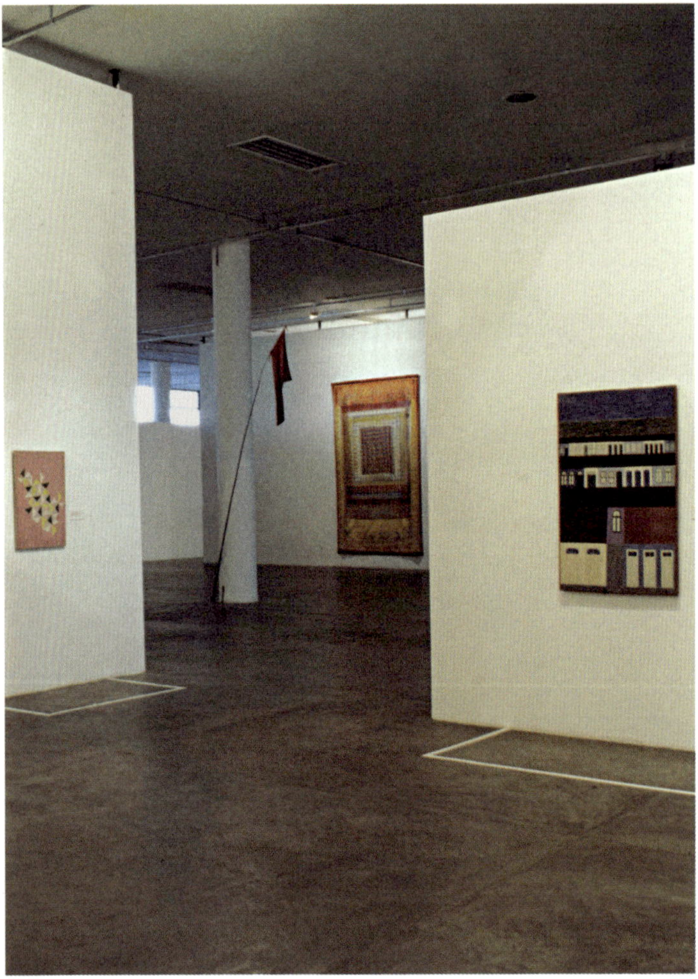

fig.91

Leaving the Alfredo Volpi display at the entry point, with his *Concretos* (mid-1950s) to the left and *Casario de Santos* (1952) to the right, Antonio Dias's *The Invented Country (God-Will-Give-Days)* (1976) was visible against the central pillar, with Delson Uchôa's *Tear* (*Loom*, 1989) on the wall behind.

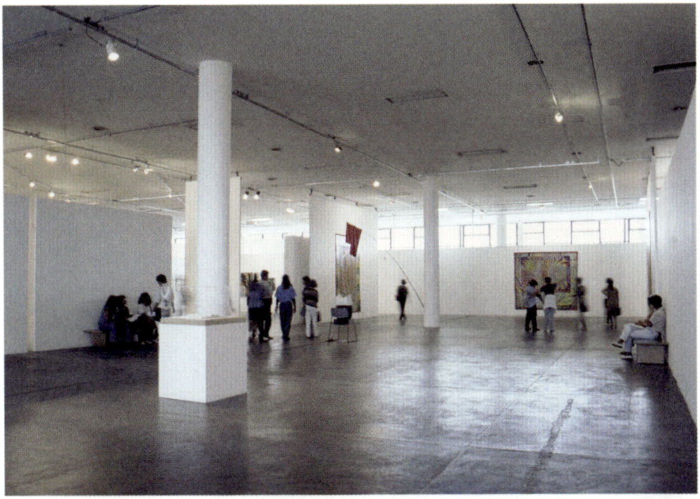

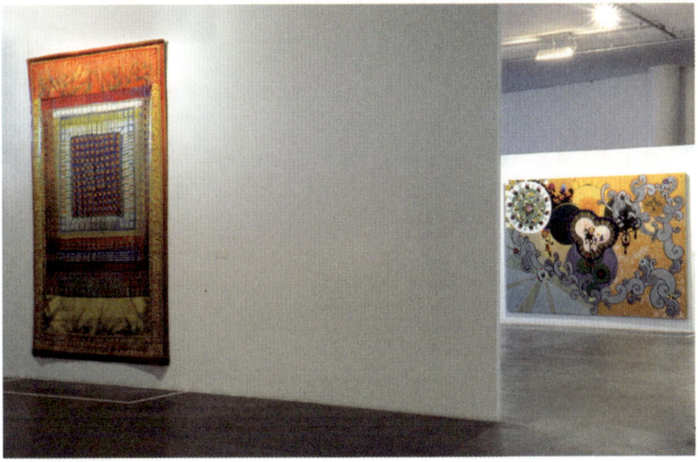

fig.92 and 93

Moving into the next space and looking left to the rear walls, viewers saw a display of Delson Uchôa's work, visible here on the far walls, from left: *Sudário Caeté* (*Caete Burial Shroud*, 1989) and *Roi Roi* (*King King*, 1989) (fig.92). Beatriz Milhazes's work was shown in an adjoining space. Here, her *Gavião e passarinhos* (*The Sparrow-Hawk and the Little Birds*, 1998) s visible beyond Uchôa's *Tear* (*Loom*, 1989) (fig.93).

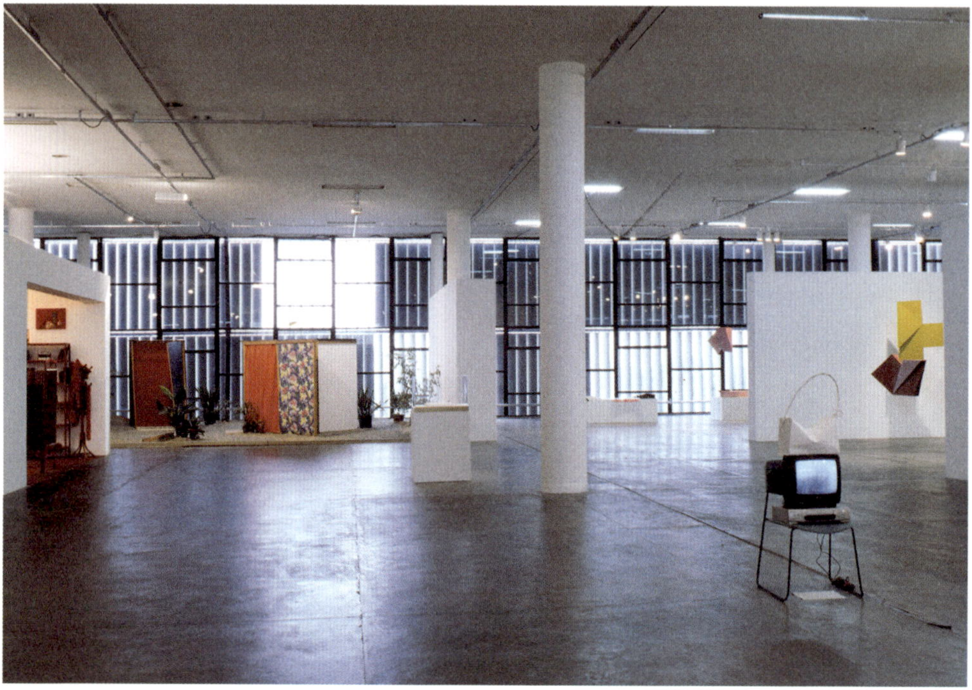

fig.94

In the opposite direction, an installation of Hélio Oiticica's *Tropicália* (1968), including *Penetráveis PN2 Pureza é um mito* and *PN3 Imagético*, was visible at the rear of the space, and two partitions on the right marked off a corridor containing works from his series *Bilaterais* (*Bilaterals*, 1959) and *Relevos Espaciais* (*Spatial Reliefs*, 1960). In the foreground is Franz West's *Paulo Herkenhoff in his Everyday* (1998), an inclusion described in the catalogue as a 'contamination'.

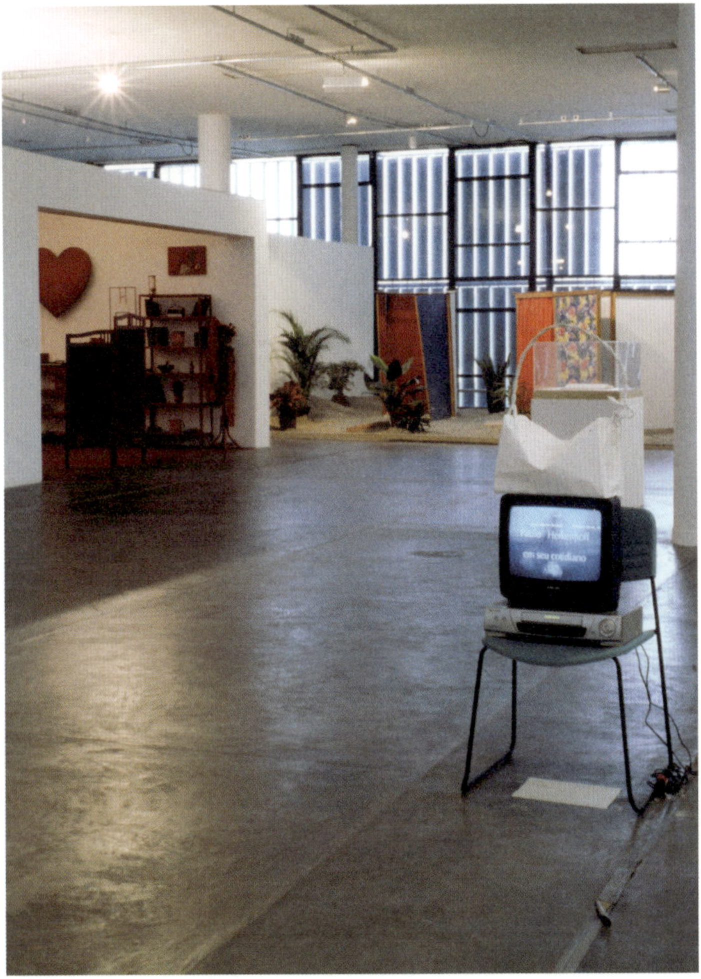

fig.95

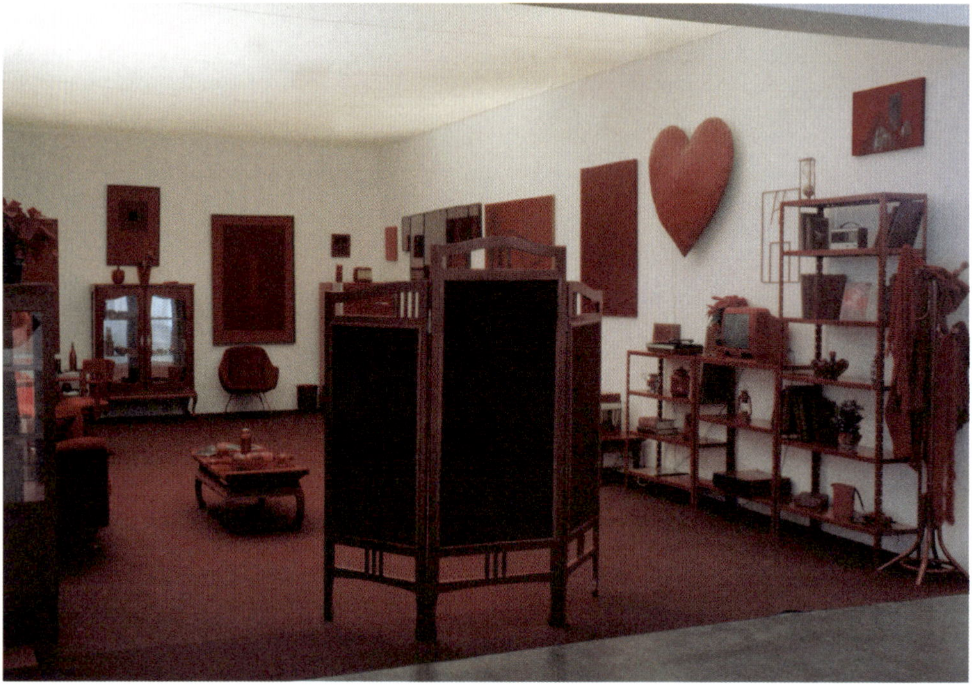

fig.96

To the left, within a walled structure, Cildo Meireles assembled a re-presentation of his immersive installation *Desvio para o vermelho* (*Red Shift*, 1967–84).

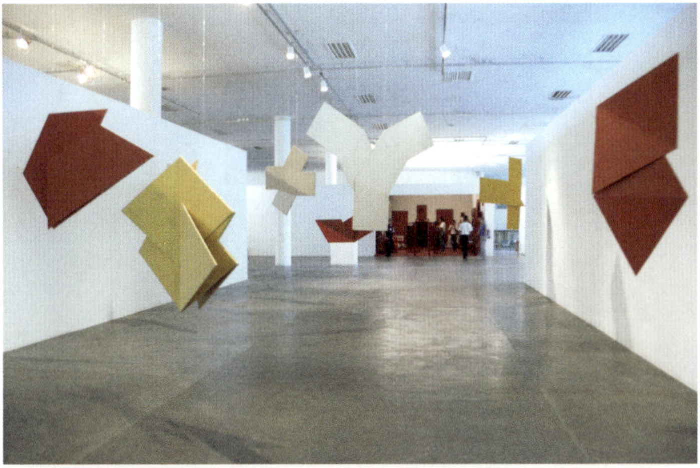

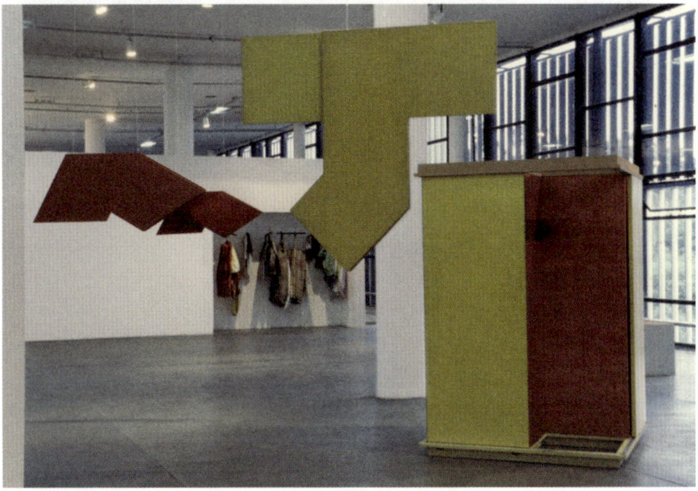

fig.97 and 98

Facing Cildo Meireles's *Desvio para o vermelho* (*Red Shift*, 1967–84), here seen in the distance, the following Hélio Oiticica works, from left to right, were presented in an open corridor-like space: *Relevo espacial (vermelho)* (*Spatial Relief (red)*, 1960), *Relevo espacial (amarelo)* (*Spatial Relief (yellow)*, 1960), *Bilateral Clássico* (1959), *Bilateral* (1959), *Maquette para Relevo espacial 23* (*amarelo*) (*Maquette for Spatial Relief 23* (*yellow*), 1960) and *Relevo espacial* (*vermelho*) (*Spatial Relief* (*red*), 1960) (fig.97). In a space adjacent to the corridor, additional works from Oiticica's series *Relevo espacial* (*Spatial Relief*, 1960) were presented alongside several of his *Parangolés* (1964–79) and *Penetrável PN1* (1960) (fig.98).

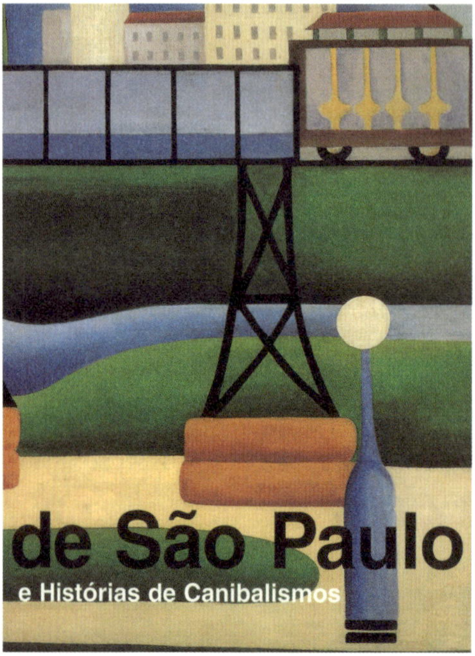

fig.99

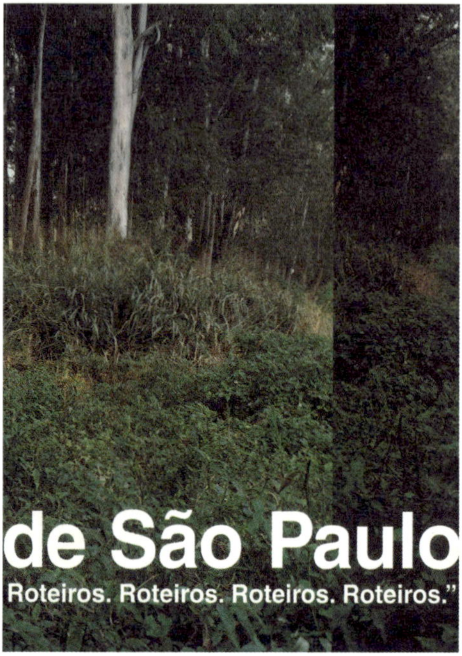

fig.100

Covers of the four volumes of the 24th Bienal de São Paulo catalogue.

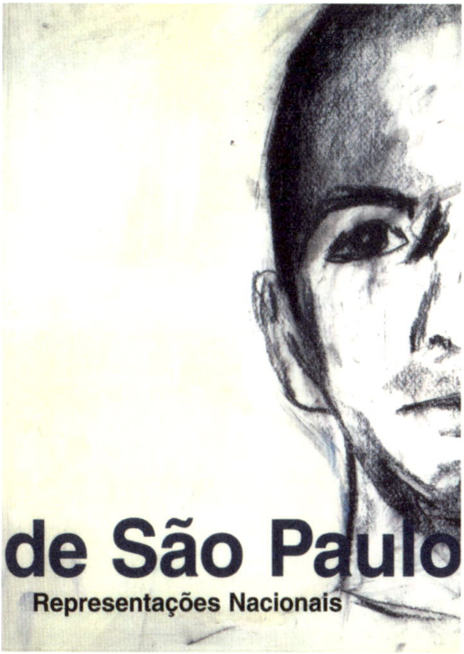

fig.101

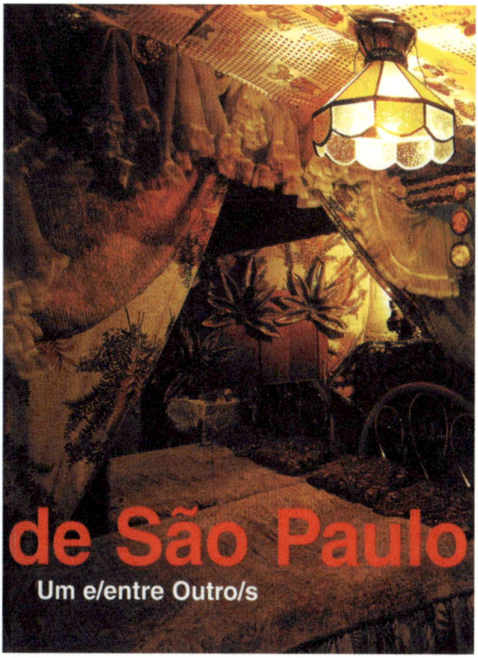

fig.102

The Epistemological Leap of Anthropophagy After the 24th Bienal de São Paulo — Mirtes Marins de Oliveira

If one of the fundamental 'functions of criticism is the attempt to recreate artistic products and make past work and past places our contemporary',[1] as Sérgio Buarque de Holanda wrote in 1940, it is possible to say that the notion of anthropophagy has actually expanded throughout time and space. When analysing the relations between poetry and criticism, Buarque de Holanda underlined this coexistence that results from criticism, in which a 'simultaneous order' is established 'with all the other authors from the past and present, even if they might mean for us something very different from what they meant to the men of their times'.[2] Adopted and considered by different disciplines, anthropophagy has proven its hermeneutic potential since the beginning of the twentieth century, instituting a simultaneous order that has constantly been revisited.[3] By choosing it as the curatorial concept of the 24th Bienal de São Paulo, Paulo Herkenhoff established his own role as an interlocutor in that order, expanding the category beyond its literary origins to contemporary artistic and curatorial practice. The critical reception of the 24th Bienal, both in the press and in academia, has shown a recurrent polarity in the analysis of the exhibition: its insertion in an anthropophagic order and, through it, in an order promoted by the international circuit of exhibitions that, in the 1980s and 90s, proposed a revision of the idea of the 'primitive' and its modern appropriation in the framework of globalisation's financial and political shifts.

Locating the 24th Bienal at the intersection between these two orders could explain its reception, which has focused on a discussion of anthropophagy rather than an attempt to understand the relationships of 'contamination' between the exhibited works that Herkenhoff had adopted as the key strategy for display.[4]

—

[1] Sérgio Buarque de Holanda, 'Poesia e crítica' (1940), in *O Homem Cordial* (ed. Lilia Moritz Schwarcz), São Paulo: Penguin, 2012, pp.39–43. Except where noted, texts originally in Portuguese have been translated for this volume.

[2] *Ibid.*, p.41.

[3] It is possible to think of the simultaneous order of cannibalism and anthropophagy as being active well before the twentieth century in the actions of European metropolises in the colonised territories of South America and Africa. In the twentieth century, the 'Manifesto antropófago' (1928) created its own simultaneous order. See Carlos A. Jáuregui, *Canibalia: Canibalismo, calibanismo, antropofagia cultural y consumo en América Latina*, Madrid and Frankfurt a.M.: Iberoamericana and Vervuert, 2008.

[4] Editors' Note: On 'contamination' in the exhibition, see Lisette Lagnado, 'Anthropophagy as Cultural Strategy: The 24th Bienal de São Paulo, 1998', in this volume, pp.19–20.

During the time of the exhibition there were several polemics, more intense in the local context and more nuanced in the international press. In the years that followed, while there was plenty of discussion about the visibility gained by the curator, there was otherwise considerable silence. In that period, Brazilian universities only timidly addressed Herkenhoff's proposals. The eventual return of interest in the show in the international arena, more than ten years after the event, is therefore somewhat surprising. The 24th Bienal has leapfrogged from being misunderstood to becoming institutionalised within an a-critical pantheon, as evidenced in its recent inclusion through installation views and catalogue covers in publications attempting to establish a canon of exhibitions of contemporary art.[5]

In the context of the globalisation of the 1980s and 90s, some curatorial proposals attempted to 'promote an internationalist vision of art through terms that could be shaped and understood locally'.[6] Some relevant examples are: '"Primitivism" in 20th Century Art: Affinity of the Tribal and the Modern' (1984–85) at the Museum of Modern Art (MoMA) in New York, the third Bienal de La Habana (1989), 'Magiciens de la Terre' (1989) at the Centre Georges Pompidou and the Grande Halle de La Villette in Paris and 'The Other Story: Afro-Asian Artists in Post-War Britain' (1989) at the Hayward Gallery in London.[7] This list could also include documenta X, from 1997, curated by Catherine David, who did not develop that exhibition in relation to the debate about primitivism but did explore operations defining relations of difference, of all those whom globalisation, after the fall of the Berlin Wall, allowed to become visible. David's project also intended to demonstrate the critical potential of artistic practices as tools that trouble the economic operations through which globalisation functions.[8] Both documenta X and the 24th Bienal were developed under the expectation of offering responses to the end of a century. In the case of the 24th Bienal, inscribing Brazilian artists into the international circuit at the time of globalisation was not enough – the curatorial project needed to rewrite established history.

—

[5] See Bruce Altshuler, *Biennials and Beyond: Exhibitions that Made Art History, 1962–2002*, London: Phaidon, 2013, pp.355–70; and Jens Hoffman, *Showtime: The 50 Most Influential Exhibitions of Contemporary Art*, London: Thames & Hudson, 2014, pp.128–31.

[6] Charles Esche, 'Making Art Global: A Good Place or a No Place?', in Rachel Weiss et al., *Making Art Global, Part 1: The Third Havana Biennial 1989*, London: Afterall Books, 2011, p.8.

[7] '"Primitivism" in 20th Century Art: Affinity of the Tribal and the Modern', 27 September 1984 to 15 January 1985, curated by William Rubin and Kirk Varnedoe; the third Bienal de La Habana, 1 November to 31 December 1989, curated by Gerardo Mosquera and others (for more on this exhibition, see R. Weiss et al., *Making Art Global, Part 1*, *op. cit.*); 'Magiciens de la Terre', 18 May to 14 August 1989, curated by Jean-Hubert Martin (for more on this exhibition, see Lucy Steeds et al., *Making Art Global (Part 2): 'Magiciens de la Terre' 1989*, London: Afterall Books, 2013); and 'The Other Story: Afro-Asian Artists in Post-War Britain', 29 November 1989 to 4 February 1990, curated by Rasheed Araeen.

[8] See Catherine David, 'Introduction', in *documenta X: Short Guide*, Ostfildern-Ruit: Verlag Gerd Hatje, 1997, pp.7–13.

In this arena, Herkenhoff chose anthropophagy as a concept operating amidst other cultural proposals that attempted to mediate between the West and the East, the South and the North, the centre and the periphery. In recuperating the debate originating in Oswald de Andrade's 'Manifesto antropófago' of 1928, Herkenhoff also brought forth the constellation Andrade built in relation to that concept: patriarchy and matriarchy, myth and reason, metropolis and colony. The curatorial project gave new life to the corrosive and irreverent critique the 'Manifesto' made of academicism, and of grand linear and hegemonic historical narratives. Also, strategically, it intended to represent a historical emblem that was supposed to characterise Brazilian identity – the anthropophagic, the act of devouring – within a set of approaches to cultural appropriation. But the chosen emblem, in contrast to what some responses to the exhibition have stated, is not a founding myth that is as obvious and homogeneous as a national narrative. Rather, until the 1950s, the 'Manifesto' and its author were relatively obscure, until their rehabilitation by the São Paulo Concretist poets (Augusto de Campos, Haroldo de Campos and Décio Pignatari) in the 1960s, and, later, by the mass visibility of Andrade's *O Rei da Vela*,[9] when it was staged by Teatro Oficina in 1967. Directed by José Celso Martinez Corrêa, the staging of the play used parody to address a sharp criticism to the petit bourgeoisie's behaviour during the dictatorship, and immediately became a reference for the actions of Tropicalismo.

In that period, the Bienal de São Paulo suffered from being used as the cultural and diplomatic arm of Brazilian governments. After the international boycott of the tenth Bienal, in 1969, by artists and intellectuals,[10] the exhibition recovered its intellectual legitimacy thanks to the efforts of Walter p.38 Zanini, curator of the sixteenth and seventeenth editions, in 1981 and 1983 (still in the final years of the dictatorship). The 1990s began with Brazil full of vitality; social and political movements led, through a democratic process, to the impeachment of President Fernando Collor de Mello on charges of corruption in 1992. But this vitality was accompanied by intense processes

—

[9] The theatre piece, written by Andrade in 1933, was published in 1937 but censored by the Getúlio Vargas government, ignored by directors and theatre critics during the 1940s, and first staged in the 1960s. It revolves around the anthropophagic paradigm. See Christopher Dunn, *Brutalidade Jardim: A Tropicália e o surgimento da contracultura brasileira*, São Paulo: Editora da Universidade Estadual Paulista, 2009, p.99.

[10] Led by Pierre Restany in France and Gordon Matta-Clark in the US. See Renata Zago, 'A Bienal de São Paulo ou Pré Bienal de 1970', lecture given at the conference 'VI Encontro de História da Arte do Instituto de filosofia e Ciências Humanas da Universidade Estadual de Campinas', Centro de História da Arte e Arqueologia (CHAA) da Universidade Estadual de Campinas (UNICAMP), São Paulo, 30 November to 3 December 2010, available at http://www.unicamp.br/chaa/eha/atas/2010/renata_cristina_oliveira_maia.pdf (last accessed on 16 February 2015). See also the visceral letter by Matta-Clark, dated 19 May 1971, which was reproduced in the catalogue for the 27th Bienal de São Paulo, available at http://issuu.com/bienal/docs/27a_bienal_de_sao_paulo_guia_2006 (last accessed on 16 February 2015).

of privatisation, begun during Collor's government and continuing through those that followed. The Fundação Bienal didn't avoid such dynamics. In institutional terms, in the 1980s and 90s it engaged in gigantism and spectacularisation under the presidency of Edemar Cid Ferreira. He was followed, for the 24th Bienal, by Julio Landmann, who established, in collaboration with Herkenhoff, new professional parameters for giving shape to the exhibition.[11]

In 1998, the Brazilian press, accustomed to the profile of previous editions of the Bienal, offered an anecdotal reading of the exhibition, exploring the cannibalistic analogies and criticising what they saw as the imposition of an arbitrary curatorial eye on 'helpless' artistic production.[12] It is worth remembering that a conception of curating as knowledge production – Herkenhoff's position[13] – was in strong contrast to the ideas presented in the 23rd Bienal, which merely reheated the notion of dematerialisation in reference to art production from the late 1960s and early 70s, as shaped by Lucy Lippard and John Chandler in the US and Oscar Masotta in Argentina.[14] This anecdotal reaction has recurred in unsuspected places, such as the book published by the Fundação Bienal on the fiftieth anniversary of the Bienal.[15] In *Bienal 50 anos: 1951–2001*, the Fundação echoes the local misunderstandings, failing to construct an institutional discourse of its own:

> *The daring act of curator Paulo Herkenhoff, responsible for the most radical experience after the Great Canvas in 1985, was not discussed as it deserved by the local media, even though it received great international recognition. What emerged was a generalised discomfort among the local artistic scene in response to what they considered an emphasis on the figure of the curator that eclipsed the work of art, when it should instead increase its worth.*[16]

The hailstorm that flooded São Paulo in the first week of October 1998, when the exhibition opened, damaging several windows and the roof of the Ciccillo Matarazzo Pavilion, was reported by the press with no generosity: perceiving Brazil's international image as stained, they blamed the Fundação for its lack of preparation for such a crisis. The financial and management scandals that had affected previous editions also prepared the way for another area of interest: the new forms of cultural marketing and popularisation adopted by

—

[11] In relation to the collaborative work and mutual support between the curator and the presidency, see Paulo Herkenhoff, 'Bienal 1998: princípios e processos', *marcelina,* vol.1, São Paulo, 2008.
[12] Examples of some of the headlines printed in Brazilian journals and magazines: 'A angústia da autofagia' ('The Anguish of Self-Devouring'), 'Receita à moda da casa' ('Home Recipe'), 'Miscelânea no 1o andar' ('Miscellany on the First Floor'), 'O cardápio antropofágico' ('The Anthropophagic Menu').
[13] P. Herkenhoff, 'Bienal 1998: princípios e processos', *op. cit.*
[14] Lisette Lagnado, 'As tarefas do curador', *marcelina*, vol.1, 2008, p.16.
[15] See *Bienal de São Paulo 50 anos, 1951–2001 / 50 years of the São Paulo Biennial,* São Paulo: Fundação Bienal, 2001.
[16] *Ibid.*, p.259.

the 24th Bienal, echoing practices from other cultural contexts. The amount of money spent on the production of the exhibition – almost R$15 million, which in 1998 amounted to US$15 million[17] – was widely publicised and discussed, as was the unfulfilled promise by Telesp, the public telecommunication network of the State of São Paulo, to contribute funding to that edition.[18]

In the international press, the critical reception was more complex, and contributed to the dissemination of anthropophagy as a hermeneutical category beyond Brazil. In this respect, Edward Leffingwell's essay 'Cannibals All', published in *Art in America,* in May 1999, is exemplary: he attempted to locate anthropophagy in the materiality of the exhibition and the books published by the team, organised by Herkenhoff together with associate curator Adriano Pedrosa. Leffingwell pointed to the coherence between the exhibition and the catalogues, which, through contamination, presented 'interpolations of image or text that critically illustrate themes' around anthropophagy,[19] for example:

fig.99

> *Géricault's* Raft of the Medusa [1818–19], *reproduced on the inside front cover of the 550-page principal volume, set forth the notion of cannibalism with its internal reference to a nineteenth-century example. It was accompanied by an appropriate quote from Rabelais's* Gargantua and Pantagruel [1532] *that reads in part, 'Taste this chapter, swallow this gloss.' Readers are invited to similarly 'devour' the catalogue in their hands.*[20]

The essay also describes several other ways through which contamination occurred in the exhibition space:

fig.78

fig.94–95 and 97–98

fig.46–48

fig.41 and 43

> [Mary Jane] *Jacob's selection of materials-centred* Non-Sites *by Smithson and objects by Hesse seemed apposite to the presentation of similarly process-oriented works by Hélio Oiticia and Lygia Clark, artists who are in a sense counterparts in production and legend to Smithson and Hesse in the United States. The language of installation design further linkedClark and Bourgeois to Maria Martins, whose Surrealist plasters and bronzes populated a banquette flanking one of the major ramps, facing a similarly installed gathering of Giacometti bronzes, perhaps in an attempt to support the current rehabilitation of Martins's career.*[21]

—

[17] In July 1994, the real became the Brazilian currency. The Central Bank of Brazil set its value as equal to the US dollar.

[18] In 1996, during the privatisation and the fragmentation of the Sistema Telebrás, of which Telesp was part, Minister of Communication Sergio Motta promised to contribute R$1 million to the 24th edition. Motta passed away in April 1998, and the donation did not take place. Regarding the financial problems of the Bienal, see Cassiano Elek Machado, 'Exposição: Bienal tem rombo de R$ 1,4 milhão', *Folha de S. Paulo*, 14 November, 1998.

[19] Edward Leffingwell, 'Cannibals All', *Art in America*, vol.87, no.5, May 1999, pp.47–55.

[20] *Ibid.*, p.47.

[21] *Ibid.*, p.48.

The critic also perceived that the re-presentation of Cildo Meireles's *Desvio para o vermelho* (*Red Shift*, 1967–84) allowed for new readings: this, its third installation, was its first since the end of the dictatorship; it also echoed Henri Matisse's *L'Atelier rouge* (*The Red Studio*, 1911).[22] Leffingwell also wrote about the exhibition's presence in the city through the pedagogical activities of Brian Maguire's workshops in the favela of Vila Prudente, and in concurrent exhibitions at the Museu de Arte Contemporânea (MAC USP), Museu de Arte Moderna de São Paulo (MAM SP) and the Museu de Arte de São Paulo (MASP),[23] in addition to others in commercial spaces, which all created a backdrop against which to understand more deeply what was exhibited in the Bienal. fig.96

More analytical readings were offered elsewhere at the time, such as Lisette Lagnado's in *Third Text*,[24] in which the description of the relations between works in the exhibition, beyond the 'Núcleo Histórico' ('Historical Nucleus'), was accompanied by analyses that revealed the different forms in which the various conceptions of anthropophagy were presented via the curatorial platform. Lagnado also accounted for the misunderstandings of both critical and public audiences, noting that the 'gigantic scale of the building contributed to an engulfing of the smaller curatorial "embroideries" offered to a public always out of step with contemporary issues'.[25] pp.*114–73*

Interviewed by Rosa Olivares for *Lápiz*,[26] Herkenhoff identified the deconstruction of a hegemonic historical narrative as the exhibition's greatest intellectual contribution, a point he repeated in several other places.[27] Particularly in relation to the 'mission' of the institution – to show the newest and the most experimental contemporary art – the success of the 'Núcleo Histórico' over the contemporary displays might be understood as a crisis for the Bienal: 'The bigger the success of the historical section, the bigger the crisis of the institution.'[28] For the curator, the institutional crisis materialised in the fact that it was more difficult to 'keep a video running than the air conditioning

—

[22] *Ibid.*, p.49.

[23] These were: 'Heranças contemporâneas' ('Contemporary Inheritances'), MAC-USP, 25 September to 5 December 1998; 'Arte Construtiva no Brasil: Coleção Adolpho Leirner' ('Constructivist Art in Brazil: Adolpho Leirner Collection'), MAM-SP, 2 October to 20 December 1998; and 'O moderno e contemporâneo na arte brasileira – Coleção Gilberto Chateaubriand Collection' ('The Modern and the Contemporary in Brazilian Art – Gilberto Chateaubriand Collection'), MASP, 6 October to 13 December 1998.

[24] L. Lagnado, 'On How the 24th São Paulo Biennial Took on Cannibalism', *Third Text*, vol.13, no.46, 1999, pp.83–88.

[25] *Ibid.*, p.88.

[26] Rosa Olivares, 'Ahora es necesario olvidar la historia: Entrevista a Paulo Herkenhoff', *Lápiz*, no.149/150, January–February 1999, pp.153–61.

[27] See, for example, P. Herkenhoff, 'Bienal 1998: princípios e processos', *op. cit.*; and Maria Helena Carvalhaes, 'Dez anos depois: Um debate com Paulo Herkenhoff', *marcelina*, vol.1, 2008.

[28] P. Herkenhoff, 'Bienal 1998: princípios e processos', *op. cit.*

for the historical works'.[29] When he stated that 'now we need to forget about history',[30] he was certainly proposing to forget about the linear and causal approach of many historiographic perspectives, and to offer, instead, a confrontation between contemporary artistic production and an international historical tradition. In moving away from the 'Salas Especiais' ('Special Rooms') of earlier editions and proposing instead a 'Núcleo Histórico', he was attempting to substitute status for knowledge.[31]

Olivares perceived the polarisation of the debate about the exhibition:

> *The result* [of the exhibition] *has been criticised by some and praised by others. Among the former, the more conservative sector of Brazilian criticism, showing nostalgia for other times and other artistic demonstrations, more decorative and less radical; and also proponents of the idea that history cannot be changed. Among those who have considered this Bienal a rupture with the traditional decline of such exhibitions are the international critics and the hundreds of thousands of spectators who were able to approach contemporary art in a friendlier and more critical manner, understanding that it is much closer to their own lives than they could have ever imagined.*[32]

Writing in 2009, in a retrospective evaluation for *Asociación Internacional de Críticos de Arte–Paraguay* (*AICA–PY*), and looking to analyse the impact of globalisation on cultural dynamics, Jacques Leenhardt presented the curatorial project of the 24th Bienal as exemplary in the incorporation of transcultural problematics. For the author, the choice of anthropophagy as a conceptual axis made evident 'the place of the curator': '[the] point of tension between a local problematic, needed for the local public to be interested in the manifestation, and a global problematic open for others, especially for the specialised public and art critics, who have no alternative today but to be open to a globalised art space'.[33]

Globalisation processes demanded a different terminology, newly coined or recuperated from the past, in order to provide instruments for interpreting culture. *Syncretism*, *hybridisation*, *miscegenation*, *fusion*, *creolisation*: these terms were activated during the 1980s and 90s to refer to the cultural dynamics between the West and Latin America, to the legacy of the relationship between metropolis and colony.[34] The physical and cultural violence of colonisation would be avenged by Andrade's anthropophagy through the destruction of the coloniser and the inversion or carnivalisation of its impositions, offering simultaneously a daring critique of neocolonisalism.

—

[29] R. Olivares, 'Ahora es necesario olvidar la historia', *op. cit.*, p.155.
[30] *Ibid.*
[31] *Ibid.*
[32] *Ibid.*, p.153.
[33] Jacques Leenhardt, 'El papel del comisario en las exposiciones internacionales', *AICA-PY*, Year 2, no.2/3, December 2009–January 2010, p.11.
[34] See Néstor García Canclini, *Culturas Híbridas: Estratégias para entrar e sair da modernidade,* São Paulo: Universidade de São Paulo, 2013, p.32.

Demystifying such approaches, Gerardo Mosquera tackled anthropophagy in 2011 as a modernist metaphor that legitimised both anti-colonial resistance and the appropriation of European tropes.[35] Mosquera recognised the strength of the metaphor, as an emblem of the cultural dynamics of the whole of Latin America.[36] However, in relation to the 24th Bienal, he attempted to distinguish between the anthropophagic approach as outlined by Andrade and Brazilian artistic production in the 90s. In an interview with Cildo Meireles, he explained:

> *Latin American culture has specialised in appropriating, digesting and re-signifying the production of other cultural centres of the world. This is the notion of 'anthropophagy' or cultural 'cannibalism' coined by the Brazilian poet Oswald de Andrade in 1928. In your work and that of other contemporary Brazilian artists this process is reversed. You are making 'international' art in a Brazilian way: your cultural identity is not represented by vernacular or local components, but it determines a different way of making the 'international'. It is an 'anti-samba' art which generates its difference not through representation – the common strategy among contemporary Mexican and Cuban artists – but through action.*[37]

Referring to Herkenhoff's choice of anthropophagy as his curatorial concept, Mosquera pointed at its incapacity to function critically, as, in its own definition, it would incorporate the 'contradictions of dependency'.[38] In his analysis of the notion as an explanatory and legitimising key for cultural relations, Mosquera incorporated the fierce criticism that Heloísa Buarque de Hollanda made of its adoption in the cultural field as the universalisation of a contradictory foundational project: the lack of a past with black or indigenous traits, dissipated in the figure of the mestizo and in the notion of 'racial democracy'. For her, 'Brazil has several imaginations, as a nation whose identity lies on the capacity to eternally delay its definition'.[39]

—

[35] Gerardo Mosquera, 'Beyond Anthropophagy: Art, Internationalization and Cultural Dynamics', available at http://www.summeracademy.at/media/pdf/pdf776.pdf (last accessed on 16 February 2015). The text is the result of the symposium 'Global Art' that took place on 30–31 July 2011 at the Salzburg International Summer Academy of Fine Arts and the Austrian and Swiss sections of the Association Internationale des Critiques d'Art (AICA).

[36] *Ibid.*, p.6.

[37] 'Gerardo Mosquera in conversation with Cildo Meireles', in Dan Cameron, P. Herkenhoff and G. Mosquera, *Cildo Meireles*, London: Phaidon, 1999, p.28.

[38] Mosquera has developed this analysis in additional articles, interviews and conferences, such as G. Mosquera, 'From Latin American Art to Art from Latin America' (trans. Michèle Faguet), *Art Nexus*, issue 48, April–June 2003, available at http://artnexus.com/Notice_View.aspx?DocumentID=9624; and Juan Pablo Pérez, 'Contra el arte latinoamericano: Entrevista a Gerardo Mosquera', *Arte Nuevo*, June 2009, available at http://arte-nuevo.blogspot.com.br/2009/06/contra-el-arte-latinoamericano.html (both last accessed on 16 February 2015).

[39] Heloísa Buarque de Hollanda, 'Um problema quase pessoal' (1998), available at http://www.heloisabuarquedehollanda.com.br/um-problema-quase-pessoal/ (last accessed on 16 February 2015).

In anthropophagy, there is to be found a recurrent identification of 'a horizontal solidarity, around goals and interests that are common to different classes, races or professional and sexual categories, masking multiple differences'.[40] The anthropophagic model, defined by modernism as the fundamental trait of Brazilian culture, has an anti-confrontational character, which dilutes difference and the other. For Buarque de Hollanda, in the anthropophagic myth and its derivations, Brazil emerges as the kingdom of cordiality, in which there is 'a difficulty to instrumentalise clearly, until very recently, the differences in interest between the social classes and the ethnic or gender groups'.[41] This criticism has been used by Mosquera to point out the insufficiency of the concept proposed for the exhibition. Mosquera's criticism can be linked to the anti-colonial cultural tradition developed in relation to the Caribbean starting in the 1930s, and in the works of Aimé Césaire and Édouard Glissant. Glissant identified the 'hybridity' characterising Caribbean identity as a cultural form that would allow for new voices in the debates and conflicts between cultures.[42] Although hybridity and anthropophagy can be seen as conceptually close in many ways, Mosquera's perspective also reinstates the premises upon which, with his involvement, the Bienal de La Habana was founded in 1984: as a deliberate attempt to oppose positions like that seen – later – at the 24th Bienal.[43]

During the 24th Bienal, Annateresa Fabris, a historian at the Universidade de São Paulo (USP), pointed out the insufficiency of anthropophagy as a hermeneutic tool[44] in her discussion of the exhibition in the pages of the *Folha de S. Paulo*. She asked whether the 'Manifesto antropófago', decontextualised from its modernist origins, could articulate a contemporary vision. Was adopting a concept defined in relation to a national identity appropriate in a moment of redefining the national under the pressure of globalisation? Hadn't the depersonalisation imposed by globalisation erased from the horizon the question of the relationship between the national and the international? 'A banalisation is taking place when the concept of anthropophagy imposes itself on the wide dialogical relations between different cultures'; furthermore, its potential alignment with the critique of Eurocentrism was problematic, since giving centrality to the periphery, at that time, was an operation 'proclaimed by the cultural institutions from the centre' – meaning Europe and the US.[45] Analysing the different ways in which the curators of 'Roteiros. Roteiros. Roteiros. Roteiros. Roteiros.

—

[40] *Ibid.*

[41] *Ibid.*

[42] Édouard Glissant developed his work on hybridity beginning in the 1950s and acquired considerable visibility in the 1990s through titles such as *Traité du Tout-Monde,* Paris: Gallimard, 1997.

[43] Terry Smith makes the point that the Bienal de La Habana was planned in opposition to the Bienal de São Paulo, with Mosquera holding a central role in the early editions of the former. See T. Smith, *What Is Contemporary Art?*, Chicago and London: University of Chicago Press, 2009, p.154.

[44] Annateresa Fabris, 'Bienal', *Folha de S. Paulo*, 10 October 1998.

[45] *Ibid.*

Roteiros. Roteiros.' understood and tackled anthropophagy, Fabris located areas of inconsistency and ambiguity. For her, a single perspective originating in the 'Manifesto antropófago' resulted in opposing curatorial projects, from Rina Carvajal's 'enthusiastic adhesion' in the selection of Latin American artists to Bart de Baere and Maaretta Jaukkuri's European 'perplexity': 'If Latin America recognises itself in that proclamation of singularity attempted by Oswald de Andrade in 1928, Europe, which shaped modern perception and continues to develop a fundamental role in the postmodern debate, just felt dislocated within a discussion that precisely confirmed its centrality, even in a situation like today's, characterised by globalisation and multiculturalism.'[46] pp.*100–13*

The criticism by Fabris is exemplary of the efforts of leading intellectuals in São Paulo in the 1980s and 90s to understand the effects of globalised culture. The frame has since shifted, as is apparent in the responses of Brazilian academia – a reaction that arrived, given the speed of institutional processes, with a certain delay. If Brazilian universities, and in particular USP, were present in the show through a number of researchers responsible for curatorial projects within the 'Núcleo Histórico', including Aracy Amaral, Ana Maria Belluzzo and Sônia Salzstein,[47] among others, this has not secured the legitimisation of the 24th Bienal within the academic system: there was no apparent increase of new research about the relation between anthropophagy and contemporary art or about the exhibition itself. The number of doctoral theses that, since 1998, have directly addressed the exhibition are few.[48] fig.88–91 fig.52–57 and 83–87

—

[46] *Ibid.*

[47] Amaral, who was Professora Titular of Art History at the School for Architecture and Urbanism, was the guest curator for Alfredo Volpi's participation; Belluzzo, Professora Titular of Art History at the School for Architecture and Urbanism, was responsible for the selection of Albert Eckhout's work (together with Jean-François Chougnet); and Salzstein, Professora Titular of Art History and Art Theory in the Fine Arts Department of the School of Communication and the Arts, was responsible for the selection of Tarsila do Amaral's work.

[48] Among the first relevant pieces of research to address the exhibition was a 2002 doctoral thesis by Elisa de Sousa Martínez presented at the Programa de Estudos Pós-graduados em Comunicação e Semiótica of the Pontifícia Universidade Católica of São Paulo, titled 'Textualização antropofágica: A curadoria do Espaço Museológico da XXIV Bienal de São Paulo' ('Anthropophagic Textualisation: The Curation of the Museological Space at the XXIV Bienal de São Paulo'), which studied the relationship between the works and the wall texts in the 'Núcleo Histórico' (Martínez currently teaches in the Programa de Pós-Graduação em Artes Visuais – Universidade de Brasília). Other studies since have discussed the curatorial project in relation to the Brazilian literary tradition (for example, Luiza Oliveira da Silva's 'Configurações identitárias na arte contemporânea: A Bienal de São Paulo de 1998' ('Identity Configurations in Contemporary Art: The Bienal de São Paulo 1998'), Curso de Pós-Graduação em Letras of the Universidade Federal Fluminense, 2006) or multiculturalism (Helena Pereira de Queiroz's 'Antropofagia ou Multiculturalismo? Oswald de Andrade na XXIV Bienal de São Paulo' ('Anthropophagy or Multiculturalism? Oswald de Andrade at the XXIV Bienal de São Paulo'), Programa de Pós-Graduação Interunidades em Estética e História da Arte, Universidade de São Paulo, 2011).

How can we explain this lack of attention to the alleged relevance of the 24th Bienal? It is possible to venture that the study of curatorial practice is still taking its first steps in Brazil. And, when exhibitions are actually studied, thematic aspects, as well as analysis of the works exhibited, are given priority, rather than the materiality of the exhibition and the specific relations that are set up by the display, or between the display and discourse, publications or other elements of the curatorial project.

In 2008, with the goal of offering balanced critical reflection on curatorial practice, a curating seminar dedicated to the 24th Bienal was organised by Lisette Lagnado at Faculdade Santa Marcelina in São Paulo, with the participation of Paulo Herkenhoff.[49] The proceedings were gathered in the first issue of the magazine *marcelina*, which was subtitled *[antropofágica]*.[50] With the increasing local demand for short courses to train curators, the idea of the 'Seminários Curatoriais' was to contribute an opposing movement, generating materials that would live beyond the recurrent superficiality.[51]

Writing in the same year, precisely a decade since the show and from an anthropophagic perspective, Carlos A. Jáuregui characterised cannibalism as a modern cultural metaphor that also suggests a 'fear of the dissolution of identity and, inversely, a way to appropriate difference'.[52] For him, the many attempts to reactivate the anthropophagic paradigm have, in their majority, voided the political capacities of the metaphor.[53] A whole chapter of his book *Canibalia: Canibalismo, calibanismo, antropofagia cultural y consumo en América Latina* (*Canibalia: Cannibalism, Calibanism, Cultural Anthropophagy and Consumption in Latin America*) is dedicated to the 24th edition, presented as exemplary of this depoliticisation: 'The discourses from and about the Bienal by the organisers, the press and critics are diverse and contradictory; a large part of them refer to the entrepreneurial project that it involved, others to its happenstances and occurrences, and the majority of them to the degree of misunderstanding of the proposal, both for the public and for the critics.'[54] Jáuregui's conclusion is that what was articulated in the publications and the exhibition was contradictory – as captured in the statement appearing on bumper stickers sold during the exhibition: 'Só a antropofagia

—

[49] The 'Seminários Curatoriais', at which Lagnado was a teacher, were organised by the Mestrado em Artes Visuais at Faculdade Santa Marcelina in São Paulo.

[50] See *marcelina*, vol.1, São Paulo, 2008, available at www.sophiamarchetti.com.br/index.php/PDF/1/32/ (last accessed on 16 February 2015).

[51] In 2012, the Fourth Seminar of Researchers at the Programa de Pós Graduação em Artes – Universidade Estadual do Rio de Janeiro presented work dealing with the 'expansion of the notion of anthropophagy proposed by the 24th Bienal de São Paulo'. 'Vômito e não: Práticas antropoêmicas na arte e na cultura' ('To Vomit and not to Vomit: Anthropoemic Practices in Art and Culture') addressed the incorporation of anthropophagy by capitalism. The organisers proposed *anthropoemy* as an inventive and productive relation in cultural contact.

[52] C.A. Jáuregui, *Canibalia: Canibalismo, calibanismo, antropofagia cultural y consumo en América Latina*, *op. cit.*, p.15.

[53] *Ibid.*, p.342.

[54] *Ibid.*, p.548.

nos une' ('Only anthropophagy unites us'). The exhibition worked on two levels, in Jáuregui's estimation: one oriented towards popular consumption, towards an audience that would be educated in Dada or Surrealism for instance; the other functioning as 'elitist banquet for a public who already has that cultural capital'.[55] fig.70–72

Jáuregui's interpretive tools for analysing the exhibition operate from fixed polarities – South America versus Europe, consumption versus concept, curators versus artists, elite versus popular – considered as internal contradictions and, therefore, weaknesses. In this way, his discourse constructs a binary logic that, however critical, cannot capture the ironies and possibilities of interference at play in globalisation processes. Should anthropophagy's internal coherence and verisimilitude, now that it functions as an expanded metaphor, be necessarily referred back to the original formulation? Furthermore, is it possible to free anthropophagy, as a metaphor for modern cultural practices, from the processes of the expansion of capital?

Potential answers can be found in Arthur Danto's response to the Bienal. Even without having seen the exhibition, Danto perceived its density in the way it reverberates within multi-volume catalogues.[56] For Danto, anthropophagy fulfilled its role as a mediator within a broad discussion about transformations of contemporary culture. That could be what Herkenhoff considered one of the most important curatorial tasks, the production of 'epistemological leaps affecting knowledge about art and the ways of thinking about it'.[57] Through the similarities and differences among the various ways in which anthropophagy materialised in the 24th Bienal, the exhibition reconfigured and expanded the anthropophagic landscape, reinforcing its historical viability, creating the simultaneous order Sergio Buarque de Holanda proposed, and inaugurating a set of material effects that helped create new ways of understanding artistic and curatorial practice.

Translated from Portuguese by Pablo Lafuente.

---

[55] *Ibid.*, p.549.

[56] See the critic and curator Felipe Chaimovich's interview with Arthur Danto for *Folha de S. Paulo*: 'As novas feiras: Para o crítico Arthur Danto, as bienais de arte substituíram as exposições internacionais', 21 May 2001, available at http://www1.folha.uol.com.br/fsp/especial/fj2005200112.htm (last accessed on 16 February 2015).

[57] P. Herkenhoff, 'Bienal 1998: princípios e processos', *op cit.*, p.23.

Out of the *cantinho* – Art Education at the 24th Bienal de São Paulo
— Carmen Mörsch and Catrin Seefranz

In 1975, the year of the 13th Bienal de São Paulo, a group of artists, including Fred Forest, gathered footage, interviews and material traces from around Ibirapuera Park to produce artefacts for the 'Bienal do Ano 2000', an archaeological projection of the future of the Bienal.[1] In fact, a Bienal would not be held in 2000: the edition planned for the millennium was postponed twice. There was a huge shortfall in the budget; the designated curator, Ivo Mesquita, was let go; and the Fundação Bienal's president ended up in a fist fight with an artist.[2] As has been written, the Fundação was 'in perhaps the greatest crisis since its inception'.[3] When the 25th edition was finally held, in 2002, it received a lukewarm reception.[4] But, four years earlier, there was a Bienal de São Paulo with far more potential for an archaeology of the future of exhibiting, as well as for the future of art education.[5]

Among the relics of the 24th Bienal, let us imagine an unspectacular metal and glass booth, covered in Ibirapuera's vegetation, with HBSC's logo peeping
fig.5 out from beneath the undergrowth: a remnant of the Sala Educação, a structure set up on the ground floor of the Ciccillo Matarazzo Pavilion, once the operational base for the Bienal's educational initiatives – one of the

—

[1] Media artist Fred Forest was part, with Hervé fischer and Jean-Paul Thenot, of the Collectif d'art sociologique, which developed a practice of artistic research based on sociological theory. Forest had already participated in the Bienal de São Paulo in 1973, in the section planned by Vilém Flusser, 'Arte e comunicação' ('Art and Communication'), and was arrested by the police during one of his actions. In 1975, he produced the 'Bienal do Ano 2000' for the Museu de Arte Contemporânea da Universidade de São Paulo (MAC-USP). See Isobel Whitelegg, 'The Bienal de São Paulo: Unseen/Undone (1969–1981)', *Afterall*, issue 22, 2009, pp.107–13.
[2] Celso Fioravante, 'Feud for thought', *Artforum*, vol.39, no.3, 2000, p.37.
[3] *Ibid.*
[4] The 25th and 26th editions were curated by Alfons Hug, who reintroduced the 'Venetian' order of national representations, and this resulted in negative criticism. 'The "Bienal da Antropofagia" [...] received immense international attention and praise, but this was not enough to save the exhibition from entering an acute period of crisis in the years that followed.' Kiki Mazzucchelli, 'The São Paulo Biennial and the Rise of Brazilian Contemporary Art', in Hossein Amirsadeghi (ed.), *Contemporary Art Brazil*, London: Thames & Hudson, 2012, p.22.
[5] We, the authors, would like to note that this text offers a perspective shaped by our engagement with contemporary large-scale exhibitions such as documenta X and 12. We cannot assert first-hand knowledge of the complexities of the Bienal de São Paulo's editions in recent decades. We have concentrated on archival documents on the art education programme, as well as on oral histories that are certainly not fully representative of the concrete work of the roughly 160 art educators who participated in the 24th Bienal. The question of how affirmative or critical the art education actually was in practice, and whether there were institution-critical twists to it (albeit not foreseen in the overall thrust of the programme), would need to be further appraised through interviews with the protagonists – the audience, art educators, teachers and others.

rarely examined but most relevant aspects of this now-familiar exhibition. This *cantinho*, or corner, for art education was intended primarily as a space to enable exchanges and provide information for visiting teachers (initially it was called the Sala do Professor). It signalled much more: at the 24th Bienal, education had, indeed, become a fundamental pillar of the Bienal as a whole. This role, however, came accompanied by some ambivalences. After all, the Sala was located on the pavilion's ground floor, in the service area, which was also used during the 24th Bienal to showcase its sponsors and partners, through, for example, stands for collaborating magazines and newspapers and photographic printers such as Kodak. fig.6

Taking this image of the discarded container dug up from the depths as a point of departure, we can write a modest archaeology of education at the 24th edition, reconstructing and contextualising its policy and practice of art education, which was ambitious and advanced in manifold ways. What dared to come 'out of the *cantinho*' entered a cultural force field of overlapping political, curatorial, economic, public policy and art educational interests. This archaeology reveals continuities that have played a significant role in the history – characterised by massive caesuras – of this notoriously 'unstable institution'.[6]

1. A 'Curatorial Difference'

Education at the 24th Bienal de São Paulo was implemented from above, flourishing high on the banners of its institutional policy and curatorial approach. This was unusual, despite the Bienal's long-standing educational commitment, as Evelyn Ioschpe, director in charge of education for the 24th edition, has explained: 'Whereas usually the educational aspect is subordinated to the curatorial, or even clashes with it, here at this zero point we see the clear will of the institution and the curator to position an important educational initiative.'[7] Julio Landmann, president of the Fundação Bienal de São Paulo at the time of the 24th Bienal, has since described the educational imperative he and the exhibition's curator, Paulo Herkenhoff, agreed to:

> *As early as the first month of our preparation, we produced a document listing its main functions. There were about twenty of them – from temporary museum to symbolic representation of the city of São Paulo, from educating the gaze of young artists to showing Brazilian art on the international scene. The 24th Bienal was set on a tripod – exhibiting, publishing, educating – and the Bienal began to be seen as an instrument for art education.*[8]

—

[6] We borrow this term from Carlos Basualdo. See 'The Unstable Institution', *MJ – Manifesta Journal*, no.2, 2003–04, pp.50–61.
[7] Evelyn Ioschpe, 'Bienal e educação', Revista USP, no.52, 2001–02, pp.108–15, available at http://www.usp.br/revistausp/52/13-evelyn.pdf (last accessed on 15 April 2015). Except where noted, the translations in this essay are based on the translations into German by Catrin Seefranz from the original Portuguese.
[8] See Julio Landmann's reflection in *Bienal de São Paulo 50 anos, 1951–2001/ 50 years of the São Paulo Biennial*, São Paulo: Fundação Bienal, 2001, p.323.

The particular constitutive status accorded to art education for this edition is indicated by the creation of the position of director of education within the Fundação Bienal. As the minutes from an internal meeting attest, the decision 'recognised the importance of this aspect of the exhibition and aimed to extend it beyond the duration of the exhibition'.[9] However, in practical terms, it took ten more years for a permanent education department ('educativo permanente') to finally be established, in 2009.

Just as the Fundação's newfound focus on art education might be interpreted as a new institutional policy in a phase of strategic expansion, symbolic and economic investment in art education perhaps constituted a curatorial position (according to Landmann, the financial investment amounted to more than R$1 million, equivalent to approximately US$1 million at the time, out of a total exhibition budget of R$15 million). At the initial meeting on the 'Art Education Project', Herkenhoff reflected, according to the minutes, 'on the importance of the Bienal in São Paulo, where economic capital is transposed into symbolic capital, and on the Bienal as a large educational institution'.[10] This suggests he applied a critical eye to the Bienal as a hegemonic representational apparatus that could gain democratic or critical potential through according space to its educational programme; this process could also legitimate his own position as an engaged curator, entangled in all kinds of power relations by virtue of working on such a project. With hindsight, Herkenhoff has summarised his reconfiguration of the institution's parameters by opposing his project to the notion of an 'art hotel': 'I was not going to execute the Bienal according to its consolidated parameters ... the Bienal shouldn't be an art hotel, but a process constituting a reflection around art from a particular focus.'[11]

In Herkenhoff's work for the 24th Bienal, the museum was the locus in which this reflection on art – this critical intervention within the dominant paradigms of art history and this decentring of hegemonic modernism – became possible, in what was indubitably a rewriting of (art) history. The 24th Bienal entrusted its new, decidedly postcolonial narrative and 'epistemological leap' to the invention of the museum, permeated by the colonial project.[12] In the

—

[9] Fax dated 14 December 1998 with minutes from the constitutive meeting in December 1997, Arquivo Histórico Wanda Svevo / Fundação Bienal de São Paulo.

[10] *Ibid.*

[11] Paulo Herkenhoff, quoted in Hossein Amirsadeghi, *Contemporary Art Brazil*, London: Thames & Hudson, 2012, p.168. There was also a pragmatic reason for emphasising the educational dimension at the 24th Bienal: 'In the multifaceted negotiations of loans from foreign museums, there was always much more willingness to cooperate as soon as the educational project was mentioned'. P. Herkenhoff, 'Bienal 1998: princípios e processos', in *trópico*, 22 April 2008, unpaginated, available at http://www.revistatropico.com.br/tropico/html/textos/2973,1.shl (last accessed on 15 April 2015).

[12] *Ibid.* The 24th Bienal was indeed characterised by reflectivity *vis-à-vis* the institution of the museum and attempted to question the symbolic violence often inscribed in the exhibition space, for example through addressing hierarchies: 'If the exhibition space signifies language and power in the Bienal, then it was necessary to de-hierarchise spaces, to de-hierarchise countries.'

spirit of an 'institution of critique',[13] it created a blueprint for a reflective, critical museum – an 'open place and public institution'[14] – devoted to education, in part drawing its public duties from public financing.[15] This Bienal was therefore designed as a museum-style educational machine, a machine that was conceived in superlative terms; it was, after all, to mobilise an audience of school pupils the size of a small city.[16] A few years on, the education-based curatorial stance announced by the 24th Bienal had become the status quo in Brazil. Herkenhoff proposes to read this as the 'Brazilian curatorial difference', as a committed attitude that is 'part of a social conscience that characterises Brazil, whereby an art exhibition can contribute to creating *cidadania* (citizenship), a process driven ahead by the curator as an agent, and in which education is fundamental'.[17]

2. Subterranean History

If the education engagement of the 24th Bienal appears, in the statements cited earlier, to have been a brand-new initiative, it was actually built upon considerable history that had long remained 'subterranean'.[18] It has been written that 'from the beginning, [the Bienal] fulfilled a pedagogical function':[19] from the first Bienal onwards, a range of tours were offered,[20] and generations of art students took on the task of teaching 'visual literacy',[21] in other

—

[13] Andrea Fraser, 'From the Critique of Institutions to an Institution of Critique', *Artforum*, September 2005, vol.44, no.1, pp.278–83.

[14] Martin Grossmann, 'O Anti-museu' (1989), *Revista Forum Permanente 1*, 2012, available at http://www.forumpermanente.org/revista/numero-1/museu-ideal/martin-grossmann/o-anti-museu (last accessed on 15 April 2015).

[15] 'The conviction that the money invested gave rise to public costs led to plans for a project in the sector of public education.' P. Herkenhoff, 'Bienal 1998: princípios e processos', *op. cit.*

[16] 'The educational project of the Bienal is held to be the largest art education programme associated with an art event anywhere in the world. It is tantamount to mobilising a medium-sized city for an art exhibition'. E. Ioschpe, fax to Cynthia [surname missing], a member of the Fundação Bienal, 30 March 1998, Arquivo Histórico Wanda Svevo / Fundação Bienal de São Paulo.

[17] P. Herkenhoff, in 'Dez anos depois: um debate com Paulo Herkenhoff', *trópico*, 22 April 2008, available at http://www.revistatropico.com.br/tropico/html/textos/2972,1.shl (last accessed on 15 April 2015).

[18] Lilian Amaral used this term in speaking with Mary Lourdes Setsuko Yamanaka, in 'A experiência visível: Entrevista com Lilian Amaral', available at http://www.emnomedosartistas.org.br/FBSP/en/Educativo/Pages/Educativo-da-Bienal.aspx (last accessed on 15 April 2015). The general contours of this art education history can be found in the oral history of the Bienal de São Paulo recently made publicly available. See 'Seminário Arte em Tempo', available in different chapters on YouTube, and as quoted in several footnotes to this essay.

[19] K. Mazzucchelli, 'The São Paulo Biennial and the Rise of Brazilian Contemporary Art', *op. cit.*, p.18. See also V. Spricigo, *Modes of Representation of the São Paulo Biennial / Modos de Representação da Bienal de São Paulo*, São Paulo: Hedra, 2011.

[20] E. Ioschpe, 'Projeto Núcleo Educação Bienal/SESC', in *XXIV Bienal de São Paulo: Arte Contemporânea Brasileira: Um e/entre Outro/s* (exh. cat.), São Paulo: A Fundação, 1998, p.206.

[21] See Aracy Amaral's commentary on the early editions of the Bienal, in '30xbienal,

words, instructing those members of the audience who were keen to be educated 'in the right way of seeing'.[22]

During its first decades, the Bienal seems to have served as a kind of particularly intensive, and also particularly high-quality, temporary academy for those hired as art educators.[23] Up until the 1980s, the art education programme had concentrated on the classical tour format, and tended to be affirmative in its approach to the exhibition apparatus and its narratives; yet individual deviations from the script were possible, for example with tours given in drag in the 1960s.[24] According to Ivo Mesquita, 'the system was completely different from the one today', focused entirely on art history.[25]

During the military rule, which lasted from 1964 to 1985 (and when, despite the regime, dissident articulations were manifest at various Bienals[26]), art education for school-age viewers became part of the education programme of the Bienal. This was, according to his own account, thanks to the initiative of Antonio Santoro Júnior, who came from a family of professional clowns, was a Bienal aficionado, and later became a professor of art. The programme he organised for schools in the vicinity of Ibirapuera Park can be seen as an early predecessor to the large-scale school-visit programme of the 24th Bienal. After that, student attendance increased throughout the years, from 20,000 in 1975 (achieved via a cooperation scheme with a newspaper) to 130,000 in 1998 (110,000 from public schools and 20,000 from private schools through a cooperation system with the city and state of São Paulo).[27] When military rule became civilian rule in 1985, initiatives in the realm of formal education continued, but under conditions that, compared to those that would be seen at the 24th edition, seemed almost informal. As art educator Chaké Ekisian has recounted regarding the

—

década de 90', 2013, available at https://www.youtube.com/watch?v=kN6nBJ45H8M (last accessed on 15 April 2015).

[22] See Simon Sheikh, 'Letter to Jane (Investigation of a Function)', in Paul O'Neill and Mick Wilson (ed.), *Curating and the Educational Turn*, London: Open Editions, 2010, pp.61–75.

[23] Participants in the training often participated as volunteers, but were sometimes paid; art historian Cristina Freire recalls the generous conditions of a one-year training programme for which a grant was available in '30xbienal, década de 80', 2013, available at https://www.youtube.com/watch?v=AkXvNBncozc (last accessed on 15 April 2015).

[24] Former art educator Luiz Munari recalls the 'deusa' (goddess) Ricardo, 'obvio um travesty' (obviously a transvestite), who led tours in drag with the curator's permission, in '30xbienal, década de 60', 2013, available at https://www.youtube.com/watch?v=Os-JW-HCSn4 (last accessed on 15 April 2015).

[25] Ivo Mesquita, in '30xbienal, década de 70', 2013, available at https://www.youtube.com/watch?v=Sv_lEgHThZE (last accessed on 15 April 2015). Mesquita has occupied a variety of roles across different editions, from art educator for the 15th, in 1979, to curator of the 28th, in 2008.

[26] See I. Whitelegg, 'The Bienal de São Paulo: Unseen/Undone (1969–1981)', *op. cit.*

[27] See Maria Hirszman, 'Bienal tem menos publico, mas balanço é considerado positivo', *O Estado de S. Paulo*, 19 December 1998.

18th Bienal in 1985, curated by Sheila Leirner, the first thing that the art education team did was buy a map of the city to find schools in the vicinity of the park.[28]

Walter Zanini's celebrated 16th Bienal, in 1981, offered a scope of paradigm shifts, which filtered through into art education. Zanini resolutely conceived the exhibition as a medium, following a line of thinking that philosopher Vilém Flusser had traced out in his advisory role to the Bienal in the early 1970s.[29] This also led to reflections on the 'process of communication between the arts and the people',[30] by then long debated in the field of art education; thus, a shift in and examination of power relations began. In discussing the 18th edition, Chaké Ekisian recalled: 'We had very clear requirements for the art educators. We are not there to tell people what we think. We are also not there to tell people what they saw.'[31] p.38

There was also a resolute focus in those years on tackling territorial power relations between curators and art educators, with the latter enjoying more leeway and freedom, at least in some cases, than proved conceivable in later editions. For example, in the 18th and 19th Bienals, both curated by Leirner in 1985 and 1987, space was secured for workshops for school students and workers from 'several factories'[32] that were connected to the exhibition. These workshops took place in the exhibition itself, albeit only in the morning and 'very carefully', and there was scope to exhibit the results subsequently. For Lilian Amaral, a workshop at the 19th Bienal marked a decisive moment: 'To my mind an enduring change came about there, a shift from "before" to "after". The Bienal changed its discourse, work with it became more visible and the audience was so affected by the art that they began to make art themselves. Having a place to practice art is fundamental, enormously important; it changed my relationship to art education.'[33]

As head of art education for the 23rd Bienal in 1996, Amaral continued the territorial debates with the clear intention 'that the curators should share their space and reduce their hegemonic claims'. Subverting 'curatorial authority', 'semi-clandestine' teaching materials were produced 'as the curators did not allow us to write any critical texts'.[34] Similarly, the project 'Mapas urbanas:

---

[28] 'We were only out-and-about in the close environs', within a limited radius. 'Entrevista com Chaké Ekisian', *Educativos – uma história*, available at http://www.emnomedosartistas.org.br/FBSP/en/Educativo/Pages/Educativo-da-Bienal.aspx (last accessed on 15 April 2015).

[29] In the 1973 edition, Flusser's concepts were only partially implemented, for example in the works by Fred Forest cited at the start of this essay and in the 'Art and Communication' section.

[30] V. Spricigo, *Modes of Representation of the São Paulo Biennial/Modos de Representação da Bienal de São Paulo*, *op. cit.*

[31] 'Entrevista com Chaké Ekisian', *op. cit.*

[32] C. Ekisian, in '30xbienal, década de 80', *op. cit.*

[33] 'A experiência visível: Entrevista com Lilian Amaral', *op. cit.*

[34] *Ibid.*

Arte contemporânea, a cidade e público' ('Urban Maps: Contemporary Art, the City and the Public'), consisting of 120 boards featuring drawings by education workshop participants displayed across São Paulo and at the workshop venue Paço das Artes, was realised almost behind the curators' backs.[35] Amaral also implemented an ambitious school project; the thousands of schoolchildren the scheme brought to the exhibition contributed to attaining the record visitor numbers the directorship was keen to achieve.[36] Therefore, the field on which the 24th Bienal built its *cantinho* and succeeded in implementing its ambitious art education programme was already seeded; and its activities in 1998 would lay the groundwork for future editions. The 'Bienal of the Future', if it had indeed been held in the year 2000, would have placed education at the heart of its concerns. As the designated curator Ivo Mesquita announced, 'the curator's prime concern was, in any event, education'.[37]

3. A 'Big School'

The imaginary counterpart of the artworks in the 24th Bienal is the 'mass'[38] of *nao-iniciados*[39] (non-initiates), comprising, for the most part, students from the public school system, an audience group that has been referred to in subsequent editions as *periferia*[40] (periphery) or *comunidades*[41] (communities).

This 'mass' from 1998 can only be imagined and understood through the conceptualisation of the 24th edition as a 'big school', as it was termed by members of the art education team.[42] Only the public education sector and its protagonists – the officials, teachers and pupils of public schools in the

—

[35] The Paço das Artes, an exhibition space at the University of São Paulo fifteen kilometres away from Ibirapuera Park, was accessible by a specially arranged bus four times a day.

[36] 'We had Edemar Cid Ferreira as president and he was crazy, he wanted to break the visitor record at any cost. If Rodin and Monet could mobilise 500,000 people in Rio and São Paulo, if there were queues outside the Pinacoteca, why shouldn't the Bienal break records? [...] So every morning we had 6,000 pupils from public schools. It had to be in the morning so they didn't mingle with the normal paying audience. He had the idea that children create disorder anyhow, let alone pupils from public schools, who he thought would really cause problems.' 'A experiência visível: Entrevista com Lilian Amaral', *op. cit.*

[37] I. Mesquita, quoted in M. Hirszman, 'Bienal investe na "clareza pedagógica"', *O Estado de São Paulo*, 19 December 1998.

[38] P. Herkenhoff, 'Bienal 1998: princípios e processos', *op. cit.*

[39] E. Ioschpe, 'Bienal e educação', *op. cit.*, p.110.

[40] Denise Grinspum, 'A 27a Bienal de Sao Paulo e seu projeto educativo', in *27a Bienal de São Paulo: Seminários*, São Paulo: cobogó, 2006, p.393.

[41] See '29a Bienal de São Paulo – Entrevista com Stela Barbieri', 2010, available at http://www.stelabarbieri.com.br/edu/bienal_entrevista.htm (last accessed on 15 April 2015). The underlying political views of this semantic shift demand further research. The public school system in Brazil is used by sectors of the population with limited resources, and the schools themselves are highly under-resourced, both in material and human terms.

[42] See Luiz Guilherme Vergara's commentary in '30xbienal, década de 90', *op. cit.*

city and state of São Paulo – were specifically addressed. In the light of the extreme class segregation of the educational system in Brazil (which holds to this day), this was a resolute statement. 'Concentrating on the public school sector was a political and social decision',[43] recalls Milene Chiavatto, who was in charge of coordinating the guided tours. It was made against a backdrop of transformations in educational policy during this period. In 1996, art education became compulsory for all school classes,[44] after the approval of the Nova Lei de Diretrizes e Bases da Educação Nacional (New Law of Guidelines and Bases for National Education). In 1998, the Ministry of Education was working on a revised version of the Parâmetros Curriculares Nacionais (National Curricular Parameters); the 24th Bienal was keen to intervene in this process.

Planning to contribute to a process of 'creating citizenship'[45] through art education, the 'Núcleo Educação' ('Education Nucleus') developed a concept according to three priorities: training teachers from the public school system as experts on the Bienal as well as 'audience multipliers' (school visits accounted for more than half of the expected audience for the guided tours); developing an art education programme in the exhibition itself; and presenting a concurrent education platform online. As can be read in a concept paper from the 'Núcleo Educação', the art education machine of the 24th Bienal worked on the premise of an advanced and thoroughly 'deconstructive' concept of art education, with the intention to devour and digest the curatorial agenda in an act of (art) pedagogical anthropophagy: 'The discourse of the "Nucleo Educação" had absorbed the curatorial discourse [...] in a productive fusion, in which the art educators flung themselves ravenously upon the curator's banquet and threw themselves with passion into educating people about it.'[46] Milene Chiovatto has recalled these moments of art educational incorporation as evidencing appetite for the king's head: 'It was maximum *antropofagia*, the way in which we, in a sense, gobbled up Paulo's head, the whole crazy dream he had in there suddenly became tangible for us.'[47]

This gave rise to a detailed theoretical system, formulated by Luiz Guilherme Vergara, a member of the Bienal's art education team and also director of education at the Museu de Arte Contemporânea de Niterói at that time. This system drew on phenomenology and critical pedagogy as well as the art pedagogue Ana Mae Barbosa's newly established *metodologia triangular* (triangular methodology).[48] The objective was 'to create a (trans-)cultural,

—

[43] '30xbienal, década de 90', *op. cit.*

[44] This wasn't the first time, as a similar legislation was passed in 1971. This was followed, at least since 1983, by a series of attempts to eliminate the discipline.

[45] P. Herkenhoff, in 'Dez anos depois: um debate com Paulo Herkenhoff', *ibid.*

[46] E. Ioschpe, 'Bienal e educação', *op. cit.*, p.112.

[47] '30xbienal, década de 90', *op. cit.*

[48] Barbosa was also a consultant to the 24th Bienal. What began as *metodologia triangular* and later became *proposta* (proposal) and finally *abordagem* (approach) to art education consists of a combination of *apreciar* (looking/appreciating), *contextualisar* (contextualising) and *experimentar* (experimentation). It remains a

critical and poetic consciousness through art',[49] taking the dimension of *estranhamento* (estrangement), as its point of departure 'in order to tap into the potential of the communicative tension of art'.[50]

The focus was on activating a 'diversified audience',[51] who, through engaging with art and stimulated by art educators, were to be empowered as 'producer[s] of meanings': 'Art education linking these experiences with one's own individual life circumstances can prove enriching by enhancing an awareness of belonging to a collective and being a producer of meanings, in the light of art, culture and one's own life.'[52] In conceptual terms, their approach to art education shifted away from *educação bancária*, to use Paulo Freire's term for an accumulation style of education that reproduces power relations – a banking concept of education – and moved towards an *educação problematizadora* – problem-posing education as an emancipatory and critical agenda that attempts to take alienation as a productive starting point.[53] For this politicised process of subject construction, Vergara proposed the term *antropofagias contínuas* (continuous anthropophagies) to describe a process to be set in motion by art educators: 'This anthropophagic attitude is not passive, but instead demands an individual mobilisation to exchange and share significant experiences related to one's own life circumstances'.[54] The so-called *curadorias educativas* (education curatorships) were introduced in order that the curatorial concepts would be translated into educational 'proposals for thematic routes', and through them, it was hoped, art education at the Bienal would take up a thoroughly self-aware and power-conscious stance (although the notion of the *curadoria educativa* found scarce resonance in the exhibition's public discourse).

On the basis of materials kept in the Arquivo Histórico Wanda Svevo at the Fundação Bienal, it is difficult to reconstruct the extent to which the concepts elaborated above were actually included in the teaching programme of the 'big school' that developed at the exhibition. Another question that remains unanswered here relates to the way in which the outline of the underlying concept, with its advanced theoretical framings, could actually be transposed into the concrete practice of art education, with the thousands and thousands of tours that set the art education programme moving

—

much-discussed and practised paradigm of art education in Brazil. See Ana Mae Barbosa, *A imagem do ensino da arte: anos oitenta e novos tempos*, São Paulo: Perspectiva, 1991.

[49] Núcleo Educação (ed.), *Conceitos e Metas – XXIV Bienal de São Paulo: Curadoria Educativa*, 1998, unpublished manuscript from Fundação Bienal Archive, p.9.

[50] E. Ioschpe, 'Bienal e educação', *op. cit.*, p.112.

[51] Núcleo Educação (ed.), *Conceitos e Metas - XXIV Bienal de São Paulo: Curadoria Educativa, op. cit.*, p.8.

[52] *Ibid.*, p.8.

[53] See Paulo Freire, *Pedagogy of the Oppressed* (1970, trans. Myra Bergman Ramos), New York: Continuum, 2005.

[54] Núcleo Educação (ed.), *Conceitos e Metas – XXIV Bienal de São Paulo: Curadoria Educativa, op. cit.*, p.10.

like a 'crazy turnstile'.[55] Nonetheless, it does appear that the attempt to implement a basic level of (self-)reflection in this educational machine was deemed successful:

> *We established the fields in which we wished to work with greater clarity about how and what we wished to do. Not starting from the assumption – and I believe for the first time in a consistent fashion – that in art education we would simply be leading people through the exhibition space. I think that was a huge revolution in the Bienal's mentality and, to my mind, that of all contemporary cultural institutions.*[56]

The project 'A Educacão Pública e a XXIV Bienal de São Paulo', coordinated and comprehensively documented by Iveta Fernandes, lay at the heart of the 'big school',[57] offering a comprehensive educational programme to a range of professionals in the public education system – teachers of art and other disciplines for various age groups in various types of schools; delegates broadly spread out across the pedagogical field of the city and state of São Paulo. According to Evelyn Ioschpe, over 3,000 teachers were involved from more than 140 districts in the state of São Paulo.[58] The project began with a video conference in cooperation with TV Cultura, which offered participating schools scope for interaction. A series of events, seminars and courses (after which participants received a certificate), aimed to stimulate an educational engagement with the 24th Bienal, were offered in conjunction with institutions such as the Museu Lasar Segall, Museu de Arte São Paulo (MASP), Museu de Arte Moderna (MAM SP), Serviço Social do Comércio (Social Service of Commerce, or SESC)[59] and Museu de Arte Contemporânea da Universidade de São Paulo (MAC USP).

These sessions primarily focused on the 24th edition itself, in anticipation of the groups' subsequent visits to the exhibition, where they would also, to a large extent, make use of the art education features available. The programme's focus also extended beyond, seeking to intervene actively in the process of repositioning contemporary art within the general educational system. This allowed for the creation of a cooperation agreement, vital for a project on this scale, with the Department of Education of the state of São Paulo. The production of teaching materials was a central component in the programme: 15,000 copies of a collection of 20 posters with images from the 'Núcleo Histórico' section of the exhibition and a set of questions and information were printed and distributed to schools around the state.

—

[55] M. Chiavatto, in '30xbienal, década de 90', *op. cit.*

[56] *Ibid.*

[57] See Iveta Fernandes, *Relatório do Projeto A Educação Pública e a XXIV Bienal de São Paulo*, 1998, Arquivo Histórico Wanda Svevo / Fundação Bienal de São Paulo.

[58] E. Ioschpe, 'Projeto Núcleo Educação Bienal/SESC', *op. cit.*, p.204.

[59] The SESC is a private non-profit institution dedicated to culture, health and leisure. It is funded through a payroll tax taken from the salaries of workers in the corporate sector. There are around thirty SESC units in the state of São Paulo, half of them in the metropolitan area of the capital.

The 24th Bienal, with its 'postulation of a non-Eurocentric vision'[60] and, more generally, its attempt to intervene in the canon, thus landed in many classrooms, if not on the curriculum *per se*. This *Material de apoio educativo para o trabalho do professor com arte* (*Educational Support Material for the Teacher's Work with Art*) certainly provided concrete starting points in this undertaking. Referring to a painting by Tarsila do Amaral, it proposed, for example, how reflections on the representations and realities of Brazil's indigenous population could be developed; or how works by Leonilson could provide a foundation for integrating the topic of homosexuality into teaching (a subject also addressed in the new curriculum).[61] The material was produced by various authors, which led to a 'wealth of polyphonic readings' and to a set of resources that ended up being 'very much in demand and frequently used to this day'.[62]

fig.83-87
fig.26

Continuing with Bienal tradition, guided tours were a central art educational format at the 24th Bienal, based on the concept of *curadoria educativa*. The three-month training scheme for 160 educators (selected from a total of 800 applicants who were asked to articulate their position on Brazilian modernism as part of the selection process) was run in cooperation with SESC São Paulo. Both 'stationary' and 'mobile' tours were planned (it was estimated that 146,000 would be required): art educators were positioned at particular points to answer visitors' questions[63] whilst individually designed tours that moved through the exhibition were also on offer. All the educators were paid a fixed wage (a stationary *monitoria junior* received R$500 for a six-hour day, and a mobile *monitoria senior* R$730 for four hours), and their working conditions were regulated by the Fundação Bienal.[64]

In addition, the Bienal's art educators developed the format of 'Conversas com Arte' ('Conversations with Art'), specific thematic workshops taking place during the exhibition, and musician Hélio Ziskind and critic and curator Lisette Lagnado were responsible for an audio guide. Rental revenue from the audio guide was used to support teachers' development of projects relating to the Bienal in their schools.

—

[60] Lisette Lagnado, 'On how the 24th São Paulo Biennial took on Cannibalism', *Third Text*, vol.13, issue 46, 1999, p.83.

[61] See Núcleo Educação (ed.), *Material de apoio educativo para o trabalho do professor com arte*, São Paulo: Fundação Bienal, 1998.

[62] See L.G. Vergara's and I. Fernandes's commentaries in '30xbienal, década de 90', *op. cit.*

[63] In addition, T-shirts were produced with the polysemic slogan 'Tira-Dúvidas' (clarify or eliminate doubts or questions), which did somewhat reinforce the authority of the explanations given by the educators.

[64] 'Relatório de Previsão de custos com Pessoal', fax from Mia Chiovatto to E. Ioschpe, 14 April 1998, Arquivo Histórico Wanda Svevo / Fundação Bienal de São Paulo.

4. Non-synchronicity

The discussion and practice of public art education at events of comparable size in continental Europe at the time – documenta X, Skulptur Projekte Münster and the 47th Venice Biennale, all in 1997 – lagged significantly behind those developed around the 24th Bienal de São Paulo.[65] At the European events, education was not at all conceived in terms of its conceptual or programmatic importance for the curatorial approach. Instead, it was understood as a conventional 'visitor service': a service-oriented transmission of an authorised explanatory text to as many clients as possible, from non-experts to VIP guests. The efforts on this front were particularly sparse in Venice to the extent that they can be reconstructed through archival research and interviews.[66] In Münster, various tour formats and suggested routes through the exhibition were proposed, as well as a limited number of workshops for school classes.[67] In Kassel, for documenta X, a subcontracted firm offered various tour formats and introductory lectures 'on an entrepreneurial basis' and 'guided over 150,000 people around documenta with 70 staff'; in addition, the city of Kassel's Museum Pedagogy Service offered a small programme for children.[68]

In contrast, there are numerous correspondences between the 24th Bienal's self-image as an educational undertaking, including the design of its art education as an autonomous cultural and critical practice, and the status of art education in other geopolitical regions, namely the US and England. Since the nineteenth century, Anglo-American educational practice has developed through a framework based on an ambivalent relationship between discipline and emancipation. From the 1970s onwards, efforts to realise the latter were to a large extent shaped by relationships between artists working in education and activists connected to the civil rights movement.[69]

—

[65] While Herkenhoff would identify Venice and Kassel as his major models for the 24th Bienal, it is also worth noting a much earlier history of biennials integrating discursive and other non-exhibition initiatives in the Global South: see Anthony Gardner and Charles Green, 'Biennials of the South on the Edges of the Global', *Third Text*, vol.27, no.4, 2013, p.454.

[66] In the archives of the Venice Biennale, very few references to art education for the 1997 edition are to be found. In the three catalogues produced for the exhibition, there is only one page devoted to art education, with very brief and exclusively practical information. See Germano Celant (ed.), *La Biennale di Venezia XLVII Esposizione Internazionale d'Arte* (exh. cat.), Milan: Electa, 1997, p.16.

[67] See the Skulptur Projekte Münster website: http://www.lwl.org/skulptur-projekte-download/muenster/97/index.htm (last accessed on 15 April 2015).

[68] 'Der Berliner Galerist Matthias Arndt setzt auf Vermittlung (Interview)', *Der Tagesspiegel*, 12 November 1999, available at http://www.tagesspiegel.de/kultur/der-berliner-galerist-matthias-arndt-setzt-auf-vermittlung-interview/104170.html (last accessed on 15 April 2015). An analysis of the art education work at documenta X can be found in Carmen Mörsch, '100 Tage Sprechen: Als Künstlerin auf der documentaX', available at http://www.kunstkooperationen.de/pdf/100TageSprechen.pdf' (last accessed on 15 April 2015).

[69] See Felicity Allen, 'Situating Gallery Education', in David Dibosa (ed.), *Tate Encounters [E]dition 2: Spectatorship, Subjectivity and the National Collection of British Art*, vol.2, 2008, available at http://www2.tate.org.uk/tate-encounters/edition-2/papers.shtm (last accessed on 15 April 2015).

These movements, as well as education in anglophone art institutions, have drawn a lot from Paulo Freire's pedagogy of liberation. The intensive exchanges between the instigators of the 24th Bienal's conceptual approach to art education and anglophone strands of gallery education and 'Education Through Art'[70] are well-documented: Luiz Guilherme Vergara had studied on the studio and environment art programme at New York University in addition to leading the art education programme at MAC de Niterói; and Ana Mae Barbosa wrote a doctoral thesis in 1979 at Boston University on the US influence on Brazilian art pedagogy.[71]

Having spent time intermittently as president of the International Society for Education in the Arts (InSEA), founded by Herbert Read, Barbosa has long been part of a professional community decisively influenced by art education movements from the English-speaking world.[72] Her book *A imagen no ensino da arte* (1991) focused on education work in art museums, and was a formative text for the 24th Bienal team;[73] it considers the Escuelas al Aire Libre movement of outdoor schools in post-revolutionary Mexico and the development of British critical studies and the 'discipline-based art education' pursued by the Getty Center for Education in Arts in Los Angeles during the same period.[74]

Luiz Vergara has outlined, in 'Curadoria educativa: percepção imaginativa/ consciência do olhar' ('Education Curatorship: Imaginative Perception/ Awareness of Seeing'),[75] the basis for his art education concept for the 24th Bienal. The text includes numerous references to, on the one hand, John Dewey (who was also addressed in Barbosa's dissertation), and, on the other, the interface between art and activism from a curatorial perspective in the US during the 1990s, as postulated by Suzanne Lacy in her term 'New Genre Public Art'.[76] In keeping with this, the 24th Bienal's art education programme had to steer a course between contradictions analogous to those

—

[70] See Herbert Read, *Education Through Art*, London: Faber & Faber, 1943.

[71] See Ana Mae Tavares Bastos Barbosa, 'American Influence on Brazilian Art Education: Analysis of Two Moments, Walter Smith and John Dewey', 1979, doctoral thesis, Boston University.

[72] This community also recognised Barbosa's achievements with a series of awards and appointments, among them: the Sir Herbert Read Award, UNESCO's International Society for Education through Art (1999); Distinguished Fellow, National Art Education Association, US (1997); and the Edwin Ziegfeld International Award, United States Society for Education through Art (1992).

[73] See A.M. Barbosa, *A imagem no ensino da arte: Anos 1980 e novos tempos*, São Paulo: Perspectiva, 2009.

[74] See Maria Christina Rizzi, 'Reflexões Sobre a Abordagem Triangular do Ensino da Arte', in A.M. Barbosa (ed.), *Ensino da Arte – memória e história* (exh. cat.), São Paulo: Perspectiva, 2008, pp.335–48.

[75] See L.G. Vergara, 'Curadorias educativas: A consciência do olhar: Percepção imaginativa, perspectiva fenomenológica aplicadas à experiência estética', *Anais ANPAP-Congresso Nacional de Pesquisadores em Artes Plásticas*, vol.3, 1996, pp.240–47.

[76] See Suzanne Lacy, *Mapping the Terrain: New Genre Public Art*, Seattle: Bay Press, 1994.

found in these US artistic movements or in British gallery education and socially engaged art movements, which, in the UK in 1997, if not before, were appropriated by New Labour as part of its neoliberal agenda. Vergara's ambitious programme, with a discourse directed against *educação bancária* and drawing on a lengthy theory and practice of critical (art) pedagogy, also owed its realisation to the neoliberal transformation of Brazilian cultural policy following a US model: the capitalisation and privatisation of culture implemented on a massive scale in the 1990s and manifested in the adoption of the Rouanet Law, a tax-incentive system for corporate cultural sponsorship. This legislation signified 'a radical break with the modes of cultural financing through the hallmark of a "new logic of financing"', which 'privileged the market but in the process almost always used public money'.[77] In 1995, the Brazilian Ministry of Culture published the brochure *Cultura é um bom negócio* (*Culture Is Good Business*), which pithily characterised the neoliberal paradigm shift.[78]

The Bienal de São Paulo has operated as a (geo-)politically overdetermined enterprise since its inception,[79] and its shifting representational policies, specifically in connection with the art field's capitalisation and globalisation, have been convincingly depicted by Vinicius Spricigo as an ideational machine to transform real capital into its symbolic counterpart and to generate a return on investment.[80] Art education plays an active role in this undertaking: all the more so when its 'audience has a specific quality, and additional value: children, young people, those who are excluded in a whole host of different ways, and beginners – everyone who can be counted in the balance sheet as part of the social responsibility of foundations and patrons'.[81] The 24th Bienal can therefore also serve as an example of the issues facing critical theory and the practice of art education: its consolidation and institutionalisation, especially since the 1990s, has taken place within the context of the capitalisation of culture; or rather, with the creative turns of a cognitive capitalism.[82]

—

[77] Antonio Albino Canelas Rubim, 'Políticas culturais no Brasil: Tristes tradições', *Revista Galáxia*, vol.13, 2007, p.24 and pp.101–13.

[78] See *Cultura é um bom negócio*, Brasília: Ministério de Cultura, 1995. Since Latin America (first and foremost Chile), since the 1970s, often in alliance with the military dictatorships, had been a testing ground for neoliberal policies (and perhaps just as much for resistance to such policies), a trans-local engagement with the effects in the cultural field, precisely concerning the educational turn too, would appear to offer a useful perspective for further research.

[79] See Michael Asbury, 'The Bienal de São Paulo: Between Nationalism and Internationalism', in *Espaço Aberto / Espaço Fechado: Sites for Sculpture in Modern Brazil* (exh. cat.), Leeds: The Henry Moore Institute, pp.72–83.

[80] See V. Spricigo, *Modes of Representation of the São Paulo Biennial / Modos de Representação da Bienal de São Paulo*, *op. cit.*

[81] Cayo Honorato, 'Expondo a mediação educacional: Questões sobre educação, arte contemporânea e política', *ars*, vol.9, 2007, p.115, available at http://www.revistas.usp.br/ars/article/view/2989/3679 (last accessed on 15 April 2015).

[82] The research network Another Roadmap takes this as its point of departure and examines policies and practices of art education and their genealogies from a trans-local and trans-disciplinary perspective. See http://another.zhdk.ch (last accessed on 15 February 2014).

That the first initiative to establish the Fundação Bienal's permanent art education department stemmed from a sponsor, the Fundação Vitae, fits into this scenario (the proposal was rejected by the president during the 21st Bienal, Maria Rodrigues Alves, for unspecified reasons).[83] Against this backdrop, the anthropophagic borrowings of the 24th Bienal's art education programme could be subjected to a critical reading similar to that conducted by Suely Rolnik in the Bienal's catalogue to address the concept of anthropophagy. Rolnik emphasises the ambivalence of this term; it is generally automatically classed as radical, but it is precisely the Bienal's anthropophagic capacity that makes it 'so at ease in the contemporary neoliberal scene', offering the dubious potential 'for us to become the best flexibility athletes in the world'.[84] To a large extent, 'flexibility' is a transfer effect, often invoked as a unique selling proposition of art education,[85] which 'seeks to engender creative, flexible subjectivities, with a willingness to learn, which are up to dealing with the post-Fordist regimen and system-preserving precarisation'.[86]

Even if idealising art education at the 24th Bienal is inappropriate, especially in the light of these problematics, it is important to note that the approach adopted there was ten years ahead of the conceptual and political positioning of art education at large-scale exhibitions in places such as continental Europe.[87] In the light of the notorious devaluation of art education, here the non-'unilateral'[88] alliance of curatorial and pedagogical work proclaims a 're-definition of the status of art education',[89] which would not be realised

—

[83] See 'Interview with Chaké Ekisian', *op. cit.*

[84] Suely Rolnik, 'Anthropophagic Subjectivity', in *XXIV Bienal de São Paulo: Arte Contemporânea Brasileira: Um e/entre Outro/s*, *op. cit.*, p.144. She would develop this line of argument in more detail a decade later. See S. Rolnik, 'The Geopolitics of Pimping', *transversal*, vol.10, available at http://eipcp.net/transversal/1106/rolnik/en (last accessed on 15 April 2015).

[85] '21st-century societies are increasingly demanding workforces that are creative, flexible, adaptable and innovative and education systems need to evolve with these shifting conditions. Arts Education equips learners with these skills, enabling them to express themselves, critically evaluate the world around them and actively engage in the various aspects of human existence.' UNESCO, 'Roadmap for Arts Education', report compiled from 'The World Conference on Arts Education: Building Creative Capacities for the 21st Century', Lisbon, 6 to 9 March 2006, available at http://www.unesco.org/new/fileadmin/MULTIMEDIA/HQ/CLT/CLT/pdf/Arts_Edu_RoadMap_en.pdf (last accessed on 15 April 2005). For a critical account, see Pen Dalton, *The Gendering of Art Education: Modernism, Identity and Critical Feminism*, Maidenhead: Open University Press, 2001.

[86] Catrin Seefranz, 'Causing Trouble: Zum Forschungsvorhaben Another Roadmap', *Bildpunkt* 2, 2013, available at http://www.igbildendekunst.at/bildpunkt/bildpunkt-2013/unvermittelt/seefranz.htm (last accessed on 15 April 2015).

[87] The situation is different when it comes to art education in self-organised contexts and smaller institutions. In the German-speaking world, a critical art education practice began to emerge in the late 1990s, and was in turn able to draw on examples from the 1970s.

[88] Ana Helena Curti, in '30xbienal, década de 90', *op. cit.*

[89] C. Honorato, 'Expondo a mediação educacional', *op. cit.*

in Europe until 2007, at documenta 12, through the integration of the educational dimension into the curatorial concept, intermeshed with a form of art education based on (self-)deconstruction, performativity, participation and an exploratory, interrogatory quest.[90] Similar approaches can be identified elsewhere, for example in Columbia in 2011 at the Encuentro Internacional de Medellín (MDE 11), which consisted of a three-month series of workshops, seminars, participatory art projects, media labs and a large exhibition, all under the title 'Enseñar y aprender: Lugares del conocimiento en el arte' ('Teaching and Learning: Places of Knowledge in Art').[91]

The 24th Bienal continues to offer opportunity to consider art education in all its complexity. Viewed as an anti-elitist initiative within the frame of an international art event, the visibility of the Sala Educação and its protagonists fig.5 and users, as well as the wide impact of the whole programme, was decidedly a result of a willingness to make an intervention. As described above, the substantive thrust of the material produced in this context tapped into the potential for political education within the frame of art education. In programmatic terms, the art education programme distanced itself, just as Herkenhoff and the 24th Bienal as a whole did, from the 'fetishisation of the market'[92] and the dictates of audience maximisation.[93]

5. Back to the Future

The art education policy and practice set up for the 24th Bienal was taken up again 2006, for the 27th Bienal, when Denise Grinspum was given the newly created position of education curator.[94] In contrast to the 24th Bienal, the 27th, curated by Lisette Lagnado, extended beyond the museum paradigm in an aesthetic-political exploration of the title of 'Como viver

—

[90] See C. Mörsch et al. (ed.), *Kunstvermittlung: Zwischen kritischer Praxis und Dienstleistung auf der documenta 12, Ergebnisse eines Forschungsprojekts*, Zürich and Berlin: diaphanes, 2009. Likewise, in 2007, a press release from Skulptur Projekte Münster announced: 'Never before in the 30-year history of the *Skulptur Projekte* has arts education played as important a role as it did during the 2007 exhibition.' Available at http://www.skulptur-projekte.de/besucher/?lang=en (last accessed on 15 April 2015). Also, since its 52nd edition in 2007, the Venice Biennale appears to have an education consultant.

[91] Curated by Nuria Enguita Mayo, Eva Grinstein, Bill Kelley, Jr and Conrado Uribe.

[92] 'Dez anos depois: Um debate com Paulo Herkenhoff', *op. cit.*

[93] When visitor attendance at the 24th Bienal proved lower than expected, references were made in the media to the success of the ambitious educational programme and its long-term impact: 'Uninterested in figures and in the idea of breaking records, Landmann views the educational project as a central success of the exhibition, enabling an exhibition visit with professional art education for 110,000 pupils from public-sector schools and 20,000 from private schools. A further 17,000 visitors booked tours and more than 15,000 used the digital guide.' See M. Hirszman, 'Bienal tem menos publico, mas balanço é considerado positivo', *op. cit.*

[94] 'Our point of departure was the projects developed by the 24th edition.' D. Grinspum, 'A 27a Bienal de São Paulo e seu projeto educativo', *op. cit.*

junto' ('How to Live Together'). Correspondingly, with its 'Centro-Periferia' programme, implemented by Guilherme Teixeira, the art education programme moved into new terrain, addressing the fault lines between centre and periphery – and Bienal and city – from a clearer institutional-critical and transformative perspective. This approach was already present at the 24th Bienal in the conceptualisation of exhibiting and art education as 'creating citizenship'.[95] The idea of institutionalising art education through a director of education at the Fundação Bienal, as formulated in 1997, was finally put into practice in 2009 with the creation of a permanent education team, thus definitively overcoming the art education *cantinho*.[96] This has provided the art education programme considerably more space to develop across editions of the Bienal, as demonstrated in, for example, initiatives to produce historical accounts of art education work at the exhibition.[97]

However, the institutionalisation and consolidation of art education work has not rendered old struggles insignificant. That this process goes hand in hand with regulation and/or precarisation, opening up new battlegrounds, was demonstrated in 2013 by the art educators' strike during the 9th Bienal do Mercosul in Porto Alegre.[98] The strike echoed the local political mood. A year later, lines of divergence and confrontation similarly emerged at the 31st Bienal de São Paulo between the educators and the coordinators of the education team, as well as between the educators and the Bienal institution. Questions about the role of education in relation to the curatorial project and the respective capacities for initiative and agency were amplified by a perception of unfair labour conditions and a feeling of instrumentalisation, of both the educators and the education activities, for the benefit of the institution and its self-reproduction. Considering the way the political and economic situation is evolving in Brazil, and the way the system of contemporary art consolidates around specific market practices and class structures, these conflicts are likely here to stay.

Translated from German by Helen Ferguson.

—

[95] 'Dez anos depois: Um debate com Paulo Herkenhoff', *op. cit.*

[96] In 2009, Stela Barbieri was appointed Curador Educativo ('art education curator') and a permanent art education department was established. Barbieri held this position until mid-2014.

[97] These include the research undertaken on the occasion of the '30xbienal' exhibition in 2013, made available through videos posted online (which have been cited in numerous earlier footnotes to this essay).

[98] On this point, see 'Quando falhas operacionais são desigualdades estruturais – por que o Coletivo Autônomo de Mediadores realizou uma paralisação na 9ª Bienal do Mercosul/Porto Alegre', an account from a participating art educator available at http://coletivoam.wordpress.com/2013/11/30/quando-falhas-operacionais-sao-desigualdades-estruturais-por-que-o-coletivo-autonomo-de-mediadores-realizou-uma-paralisacao-na-9a-bienal-do-mercosulporto-alegre (last accessed on 15 April 2015).

The (Re)turn of the Anthropophagites: Reconnecting Oswald de Andrade's Proposal to Amerindian Art-Thought[1] — Renato Sztutman

A poesia existe nos fatos / Poetry exists in facts
Oswald de Andrade, 'Manifesto Pau-Brasil', 1924

In his 'Manifesto antropófago',[2] Oswald de Andrade takes anthropophagy as metaphor – or, rather, as allegory – for creative processes, and particularly those applied in Brazilian cultural production. For Andrade, to devour the Other is to absorb cultural elements from another world, as opposed to being subordinated to them: this is an active process of creation, to digest foreign culture and return it in a new form. The subject of cannibalism had been explored by various avant-garde artists in the early twentieth-century (such as Francis Picabia, founder of the Dadaist journal *Cannibale* in the early 1920s) but Andrade took the image of humans devouring humans from a real-life practice: the cannibal ritual of the Tupinambá, indigenous to what is now Brazil, who were known to colonisers for executing enemy warriors and eating their flesh amid lively feasting. As shown by the burgeoning anthropological research of the second half of the twentieth century, anthropophagy among the Tupinambá went beyond its literal, 'cannibal' sense: here, eating the Other was imbued with powerful symbolism (and quite unrelated to diet, as Andrade had clearly realised). To eat someone was to constitute oneself from alterity.[3]

Andrade had always taken an interest in anthropology, paying particular attention to reports compiled by explorers who studied the Tupi-Guarani peoples on the Brazilian coast. However, his approach – unlike that of his contemporary and fellow modernist poet Mário de Andrade – did not involve going on expeditions or collecting objects from folk or indigenous cultures.[4]

—

[1] This essay is an extended version of a talk given at the symposium 'XXIV Bienal de São Paulo: Anthropophagy and Cannibalism Histories', Escola São Paulo, 13 April 2013, organised by Lisette Lagnado and Mirtes Marins de Oliveira in collaboration with Afterall. Except where noted, texts originally in Portuguese have been translated for this volume.

[2] See Oswald de Andrade, 'Manifesto antropófago' / 'Anthropophagite Manifesto' (trans. Adriano Pedrosa and Veronica Cordeiro), in *XXIV Bienal de São Paulo: Núcleo Histórico: Antropofagia e Histórias de Canibalismos* (exh. cat.), São Paulo: A Fundação, 1998, pp.532–539, and this volume, pp.222–29.

[3] For two different anthropological perspectives on this, see Carlos Fausto, 'Cinco séculos e meio de carne de vaca: Antropofagia literal e antropologia literária', in J. Ruffinelli and J.C.C. Rocha (ed.), *Antropofagia hoje? Oswald de Andrade em cena,* São Paulo: Realizações Editora, 2011; and Oscar Calavia Saez, 'Antropofagias comparadas', *travessia,* no.37, July–December 1998, available at https://periodicos.ufsc.br/index.php/travessia/article/view/14919/13583 (last accessed on 5 February 2015).

[4] Mário de Andrade was one of the primary organisers of the 1922 Week of Modern Art in São Paulo, which is often historicised as the foundational event

Although Andrade had studied the period's extensive anthropological literature, his 'Manifesto' was still based on ethnocentric concepts such as 'evolution' and 'pre-logical mentality', and had very little to say specifically about the Tupi-Guarani-speaking peoples of the South American lowlands. Andrade took the realm of the Tupinambá as an allegory or even as a lesson (a kind of utopia) for 'our own' private world, in the sense that it would only be worthwhile if it could actually affect or change the world we live in.

Now that today's anthropologists, as part of their struggle against ethnocentrism, have acknowledged many artistic treasures in indigenous realms – artworks that continue to feature images of cannibalism – to what extent may we reconnect the indigenous concept of anthropophagy with the 'modernist' version as spawned by Andrade? And what potential does this – or do these – notion(s) of anthropophagy hold now?

—

The relative absence of work by Brazil's indigenous peoples at the 24th Bienal de São Paulo is intriguing, to say the least. There were pieces from other non-Western populations historically viewed, mistakenly, as 'primitive', such as indigenous artists from Australia and Canada, some of whom had by 1998 become well known in certain Western artistic circles for their ritual objects: abstract paintings by the former, which gained traction in the art market, and zoomorphic masks (which the Surrealists used so extensively) in the case of the latter.[5] At the same time, together with the phenomenon of art-market appreciation and absorption of these so-called 'traditional' arts, a new figure emerged in Australia and North America: the 'contemporary indigenous artist', whose exploratory pieces in their own way recreated an anthropophagic gesture by appropriating hegemonic languages with a rebellious or oppositional twist.[6] This dual process is still at an incipient stage

—

for Brazilian modernism. Together with Claude Lévi-Strauss and Dina Dreyfus, Mário de Andrade founded an ethnography and folklore society in São Paulo, the Sociedade de Etnografia e Folclore, which lasted from 1935 to 1938. See Luísa Valentini, *Um laboratório de antropologia: O encontro entre Mário de Andrade, Dina Dreyfus e Claude Lévi-Strauss (1935–1938),* São Paulo: Alameda, 2013.

[5] In this respect, see two pieces from the Bienal catalogue: Jean-Hubert Martin's reflection on the art-religion relationship and Australian aboriginal art ('A religião, herética para a arte moderna' / 'Religion, heretical for modern art' in *XXIV Bienal de São Paulo: Núcleo Histórico: Antropofagia e Histórias de Canibalismos, op. cit.*, p.518); and Deborah Root's discussion of the ritual masks of the Kwakiutl people and their appropriation by modern artists ('Devorando o cannibal: um conto de precaução da apropriação cultural' / 'Eating the cannibal: a cautionary tale on cultural appropriation', in *XXIV Bienal de São Paulo: Roteiros. Roteiros. Roteiros. Roteiros. Roteiros. Roteiros. Roteiros.* (exh. cat.), São Paulo: A Fundação, 1998, p.180).

[6] For instance, at the Bienal itself, 'Roteiros Oceania' featured a work by Francis Jupurrurla, a member of the Warlpiri Media group in Australia, which, as described by Louise Neri in the catalogue, shows the Warlpiri people's cosmological discourse transposed to the language of video so that it becomes a political tool denouncing a history of massacres and territorial claims. In her catalogue essay, Deborah Root defines the new 'indigenous artists' as those who are exploring hybridism, such as the painter Lawrence Paul, who 'toys with the Surrealists being fascinated by

in Brazil; nonetheless, indigenous arts have become part of the art scene and market (which is always problematic, given the risk of decontextualised instrumentalisation and objectification of their particularly ritual and relational character) and politicised indigenous artists have emerged (reacting to stereotypes, rejecting both aesthetic and economic subordination). Indeed,the art of Brazil's indigenous peoples, with rare exceptions, remains among the planet's least known.[7] Unlike those in Africa, Asia, Australasia and North America, and relative to other South American countries, their work remained practically absent from the exhibitions of the avant-garde period. However, their practices convey a powerful anthropophagic meaning that now enables us to reconnect with the ethical, aesthetic and metaphysical proposal of Andrade's 'Manifesto'.

Allegory and utopia

To describe Andrade's anthropophagy as allegorical is not to claim that it breaks new ground in terms of recorded knowledge of non-Western peoples. Andrade was a tireless reader of primary sources, of sixteenth century literature on Tupi-Guarani people and such anthropological studies as were available at the time, references to which can be found in both his 'Manifesto Pau-Brasil' of 1924 and the 'Manifesto antropófago' of four years later, as well as being evident in his more theoretical pieces written several decades later, such as 'A crise da filosofia messiânica' ('The Crisis of Messianic Philosophy', 1950) or 'A marcha das utopias' ('The March of Utopias', 1966, published posthumously).[8]

—

northwest-coast patterns as a way of both complicating and subverting the premises of Western science'. See L. Neri, 'Roteiros Oceania', in *XXIV Bienal de São Paulo: Roteiros. Roteiros. Roteiros. Roteiros. Roteiros. Roteiros. Roteiros., op. cit.*, p.40; and D. Root, 'Devorando o cannibal: um conto de precaução da apropriação cultural' / 'Eating the cannibal: a cautionary tale on cultural appropriation', *op. cit.*

[7] This situation has changed over the last few years. There have, for example, been two paradigmatic exhibitions of works by Brazilian indigenous artists: 'Histoires de voir, Show and Tell', Fondation Cartier pour l'Art Contemporain, Paris, 15 May to 21 October 2012; and 'Mira! Artes visuais contemporâneas dos povos indígenas' ('Look! Contemporary Visual Arts of Indigenous Peoples'), which opened in July 2013 at Centro Cultural UFMG, Belo Horizonte, and will be travelling to several cities in Brazil (see http://projetomira.wordpress.com, last accessed on 5 February 2015). See also Sophie Moiroux, 'Painting the Xingu: Amati Trumai's Images as Memory of Traditions' (UpperXingu, Central Brazil), unpublished manuscript submitted to the seminar 'Arts and Belonging in the Americas Today', Senate House, London, 12 to 13 April 2013.

[8] See O. Andrade, *Obras Completas VI: Do Pau-Brasil à Antropofagia e às Utopias,* Rio de Janeiro: Civilização Brasileira, 1972. For more on these works, particularly the crisis of messianic philosophy, see Benedito Nunes, 'Antropofagia ao alcance de todos', in *A utopia antropofágica*, São Paulo: Globo, 1990; and *Oswald Canibal,* São Paulo: Perspectiva, 1979. Antonio Candido recalled that Andrade submitted 'A crise da filosofia messiânica' as part of a competitive selection procedure for a philosophy appointment at Universidade de São Paulo, but the National Education Council rejected the book and demanded the applicant show a degree-level diploma specifically in philosophy. See A. Candido, 'Digressão sentimental sobre Oswald de Andrade', in *Vários escritos*, São Paulo, Rio de Janeiro: Duas Cidades, Ouro sobre Azul, 2004.

While the 'Manifesto antropófago' poses a programme for an anthropophagous approach to artistic creation, Andrade's later writings aspire to an entire 'conception of the world', a cannibalistic philosophy as such, based on a dialectical synthesis of savage and civilised worlds, low and high culture, freedom and technique. Such a conception sharply opposes the philosophies and religions of transcendence – here termed 'messianic' – which have emerged in the wake of political forms that owed much to patriarchal models.

Andrade's later theoretical writings developed the allegories found in the 'Manifesto antropófago', using ideas such as 'primitive matriarchy' or 'participatory consciousness' that he borrowed from the writings of late-nineteenth and early-twentieth century anthropologists.[9] Whilst Andrade's use of notions that now seem outdated or even mistaken must be treated with due care, his position as a thinker and artist perhaps allows these aspects to be revisited more readily than if he were writing as a scholar or anthropologist.

Among its aphorisms, the 'Manifesto' contains an important reference to an allegorical 'Pindorama matriarchy'. *Pindorama* is a Tupinambá word meaning 'region or country of the palm trees', yet here Andrade owes more to a book by the Swiss anthropologist and jurist Johann Jakob Bachofen concerning purportedly maternal rights in the 'ancient world' than to historical descriptions of Tupinambá society itself.[10] Bachofen rejected patriarchy as a universal form of society – against his British contemporary Henry James Sumner Maine's theses of patriarchal domination as a property-derived primordial right – suggesting that matriarchal regimes had existed in the remote past and were neither despotic nor based on private property.

A direct association between the theme of matriarchy and anthropophagy was to return in a passage from 'A crise da filosofia messiânica'. In this essay, Andrade opposed a matriarchal world, in which cannibalism was customary, to a patriarchal one in which subordination would take the form of slavery or class rule. Surely influenced by Friedrich Engels's interpretation of nineteenth-century anthropology,[11] Andrade embraced an idea of dialectical and predictably evolutionary progress from simple to more complex societies.

—

[9] In the second half of the twentieth century, anthropologists rejected both Johann Bachofen's 'primitive matriarchy' hypothesis and Lucien Lévy-Bruhl's notion of 'participatory consciousness'. In the first instance, they pointed to confusion between regimes in which matrilineal descent prevailed and the hypothesis that women had governed society. The struggle against the idea of 'participatory consciousness' and also against 'pre-logical thought' is closely associated with Claude Lévi-Strauss, who argued instead for an enlarged or broadening universal rationality.

[10] See Johann Jakob Bachofen, *An English Translation of Bachoffen's Mutterrecht (Mother Right) (1861): A Study of the Religious and Juridical Aspects of Gynecocracy in the Ancient World: Volume I "Lycia," "Crete," and "Athens"* (trans. David Partenheimer), London: Edwin Mellen Press, 2007.

[11] See Friedrich Engels, *The Origin of the Family, Private Property, and the State* (1884, trans. Robert Vernon), Atlanta: Pathfinder Press, 1972.

However, the most interesting aspect of his view is the idea that domination – by the Father, the One, the State, figures of a messianic philosophy as such – is not the essential 'law of Man' but there are other laws, such as 'the law of the anthropophagite', which primarily means recognising equality of conditions and constitutive freedom.[12] Andrade insisted that patriarchy and its forms had not always existed but were introduced in the distant past following the downfall of a prior system of matriarchy; equally, that subordination was not inherent to humanity but could be rejected through the devouring practice of anthropophagy.

In Andrade's 'A marcha das utopias', matriarchy is depicted quite differently, not as something confined to the past but as a utopia. He proposes this as both a dream and a protest, quoting Lenin – 'If there is some connection between dreams and life then all is well', then adding: 'Utopia is always a sign of nonconformism and a harbinger of revolt.'[13] This essay finds Andrade somewhat remote from Marxist orthodoxy: his vision of utopia involves the return of matriarchy, this time under the sign of technology, which could end labour as an imposition giving rise to inequality. In Andrade's words, 'human labour leads to idleness. The paradisiacal stage of matriarchy.'[14] Here, again, we find the 'technicised barbarian' of the 'Manifesto': matriarchy had been overthrown by patriarchy and freedom reduced to subordination, but technology would then restore matriarchy and human freedom by minimising toil. Here Andrade reflects his generation's faith in the power of technology and science but projects it onto a different image of the world that is capable of combining modernisation with primitivism to reach the utopia outlined in Marx and Engel's *German Ideology*. In this state, people would no longer be required to labour but be fulfilled as free human beings. Andrade's anthropophagy becomes thus both thought and art, allegory and utopia, drawing its power from the possible world of Others. Rather than allegorising the world in which he found himself, he posed an allegory *for* this world.

As the 'Manifesto' points out, 'we never admitted the birth of logic among us'.[15] This statement leads Andrade explicitly to the ideas of philosopher and sociologist Lucien Lévy-Bruhl, who had described a 'participatory consciousness' in connection with experience of the sacred, which contrasts with standard rationality.[16] Lévy-Bruhl's notions of 'participatory consciousness'

—

[12] Alexandre Nodari's brilliant discussion of the 'law of the anthropophagite' in the 'Manifesto' asks how a law that succinctly acts to disable 'Law' may be understood. See A. Nodari, 'A única lei do mundo', in J. Ruffinelli and J.C.C. Rocha (ed.), *Antropofagia hoje? Oswald de Andrade em cena,* São Paulo: Realizações Editora, 2011, p.455.

[13] O. Andrade, *Do Pau-Brasil à Antropofagia e às utopias, op. cit.*, p.209.

[14] *Ibid.*

[15] O. Andrade, 'Manifesto antropófago', *op. cit.*, p.227.

[16] See Lucien Lévy-Bruhl, *La mentalité primitive* (1922), Paris: Anabet Éditions, 2007. In 'A marcha das utopias', while admitting the problematic nature of Lévy-Bruhl's reflections, Andrade notes how he revised his ethnocentric arguments in his more mature work, particularly in his *Carnets* (see *Les Carnets de Lévy-Bruhl,* Paris: PUF, 1949). For a discussion of Lévy-Bruhl's ideas and their internal development,

and 'pre-logical thought' were related to the image of the sacred that the Surrealists had appropriated in their own particular way, as well as with Sigmund Freud's concepts of instinct, impulse and drive. Andrade made these relationships explicit by presenting a singular interpretation of psychoanalytic thought, with particular reference to Freud's controversial *Totem and Taboo* (1913).[17] Andrade imagined that the Tupinambá cannibal rituals and their sacrifice of enemy warriors were sacred acts as such, conjoining killers and victims: 'Anthropophagy. Absorption of the sacred enemy. To transform him into totem.'[18] For Andrade, to transform totem into taboo is to sacralise pre-rational instincts (those that activate 'participatory consciousness', a mixture between human and non-human subjectivity) during rituals, a practice cultivated by Tupinambá anthropophagites but repressed by so-called civilised peoples. Instead of dismissing primitive peoples as neurotics incapable of suppressing primal instincts such as the Oedipus complex, as was insinuated by Freud, Andrade suggests de-repressing instincts, specifically those that instigate a return to such a participatory state.[19]

In short, Andrade's anthropophagy projects both an allegory and a utopia: the sacred act of anthropophagy emerges as a critique of bourgeois logic and a chance to retrieve forgotten experiences, to re-engage with the world passionately. In his invocation of the 'Caraíba revolution' (in Tupinambá history and mythology, the Caraíba were empowered shamans or prophets who led migrations to the so-called 'Land Without Evil') and the 'matriarchy of Pindorama', Andrade was not proposing a return to an ancestral past but rather a future – the future of 'technicised barbarianism' and experimental hybridisms.

Anthropophagous metaphysics

The difference between Oswald de Andrade's anthropophagy and its indigenous form is more than just a difference between symbolic figure and real practice; 'real life' anthropophagy is also symbolic in most cases. The act of 'literally' eating another human being is charged with symbolism, just as a symbolic act of devouring will usually have real consequences for people's lives. Cannibalism as ethics – rather than diet – has always been found among many of the indigenous peoples of South America's lowlands. However, colonisation led to 'pacification' (or ethnocide, as it might well be called) and these practices were suppressed through missionary catechesis. In general, two indigenous forms of cannibalism may be distinguished: exo-cannibalism, which involves warriors and the consumption of a sacrificed enemy's flesh

—

see Marcio Goldman, *Razão e diferença: Afetividade, racionalidade e relativismo no pensamento de Lévy-Bruhl*, Rio de Janeiro: Ed. Da UFRJ/Grypho, 1994.

[17] Sigmund Freud, *Totem and Taboo: Some Points of Agreement Between the Mental Lives of Savages and Neurotics* (1913, trans. James Strachey), London: Routledge and Kegan Paul, 1950.

[18] O. Andrade, 'Manifesto antropófago', *op. cit.*, p.230.

[19] On Andrade's 'libertarian' interpretation of Freud, see B. Nunes, *Oswald Canibal, op. cit.*

(for instance, by the Tupinambá), and endo-cannibalism, associated with funeral ceremonials (for instance, by the Yanomami).[20]

In Brazilian anthropology, in particular studies of the Tupi-Guarani speaking peoples, anthropophagy is a recurring theme. Early proto-anthropological writing – in the form of travel journals or missionaries' letters – took anthropophagy as the basis for a view of indigenous peoples through European (notably Portuguese and French) eyes. The first substantive analysis of this subject in a Brazilian context was in the 1950s, when Florestan Fernandes wrote *A função social da guerra na sociedade Tupinambá* (*The Social Function of War in Tupinambá Society*, 1952). Among the Tupinambá, Fernandes argued, war was a means of holding society together: the anthropophagous ritual sacrificing of an enemy was meant to seal group-unity and reinforce continuity between the living and their ancestors.[21]

A few decades later, Manuela Carneiro da Cunha and Eduardo Viveiros de Castro revised Fernandes's interpretation for their 1985 article 'Vingança e temporalidade' ('Revenge and Temporality').[22] They reinterpreted their predecessor's sources, critiqued his functionalist approach and rejected the notion that the purpose of war is to foster social cohesion and celebrate the ancestral. They proposed that, rather than keeping a group together, war was a vehicle for vengeance. Moreover, they argued that the killer-victim relationship, as the basis of Tupinambá social life, has to be understood in terms of its reversibility: in a circular fashion, today's killer may be tomorrow's victim. He who is to be devoured will have devoured others, and his own subjection to this event is an honour. In this ritual, the prisoner of war is treated as a free being; equally, he will never flee from his captivity. Instead, he becomes part of a family, has his name changed, is given a wife and takes part in everyday life – until the day of cannibal feasting. Devouring is a relationship between warriors mutually recognising their glory, rather than an act of subordination based on the possibility of objectification of one by another. (The idea of such an anthropophagical joy takes us back to the spirit of the 'Manifesto'.)

In the 1980s, the Amazonian Tupi-Guarani peoples were examined in a profusion of publications, among which Viveiros de Castro's study of the

—

[20] Many peoples ate their dead and still do; the point is that the one who eats the dead is never a close relative. For an overview of indigenous cannibalism, see, for instance, Carlos Fausto, 'Banquete de gente: Comensalidade e canibalismo na Amazônia', *Mana,* vol.8, no.2, 2002, pp.7–44. For ethnographic studies of cannibalism among present-day peoples, see Aparecida Vilaça, *Comendo como gente: Formas de canibalismo wari*, Rio de Janeiro: UFRJ, 1992; and Bruce Albert, 'Temps de sang, temps de cendres: Réprésentations de la maladie chez les Yanomami du Sud Est (Amazonie)', unpublished doctoral thesis, Nanterre: Université Paris X, 1985.

[21] See Florestan Fernandes, *A função social da guerra na sociedade Tupinambá* (1952), Rio de Janeiro: Globo, 2006.

[22] See Manuela Carneiro da Cunha and Eduardo Viveiros de Castro, 'Vingança e temporalidade' (1985), in M. Carneiro da Cunha (ed.), *Cultura com aspas*, São Paulo: Cosac Naify, 2009.

Araweté people of Ipixuna, in southeastern Pará, is particularly noteworthy.[23] Despite the Araweté's warrior tradition, Brazil's National Indian Foundation (FUNAI) – a governmental body who devise and enforce policy in relation to indigenous peoples – gradually persuaded this group to be pacified. The Araweté did not usually hold anthropophagous feasts to devour enemies like the Tupinambá, nor eat their own dead like the Yanomami. However, their speculations concerning fate after death described part of the human soul ascending to heaven to be devoured by cannibal gods, the Maï, at which point this soul would become a god too. Becoming a cannibal god was a posthumous destiny awaiting all Araweté, especially the great killers.

Among the Araweté, as for the Tupinambá, the enemy is a key figure. When the period of reclusion that followed a killing ended, the Araweté killers would have to sing songs they had received from their dead enemies. According to Viveiros de Castro, these songs conveyed the words of their enemies; it was the enemy that was singing, never the killer. Something similar was seen among the Tupinambá: the words they sung were always those of others. In both cases, the killer sees things from the enemy's point of view, which means that he experiences an enemy affect or 'becoming' – a condition that is quite dangerous for himself or his community. While the model for the Araweté male figure is that of a killer, the 'becoming-enemy' is a constituent part too. Taking the argument further, one might conclude that, rather than identity, 'becoming-Other' is the mark of the Araweté person. Comparing their ethnography with that of other Tupi-Guarani populations, Viveiros de Castro elucidates a cannibal ethics that defines a Tupi individual as a constantly changing 'anti-Narcissus'.[24]

In his account, Viveiros de Castro in no way poses a psychoanalytic or irrational explanation: cannibalism is not a primary instinct being realised or irrationality bursting out. Instead it is this process of 'becoming-Other' based on the logic of predation: constituting the self depends on the Other; producing identity and interiority depends on difference and exteriority. In this way, far beyond notions of diet and instinct, anthropophagy reveals an entire logic, ethics and ontology – in short, a metaphysics.

It is no coincidence that *Cannibal Metaphysics* is the title of another of Viveiros de Castro's books.[25] This metaphysics is based on the idea that the problem of being – germane to Western metaphysics – must be dissolved in the problem of becoming. To cannibalise is to occupy the position of the

—

[23] See E. Viveiros de Castro, *From the Enemy's Point of View: Humanity and Divinity in an Amazonian Society* (trans. Catherine V. Howard), Chicago: University of Chicago Press, 1992.
[24] *Ibid.*
[25] In this text, Viveiros de Castro extends aspects of his Araweté observations to the Amazon region and the South American lowlands as a whole, despite numerous linguistic and cultural variations noted in these regions. See E. Viveiros de Castro, *Cannibal Metaphysics* (trans. Peter Skafish), Minneapolis: University of Minnesota Press, 2014.

Other: for warrior cannibalism, this means taking the position of the enemy; for funerary cannibalism, devouring a non-consanguineous relative rather than an enemy is nonetheless a 'becoming-Other' since affinity (in-law relationship) and enmity are interchangeable figures in this conceptualisation. In short, all thcsc cannibalisms – and there are many more than two – pose the question of the place of alterity: 'I am interested only in what is not mine', as Andrade wrote in his 'Manifesto'. Anthropophagous metaphysics!

Warrior cannibalisms also involve 'exchanging perspectives', which recalls another major theme addressed by Viveiros de Castro: the 'Amerindian perspectivism' of the indigenous peoples of America.[26] There may be different exchanges of perspective in other contexts, too, such as the shamanism often associated with hunting, when shamans may take on the point of view of animals or other non-humans. Indeed, Amerindian shamans may shuttle between different points of view, visit the world of the dead, negotiate hunting with animal masters, or enter underwater or celestial realms. Amerindian shamans are those most likely to experience 'becoming-Other' – they sing the words of others, see through the eyes of others – which would be very dangerous, if not deadly, for ordinary humans. In both predation and perspectivism, what we have is self-alteration as a mode of inhabiting a world composed of many worlds, or a *pluriverse*, to borrow a term from the philosopher William James.[27] One can only learn or know to the extent that one takes up different perspectives, and that is a cannibal act.

Again, we may draw a parallel with Andrade's anthropophagy: to create something new there has to be a 'becoming-Other', taking a point of view as self-metamorphosis. This different metaphysics, this de-definition of being by becoming – a possibility that Gilles Deleuze had raised in more traditionally philosophical terms – requires a different theory of knowledge: not one based on the fixed and hierarchical nature of positions such as subject and object but one in which subjects interrelate and therefore may devour each other. The subject's position is not a guarantee but something to be occupied and potentially reoccupied. And having collapsed the subject-object dichotomy, it follows that the nature-culture dichotomy too is endangered. Viveiros de Castro perspicaciously suggests inverting terms: for standard modern thought, there is only one nature or world for various different cultures or 'worldviews', while for Amerindian thought there are multiple natures and worlds for one single culture or 'worldview'. Modernity sees difference in culture, in the proliferation of souls (in the

—

[26] See E. Viveiros de Castro, *A inconstância da alma selvagem e outros ensaios de antropologia*, São Paulo: Cosac Naify, 2002. In English, see, for example, E. Viveiros de Castro, 'Cosmological Deixis and Amerindian Perspectivism', *The Journal of the Royal Anthropological Institute*, vol.4, no.3, 1998, pp.469–88; and 'Exchanging Perspectives: The Transformation of Objects into Subjects in Amerindian Ontologies', *Common Knowledge*, vol.10, no.3, 2004, pp.463–84.

[27] See, for example, William James, *A Pluralistic Universe: Hibbert Lectures at Manchester on the Present Situation of Philosophy* (1909), New York: Biblio Bazaar, 2006.

sense that the body is a common measure of all existing souls); the latter sees difference in nature, in the proliferation of bodies (in the sense that all share a single soul with no particularised being). From this perspectivist standpoint, the subject is simply a position that may be occupied by any existing thing, which means that anything may be a subject – so everything may be human. In such a world, peopled by so many human subjectivities, cannibalism becomes a common horizon: everything that you eat may be human, and everything that looks at you may devour you.[28]

With his claim that perspectivism revisits Oswald de Andrade's anthropophagy in different terms, Viveiros de Castro points to an elective affinity between an artistic manifesto and indigenous thought, translated by contemporary ethnology.[29] Overall, it seems that the anthropophagous thinking Andrade pursued in his later writings could establish an unexpected and positive connection to the thought of anthropophagites themselves. But could this indigenous anthropophagous thought also be found at the level of expressive forms? In other words, could there be anthropophagous art among the anthropophagites?

Anthropophagous arts

As already noted, Andrade did not derive his concept of anthropophagy directly from Brazilian indigenous ethnographic objects. Instead he focused on descriptions of Tupi rituals and mythologies that were symbolically or artistically suggestive. From burgeoning research into expressive forms produced by indigenous Amazonian populations over the last few decades, it could be argued that these arts show distinctively anthropophagous potential. This would explain the fact that everything that has artistic value is conceived as being of 'foreign' origin for these people. Art is that which originates from the worlds of enemies, animals or spirits – the different realms of Otherness.

But in what sense may it be claimed, from a Western standpoint, that non-Western objects and performances (rituals, for instance) are artistic? Published in 1998, Alfred Gell's *Art and Agency* suggests that if the notion of art were to be extended to be relevant to all the planet's peoples, which would be a political move, it would have to relinquish classical aesthetics and symbolism and conclude that an art object is anything capable of prompting action,

—

[28] To put it another way, among different Amerindian cosmologies, cannibal spirits or soul eaters populate the cosmos. Note that the Amerindian notion of the soul is actually corporeal: souls have bodies and may be eaten, but, for that very reason, they too may devour others. On this subject, see Anne Christine Taylor, 'The Soul's Body and Its States: An Amazonian Perspective on the Nature of Being Human', *Journal of The Royal Anthropological Institute*, vol.2, 1998, pp.201–15.

[29] See E. Viveiros de Castro in conversation with Luísa Elvira Belaunde, in Renato Sztutman (ed.), *Entrevistas com Eduardo Viveiros de Castro*, Rio de Janeiro: Azougue, 2008, p.114.

anything that has agency or the ability to actively influence the world.[30] Just as Claude Lévi-Strauss extended rationality to rediscover it in 'savage' thought, there finding it to abide by its own logic of sensitive qualities, Gell too extends art and rediscovers it in life, with attendant critique of exhibition spaces and of the autonomy of artworks. By emphasising agency, Gell attempted to shift art as a whole closer to magic as technology – based on the principle of efficacy – without presupposing a transcendent reality as in the case of religion.[31] Following this reasoning, artistic objects or performances must not be reduced to their form, or to the possibility of their symbolising something; what they actually do is produce a reality – which again connects to the real-symbolic or literal-metaphorical dichotomy, as seen in relation to anthropophagy. The idea of art as agency is also seen in Gilles Deleuze and Félix Guattari's definition of art as producing and conserving affects.[32] An artistic object would be one that causes an action or produces affects in someone.

These considerations surely shed light on indigenous arts. It is often said that drawing on a surface is a way of activating it; making an object is conceiving a live body; performing a song is actualising a reality, with what is sung synaesthetically being seen. Such art is more than merely decorative: it potentiates, it produces affects. A painted or sculpted arrow makes it efficacious; a drawing or painting on a body will protect it from supernatural attack; singing makes one become like a god or a spirit. Art is inscribed here in the realm of 'becoming' and the body, rather than the realm of representation or the soul. It is inscribed in the realm of effectiveness rather than contemplation – implied in life precisely because there is no separation between art and life.[33] Not unrelatedly, shamans may be described as artists. In making connections between realms, they are prompted to invent new things or knowledge that must acquire form – visual (drawing), verbal-musical (song), choreographic (dance). There is

—

[30] Alfred Gell, *Art and Agency: An Anthropological Theory*, Oxford: Oxford University Press, 1998.

[31] There is an odd tendency to talk about indigenous arts in the realm of religion as religious arts and ceremonial arts. Gell's way of approaching them is through magic, which involves immanence. In this respect, the objects he has in mind are more ones that 'do things' and are thus designated as 'fetishes' or 'sorcery', rather than 'objects of worship' or 'veneration'.

[32] See Gilles Deleuze and Félix Guattari, *What is Philosophy?* (1991, trans. Hugh Tomlinson and Graham Burchill), London: Verso, 1994.

[33] For an introduction to the general problem of anthropological studies on indigenous arts, see Els Lagrou, *Arte indigena no Brasil: Agência, alteridade e relação*, Belo Horizonte: Com Arte, 2009; and A.C. Taylor, 'Voir comme un autre: Figurations amazoniennes de l'âme et des corps', in Philippe Descola (ed.), *La fabrique des images*, Paris: Musée du Quai Brany, 2012. For a key study of Amerindian graphic arts, see Peter Gow, 'Piro Designs: Paintings as Meaningful Action in an Amazonian Lived World', *Journal of the Royal Anthropological Institute*, vol.5, no.2, 1999, pp.229–46. On the relationship between imagery and verbal expression, examined through a study of Marubo shamanism, see Pedro Cesarino, *Oniska: Poética do xamanismo na Amazônia*, São Paulo: Perspectiva, 2011.

no discernible distinction between aesthetics and the shamans' shuttling back and forth between perspectives.[34]

It is very common to hear from different Amerindian peoples that art objects or performances, as forms invested with efficacy, originate from the worlds of enemies, animals, spirits – realms into which one enters through an exchange of perspectives, a high-risk move that may border on devouring.[35] Art would, then, be precisely a means of domesticating all this ferociousness, since being affected is not enough – these affects must be retained, tamed, transformed into something else. The idea of art domesticating the ferociousness of other realms has been developed by Lucia Hussak van Velthem in her studies of the Carib-speaking Wayana people of Pará. She rejects the imperious view of indigenous arts as repetitive and lacking innovation or invention, said to be constantly reformulating the same graphic patterns based on a supposedly finite set of motifs.[36] Instead Velthem reports that Wayana designs, or *milikut* (the term is also used to refer to writing taught in local schools), are not the property of the Wayana themselves; they belong to 'archetypal' beings, especially mythical characters that may materialise and need to be engaged with creatively.

A widespread myth in the region traces the origin of these drawings to observations of a painted ancestral *Tulupërë* (serpent, anaconda or caterpillar) – a being that is metamorphic by definition, a shape-shifting or scale-shedding creature that constitutes an enduring image of immortality. According to the myth, having trapped and killed the monster, the Wayana began copying its image in countless drawings on various supports, including basketry, pottery and their own bodies. Van Velthem summarises Wayana art with the dictum 'beauty is the beast': meaning that aesthetic experience is directly related to supernatural beings' ferociousness and the scale of their predatory activity.[37] Once again, to see this process of imprinting predatory beings solely in terms of representation would be a misunderstanding. Rather, the crucial feature is agency, since appropriation of these archetypes leads to

—

[34] The relationship between art and shamanism was specifically addressed in two of Aristóteles Barcelos Neto's books on the Wauja of the Upper Xingu region, *A arte dos sonhos: Uma iconografia ameríndia* (Lisbon: Assírio & Alvim, 2000) and *Apapaatai: Ritual de máscaras no alto Xingu* (São Paulo: Edusp, 2008), which primarily examine the visionary experience of Wauja shamans and their interaction with *apapaatai*, or pathogenic supernatural spirits. The shamans' duty is to appease these spirits in order to heal the sick. To do so, however, the same spirits must be 'represented' by patterned masks and musical instruments, and then fed in the course of elaborate rituals. Another view of the relationship between art and shamanism may be found in P. Cesarino, *Oniska: Poética do xamanismo na Amazônia, op. cit.*

[35] See, for example, Lucia Hussak van Velthem, 'Em outros tempos e nos tempos atuais: Arte indígena', in *Artes Indígenas: Mostra do Redescobrimento* (exh. cat.), São Paulo: Fundação Bienal, 2000.

[36] *Ibid.*

[37] See L.H. van Velthem, *O Belo é a Fera: a Estética da Produção e da Predação entre os Wayana*, Lisboa: Assírio & Alvim, 2003.

specific affects; it involves channelling supernatural ferociousness in order to keep it at bay.[38] Van Velthem has associated this process with a certain anthropophagous potential, given that all these forms originate in others' models and may yet become part of a shared knowledge driven by mythological narratives and shamanism. It is a matter of not just reproducing models but subjecting them to constant experimentation. Such proliferation of mythic narratives around looting or appropriation in reference to the origin of graphic markings and/or objects is not uniquely Wayana; it may be found everywhere among indigenous peoples of the Amazon region.

Els Lagrou writes of the many narratives of the Pano-speaking Kaxinawá people of the western Amazon region, according to which the origin of graphic patterns and all the world's beauty lies in loving and having sexual intercourse with strangers or foreigners – be they human or animal. Here, looting gives way to seduction, which is also a way of producing contact between remote realities.[39] The Kaxinawá themselves associate glass beads currently obtained from Westerners with the ornaments and medicinal substances which were taken from the Inka, their mythological enemies. In so doing, they take history as an extension of mythical stories and logics. Like everything of artistic value, and thus agency-related, beads come from outside, and the outside is what constitutes world and self. As Lagrou writes:

> *The Kaxinawá love of beads may be related to their fascination with the dangerously alluring beauty of their powerful 'Others'* [including Westerners and the Inka]. *In this sense, objects made from beads would not be mere 'hybridisms' but 'legitimate expressions of specific ways of producing and using substances, raw materials and objects while following specific logics of transformation and classification'.*[40]

The image of mythological, shamanic and bellicose acts of seduction and looting (since war was an important source of appropriated objects, drawings, stories and even ritual)[41] suggests that these aesthetic regimes would involve constantly experimenting with others' works rather than creating ex nihilo.

—

[38] See Barcelos Neto's research of the Wauja, who believe that *apapaatai* drawings are the outcome of their diplomatic relations with shamans, who 'imitate' the *apapaatai* in order to transform their pathogenic, or predatory, powers into art in both the aesthetic and diplomatic senses, 'creating forms' and the 'art of building relationships', respectively.

[39] Lagrou compares different ethnographic case studies and recognises one of the region's 'key symbols' as the mythical anaconda, with its power of generating all decorative motifs – the 'Big Snake' figure evoked in Andrade's 'Manifesto'. See E. Lagrou, *Arte indígena no Brasil: Agência, alteridade e relação*, Belo Horizonte: Com Arte, 2009, p.77.

[40] *Ibid.*, pp.55–56.

[41] Viveiros de Castro's aforementioned *From the Enemy's Point of View* contains an extensive analysis of Araweté warrior songs, or 'enemy songs', to show that it is the dead enemy that takes the place of enunciating subject in these songs, which are taken from the enemies in as far as the enemies sing through the mouths of their killers. The same formulation may be found among other indigenous peoples.

Regimes such as these require 'creating a different concept of creation'.[42] Hence Viveiros de Castro's suggestion of a possible connection between traditional indigenous and recent digital modes of creating; for example, sampling in music production or tools and organisations for sharing knowledge and products, such as Creative Commons. Both modes reject the idea of creating from nothing since we always start from something that already exists. In this sense, what is shamanic art if not combining created work with citations, since all its expressions are already compositions of images, voices or sounds that belong to other agents? Not coincidentally, the Araweté liken their shamans to radios, while the Yanomami talk of recorders and amplifiers in forests that broadcast the words of the spirits with whom their shamans communicate by ingesting hallucinogenic *yakoana*.[43] In short, they perform metamorphoses and ramifications rather than creations in some absolute sense. The human world may be understood in terms of the continuous imitation and improvised actualisation of mythological models – necessarily involving danger since a model can become real, and might prove monstrous. Hence, 'becoming' rather than 'being' – instead of forms being fixed (each with its own authenticity), they occupy a state of continuous transformation.

—

This discussion indicates that certain Amerindian expressive modes, understood in conjunction with a particular metaphysics, may be considered as art. This view also enables these modes and concepts to connect with what we have called 'artistic anthropophagy' in modernist and contemporary settings. Such connections were perhaps the great lacuna at the 24th Bienal de São Paulo: the absence of work by those who inspired Andrade's 'Manifesto', namely the indigenous peoples who still inhabit Brazil, remains striking.

A first step towards including the indigenous arts and their underlying thought in curatorial agendas should be to recognise their special regimes of creativity. This would mean, for example, no longer seeing them as mere repetition of unchanging and unreflective traditions. It would involve apprehending their unique forms and creative artworks, which include subtle variations and incessant appropriation of exogenous elements. As in Andrade's proposal, to say that everything that is 'mine' has come from the Other does not mean letting go of creativity. Quite the contrary: creative artwork takes place precisely as part of a relationship with the outside and the Other. In this way, indigenous arts are more radically anthropophagous than Western art, since they focus less on the autonomy of individual artists or artistic collectives and their artworks – hence less on the fierce opposition between creator-artist-subject and objectified product – and more on relational networks in which creativity emerges precisely because 'subject' and 'object' roles are interchangeable.[44]

—

[42] E. Viveiros de Castro in conversation with P. Cesarino and Sérgio Cohn, in *Entrevistas com Eduardo Viveiros de Castro*, *op. cit.*, pp.164–87.

[43] Davi Kopenawa and B. Albert, *La chute du ciel: Paroles d'un chaman yanomami*, Paris: Plon, 2010.

[44] James Leach distinguishes modes of creativity not confined to the universe we

Although this concept of anthropophagy is not exactly the same as that cultivated in contemporary art – or by the 24th Bienal – this should not prevent us from continuing to foster dialogue and trace connections. Many of the critiques levelled at art historical canons, for example, coincide with concerns posed by Amerindians. Just as indigenous artists have started to appropriate technologies, languages and spaces in contemporary art, curators have been showing interest not only in indigenous objects but also their modes of creativity.[45] The greatest challenge in engaging with these practices is the step from inspiration to alternative, from the Other as allegory to the Other as alteration of ourselves.

Writing in 2009, Pedro Cesarino noted: 'The detour toward the Other is a way of pursuing the powerful spirit, the creative potential in a state of ebullition, and constantly challenged thought.'[46] If indigenous arts do actually develop such an anthropophagous potential – materialising these cannibal metaphysics, invoking metamorphosis and 'becoming' to the detriment of identity and 'being'; insisting that soul is body and body is flesh – then they may well lead to reflection on or even extension and radicalisation of this intriguing cannibalistic tradition: the same anthropophagy that has impelled Brazilian modernist and contemporary art, as spawned by Andrade's 'Manifesto'.

Translated from Portuguese by Izabel Burbridge.

—

call 'art': while predominant modes in the modern West are 'appropriative' in relation to the idea of property, his studies of indigenous societies such as Melanesia's have found 'distributive' modes prevailing, with creativity disseminated rather than belonging to anyone. See J. Leach, 'Modes of Creativity', in Eric Hirsch and Marilyn Strathern (ed.), *Transactions and Creations: Property Debates and the Stimulus of Melanesia*, New York: Bergham Books, 1990.

[45] I have at least two recent exhibitions in mind. One is 'Yanomami, l'esprit de la forêt', Fondation Cartier pour l'Art Contemporain, Paris, 14 May to 12 October 2003, curated by Hervé Chandès and the anthropologist Bruce Albert. The exhibition resulted from an encounter between Yanomami shamans and contemporary artists aiming to trigger 'free associations' across different creative processes. See *Yanomami, l'esprit de la forêt* (exh. cat.), Paris: Fondation Cartier, 2003. The second is the 'Hidden State', curated by Rodrigo Moura in dialogue with the anthropologist Paulo Maia, at the 43 Salón (inter) Nacional de Artistas, Medellín, Columbia, 6 September to 3 November 2013. The curatorial proposal questioned the meaning of art based on the dialogue between indigenous objects and contemporary artworks, with indigenous artists and film-makers participating. See http://universes-in-universe.org/eng/bien/sna_colombia/2013_medellin/tour/mamm_2 (last accessed on 5 February 2015). Both exhibitions focused on interesting ideas of collaboration involving the chance to instigate creative alterations and contaminations in both parties. Pointing to the possibilities these collaborations suggested is more important than judging their materialisation (there will always be asymmetry in the background, since the spaces focused on are always 'ours').

[46] P. Cesarino, 'Atualidade e alteridade', *Atual: o Último Jornal da Terra*, 1 May 2009.

Manifesto antropófago[1] — Oswald de Andrade

Só a antropofagia nos une. Socialmente. Economicamente. Filosoficamente.

Única lei do mundo. Expressão mascarada de todos os individualismos, de todos os coletivismos. De todas as religiões. De todos os tratados de paz.

Tupi, or not tupi that is the question.

Contra todas as catequeses. E contra a mãe dos Gracos.

Só me interessa o que não é meu. Lei do homem. Lei do antropófago.

Estamos fatigados de todos os maridos católicos suspeitosos postos em drama. Freud acabou com o enigma mulher e com outros sustos da psicologia impressa.

O que atropelava a verdade era a roupa, o impermeável entre o mundo interior e o mundo exterior. A reação contra o homem vestido. O cinema americano informará.

Filhos do sol, mãe dos viventes. Encontrados e amados ferozmente, com toda a hipocrisia da saudade, pelos imigrados, pelos traficados e pelos touristes. No país da cobra grande.

Foi porque nunca tivemos gramáticas, nem coleções de velhos vegetais. E nunca soubemos o que era urbano, suburbano, fronteiriço e continental. Preguiçosos no mapa-múndi do Brasil.

Uma consciência participante, uma rítmica religiosa.

Contra todos os importadores de consciência enlatada. A existência palpável da vida. E a mentalidade prélógica para o Sr. Lévy-Bruhl estudar.

Queremos a Revolução Caraíba. Maior que a Revolução Francesa. A unificação de todas as revoltas eficazes na direção do homem. Sem nós a Europa não teria sequer a sua pobre declaração dos direitos do homem.

A idade de ouro anunciada pela América. A idade de ouro. E todas as girls.

Filiação. O contato com o Brasil Caraíba. *Oú Villegaignon print terre.* Montaigne. O homem natural. Rousseau. Da Revolução Francesa ao Romantismo, à Revolução Bolchevista, à Revolução surrealista e ao bárbaro tecnizado de Keyserling. Caminhamos.

—

[1] Editors' Note: This text was originally published in *Revista de Antropofagia*, May 1928, São Paulo.

Nunca fomos catequizados. Vivemos através de um direito sonâmbulo. Fizemos Cristo nascer na Bahia. Ou em Belém do Pará.

Mas nunca admitimos o nascimento da lógica entre nós.

Contra o Padre Vieira. Autor do nosso primeiro empréstimo, para ganhar comissão. O rei analfabeto dissera-lhe: ponha isso no papel mas sem muita lábia. Fez-se o empréstimo. Gravou-se o açúcar brasileiro. Vieira deixou o dinheiro em Portugal e nos trouxe a lábia.

O espírito recusa-se a conceber o espírito sem corpo. O antropomorfismo. Necessidade da vacina antropofágica. Para o equilíbrio contra as religiões de meridiano. E as inquisições exteriores.

Só podemos atender ao mundo orecular.

Tínhamos a justiça codificação da vingança. A ciência codificação da Magia. Antropofagia. A transformação permanente do Tabu em totem.

Contra o mundo reversível e as idéias objetivadas. Cadaverizadas. O stop do pensamento que é dinâmico. O indivíduo vítima do sistema. Fonte das injustiças clássicas. Das injustiças românticas. E o esquecimento das conquistas interiores.

Roteiros. Roteiros. Roteiros. Roteiros. Roteiros. Roteiros. Roteiros.

O instinto Caraíba.

Morte e vida das hipóteses. Da equação *eu* parte do *Kosmos* ao axioma *Kosmos* parte do *eu.* Subsistência. Conhecimento. Antropofagia.

Contra as elites vegetais. Em comunicação com o solo.

Nunca fomos catequizados. Fizemos foi Carnaval. O índio vestido de senador do Império. Fingindo de Pitt. Ou figurando nas óperas de Alencar cheio de bons sentimentos portugueses.

Já tínhamos o comunismo. Já tínhamos a língua surrealista. A idade de ouro.

Catiti, Catiti,
Imara Notiá,
Notiá Imara,
Ipejú

A magia e a vida. Tínhamos a relação e a distribuição dos bens físicos, dos bens morais, dos bens dignários. E sabíamos transpor o mistério e a morte com o auxílio de algumas formas gramaticais.

Perguntei a um homem o que era o Direito. Ele me respondeu que era a garantia do exercício da possibilidade. Esse homem chamava-se Galli Mathias. Comi-o.

Só não há determinismo – onde há mistério. Mas que temos nós com isso?

Contra as histórias do homem que começam no Cabo Finisterra. O mundo não datado. Não rubricado. Sem Napoleão. Sem César.

A fixação do progresso por meio de catálogos e aparelhos de televisão. Só a maquinaria. E os transfusores de sangue.

Contra as sublimações antagônicas. Trazidas nas caravelas.

Contra a verdade dos povos missionários, definida pela sagacidade de um antropófago, o Visconde de Cairu: – É mentira muitas vezes repetida.

Mas não foram cruzados que vieram. Foram fugitivos de uma civilização que estamos comendo, porque somos fortes e vingativos como o Jabuti.

Se Deus é a consciênda do Universo Incriado, Guaraci é a mãe dos viventes. Jaci é a mãe dos vegetais.

Não tivemos especulação. Mas tínhamos adivinhação. Tínhamos Política que é a ciência da distribuição. E um sistema social-planetário.

As migrações. A fuga dos estados tediosos. Contra as escleroses urbanas. Contra os Conservatórios e o tédio especulativo.

De William James e Voronoff. A transfiguração do Tabu em totem. Antropofagia.

O pater famílias e a criação da Moral da Cegonha: Ignorância real das coisas + falta de imaginação + sentimento de autoridade ante a pro-curiosa.

É preciso partir de um profundo ateísmo para se chegar à idéia de Deus. Mas a caraíba não precisava. Porque tinha Guaraci.

O objetivo criado reage com os Anjos da Queda. Depois Moisés divaga. Que temos nós com isso?

Antes dos portugueses descobrirem o Brasil, o Brasil tinha descoberto a felicidade.

Contra o índio de tocheiro. O índio filho de Maria, afilhado de Catarina de Médicis e genro de D. Antônio de Mariz.

A alegria é a prova dos nove.

No matriarcado de Pindorama.

Contra a Memória fonte do costume. A experiência pessoal renovada.

Somos concretistas. As idéias tomam conta, reagem, queimam gente nas praças públicas. Suprimamos as idéias e as outras paralisias. Pelos roteiros. Acreditar nos sinais, acreditar nos instrumentos e nas estrelas.

Contra Goethe, a mãe dos Gracos, e a Corte de D. João VI.

A alegria é a prova dos nove.

A luta entre o que se chamaria Incriado e a Criatura – ilustrada pela contradição permanente do homem e o seu Tabu. O amor quotidiano e o modus vivendi capitalista. Antropofagia. Absorção do inimigo sacro. Para transformá-lo em totem. A humana aventura. A terrena finalidade. Porém, só as puras elites conseguiram realizar a antropofagia carnal, que traz em si o mais alto sentido da vida e evita todos os males identificados por Freud, males catequistas. O que se dá não é uma sublimação do instinto sexual. É a escala termométrica do instinto antropofágico. De carnal, ele se torna eletivo e cria a amizade. Afetivo, o amor. Especulativo, a ciência. Desvia-se e transfere-se. Chegamosao aviltamento. A baixa antropofagia aglomerada nos pecados de catecismo – a inveja, a usura, a calúnia, o assassinato. Peste dos chamados povos cultos e cristianizados, é contra ela que estamos agindo. Antropófagos.

Contra Anchieta cantando as onze mil virgens do céu, na terra de Iracema – o patriarca João Ramalho fundador de São Paulo.

A nossa independência ainda não foi proclamada. Frape típica de D. João VI: – Meu filho, põe essa coroa na tua cabeça, antes que algum aventureiro o faça! Expulsamos a dinastia. É preciso expulsar o espírito bragantino, as ordenações e o rapé de Maria da Fonte.

Contra a realidade social, vestida e opressora, cadastrada por Freud – a realidade sem complexos, sem loucura, sem prostituições e sem penitenciárias do matriarcado de Pindorama.

Oswald de Andrade
Em Piratininga
Ano 374 da deglutição do Bispo Sardinha.

Anthropophagite Manifesto[1] — Oswald de Andrade

Only anthropophagy unites us. Socially. Economically. Philosophically.

The world's only law. The masked expression of all individualisms, of all collectivisms. Of all religions. Of all peace treaties.

*Tupi, or not tupi that is the question.**

Against all catechisms. And against the mother of the Gracchi.

I am interested only in what is not mine. Law of man. Law of the anthropophagite.

We are tired of all the suspicious Catholic husbands put in drama. Freud put an end to the enigma of woman and to other frights of printed psychology.

What hindered truth was clothing, the impermeable coat between the interior world and the exterior world. The reaction against the dressed man. American cinema will inform us.

Sons of the sun, mother of the living. Found and loved ferociously, with all the hypocrisy of nostalgia, by the immigrants, by those trafficked and by the *touristes.*[3] In the country of the big snake.

It was because we never had grammars, nor collections of old plants. And we never knew what was urban, suburban, frontier and continental. Lazy men on the world map of Brazil.

A participating consciousness, a religious rhythm.

Against all importers of canned consciousness. The palpable existence of life. And the pre-logical mentality for Mr Lévy-Bruhl to study.

We want the Caraíba revolution. Bigger than the French Revolution. The unification of all efficacious rebellions in the direction of man. Without us Europe would not even have its poor declaration of the rights of man.

The golden age proclaimed by America. The golden age. And all the *girls.**

—

[1] Editors' Note: This is a lightly revised version of the translation by Adriano Pedrosa and Veronica Cordeiro that was published in *XXIV Bienal de São Paulo: Núcleo Histórico: Antropofagia e Histórias de Canibalismos* (exh. cat), São Paulo: Fundaçao Bienal, 1998, pp.536–39; the original was published in *Revista de Antropofagia*, May 1928, São Paulo. For notes on translation issues see, for instance, Steve Berg, 'An Intro-duction to Oswald de Andrade's *Cannibalist Manifesto*', *Third Text*, vol.13, no.46, Spring 1999, pp.89–91; and Leslie Bary, '*Cannibalist Manifesto* by Oswald de Andrade', *Latin American Literary Review*, vol.19, no.38, July–December 1991, pp.38–47.

* Indicates language used in original.

Filiation. The contact with Caraíba Brazil. *Oú Villegaignon print terre.** Montaigne. The natural man. Rousseau. From the French Revolution to Romanticism, to the Bolshevik Revolution, to the Surrealist Revolution and Keyserling's technicised barbarian. We walk.

We were never catechised. We live through a somnambular law. We made Christ be born in Bahia. Or in Belém do Pará.

But we never admitted the birth of logic among us.

Against Father Vieira. Author of our first loan, to gain his commission. The illiterate king had told him: 'Put this on paper but don't be too wordy.' The loan was made. Brazilian sugar was recorded. Vieira left the money in Portugal and brought us wordiness.

The spirit refuses to conceive the spirit without body. Anthropomorphism. The need for an anthropophagical vaccine. For the equilibrium against the religions of the meridian. And foreign inquisitions.

We can only attend to the oracular world.

We had justice, the codification of vengeance. And science, the codification of Magic. Anthropophagy. The permanent transformation of Taboo into totem.

Against the reversible world and objectivised ideas. Cadaverised. The *stop** of thought that is dynamic. The individual victim of the system. The source of classical injustices. Of the romantic injustices. And the forgetting of interior conquests.

Routes. Routes. Routes. Routes. Routes. Routes. Routes.

The Caraíba instinct.

Death and life of the hypotheses. From the equation *I*, part of the *Kosmos,** to the axiom *Kosmos*, part of *I*. Subsistence. Knowledge. Anthropophagy.

Against vegetable elites. In communication with the soil.

We were never catechised. What we did was Carnival. The Indian dressed as a Senator of the Empire. Pretending to be Pitt. Or featuring in Alencar's operas, full of good Portuguese feelings.

We already had communism. We already had the Surrealist language. The golden age.

> *Catiti, Catiti,*
> *Imara Notiá,*
> *Noliá lmara,*
> *Ipejú**

Magic and life. We had the relation and the distribution of physical goods, of moral goods, of noble goods. And we knew how to transpose mystery and death with the aid of some grammatical forms.

I asked a man what the Law was. He replied it was the guarantee of the exercise of possibility. That man was called Galli Matias. I ate him.

Determinism is only absent where there is mystery. But what do we have to do with this?

Against the stories of man, which begin at Cape Finisterra. The undated world. Unsigned. Without Napoleon. Without Caesar.

The fixation of progress through catalogues and television sets. Only machinery. And the blood transfusors.

Against the antagonistic sublimations. Brought in caravels.

Against the truth of missionary peoples, defined by the sagacity of an anthropophagite, the Viscount of Cairu: 'It is the often repeated lie.'

But they who came were not crusaders. They were fugitives from a civilisation that we are eating, because we are strong and vengeful like the Jabuti.

If God is the consciousness of the Uncreated Universe, Guaraci is the mother of the living. Jaci is the mother of plants.

We did not have speculation. But we had the power of guessing. We had Politics which is the science of distribution. And a social-planetary system.

The migrations. The escape from tedious states. Against urban sclerosis. Against Conservatories, and tedious speculation.

From William James to Voronoff. The transfiguration of Taboo into totem. Anthropophagy.

The paterfamilias and the creation of the Morality of the Stork: Real ignorance of things + lack of imagination + sense of authority in the face of the pro-curious.

It is necessary to depart from a profound atheism to arrive at the idea of God. But the Caraíba did not need to. Because he had Guaraci.

The created objective reacts as the Fallen Angels. Afterwards, Moses wanders. What have we got to do with this?

Before the Portuguese discovered Brazil, Brazil had discovered happiness.

Against the Indian with the torch. The Indian son of Mary, godson of Catherine de Médici and son-in-law of Dom Antônio de Mariz.

Happiness is the proof of the pudding.

In the matriarchy of Pindorama.

Against Memory as source of habit. Personal experience renewed.

We are concretists. Ideas take hold, react, burn people in public squares. Let us suppress ideas and other paralyses. Through the routes. To believe in signs, to believe in the instruments and the stars.

Against Goethe, the mother of the Gracchi, and the court of Dom João VI.

Happiness is the proof of the pudding.

The struggle between what one would call the Uncreated and the Creature – illustrated by the permanent contradiction between man and his Taboo. Everyday love and the capitalist modus vivendi. Anthropophagy. Absorption of the sacred enemy. To transform him into totem. The human adventure. The mundane finality. However, only the pure elites managed to realise carnal anthropophagy, which brings with it the highest sense of life, and avoids all evils identified by Freud, catechist evils. What happens is not a sublimation of the sexual instinct. It is the thermometric scale of the anthropophagic instinct. From carnal, it becomes elective and creates friendship. Affectionate, love. Speculative, science. It deviates and transfers itself. We reach vilification. Low anthropophagy agglomerated in the sins of catechism – envy, usury, calumny, assassination. Plague of the so-called cultured and Christianised peoples, it is against it that we are acting. Anthropophagi.

Against Anchieta singing the eleven thousand virgins of the sky, in the land of Iracema – the patriarch João Ramalho, founder of São Paulo.

Our independence has not yet been proclaimed. Typical phrase of Dom João VI: 'My son, put this crown on your head, before some adventurer does!' We expelled the dynasty. It is necessary to expel the spirit of Bragança, the law and the snuff of Maria da Fonte.

Against social reality, dressed and oppressive, registered by Freud – reality without complexes, without madness, without prostitutions and without the prisons of the matriarchy of Pindorama.

Oswald de Andrade
In Piratininga
Year 374 of the swallowing of the Bishop Sardinha.

Incomplete Glossary of Sources of Latin American Art[1]
— Paulo Herkenhoff

BANANA. Plant originally from Asia, from the family of the *Musaceae*. It was introduced in America in the sixteenth century. In popular culture it has a very broad set of meanings (erotic, depreciative, etc.). Brazilian Modernism was very dependent on bananas, while nineteenth-century academicism (Agostinho José da Mota and Estêvão Silva) preferred watermelons. (See *WATERMELON.*) In one of the very few important paintings that she made in Brazil after returning from New York, Anita Malfatti presents, in her canvas *Tropical* (c.1917), a basket of fruits from bananas to pineapples. 'It is certainly the first time that the national theme is focused within modern art in Brazil', says Malfatti's biographer, Marta Rossetti Batista. Right after his definitive immigration to Brazil (1923), Lasar Segall introduced a joyful expressionistic landscape of a banana plantation with a certain post-Cubist spatial character. In the 'Antropofagia' of the late twenties (see *CANNIBALISM*), large banana-tree leaves with vegetal bodies dwell in the anthropophagous native landscape of Tarsila do Amaral (since *A Negra*, 1923). These same leaves will appear in Livio Abramo's early anthropophagous period woodblock prints. In the late sixties, Brazilian Antônio Henrique Amaral, after his Pop departure, slowly moved to a hyperrealistic amplification of bananas which are being submitted to painful operations (like being tied up or hung with string, or cut with forks and knives) as a metaphor for the dark political times of the prevailing dictatorship of torture and murder. The negative symbolism of Latin American countries as 'banana republics' (as a post-Colonial alliance of local corrupt oligarchies, either civilian or military, with foreign interests and presently with United States interventionism) finally finds a morbid yet truthful portrait, in spite of some efforts of modernisation in certain societies of the continent.

BODY. O corpo é o motor da obra. (The Body is the motor of the work.)

BRASIL. Also once called *Pindorama.* (See *WOMEN.*) Not to be mistaken with the island Brazil, in the same latitude as the south of Ireland and consisting of an enormous ring of earth around a sea full of islands. Common mortals cannot see this island (Angelinus Dalorto, 1325, *apud.* Manguel and Guadalupi). Since Latin American Brazil is the country of the author of this glossary, the predominance of Brazilian examples is not intended to indicate the greater importance of this country, rather, it indicates the limitations of his horizons.

BRASILIDADE. See *CANNIBALISM.*

—

[1] Editors' Note: This text was first published in Ivo Mesquita, Paulo Herkenhoff and Justo Pastor Mellado (ed.), *Cartographies* (exh. cat.), Winnipeg: Winnipeg Art Gallery, 1993, and has been edited for this volume. It is reproduced here by kind permission of the author and publisher.

CANNIBALISM. The indigenous cultural pattern of cannibalism has provided Brazilian artists and writers of the twentieth century with a source for a modern theory of cultural absorption: 'Antropofagia' (= cannibalism). The 1928 'Manifesto antropófago' by poet Oswald de Andrade, taken from the painting *Abaporu* (1928) by Tarsila do Amaral states that only cannibalism unites Brazilians socially, economically and philosophically. The law of the man-eater indicates an interest in Otherness, unlike the importation of canned consciousness. In this stage of Brazilian modernism, it was no longer enough to update art with the international scene. A national culture would be open to devour any influence, to digest it for new meanings and possibilities. The primitivist model is transformed into a barbarian pattern against the oppressive censorship of civilisation. Andrade advocates the permanent transformation of taboo into totem. References to Freud and Surrealism indicate the precedent he finds in Picabia's cannibalism. In Brazil, the 'Antropofagia project' has both historical and contemporary validity. It is a dialectic method which is far deeper than the superficial postmodern principle of image quotations.

CARTOGRAPHIES. Artists in Latin America have used maps as a reference to the controversial social reality, rather than the flag, a conventional and unifying symbol of a nation, subjected to political manipulation. For Borges the map (in 'Del rigor de la ciencia') offered the possibility of substituting the failure of rational knowledge for the actuality of adjusting metaphor to reality, whereas Torres-García practices the inversion of the map (1936), with the intention of breaking the mirror (see *ESPEJISMO*) in a return to Latin America's own values. The perpetuation of Mercator's topographical conventions and distortions, in a science developed by the Conquest, are not innocent. The maps of Anna Bella Geiger register cultural domination with hegemonies and marginality. The painting of Guillermo Kuitca draws on many sources, from a Russian film (Eisenstein), a German dancer (Bausch) or an English song (The Beatles), overflowing the geographic borders or any boundary between the realms of artistic languages. The maps fix no point as they confirm a transiency of meanings from culture to the fantasmatic. Their function is inverted. It is no longer a description. Kuitca operates the revelation of the irreducible fluidity of the space of doubt and quest, of a world glowingly transitional and challenged by the awareness of the Otherness. Time is 'never finished and is constantly changing' in the work of Kuitca (Rina Carvajal). Kuitca then has the opportunity to transform the map, in the Borges tradition, from the passive possibilities of the mirror into the crystalline action of the prism.

CENSORSHIP. See different forms of censorship in *CANNIBALISM, COLONIALISM* and *WOMEN.*

CHANGE. 'Change is the essential condition of existence' (Lucio Fontana, 'Manifiesto Blanco', Buenos Aires, 1946).

COLONIALISM. 'Art is no longer an instrument of intellectual domination', said Hélio Oiticica (1967). It is up to the artist to overcome postcolonialist aesthetics, in spite of the remnants of colonialism in the international circulation of art. Both the exclusion from history and an interpretation that includes references only to European sources are forms of colonialist censorship.

COLOUR. The undeniable alignment of Latin American artists with the Western history of colour could lead to such clear relationships as Soto or Oiticica with Malevich or Mondrian. Within this tradition (sometimes touching the question of the monochrome) we may still quote the concretist, constructive or optical choices of colour in Cruz-Diez (Venezuela), Negret (Colombia), Weissmann and Carvão (Brazil), among others. A picturesque colour may descriptively derive from reality as in the Mexican painter Rivera or the Colombian sculptor Botero. It can be emblematic, within national conventions and codes of tradition, like the Orixas' heraldic colours in Cuba or Brazil. Archeological colour rules the earthy palette of Brazilian Rêgo Monteiro, with reference to Amazonian Marajó civilisation, whereas Andean artists Szyszlo (Peru) and Viteri (Ecuador) articulate historical colour from the fabrics, dolls and other sources in material culture and spiritual symbolism of the Incas and other groups. In Brazil, the purification of a colour system derived from popular culture established an anthropological dimension. It starts with the landscapes of the Pau-Brasil period (1924), by Tarsila do Amaral, through the reductive and constructive colour architecture of Alfredo Volpi (1950/1970s) and the sensory experience of colour as space and materiality in Oiticica (1960s). The harmonious colour compositions of a native naiveté by Tarsila do Amaral and Volpi synthesise a certain rural taste. In other areas, contemporary colour sensibility might call for more bright and strident combinations, as vigorous efforts to guarantee extreme visibility, like the recent work of Delson Uchôa in the Northeast and Emmanuel Nassar in Amazonia. A crisis of colour finds a moral severity in the almost black-and-white portraits of Mexican Siqueiros, such as *The Proletarian Mother* (1930) and *Ethnography* (1939). Here the extreme scarcity of light and colour induces a political judgment. Ethical severity also impels the woodblock prints of Brazilian Goeldi. The anguished light is the presentation of a moral night, melancholic in the urban drama of Rio de Janeiro and naturalistic, yet mythical, in the Amazonian scenario. The painful extreme of tropical light is approached by the opposition of the sombre Goeldi to the solar Reverón in a complementary dimension like day and night. The antinomy of light/colour in Reverón's paintings lays in the scarceness of pictorial matter. The Venezuelan brings the excess of light as an approach to blindness. The experience of visual bewilderment leads the gaze to the possibility of its own nullification.

CONTINENTALISM. See *NATIONALISM.*

CRISIS. 1492 sets a dual crisis. A multilevel crisis, from religion to knowledge, reaches Europe. A Portuguese map (1519) by Lopo Homem creates a southern territorial link between America and Africa, as a last effort to re-validate the Ptolemaic geographic notions. A permanent crisis was set for the natives of the Americas, from cultural survival to life itself. After independence, Paraguay underwent genocide and strangulation from its neighbours. (See *WAR.*) Brazilian Mário Pedrosa discussed the 'Crisis of the

Artistic Conditioning' (1966) due to the use of alien cultural roots. Pedrosa added that this crisis of modern art was due to the crisis in the levels of social function and communication (1972). (See *POSTMODERN.*) Argentinian Jorge Romero Brest wrote *La Crisis del Arte en Latinoamerica y en el Mundo* (1974). He discussed the notions of crisis and development in art and stressed a dialectic contradiction between the order of human needs and the order of artistic demands. Besides the many specific crises that Latin American artists are dealing with, like perception (Waltercio Caldas and Alfred Wenemoser), the critic Nelly Richard points to a fundamental contemporary crisis. The Chilean group CADA (Colectivo de Acciones de Arte – Collective for Art Actions) (Raúl Zurita, Diamela Eltit, Juan Castillo, Lotty Rosenfeld and Fernando Balcells) in the postulation of a 'discourse of the crisis', 'had learned to mistrust any new illusion of "totalitarian totality": may we call it either revolutionary utopia, myth or ideology' (Nelly Richard). (See *UTOPIA.*)

DIFFERENCE. 'Here I leave murdered distance', says the Peruvian writer Alberto Hidalgo, 'I am urged to declare that Hispanic-Americanism is repugnant to me. This is something false, utopic and mendacious [...] Besides, there is not even similitude of characters between the Hispanic American countries. [...] The abyss that can be glimpsed between an Argentinian and a Colombian is incommensurable. That all are Spanish descendants, this is the least. The conquerors have imposed the idiom but not the spirit. The predominating influence is the land, the haphazard of the tribe with which the crossing was produced. [...] The immigrant from Russia, Italy, Germany, etc. is making or has made the truthful independence. Within a few years there will be more American children of Russian or Italian descent than the children of Spanish [...]' (1926). Latin America is difference. It is an internal difference (countries, regions, groups, individuals) and an external difference. Latin America remains for the West as a reserve of difference exotic and at the same time 'fantasmatic'. Yet, Latin America makes no promise of either staying or even being 'Latin American'. A 'Latin American' art of Latin America ('the essentially Latin American issues which it raises', as proposed by Oriana Baddeley and Valerie Fraser) is either a European 'fantasmatic' construction or Latin American control. However, Latin American art does not confirm this European notion of history, of the 'realisation of civilisation', which is now Latin America's, and no longer the modern European man (for this thought I'm indebted to Gianni Vattimo). The search for a single Latin America history can lead to fixed anthropological idealisations and also to the obtuseness of exploitation, internal colonialism and class conflicts, ignoring the variety of historical times and cultural perspectives. (See *EVERYTHING.*)

DISORDER. The source of disorder in Brazil could be found in an initial reference to the flag, with its motto 'Order and Progress'. A parallel historical line could be traced with Flávio de Carvalho, Hélio Oiticica and Tunga, representing three different generations. Flávio de Carvalho disrupted the social codes with two performances: a) wearing a hat in a procession (1931) and b) wearing a costume for tropical weather, which included a skirt (1956). He provoked both the religious ideological set of values and the masculine role, thus inflicting disorder in two main codes of social stability.

Hélio Oiticica defined a level of metaphor between values from the art system and challenges to a social order that reflected an authoritarian regime. He dealt with a concept of 'cultural diarrhea'. *Favelados* and samba-school dancers were brought inside the Museum of Modern Art in Rio (1965) as a rupture to the spatial feud of art. In his Bólide *Homenagem a Cara de Cavalo* (1965–66) a transparent pillow of a vivid pure-red pigment becomes a metaphor for the flesh of the bandit as 'live mud', as writer Clarice Lispector named it, for another bandit. Contemporarily, Tunga takes art as a model in crisis. His violent poetics is 'outside of the formalist model', dealing with an *inquiétante étrangeté*. Things play 'between the real and the irreal, the conscious and the unconscious, the rational and the irrational'. (The author is indebted to Catherine David in the development of this entry.)

DUALITY. Where does the Third World end and the First World begin in this world? (Or vice versa.) Is Latin American art in alignment with European and North American art? Or is it the setting of a local tradition? The Shakespearean dilemma evolves to 'Tupi, or not tupi that is the question' (pronounced 'to pe'), where the name of this Native people gives Brazilian poet Oswald de Andrade the possibility of condensing in a synthesis the fundamental doubt of national identity at the crossroad of cultures and historical times. (See *CANNIBALISM.* See also *PERVERSIONS OF HISTORY.*) Tunga's installation *Palindrome Incest* (1990) claims to have the structure of the human mind. 'I'm trying to annul the terms of exterior and interior, of inconsequential and consequential', the artist devises. (See *DISORDER.*)

ESPEJISMO. Spanish term derived from *espejo* (mirror) to describe that tendency in Latin American culture of reflecting foreign dependency or influence, usually from the hegemonic Northern hemisphere countries. Jorge Luis Borges speaks of the 'passive aesthetics' of the mirrors and the active aesthetics of the prism. For a theory of cultural absorption, see *CANNIBALISM.* The trend of 'quotations' in art in the eighties distorts the 'reflecting' character of many artists.

EVERYTHING. 'Everything human is ours', said the Peruvian José Carlos Mariátegui (1926). In the prologue of *The Book of Imaginary Beings*, Borges writes: 'the name of this book would justify the inclusion of Prince Hamlet, the point, the line, the surface, the hyper cube, all generic words and maybe each one of us and the divinity. On the whole, almost all of the universe.' Elsewhere Borges says that 'We may touch all European themes, and to touch them without superstitions [...] I repeat that we should not fear, we should think that the universe is our patrimony and try all themes.' For Borges, Xul Solar lived recreating the Universe. One may now conclude that everything could be a genuine source for art in Latin America, because it has the right to the universe, plus it holds a secret. Borges offers the broadest challenges to the imagination of many artists, be they Argentinians (Kuitca, Porter or Bedel) or non-Latin American (Kosuth). In his Biblioteca de Babel, Borges deals with a library where we may find that everything expressible in any language has been printed. One generation after the other has gone through the library in search of the Book. Some called this library Universe.

EXCLUSION. The writing of art history is an exercise in power of exclusion as well as inclusion. Someday, like the history of the defeated proposed by Walter Benjamin, one should write the history of those excluded from the dominant art history. This would include such artists as Gego in Venezuela, Oiticica, Lygia Clark, Lygia Pape and Amílcar de Castro in Brazil, or some from the Madí group in Argentina.

FOLKLORE. In Latin American Modernism folklore played a major role in the realisation of the national project. In 1920, composer Darius Milhaud advised Brazilian composers of the richness of popular and folkloric sources. Heitor Villa-Lobos and Francisco Mignone researched folklore themes like the Argentinian Alberto Ginastera in his early oeuvre. Tarsila do Amaral has taken the sense of colour in peasant architecture, while Uruguayan Pedro Figari painted the Afro dances of Candombe in his exile. Writers, from Mário de Andrade to Guimarães Rosa listened to the popular voice. Mexican Orozco was critical of certain nationalist relationships between the art of the muralist and folk art: 'Painting in its higher form and painting as a minor folk art differ essentially in this: the former has invariable universal traditions from which no one can separate him ... the latter has purely local traditions.' The recourse to folklore became an easy conservative and reductive cross-cultural experience. Against this impoverishment, Hélio Oiticica would warn that the capes *Parangolés* 'rises up since 1964 against the oppressive folklorisation used the same material which formerly would be folk-Brazil'. Yet, Oiticica never ceased his reference to genuine cultural exchange, as in his transparent Yemanja tent in *Eden* (1968–69), rich in sensual experiences connected to symbolic meanings. On the political level, critic Nelly Richard observed that the artistic action of CADA, the Chilean group Colectivo de Acciones de Arte, and the Avanzada did not seem as threatening to the dictatorial authorities in the Pinochet regime as popular forms of communicating such as theatre and folklore.

FUTURISM. First great door to Modernism in Latin America, perhaps because its direct rhetoric is so clearly connected with the industrialisation and modernisation of society. Chronology: 20 February 1909: Marinetti publishes the 'Futurist Manifesto' (*Le Figaro*, Paris); one month later (26 March) Romulo Duran publishes an interview with him (in *Comœdia* magazine), and later (13 November 1909) an article about this new literacy school in Tegucigalpa, Honduras; less than 45 days after (5 April), Rubén Darío discussed Futurism in Buenos Aires (the poems of Marinetti are 'violent, sonorous and wild') and in the following days Sousa Pinto commented on it in Rio de Janeiro; in August, Mexican Amado Nervo mentions 'the iconoclast vanity' of the new literary school; Henrique Soublette in Venezuela (July 1910) and Chilean poet Vicente Huidobro (1914) discuss Marinetti in their countries. 1921 is a curious year. It witnesses a radical rejection and a fruitful adoption of Futurism in the cultural strategies of Latin America. In May 1921, Borges refers to the passive aesthetics of the mirror and to the active aesthetics of the prism. 'In the present literary renovation, Futurism with its exaltation of the cinematic objectivity of our century, represents the passive, tame tendency of submission to the medium.'

Yet to the art historian Annatereza Fabris, 'Futurism is assumed by Brazilian Modernists in São Paulo as a combat weapon, since 1921, due to the negative charge which it contained.'

GLOSSARY. This glossary comprises a selection of entries and is necessarily incomplete due to the vastness of the object (see *UNIVERSE*) and to the universe of references that one single artist can always involve. A second level of incompleteness is in each entry, quite often vast fields in themselves. Therefore most entries are presented in abridged form or with partial examples. This is either due to space limitations or because most entries indicate the possibility of an issue. Hardly any entry would either exhaust the theme as an absolute source or be universal in Latin America. The internal differences have to be considered at this point, even between areas of a single region. Deep social contradictions in a society of class affect art and the question of its neutrality. There is a plurality of responses besides mere 'engagement'. On the other hand, innumerable sources are neither exclusive to Latin America nor even situated within the continent. There is no purity or impurity in the process of enrichment of experience. Geopoliticising is a 'coarse solution', as alluded by Tunga. However, this historical, political, social and cultural territory, in spite of its moving boundaries (see *LATIN AMERICA*), is a geographical frame of the discussion that is surveyed by History. In technical terms Latin America is a geographic subcontinent of the Western hemisphere, yet it is dealt with here as a cultural continent. Latino-americanidad should not serve the idea of multiculturalism as a policy of compartmentalising the ethnicities, by separating and dividing the one oppressed in relation to the other oppressed, under the same perspective of devaluation. Multiculturalism should be denounced when it imposes opacity over determinant class differences. Cross references serve also to eliminate repetitions. Yet certain fundamental quotations might have been brought in more than one entry, due to the autonomous character of a source. A reiteration of certain paradigmatic names occurs. This is due to the reality that artists, even if not compared, have different qualities and that some are founders of the local tradition of art, or are sustaining positions of radical or unmatched importance. The given examples do not encompass all the possibilities for a certain subject. This glossary was written for the Winnipeg Art Gallery (Canada) in complement to the exhibition 'Cartographies', curated by Ivo Mesquita. However, the text does not discuss exclusively the participating artists in this show. Some widely accepted or known terms, like Futurism, are not explained on the assumption that the public is aware of their meaning. This glossary doesn't intend to be a general theory of the origins of Latin American art. It is intended to address the general public, and less the scholarly or initiated audience. There, the text ends up being a list of the author's doubts. Sometimes the entries are collages or converging positions, or they might be the ongoing building of a problematic issue. The entries are then scattered notes on diverse themes in alphabetical order. The author is deeply indebted to Ivo Mesquita, Jon Tupper and to the Winnipeg Art Gallery. The initial commission of a ten-page paper on the theme of sources of Latin American art evolved into this Glossary as an autonomous publication. The author also wishes to allude to the extreme openness of those individuals in accepting a personal way of writing which allows a level of play and implies, in that confession, deep insufficiency, what Theodor Adorno mentions in his *Minima Moralia* (1951). The author wished a transparent operation with his net of prejudices, intuitions, apprehensions, selfcorrections, anticipations and exaggerations, as Adorno has appended, which are never clear in the process of production of knowledge. The author did not invent the *UNIVERSE* (see entry), therefore many art critics are purposely quoted in order to denote a network of investigative thought around Latin American culture, which is sometimes very controversial. The limited horizons of the author are also dealt with in the entry *BRASIL,* and therefore omissions in examples should not be seen necessarily as discrimination. They conform to the part of the announced incompleteness of this glossary. Counterpoising the numerous mentions of Brazilian artists, the specific entry about Brazil somehow hides the country. An initial limitation results from the fact that it was originally written in English, when Portuguese is the mater language of the author. Hopefully, cataloguing a mutable taxonomy in alphabetical order will not send the reader away, even if it is an incomplete glossary under a double perspective: if it goes halfway in the recognition of a place it will have accomplished an impossibility in the ever-growing world of cultural exchanges. This glossary is an ongoing project. Published here is a selection of existing entries from a list which now comprises over 250 terms. The author hopes to publish an expanded version of this text in the future.

HESSE, EVA. And also Beuys, Serra, Kiefer, Palermo, Andre, Klein, Manzoni, Kounellis, Bacon, Reinhardt, Newman, Tàpies, Johns, Warhol, Stella, Baselitz, Paladino, Cucchi, Haring, de Kooning and many more are just a few of the post-War references. The 'postmodernist' trend of quotation set the artists free regarding ghosts of influences, referents and plagiarism. A world without boundaries, in spite of the challenge of the differentiation within a totalitarian trend, makes no shame in claiming interest in a non-Latin American artist. This means neither a denial of specificities and cultural tradition of its own in Latin America, nor an uncritical approach (to anyone from anywhere). There is hardly any difference between a regionalist purity of sources and an interest in Bataille or Klossowski. In one of his many texts, Hélio Oiticica made an appraisal of references (as precedents, differences, parallelisms) between Brazilians and non-Brazilians regarding 'The Transition from Colour in the Picture to the Space and the Sense of Constructivity' (1960s): Kandinsky, Tatlin, Lissitzky, Malevich, Pevsner, Gabo, Mondrian, Klee, Arp, Taeuber-Arp, Schwitters, Calder, Kupka, Magnelli, Jacobsen, David Smith, Brancusi, Picasso, Braque, Gris, Boccioni, Max Bill, Baumeister, Dorazio, Étienne-Martin, Wols, Pollock, Tinguely, Schöffer, Nevelson, Klein, Barré, Bloc, Slesinska, Pasmore, Herbin, Delaunay, Fontana, Albers, Agam, Tomasello, Kobashi, Lardera, Isobe di Teana, Vassarely, de Kooning, Rothko, Tobey. (See *UNIVERSE*.) A puritanism of Latin American sources finds no support in reality. So they are sources and resources, plus Matisse (with talc). Brazilian Waltercio Caldas proposed an open art book about Matisse with talc spread on top of the images. The apparent constraints to the vision blossom in the problems of perception – that of a lucid and transparent ontology of opacity.

HISTORY OF LATIN AMERICAN ART. In spite of previous denials, from the continent or abroad, the art of Latin America also substantially nourishes itself from the History of Latin America which is a tradition in its own right and can be observed in constructive art. The work of the atelier of Torres-García in Montevideo, Asociación de Arte Constructivo (1934–40), was key to the formation (as voluntary identification) of the Buenos Aires groups and Madí in the 1940s, whose artists exhibited in Rio de Janeiro (1953) and influenced the Brazilian Neoconcretist artists. The Neoconcretist group (Amílcar de Castro, Clark, Pape, Oiticica, Weissmann) is a reference for the artists of the seventies in Brazil (Cildo Meireles, Antonio Manuel, Ivens Machado, Waltercio Caldas, Tunga, Fajardo, José Carvalho, Iole de Freitas) on many levels, such as phenomenology, poetics, aesthetics, philosophy and ethics (and less in formal aspects). Younger artists (Jac Leirner, Fernanda Gomes, Ernesto Neto, Valeska Soares, Frida Baranek) refer to both previous generations as well as to other international art movements. In Brazil, this is a cultural dynamic of transformation of ideas rather than a series of aggressive ruptures.

INDO-IBERIAN AMERICA. A term proposed for Latin America in an editorial of the Mexican magazine *America Indigena* (vol.19, no.2, April 1959): 'The name Latin America can suggest that those who inhabit this great territorial extension are individuals who descend only from the so-called Latin European peoples. [...] We believe in the name Indo-Iberian America, since its inhabitants are descendants both of Indians and of ancestors from the Iberian Peninsula, or rather Spanish and Portuguese.'

INTERNATIONALISM. See *UNIVERSALISM.*

LATINO-AMERICANIDAD. Just to turn into a problematic issue what seems to be a univocal question, we may recall the Brazilian critic Ronaldo Brito who speaks of the nostalgia of a pre-logical phase: 'It is current for example, for Latino-Americanidad ideology to be marked by a desire to return to some pre-Greek period to recover the telluric forces which were crushed by rationalist European colonisation. What can be done with such a simplistic cultural proposal?' (from *Waltercio Caldas, Jr: Aparelhos*, Rio de Janeiro, 1979, p.153).

MANIFESTO. Latin America adopted the European modernist strategy of writing manifestos as tactical declarations of principles against conservative force or opponents, or as an effective social means of circulating ideas. Some hundreds of manifestos in all fields, from art to music, were written on the continent. Manifestos were intended to give 'visibility' to ideas. When art historians take exhibitions and manifestos as the sole or main historical process, they are distorting the cultural dynamics. This unconsciously reflects the Latin American literary tradition in dealing with art. Manifestos are not the absolute source of art and this produces a shadow over isolated artists like the Brazilian Oswaldo Goeldi, certainly the most rigorous Brazilian spirit in modern art from the 1910s until his death in 1962. That distortion by national historians leads to a second wave of opacity with foreign authors quoting the former. They have fallen into the trap of 'manifestism', a new manifest destiny, now in art...

MESSIANISM. Colonisation has transformed Eden into hell (Roger Bastide) and has created the field for the development of several forms of messianism. Messianism was indigenous (studied by Schaden and Metraux), popular (Euclides da Cunha) or European (transposed to America – Bastide). 'Messianism in South America never moved beyond a first draft of nationalism. And has been nothing but a dream for writers in Peru, and for the populace in Brazil', Bastide concludes. However, Bastide did not approach modernist messianism, even if sometimes it was full of irony and influenced by Futurist dreams.

MESTIZAGE. Ecuadorian painter Viteri made a work (collage on wood) called *Mestizage* (1987). His work deals with pre-Columbian colour, fabrics and materials referring to the colonial past. In this work the intricate cultural process of mestizage deals with spaces and openings, light and shadow, in a poetical, 'woven', constructive character. Mestizage, the widespread and complex cross-cultural process, is a major character of Latin American art. In this process of absorption, contribution or invention, the words of Brazilian poet Oswald de Andrade remain a key: 'Absorption of the sacred enemy. To transform him into totem.' The mythological process finds its psychological counterpart in the Freudian theory, giving a symbolic meaning to the dynamic politics of forms and an openness to the introduction of other moral values.

NATIONALISM. See *INTERNATIONALISM*.

NATIVE. The indigenous presence in Latin American art varied thematically in the early European representations, from the idea as a source and contribution to the national identity, to primitivist references, to subjectivity of native self-representation and individual self-expression. Cuba has very little native heritage, since the indigenous population was exterminated in the first decades of colonisation. Also, the mestizage process rendered different approaches to self-identification regarding the ethnic origin. The native gaze has been absorbed throughout Latin America, as in the Andean paintings of the Cuzco, Potosí and Quito schools or in the baroque of the Jesuit missions in Paraguay. Some groups have also shown their distaste for the colonisation of their people, like Guaman Poma de Ayala. The long history of indigenous art has many chapters. In the nineteenth-century Brazilian academy, as commonly as elsewhere, Indians did not correspond to their ethnic group. This anthropological falsehood was reinforced with Catholic morality. Native nudity would appear only in dying Indians and corpses (like in Victor Meirelles's *Moema* of 1866), or in a Christian situation, like *The Last of the Tamoios* (1883) by Rodolfo Amoedo. What was indigenous gained strength in Andean countries and Mexico in the last century. As early as 1855 Peruvian Francisco Laso painted *The Indian Potter*, an individual full of dignity and an inheritor of history. In Mexico, the indigenous was symbolic in nationalism and modernisation. Under the pressures of foreign oppression and exploitation national identity appeared in the last quarter of the nineteenth century in the paintings of José María Obregón, Félix Parra and Leandro Izaguirre (*Torture of Cuauhtémoc*, 1893). The muralist movement brought the indigenous to public spaces, building for Mexico the broadest set of symbolic images, with artists such as Diego Rivera, José Clemente Orozco, Siqueiros, Fernando Leal, Jean Charlot and Francisco Goitia, among others. In European primitivism there was a relatively smaller reference to the indigenous heritage of Latin America, as with Henry Moore. Returning from his long European stay, Torres-García came back to Uruguay in 1934 for his final search for universal symbolism in native culture. Modernism in the region faced the apparent contradiction of looking to the past. This movement sought to regain the identity which had been lost, distorted or constructed in the colonial past. From the Peruvian magazine *Amauta* (1926) by José Carlos Mariátegui ('El titulo no traduce sino nuestra adhesion a la Raza, no reflexa sino nuestro homenaje al Incísmo') to the painting *Abaporu* by Tarsila do Amaral and to the 'Manifesto antropófago' (1928) of Oswald de Andrade (see *CANNIBALISM*) this modernist attitude was widespread in the continent. Some contemporary artists are absorbed by the vast and silent Andean landscape as marked by the pre-Columbian cultures, others with the grief of the Conquest. The aesthetic, which searches for an indigenous metaphysical space is evidenced in the work of Peruvian Alfredo Szyszlos, Colombians Carlos Rojas, Edgar Negret and Ramírez Villamizar, Uruguayan Nelson Ramos, in the books of Argentinian Jacques Bedel and in the photography of Brazilian Sebastião Salgado. More recently some artists such as Cildo Meireles, Claudia Andujar and Bene Fonteles in Brazil and Uruguayan José Gamarra, with his literary historical landscapes aligned their work against the genocide of Indians. In spite of the richness of this theme, historical domination remains as a constraint to the self-expression of Native groups in Latin America. This appears also in the work of Chileans Gonzalo Díaz and Eugenio Dittborn. On the other hand, 'art' as a Western category is foreign to indigenous cultures. Can we call the symbolic artifacts of the ceremonial life of such cultures 'art'? As the German artist Lothar Baumgarten has dealt with in his work, this can touch, as an act of linguistic appropriation, the very first movements of the Conquest: the giving of European names to the geography of the New World.

NATIVE LATIN AMERICANS. They were born in Latin America: Lautréamont (Uruguay) (see *SURREALISM*), Lucio Fontana (Argentina) Öyvind Fahlström (Brazil), Hervé Télémaque (Haiti), Marisol and Meyer Vaisman (Venezuela) and Saint Clair Cemin (Brazil), Matta (Chile) and the Irish potato.

OTHER. 1492 was 'an astonishing revelation of Otherness (people, lands, cultures) beyond the confines of the Old World', wrote Mari Carmen Ramirez. Contemporarily, Heidegger's influence has been the awareness of an 'existence among Others' within the irremediable separation between the I and the Other. Since the early sixties, Brazilian artists developed, as a strategy for dealing with a period of social and political crisis and psychological distress, an art that was an alliance with the Other. For such artists as Lygia Clark, Hélio Oiticica and Cildo Meireles, among others, art would perfect its existence and realise its full potential as a significant period and an irreplaceable experience only through the action of the Other. At the same time, in Buenos Aires, Luis Felipe Noé published his *Antiestetica* (1965). He discusses the making of art in a chaotic reality. Art is then an adventure, involving oneself and the Other. (See *SOCIAL COMMITMENT.*) In the present system of hegemonies, the truth is that the 'Other' is always us, never they, observes Cuban art critic Gerardo Mosquera.

PERVERSIONS OF HISTORY. The first murder of a Native, the first rape, the first descent of an African slave on the continent, the experience of Otherness (see *OTHER*) is found in the perverse face of history. The complex *DUALITY.* Guy Brett has commented on the widespread proposition of 'a Latin American "subject" faced by overwhelming contradictions: on the one hand between experiences of the immensity and richness of nature', and 'on the other hand of its waste and destruction by corrupt administrations (in league with foreign interests, which have been continuously engaged in robbing the continent for more than 400 years)'. (See *UTOPIA.*) In the painting *Filho Bastardo* (*Bastard Child*, 1992) Brazilian Adriana Varejão revisits historical images, like the French painter J.B. Debret, to present perversions in history, such as a negress being raped by a priest, or an Indian woman prisoner approached by a soldier with his phallic weapons. The artist is an agent of history for the politics of gender. Chilean Juan Davila covers the male body with signs, symbols and reminiscences of a perverse personal history. The signs of degradation of the private world are visibly attached to the body like scarifications and perverse decorations.

POSTMODERN. A term coined by Mário Pedrosa in Brazil in 1966 to refer to the end of modern art ('Crise do Condicionamento Artístico', in *Mundo, Homem, Arte em Crise*, São Paulo, 1975, p.92). (See also *CRISIS* and *ROOTS.*)

POSTMODERNISM. The term postmodern had been coined and used in Latin America before the great discussion in Europe and North America (see *POSTMODERN*), however, in the post-modern debate it seems that in Latin America we are only perceiving its arrival, says Néstor García Canclini. Some others point out that the idea of postmodernity is useless in a continent where modernity has neither yet arrived at large nor come for everyone. For Canclini Latin America has a multitemporal heterogeneity, with contradictions between cultural modernism and socio-political modernisation. That temporality involves the indigenous and colonial traditions with modern political, educational and communicational activity. According to Chilean critic Justo Mellado: 'the eighties and the nineties [...] have allowed that the demarxistisation of the artistic discourse be replaced by post-structuralism, i.e. the North-American version of a group of French authors of diverse epistemological precedence, whose introduction to the American editorial space gave place to a heterodox body of discourse which has been called "postmodern theory".'

PRIMITIVISM. The impact of Futurism in Latin America in the first decades of the century was gradually replaced by primitivism as a general trend. Primitivism was closer to the reality of Latin America, more coherent to the impact of the social Darwinism of Spencer than the Futurist ideas of social progress and technology. This 'modernity offered a possibility of a connection with the past and cultural reality of Latin America. Thus, primitivism was not now an approach to the Other, but rather a search for oneself through the national identity.' Furthermore, primitivism was a filter between Latin America and some tribal societies. Tarsila do Amaral's painting *A Negra* (1923) is the major modernist work dealing with Brazilian African heritage. However she found her sources of primitivism in Brancusi's sculpture and Blaise Cendrars' ideas of 'negritude' in a sojourn in Paris that year.

PSYCHOANALYSIS. 'As artistic talent and productive ability are intimately connected with sublimation, we have to admit also that the nature of artistic attainment is psychoanalytically inaccessible to us' (Freud). This entry only makes some cross references between art and psychoanalysis as a source. Briefly applying the meaning of Freud to Surrealism, we may see, as devised by William Rubin in 'the Freud-inspired dialectic of Surrealism': 'what had been a therapy for Freud would become a philosophy and literary point of departure for Breton'. Mexico has been a realm for Surrealist visitors (Breton, Buñuel), immigrants (Wolfgang Paalen from Austria, Leonora Carrington from Britain and César Moro from Peru) and the natives (Manuel Álvarez Bravo, Diego Rivera at a certain moment, Remedios Varo, who was married to French Surrealist poet Benjamin Péret, Agustín Lazo). However Frida Kahlo and Álvarez Bravo did not consider themselves Surrealists. Dislocation has been a territory for the development of the three 'last surrealists' as named by Rubin: the Chilean Roberto Matta, the Cuban Wifredo Lam, with the Afro-Cuban orixas and the Armenian Arshile Gorky. In Brazilian modernism, the surrealist aspect brings a level of both a threshold repulse and a dynamic incorporation of Freudian psychoanalysis: 'Before the Portuguese discovered Brazil, Brazil had discovered happiness' (Oswald de Andrade, 'Manifesto antropófago', 1928). Ideally, in this land the 'beau sauvage' was not reducible to the Freudian theory because their civilisation had not experienced certain conflicts: 'Down with social reality, dressed and oppressive, registered by Freud – reality without complexes, without prostitution and without prisons of the matriarchy of Pindorama', Andrade adduces. (See *CANNIBALISM* and *WOMEN.*) The basic anthropophagous surrealism of Tarsila is a state of vigil, instead of the elsewhere predominant model of the dream. Finally, the major relationship with the theory of Freud is established in the fundamental principle that directs Brazilian culture in this century: the anthropophagous banquet, 'the permanent transformation of taboo into totem' (Oswald de Andrade). For some other reasons, we find a similar denial of Freud's positions for art with Lygia Clark in 1966: 'We refuse the Freudian idea of man conditioned by the unconscious past and we stress the notion of liberty. Contemporary Latin American art, as in other continents, is a broad field caught up with psychoanalysis. Otherwise, the psychoanalytical dimension might be raised within certain discussions of an apparently unrelated source. We should not limit the interest to Freud, since other theorists like Jung and, last but not least, Lacan, have an importance in their own right. The post-Freudian theories find their place among the sources for Latin American art. To exemplify the individual approach, under different circumstances, the 'primal scene' was chosen, as dealt with by

Juan Davila, a Chilean living in Australia, and Julio Galán, a Mexican living in his native Monterrey. This is implied in Galán's paintings like *Mi papas el dia antes que supieran que yo hiber a nacer* (1988). For Davila, the primal scene is dislocated from the narcissistic obsession, and moves toward a collective symbolisation. The primal scene is now History, in the chapter of the Conquest. Davila takes the character of Juanito Laguna, from the series of paintings of the Argentinian Antonio Berni, to create images where the boy is dressed in the make-up of the 'exotic' Latin American style of painting, says Davila with irony. The artist further writes that 'I will cast him in drawings of Balthus, of Wuthering Heights, as Cathy [...] Juanito Laguna as a half-caste, mixed breed, arrives in the 'primal scene of an English novel to enact the return of the outcast' [*sic*]. Some paintings of Galán touch deep levels of the individual topic. He plays with the symbolism of regression to areas of the 'primal scene' and he nods to the 'mirror state' (Lacan), as if the ego searched for the trauma of the constitutive moment. The exploration of these inner regions transfers the psychoanalytical reconstruction of the individual history as a pictorial visibility. Brazilian Lygia Clark's work evolved from an art connected to perception and phenomenology to an actual practice of therapy with 'relational objects', following the theory of Sapir. Such objects are defined in the relationship established with the fantasies of the subject. Prior to this, Clark had ideas of the dissolution of the figure of the artist, when proposing experiences (see *OTHER*), in such works as *Caminhando* (1964) and *Sensorial Gloves* (1968). Finally, in a radical move, she called herself a 'non-artist'.

REGIONALISM. See *CONTINENTALISM.*

RELIGION. The Catholic Church was responsible for the major colonial artistic achievements all over Latin America, such as the temples in Quito, Lima, Ouro Preto, Rio de Janeiro, Salvador, Habana or Mexico. 'The low anthropophagousness in the sins of the catechism, envy, usury, calumny, murder. Plague of the so-called cultured Christianised peoples, it is against it that we are acting' has been ironically stated by Brazilian poet Oswald de Andrade in his 'Manifesto antropófago' (See *CANNIBALISM*). Peruvian José Carlos Mariátegui applied a bruising directness in his appraisal of the Indian problem [*sic*]: 'Today, however, a religious solution is undoubtedly the most obsolete and anti-historical of all.' Religion is critically approached today by such artists as Brazilian Adriana Varejão (the embodiment of suffering) and Peruvian Moico Yaker (the perversion of the Judeo-Christian civilisation). A contemporary position is the approach to Saint Augustine (396–430 AD) to whose philosophical thoughts Brazilians Regina Vater and Tunga refer. Tunga's exhibition, 'Desordres' (Jeu de Paume, 1993) is an installation which makes reference to Saint Augustine 'either in theological discussions with meditation on the investigation of the meaning of words or in a simple anecdote which itself refers to a meditation (about the Holy Trinity)'. '*SER TE AMAVI*' (*Confessions*, Book 10, 27–38) of Augustine is the title of the installation. Tunga uses the anecdote of the angel, the ocean and the 'thimble' as a possibility for discussing the inexorable access to human language, the transcendence which, in said installation, migrates to the aesthetic fact.

ROOTS. For Mário Pedrosa (see *POSTMODERN*) the crisis of Modern Art is in the loss of its cultural roots and its submission to unstable and aleatory patterns, like those dominating the market.

SOCCER. Latin America produces no good art connected to soccer, in spite of winning the world championship seven times: Brazil (3), Argentina (2) and Uruguay (2).

SOCIAL COMMITMENT. It is quite common for the individuality of a Latin American artist to be denied or required to represent some aspect of the region. This happens both in regard to foreign expectations and local demands, to which he/she might be aligned in a 'South American sensibility' (Chantal Pontbriand). Living amidst a hard social reality, and yet in a less individualistic society, Latin American artists in general never believed in the absolute autonomy of art. Historically this belief in the social character of the cultural project has led artists to search for a national identity and to engage social change. Ida Rodríguez Prampolini reached the conclusion that 'since Mexico obtained its independence from Spain in 1821, if any quality has remained around the trajectory of critical and artistic production up to 1950s it is the entailment of art, politics and society'. This commitment has been altered by the historical process. Says Argentinian artist Luis Felipe Noé: 'As a change we are now in a society in which the artist lives with the consciousness of the 'I and the Other', and the world in front', 'I and the Others', 'I and world around mine'. This way he finds himself in adventure, not implicitly in a collective adventure but in wonder. He has the tendency to meet society, however without halting his own mission, his own sense of being.' Brazilian sculptor Carlos Fajardo, with his investigation and invention of the poetic possibilities of materiality, offers a level of sociability that is pertinent to contemporary times. Working within a tradition, the rigorousness of his project and the transparency of his method, Fajardo opens new approaches to knowledge as an experience of clarity. This is the commitment to the Other, in a contemporary social dimension.

SURREALISM. Since the 'Chants of Maldoror' (1868) of Lautréamont a video by the Uruguayan Isidore-Lucien Ducasse (1846–70), the Surrealist process of dissociation was created by 'the chance encounter of a sewing machine and an umbrella on a dissection table'. Quite often Latin America is given as a Surrealist continent, as Mexico has been a haven for the Surrealist exile, 'everyday life in Latin America proves that reality is full of the most extraordinary things', remarked Colombian writer Gabriel García Márquez. Surrealism and other affinities reinforce the idea of unconsciousness and irrationality, sometimes assigned to Latin American culture. When a Brazilian poet declares that 'we had already the surrealist language' in his 'Manifesto antropófago' (1928) (see *CANNIBALISM*), there is an indisputable historical dimension. He was in the process of establishing a national project of culture. Therefore the past and native origin (i.e. the language) had a contemporary meaning (i.e. it was Surrealist, that is to say, it had the character of the then predominant international cultural movement). This is Andrade's dialectical perspective of culture. The Shakespearean dilemma (to be or not to be) would then find a cultural migration in the pun with the Tupi native language (Tupi, or not tupi that is the question).

TRANSLINGUISTIC DETERRITORIALISATION. This glossary has been originally written in English, Portuguese being the mater language of the author. This deterritorialisation is meant to compare to the answer given by the Argentinian artist Miguel Uriburu, when asked by the British customs to spell his last name: 'You are I, be you, are you.' In such babel of otherness and identity, the artist developed his artistic project of dumping green colour in the water of important geographic points (the Hudson River in New York, the Grand Canal in Venice, etc.). Colour was the unifying element derived from visual language in a world of growing internationalism and disrupted by deterritorialisations.

UNIVERSALISM. See *REGIONALISM.*

UNIVERSE. See *EVERYTHING.*

UTOPIA. According to Sir Thomas More, Utopia was very close to South America, just some fifteen miles from its coast. Maybe that is why the Americas have been a fertile field for the projection of utopias. Since 1492, like utopia under a nightmare, the 'beau sauvage' has continuously been faced with and resisted genocide. Since the sixties, Cuba represented a real and possible social utopia for a continent of great inequalities. The Cuban artist Ricardo Brey, living in Belgium, has written about present times: 'I was born in Cuba. That was Utopia. The cathedral too. Now we need to reconsider things. Maybe there's no longer a place for cathedrals.'

WAR. Civil wars, wars among Latin American countries or wars with the Northern Neighbor (with its application of the Monroe Doctrine) are a source of art. This art, in the realm of the expansion of capitalism, is an act of resistance. The craft of the Arpilleras of Chile, under the Pinochet dictatorship (which realigned the country with capitalism) testified for the grief under the political regime. During the Paraguayan War (1865–70, which opened the country to British capital), Brazil, Argentina and Uruguay committed genocide against Paraguay (an estimated killing of 75 per cent of the population), whereas the Paraguayan soldiers resisted by printing newspapers in their camps and illustrating them with caricatures made by woodblock prints. Contemporary Uruguayan artist Luis Camnitzer takes the Mexican American War (1848), through which the United States annexed the present territory of Texas, to deconstruct the opacities of history by building coincidences between historical facts and present-day objects (like a camouflage bag inscribed with Coca-Cola that he bought from a tourist stand at the site of one of the historical events of that war). Argentinian Guillermo Kuitca painted a theatre of individual anguish towards the distant theatre of the absurdities of war.

WATERMELON. The heraldic fruit for Mexico is the watermelon. Quite often it appears as colour intensity, as in the painting of Frida Kahlo and Rufino Tamayo. The painting of Dulce Maria Nunez takes the fruits of the fertility of the land as symbols of a historicity derived from artistic tradition. There are watermelons and pineapples in *Mermaid* (1990), bananas in Dutch Huitzilopochtli or corn, deified by the ancient Natives. The Brazilian poet Murilo Mendes called the open watermelon 'the red bread suspended in front of the mouth of the poor, a spectacle to the stomach, on view'. (See *BANANA*.)

WOMEN. Brazil profited from the most radical (see *ROOTS*) participation of women throughout the twentieth century. The first Brazilian-born artist to have a one-person exhibition of modern art in the country was Anita Malfatti, in 1917. Tarsila do Amaral established the basis for a national modern art that involved local plastic values and a cosmogony where women have expended great energy for the creation of a social place for art. During the Pinochet dictatorship in Chile, Nelly Richard developed a criticism of resistance and a highly complex political analysis of the social inception of artistic language. In this country, women of different generations (Roser Bru, Virginia Errázuriz, Alicia Villarreal, Catalina Parra, Lotty Rosenfeld, Diamela Eltit and Nury González), using poetic strategies of ellipses and metaphor, effected a political project for a cultural life under surveillance. Argentinean critic Marta Traba, active in Colombia, made probably the first major attempt to understand the artistic process of Latin America within a political totality. For younger Colombian generations there is María Fernanda Cardoso and Doris Salcedo, with their perverse disturbance of the systems of objects, from nature to the domestic environment. In Mexico the new fundamentalist tendencies (with Rocio Maldonado, Dulce Maria Nunez, Georgina Quintana, Mónica Castillo and Sylvia Ordóñez, among others) overtly deal with the female presence in art and life, with the tradition of the country and with desire. They repeat the broad presence of the female gaze and imagination, as in the Surrealism of Mexico (Frida Kahlo, Remedios Varo, Leonora Carrington and María Izquierdo) (Abridged.)

WORDS. 'I insistently recommend, in face of the plastic-fact, the verbal vacuum', said Brazilian sculptor Sérgio de Camargo in this continent of the baroque. However, there are several examples in which the dialogue with an art critic has been a decisive element or a contribution to the formation of the art of certain individuals. The crucial moment of Brazilian modernism, 'Antropofagia' (See *CANNIBALISM*) had its starting point in the paintings by Tarsila do Amaral, *Abaporu* and *Antropofagia* (1928), developing its position in the 'Manifesto antropófago' (1928) by writer Oswald de Andrade. The poet Murilo Mendes in Brazil was important to the development of the work of Ismael Nery. Marta Traba said that in many cases 'The only failure of the sorcerers is that they were not perfectly followed in the rituals by officiating aids comparable to Paz for Tamayo, and later for Cuevas, or to Fuentes for Cuevas.' In Brazil Mário Pedrosa established ethical standards through in-depth dialogue with the art system. Neoconcretism in Rio de Janeiro, and Lygia Clark among the artists of the group, are very much indebted to the poet Ferreira Gullar for the organisation of their thought. Since the early 1970s, Ronaldo Brito in Rio de Janeiro has exchanged ideas and worked very closely with Sérgio de Camargo, Tunga, Eduardo Sued and Waltercio Caldas. Tunga has written that, 'More important though, is the presence of Raymond Roussel or Edgar Poe among many others. However, Lezama Lima and Godofredo Iommi as poets or 'theorists' are still found in the fundamentals of the work.' To this list Bataille and Nerval could be added. Romero Brest opened the space for free experiment in Argentina for decades, in a position in many ways similar to Pedrosa. In Peru, the critic Emilio Westphalen gave his support to the indigenous themes of painter Fernando de Szyszlo. Marta Traba identified with some painting and literature, such as Guayasamín and *Huasipungo* respectively in Ecuador, Szyszlo and Vallejo in Peru. In Colombia she compared Garcia Marquez to Alejandro Obregón (in the atemporality of the plot) and Fernando Botero (the treatment of 'normality' that is given to verisimilitude). Poetry and art were interwoven in Brazil with Poesia Concreta (Décio Pignatari, Haroldo and Augusto de Campos), with Concretism (Waldemar Cordeiro, Geraldo de Barros and others), as well as with collaborative works by Hélio Oiticica, Julio Plaza and others. Poet Raúl Zurita integrates the multidisciplinary Chilean group CADA. For Borges, after his father, Alejandro Xul Solar was the most persistent person in his memory: 'Xul has lived recreating the universe'.

Reporting from São Paulo, I'm from the United States: Five Broadcasts on the 24th Bienal de São Paulo — Andrea Fraser

In 1998, Ivo Mesquita invited me to participate in the North American section of the 24th Bienal de São Paulo, which he curated. This text is a transcript of my project for the Bienal, a series of short videotapes produced in São Paulo and edited in New York between September and December 1998. The videotapes, comprised of interviews and commentary recorded on location, were co-produced by the Fundação Bienal de São Paulo and TV Cultura, a cultural station supported by a private foundation, and were supposed to be televised nationally in Brazil by TV Cultura. Due to a number of adverse circumstances, many of which are represented on the tapes themselves, as well as scheduling conflicts created first by national elections and then by the Free Jazz Festival, shooting was not completed until three weeks after the exhibition opened and editing continued until three days before the show closed. The tapes were never broadcast.

—

1. 'The only things that interest me are those which are not mine.'[1]

> [*The opening of the 24th Bienal de São Paulo, 2 October 1998. A series of shots show the well-dressed crowd at the invitation-only pre-opening cocktail party.*]

Andrea Fraser [*voice-over*]: *Boa noite.* The 24th Bienal de São Paulo opens this evening with a private gala event at the Ciccillo Matarazzo Pavilion, in São Paulo's Parque Ibirapuera. Among the hundreds of cultural luminaries visiting from all over the world is the US artist Andrea Fraser.

> [*Cut to Andrea*[2] *standing on the central ramp of the Matarazzo Pavilion, designed by Oscar Niemeyer, with the atrium behind her. Throughout the broadcasts she is wearing the same black dress and jacket and holding a microphone bearing the TV Cultura logo.*]

AF: Andrea's project is to produce news reports about the Bienal for TV Cultura. [*Andrea turns to address an interviewee off-camera to her right.*] Andrea, what led you to select reportage as your medium for the Bienal?

> [*Cut to counter-shot of Andrea, now standing to the right.*]

—

[1] All of the segment titles, including this sentence, are quoted from Oswald de Andrade's 'Manifesto antropófago' ('Anthropophagite Manifesto'), originally published in *Revista de Antropophagia*, May 1928, São Paulo. [Editors' Note: For Andrade's 'Manifesto', see this volume, pp.222–29.]

[2] My use of first names in these shot descriptions follows the convention of the Brazilian media, where even the president is referred to by her first name.

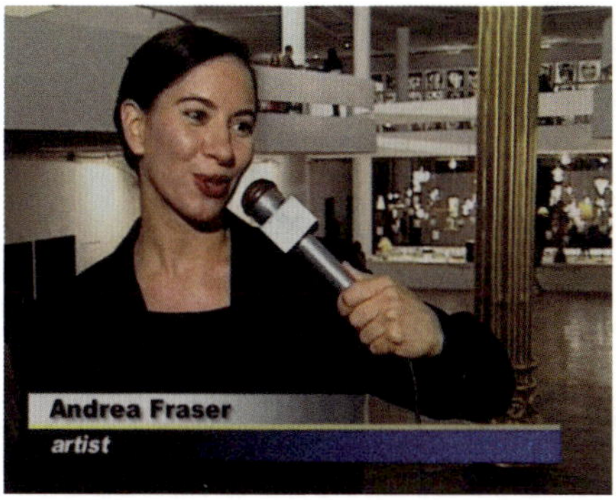

Andrea Fraser, *Reporting from São Paulo, I'm from the United States*, 1998, five-channel video installation, colour, sound; and single-channel video, colour, sound, 24min, video stills

AF: In Europe and the US I'd never be able to work on TV, so it's a great opportunity.

> [*Andrea walks back to her first position, speaks to her right, then smiles.*]

AF: That's great.

> [*Two-second freeze-frame. Cut to Andrea on the top floor of the Pavilhaõ Matarazzo (Matarazzo Pavilion), with Choi Jeong Hwa's* Encore, Encore, Encore *(1997), an inflatable column with an angel on top, all in gold, flapping its wings in the background.*] fig.10, 27 and 40

AF: The Bienal has always been about fostering international exchange. This year's instalment attempts to thematise that process by focusing on the concept of cannibalism. According to the organisers, cannibalism is not a diet, but a metaphor for our relationship to others [*cut to wide shot of ground floor from the central ramp*]: to differences of culture, identity and status [*cut to a large group of young women, all wearing black dresses and jackets, walking down the ramp*]. Anthropophagy is a process of confiscating another's values to construct one's own [*cut to the group of women in black in a reception area with Bienal logo in background; Andrea walks into the frame*], of legitimising oneself in relation to [*cut back to Andrea on the top floor*] – or opposition to – what is given as legitimate in society.[3]

—

[3] This interpretation of cannibalism was offered by Mari Carmen Ramírez in her press release for the exhibition of works by David Alfaro Siqueiros that she curated for the Bienal. Ramírez has elsewhere written: 'The efforts undertaken in the last decade to integrate Latin American countries into the dynamics of a new world order have necessitated the exchange of cultural capital for access to financial and economic privileges. One of the unacknowledged forms in which this exchange has taken place has been through art exhibitions.' Further on in the same essay, she notes: 'Whereas, in the past, the visual arts functioned as banners of prestige for nationalist states, today they can be seen to embody a type of marketing tool for Latin American neo-liberal economic elites. [...] The erasure of the conflict-ridden sixties and seventies from the ensuing mainstream account of Latin American art can only suggest two

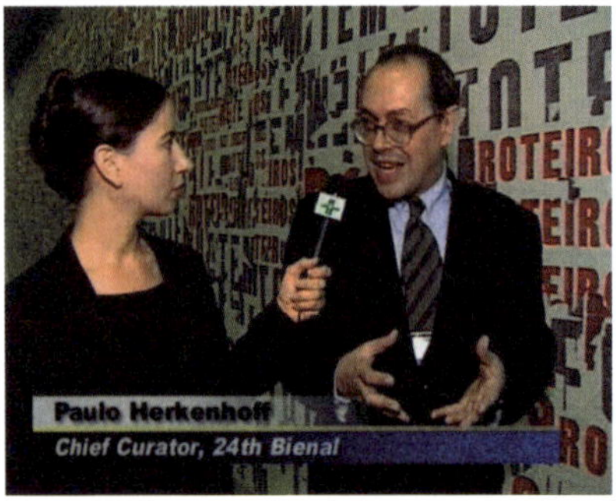

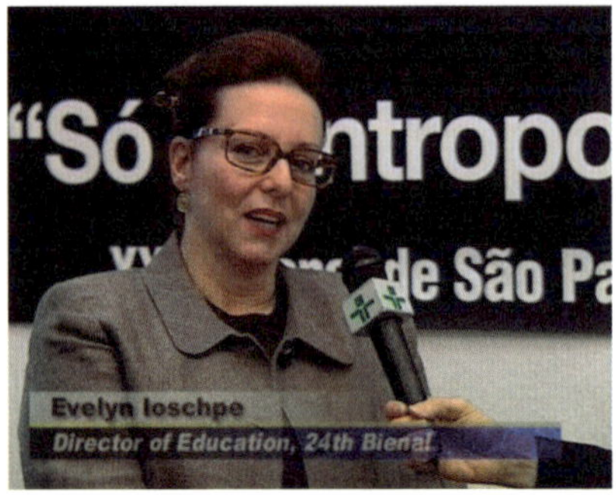

[Cut to interview with Paulo Herkenhoff, Chief Curator of the 24th Bienal. Andrea and Paulo are seen walking along an enormous wall plastered with fragments of the words 'totem', 'taboo' and 'roteiros'.]

Paulo Herkenhoff: Every cannibalistic act, every anthropophagic act, is a symbolic act. That means, eating the other in order to get the force of the other, the values of the other, into yourself.

fig.94-95 *[Cut to Andrea in front of* Tropicália Penetráveis *(1967) by Hélio Oiticica, an installation of fabric-walled huts and tropical plants on gravel and sand. One of the huts contains a television set.]*

AF: Among the hundreds of interpretations of cannibalism offered by the organisers of the 24th Bienal is of anthropophagy as a strategy of emancipation *from* a colonial past – or within a *neo*-colonial present.

[Cut to interview with Evelyn Ioschpe, Director of Art Education for the 24th Bienal. Andrea and Evelyn are seen in the Bienal offices, seated in front of a large poster with one of the Bienal's slogans: 'Only anthropophagy unites us.']

Evelyn Ioschpe: This is a perfect moment to think about this: how we – all the colonised countries – have to deal with the anthropophagy of ideas; how you as a being deal with a culture when you feel that your culture is somehow a dependent culture.

[Cut to Andrea in front of Tropicália Penetráveis. *Shortly after she begins speaking camera pans right, past the installation and around the central*

—

things: first, the neo-liberal elites' search for legitimation of their origins in an essentialist, ultimately reductive, account of the cultural achievements of the twenties and thirties; second, the recognition of the positive achievements of their modernisation project.' M.C. Ramírez, 'Brokering Identities: Art Curators and the Politics of Cultural Representation', in Reesa Greenberg, Bruce W. Furguson and Sandy Nairne (ed.), *Thinking about Exhibitions,* New York: Routledge, 1993, pp.25 and 30–31.

gallery of the 'Modernismo Brasileiro' section of the exhibition, showing its visitors and guards.]

AF: It was Fernando Henrique Cardoso who first described neo-colonialism as resulting from an internalisation of external interests and values. According to Fernando Henrique, external interests are represented and enforced internally by local elites who identify foreign values as their own. This process of internalisation led internationalised elites in peripheral countries to adopt models of development based on the consumption patterns and lifestyles of central capitalist economies.[4]

[*Cut to a photograph of Francisco 'Ciccillo' Matarazzo Sobrinho at the entrance of the Bienal offices. Camera pans left and travels down corridor to the Bienal logo. Andrea can be seen walking through frame towards camera.*]

AF [*voice-over*]: The history of the Bienal itself reveals a process of anthropophagy. Founded by the Italian-born industrialist Francisco 'Ciccillo' Matarazzo in 1951, the Bienal de São Paulo was inspired by such influences as the Venice Biennale and the Museum of Modern Art in New York.[5]

[*Cut to interview with Paulo.*]

PH: The country came out of the war with an economic surplus in the balance of payments. Of course, there was a bourgeoisie that was willing to act in a modern way.[6]

—

[4] Fernando Henrique Cardoso and Enzo Faletto, *Dependency and Development in Latin America* (trans. Marjory Mattingly Urquidi), Berkeley: University of California Press, 1979. In 'The Consumption of Dependency Theory in the United States' (*Latin American Research Review*, vol.XII, no.3, 1977, p.13) Cardoso summarised the position of 'dependentistas' as follows: 'If imperialism was embodied in the penetration of foreign capital ... it also implied a structural pattern of relations that "internalised" the external and created a state which was formally sovereign and ready to be an answer to the interests of the "nation", but which was simultaneously and contradictorily the instrument of international economic domination.' In this way 'alliances are established *within the country*, even though in contradictory form, to unify external interests with those of the local dominant groups' and, as a result, 'the local dominated classes suffer a kind of double exploitation'.

[5] Another influence was clearly Nelson Rockefeller, president of MoMA and a friend of Matarazzo. The first paragraph of a 1951 letter co-signed by Rockefeller and Matarazzo reads: 'Realising the great need for increased understanding in the field of international relations, the Museum of Modern Art and the Museu de Arte Moderna de São Paulo last October entered into an agreement to cooperate with each other in every way possible. The purpose of this agreement is to supplement the existing cooperation in the sphere of economics and politics with cultural interchange.' Letter from Francisco Matarazzo Sobrinho and Nelson A. Rockefeller to Albert V. Moore, 8 March 1951, Fundação Bienal Archive. However, after a few years of close cooperation between the Bienal – then a programme of the Museu de Arte Moderna – and MoMA in New York, Matarazzo caused a split by refusing to hire a curator recommended by Rockefeller.

[6] Herkenhoff went on to say: 'Of course, there were some models, like the Museum of Modern Art in New York, for these institutions, or the Biennale in

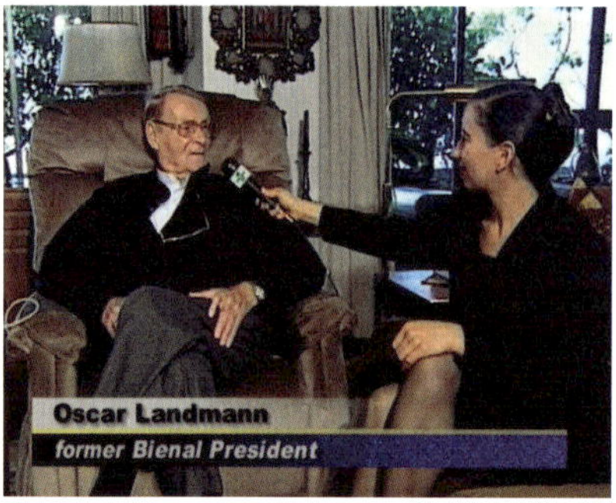

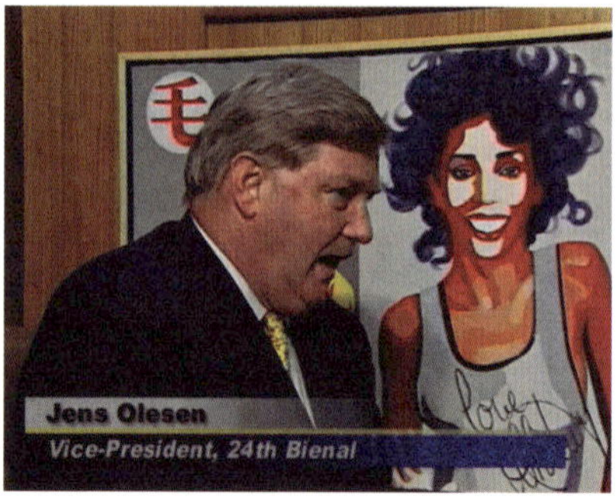

> [*Cut to interview with Oscar Landmann, the first President of the Bienal following* Ciccillo's *death and the father of the 24th Bienal's President, Julio Landmann.*]

AF: Tell me about Ciccillo. What kind of person was he?

Oscar Landmann: He was a total dictator, I would say.

> [*Cut to interview with Paulo.*]

PH: I think the Bienal educates, in a way, the bourgeoisie, and now the enterprises. No? Transforming financial capital into symbolic capital.

> [*Cut to VIPs leaving the pre-opening cocktail party in the Bienal offices. The photograph of Ciccillo can be seen in the background.*]

AF [*voice-over*]: While ranked 'tops in prestige' in its early years, the military dictatorship and the 'lost decade' of the 1980s led to a decline which the Bienal only recently began to reverse.[7]

—

Venice, but I think that with its half-century of history the Bienal has developed a history of its own. In the beginning it was a place where the country could see what was going on around the world – let's say to update itself – but nowadays it's more a place of discussion where also the world can see what [is going on in Brazil]. It has formed an audience. It has formed many artists.'

[7] In his 1967 review of the 9th edition, Hilton Kramer first blamed this 'decline' on the influence of the Bienal itself: 'Brazilians are just catching up on the impact of the last exhibition when the new one wipes the slate clean again and imposes new influences, new conceptions and new fashions. ... What one finds very, very little of is art of an authentic personal vision or cogency. One sees only synthetic ill-digested ideas often executed with a startling vulgarity and ineptitude.' Kramer then provides a stunning example of this 'influence' in action: 'It happens that the American exhibition here, called "Environment U.S.A: 1957–1967", a spectacular survey of Pop art spectacularly installed, is the smash hit of the Bienal, and in the reaction of visiting officials and artists one can see that mixture of envy, admiration, fear and outright hatred that has its political analogy the world over.' H. Kramer,

[*Cut to an interview with Jens Olesen, Vice-President of the 24th Bienal as well as President for Latin America of the advertising firm McCann Erickson. Andrea and Jens are seen seated in his office. Behind Andrea is a large yellow lithograph of Marilyn Monroe. Behind Jens is a painting depicting Mao Tse-tung and Whitney Houston.*]

AF: Jens, how long have you been involved with the Bienal de São Paulo?

Jens Olesen: I've actually been involved for the last seven years. For the 22nd Bienal I was invited to come in as the National Director and try to regain some of the prestige and respect of the Bienal in the world, to bring big names for special exhibitions, to get the big public to come, because the Bienals in the past had gotten to a level that I don't think was too satisfactory. They were not international Bienals on the highest levels. And it's not enough to have a Brazilian or Latin American Bienal. You have to have a worldwide international Bienal.[8]

[*Cut to camera following Andrea as she walks through a service corridor, past surprised service staff and cleaning supplies, into exhibition galleries, merging with the opening crowd. Cut back to interview with Jens.*]

JO: I would say overall that the Bienal is a very professional, disciplined organisation that is as good as any other international organisation in the world [*cut to a series of images of people at the opening*]. This has happened over the last six years, where now that, in terms of security, in terms of having a [*cut to a series of images of guards at the opening, ending with a caterer shutting a door on the camera*] museum that has temperature and humidity controls, and security...

[*Cut to Andrea on ground floor of the Pavilhão Matarazzo. Behind her, people and press crowd into the area where opening speeches are being delivered by various officials. Andrea addresses an interviewee off-camera to her right.*]

AF: Are you enjoying the opening this evening?

[*She steps to her right and passes the microphone to her left hand.*]

AF: Well, it's great to be surrounded by the most important people in Brazil. It's great to have the attention of the media. It's great to see people here

—

'Art and Politics in São Paulo', *The New York Times*, 24 September 1967.

[8] Roberta Smith's 1994 review of the 22nd edition continues in the same vein with remarkable seamlessness: 'Does this hodgepodge of weak art and mixed messages want to be, like its European counterparts, a survey of the artistic mainstream ... ? Does it want to redefine the megashow concept into something more egalitarian and genuinely international? Or does it want to remain the amateurish exercise in nationalism and regionalism that is had tended to be in recent years?' R. Smith, 'Signs to a Global Village in Progress', *The New York Times*, 30 November 1994.

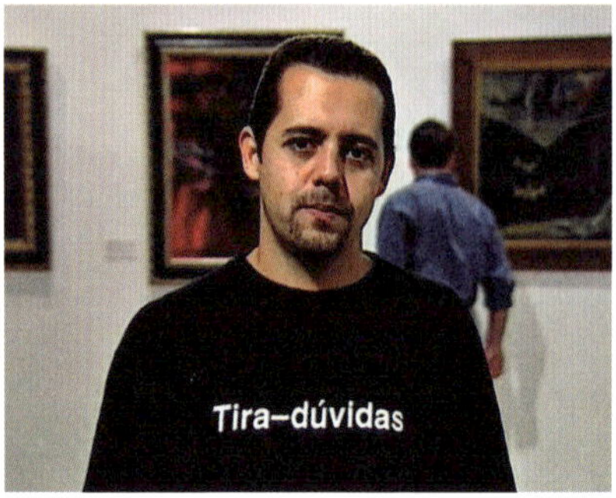

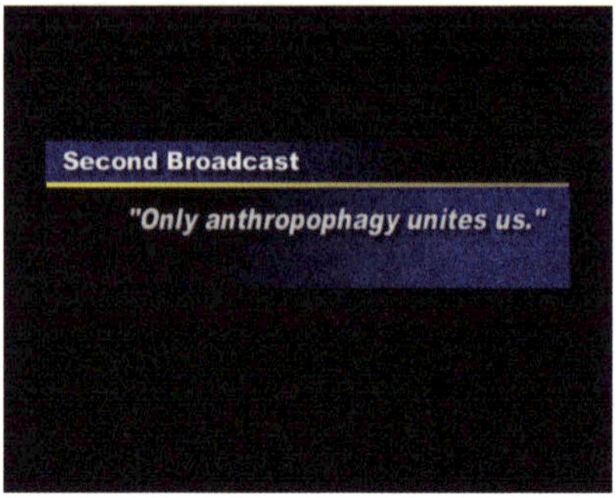

I know from all over the world. I feel like I'm who I'm supposed to be, where I'm supposed to be. I feel justified in being what I am.

[*She steps to her left and passes microphone to her right hand.*]

AF: That's great. That must be very satisfying. I envy you.

—

2. 'Only anthropophagy unites us.'

[*Cut to Andrea on the ground floor of the Pavilhão Matarazzo. The opening crowd can be seen walking towards the camera from behind her.*]

AF: This Bienal understands education as its major responsibility. Education is understood as the formation of new audiences and the integration of culture into society as well as work with schools, libraries and public networks.

[*Cut to pan of a school group walking through the pavilion's atrium, then to another school group walking towards the camera at the entrance to the Bienal.*]

AF [*voice-over*]: Half a million visitors are expected at the 24th Bienal. 40 per cent of these will be visiting an art exhibition for the first time.

[*Cut to interview with Evelyn; counter-shot of Andrea.*]

AF: What kind of experience is that, that first encounter with art?

EI: It's always a very odd experience, that people would come for the first time, and somehow I think that they're not conquered by what they see.

[*Cut to a member Bienal's education staff looking blankly at camera. He is wearing the official education staff T-shirt with the words 'Tira-duvidas' (Strip of Doubt). Cut to interview with Paulo.*]

PH: The conquering of souls for Christianity was like cannibalism: you should have this drive to devour the other into your own ideas. Of course, this is a notion from Christianity in the seventeenth century, but what I think is very interesting – that is being developed now, here, at the Bienal – is that in the 'Manifesto antropófago' there is a moment in which it says 'Only anthropophagy unites us.' It says, we need the other, the values of the other, to mingle, to mediate, to absorb. But also the manifesto says 'I am interested only in what is not mine.'

[*Cut to interview with Evelyn.*]

EI: All I'm interested in is what is not mine. That's what the Anthropophagic movement tells us. So that is what we are exploring with the teachers.

AF: To try to encourage them to look at art that way?

EI: Yes, and not… Without any bias.

[*Cut to counter-shot of Andrea, looking at the shoes, hair, etc., of interviewee.*]

EI [*voice-over*]*:* In a country as Brazil, where you have an economic gap – meaning also an educational gap [*cut back to Evelyn*] – when you're dealing with art education, you're dealing with literacy, you're dealing with all other subjects, which means social inclusion. [*Cut to counter-shot with the producer of the programme, a young black woman, sitting in as interviewer, listening.*] If you have an educated people, you will have people who fight for their rights, you will have the land reform [*cut back to Evelyn*], you will have a situation which is decent for all people.

[*Cut to interview with Paulo.*]

PH: It's about developing, let's say, a critical citizenship.

[*Cut to interview with Brazilian Minister of Culture, Francisco Weffort. Andrea and Francisco are seen standing at the pre-opening cocktail party, with a poster for the first Bienal in the background.*]

Francisco Weffort: For us Brazilians, the development of culture is among the duties of the state, as well as education, for example.

[*Cut to school group walking past the Bienal gift shop.*]

AF [*voice-over*]: The Bienal is now seen as a major educational tool in the efforts of the city, state and federal governments to improve the quality of life for all of Brazil's citizens.

[*Cut to interview with Francisco.*]

AF: How do you weigh support for traditionally 'elite' culture, like exhibitions of contemporary art, against support for more popular cultural forms?

FW: No, we don't have this kind of dilemma, the dilemma among cultural popular sectors and visual arts for elite people. [*Cut to a billboard outside of*
fig.2-3 *the pavilion with the slogan 'Only anthropophagy unites us.'*] A lot of these people are poor people of popular classes [*cut to T-shirts and tote bags in the gift shop with the slogan 'I'm only interested in what is not mine'*] and working classes in Brazil. So even if, even if the criteria is the criteria of elites [*cut back to interview*] this is a thing very open to the public.

> [*Cut to ticket booths outside of the Bienal, with the entrance turnstiles in the background. At the bottom of the screen, a title reads: 'Source: TV Cultura news report, October 4, 1998'.*]

AF: Brazilians always like to do things at the last minute. This saying is demonstrated again at this school where you can see long lines just a short while before the close of the polls. Elsewhere in the city today, an almost festive atmosphere prevailed as Brazilians from all social groups and walks of life went to the polls to exercise the democratic right – and legal obligation – to cast their votes on this election day [*Andrea turns to an off-camera interviewee to her left*]. And why did you come to vote so late today? [9]

—

—

[9] From a TV Cultura report broadcast on the programme *National*, October 1998. General elections, including presidential elections, were held throughout Brazil on the day after the opening of the 24th Bienal. Voting has been mandatory in Brazil since the country's transition from military dictatorship. In a splendid example of how a conservative press directly influences electoral politics, *O Globo* and other right-wing media consistently reported opinion polls showing the Workers' Party candidate for governor of São Paulo, Marta Suplicy, trailing a distant fourth, with Paulo Maluf, a notoriously corrupt former governor, on top. Returns, however, placed Suplicy a tenth of a percentage point behind second place, and thus shut out of second-round voting, leading many to assume that if voters had not been led to cast their ballots for the candidate they considered best placed to beat Maluf, Suplicy might have won. Instances of skewed opinion polls may have also influenced voting for governors in two other states. In addition, *O Globo* may have broken the law by releasing opinion polls predicting Cardoso's victory before polls closed on the day of elections. See Paula Schmitt in the English-language internet report 'Brazil this Week', 7 to 13 October 1998, *Net Estado*. In the week before elections, 23 to 29 September 1998, 'Brazil this Week' asked: 'Are you reading anything about [Brazil's] current crisis? About our debts and the IMF's demands? Are you seeing that on TV? We are not. (But whoever read the British *Daily Telegraph* the past week got to know that the media is hiding the economic crisis.) We also have not been informed about the pantheon of artists and intellectuals who published a manifesto in favour of Lula (Workers' Party), the opposition candidate. Among Lula's supporters are singer and composer Chico Buarque, architect Oscar Niemeyer, prominent philosophers, sociologists, economists and even important businessmen. From the media, just oblivion.'

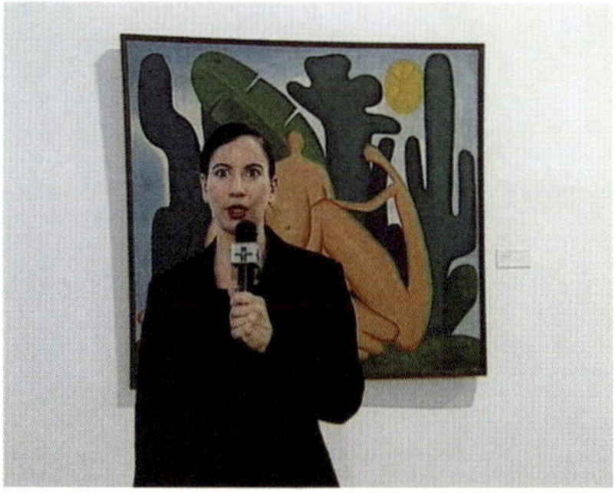 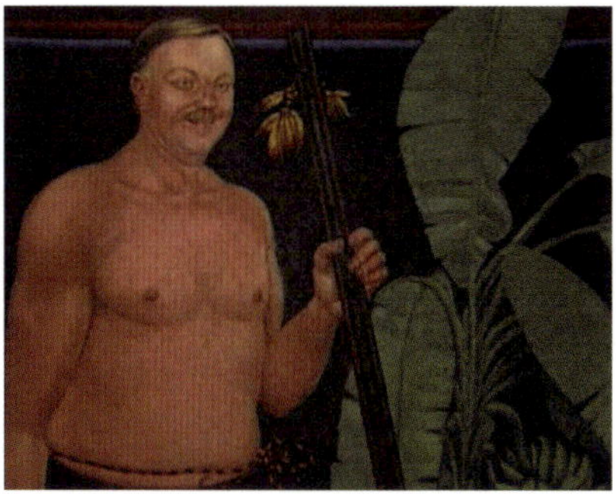

3. 'Tupy or not Tupy…'

[*The 24th Bienal's 'Núcleo Histórico' section on the top floor of the Pavilhão Matarazzo. Andrea is standing in front of Tarsila do Amaral's painting* Antropofagia *(1929).*]

AF: In what organisers describe as a political project, the 24th Bienal is the first edition in the exhibition's almost fifty years of existence to propose Brazilian culture as its starting point.

[*Cut to an interview with Julio Landmann, President of the 24th Bienal. Andrea and Julio are seen seated in the Bienal's press room. The wall in the background is painted with an image of the pavilion's central atrium and the words 'XXIV Bienal de São Paulo'.*]

Julio Landmann: I want to make a Bienal which, for the first time, explores a Brazilian concept.

[*Cut to interview with Paulo.*]

PH: In Brazil, *antropofagia* is very much concerned with our historical culture, the idea that we are formed by several cultures – the native, the European, the Afro-Brazilian – and among those cultures there was one that had the symbolic practice of cannibalism.

[*Cut to Andrea standing in front of four portraits by Albert Eckhout in the Bienal's 'Núcleo Histórico' section:* Mameluke, Tupi Woman, African Woman *and* Tarairiu Indian Woman *(all 1641).*] fig.52–53

AF: Anthropophagy is an ironic and irreverent interpretation of how foreign influences are incorporated into a native 'body'. Brazilian cultural identity has been described as the product of the aggressive, sometimes amorous encounter of Europeans, Indians and Africans, which fed on each other to produce a new being.

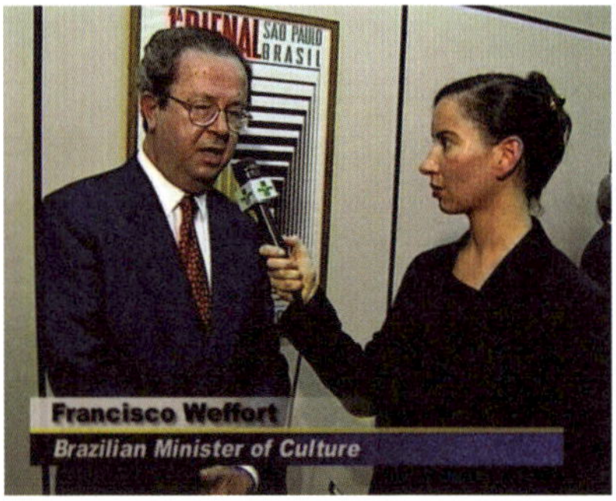

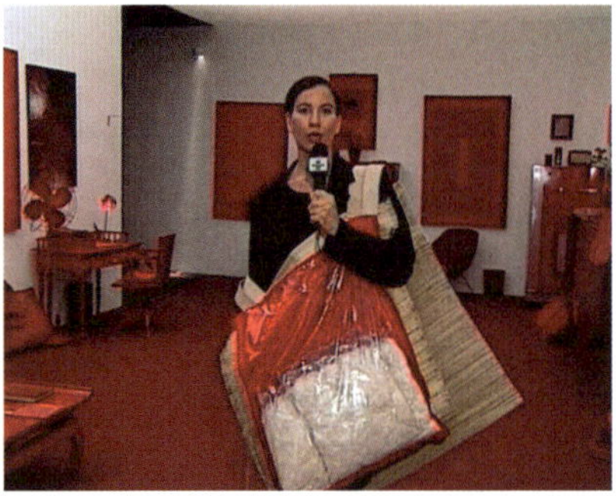

[*Cut to a wide shot of the portraits, then a series of pans up each one.*]

JO [*voice-over*]: I came to Brazil like everyone else. In the beginning, I had a very rough time, a difficult time, and then I got married to a Brazilian and I got Brazilian children. [*Cut to interview with Jens.*] Then I always loved the country, because the people, the Brazilian people, have some qualities. [*Cut to pan down a painting – after Albert Eckhout – in Jens' office of the interviewee dressed as an Indian.*] First of all they're very open, they're nice, they have no prejudices on a big scale, they're very musical, they love the outdoor life, they play good football, at least until now.[10] [*Cut to back to interview with Jens, in close-up, looking at the camera*] Brazil has… It's not a country. It's a continent.

[*Cut back to Andrea standing in front of* Antropofagia.]

AF: Anthropophagy rejects the notion of national culture, claiming instead that cultural identity is a buffet of diverse influences. But that hasn't prevented a broad range of national public figures from making it their own.

fig.87 and 96–97

[*Cut to series of shots of Cildo Meireles's* Desvio para o vermelho (Red Shift, *1967–84*). Desvio para o vermelho, *a living room furnished entirely in red with a faucet continuously pouring red liquid into a sink, was produced in response to the murder of a journalist by the military during Brazil's military dictatorship.*]

AF [*voice-over*]: According to Minister of Culture Francisco Weffort, 'Anthropophagy signifies our capacity for synchrony, openness and tolerance, therefore something intrinsically democratic in our cultural process.'[11] And, Fernando

—

[10] From the interview with Evelyn Ioschpe: 'There is a somewhat folkloric image of Brazil: carnival, soccer and popular culture. That is Brazil, but there is something else also in Brazil. There is an elite thinking [in] the country and a creating of new forms and new thoughts. So, I think those who [come to the Bienal] and the information which might get out to the world is very important. This is the Brazil that the world doesn't know.'

[11] From a speech by Francisco Weffort at a press conference for the 24th Bienal,

Henrique has said that despite the 'cultural fusion of Portuguese with African and Amerindian traditions...'

> [*Cut to Andrea standing in front of* Desvio para o vermelho *wearing a mostly red* Parangolé *by Hélio Oiticica.*]

AF: '...we Brazilians are an extremely homogenous people in cultural terms. Our regional differences are mere variations on a basic theme.'[12]

—

4. 'Against all importers of canned consciousness.'

> [*The entrance area of 24th Bienal, where Andrea is standing just inside the turnstiles. In the background, a crowd of people wait to pick up film at a Kodak booth.*]

fig.6

AF: Of the 24th Bienal's twelve-million-dollar budget,[13] approximately one third comes from private sponsors, with the remaining two thirds divided between public sources and earned income. In addition to the usual display of sponsors' logos and the privilege of throwing private parties at the Bienal, this year corporate patrons have been provided with their own spaces to display products and services: [*gesturing*] they're conveniently located in the entrance corridor, next to the education and security centres.

> [*Cut to interview with Jens.*]

JO: If you don't have sponsors, you don't have a Bienal, so therefore, you have to have sponsors. And that was a big job that we tried to do: to try to get the major Brazilian and international corporations to find out that it's worthwhile investing in art, and to invest in art is not only good business, it's good for *their* business... [*Cut to wall of names of sponsors at the top of the exterior entrance ramp.*] We let the sponsors sponsor an artist and exhibition [*cut to Kodak booth*]: a van Gogh [*cut to* Folha *booth*], or a Matisse [*cut to* Gazeta *booth*], or a Bacon [*cut to Sudameris booth*], or Giacometti [*cut to first aid booth*], or CoBrA [*cut back to interview*] or Eckhout. Just by doing that, we told them about the particular exhibitions, and then they got interested in the artist as someone who had relevance to their business. fig.6

> [*Cut to wide shot of Albert Eckhout's four portraits, then one detail of each, including a shot of body parts sticking out of a basket.*] fig.52–53

AF [*voice-over*]: Albert Eckhout is sponsored by ABN AMRO, a prominent universal banking group with a strong international focus and a worldwide network of branches and subsidiaries. Its corporate culture is based on the

—

broadcast by TV Cultura on the programme *Metropolis*, March 1998.

[12] F.H. Cardoso, inaugural speech, Brasília, January 1995.

[13] Editors' Note: A total budget of fifteen million real was reported at the time of opening, equivalent to the same amount in US dollars at the time.

four values of integrity, teamwork, respect and professionalism.[14] [*Cut to images of works in 'Núcleo Histórico': details of two etchings by Theodore de Bry depicting cannibalism from his* America *series (1592) and the painting* América *(artist unknown, c.1650), also depicting cannibalism.*] Siemens has sponsored the exhibition of art from the sixteenth to eighteenth centuries. Over the past 150 years, Siemens has grown to become one of the largest electrical engineering and electronics companies in the world. With increasing globalisation, Siemens is represented worldwide by production sites and sales organisations in over 190 countries. At Siemens, the customer always comes first.[15] [*Cut to wider shot of* América, *with a woman and child leaning in to read the wall label.*]

fig.56

[*Cut to interview with Paulo.*]

PH: We say that capitalism is savage in a country like Brazil, in the third world. So a savage capitalism can sometimes correspond to a savage sponsorship, a savage marketing. I'm not saying that this is the case with the Bienal...

[*Cut to interview with Francisco.*]

AF: Do you see corporate sponsorship of art as a necessary evil or as a positive development in itself?

FW: No, I would say that it is a positive development.

[*Cut to counter-shot with Andrea standing in front of the Banco Bradesco booth in the entrance corridor of the Bienal. A translation of a sign in the background appears at the bottom of the screen: 'Reception area for exclusive use by clients of Bradesco Bank.'*]

AF: And how will corporate sponsorship affect the kind of culture that's supported?

FW: We don't have any problem of private enterprise influence on the character of visual art. But we have, on the contrary, the chance, the opportunity, for arts to have an influence on the life of private enterprise.

[*Cut to interview with Jens.*]

AF: One of the sponsors you've been dealing with for the Bienal is Coca-Cola. Can you tell me how sponsorship fits into their marketing strategy for Brazil or for Latin America?

JO: Coca-Cola is a product which is sold to the young generation, is a product that is very much associated with art. I mean, a man like Andy Warhol

---

[14] ABN AMRO, annual report, 1997. ABN AMRO has been pursuing a particularly aggressive strategy of acquisitions in Latin America. In September 1998, for example, ABN AMRO acquired a partial stake in the Brazilian Banco Real.
[15] Siemens, annual report, 1998.

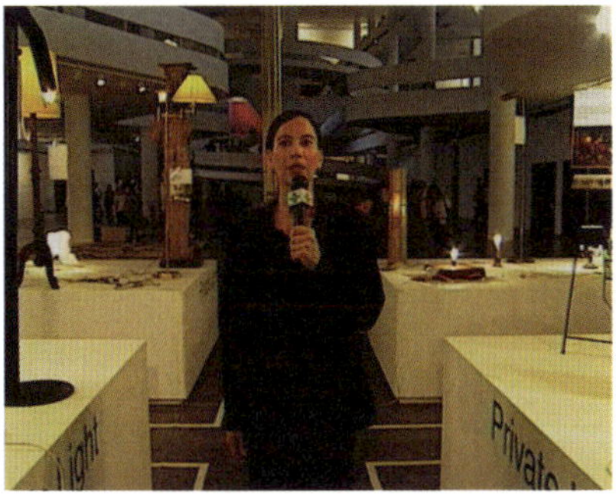 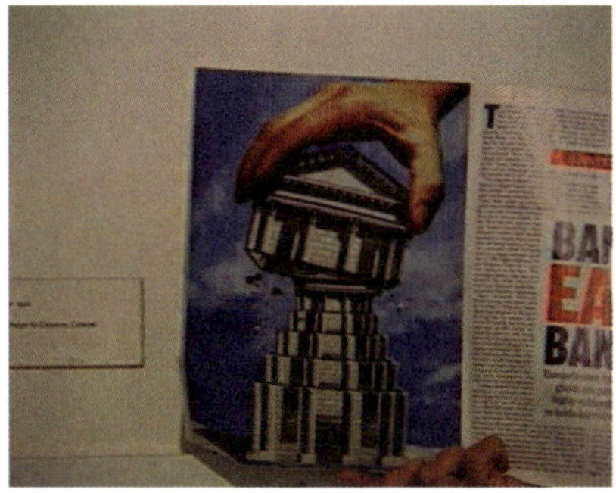

with the Coca-Cola bottle and the whole American Pop art movement was very much around Coca-Cola, one way or another. Listen to a man like Andy Warhol! You can use him for anything – on caps, on posters, on display material and all that – and it has a certain relationship. So we hope many of the Coca-Cola drinkers will come and drink Coca-Cola at the Bienal as well as see what Coca-Cola has sponsored.

> [*Cut to pan of a vitrine containing Surrealist works on paper and public-* fig.71
> *ations. Pan ends on a hand holding up an issue of* Business Week *with the headline 'Bank Eat Bank'.*]

AF [*voice-over*]: The exhibition on Dadaism and Surrealism, sponsored by Coca-Cola, introduces cannibalism as a result of 'civilisation' – celebrated, ironically, as joy and happiness and represented with greedy devourment, gluttony and vomit.[16]

> [*Cut back to interview with Jens, seen in close-up, looking at the camera.*]

JO: I'm very happy for nearly 33 years to be associated with Coca-Cola.

> [*Cut to the ground floor of the 24th Bienal, where national representatives are exhibited. Andrea is standing in the atrium. Work by the German representative, Mischa Kuball, is visible in the background.*]

AF: The United Nations released its 1998 Human Development Report this week. Canada, France and Norway top the list, which rates countries according to levels of health and education as well as wealth. [*Cut to pan of the 'Arte Contemp-*
orânea Brasileira' section, on the pavilion's first floor.] Brazil has jumped the line pp.*78–99*
from 'Medium Development' to 'High Development', moving to the 62nd place from the 68th. The bad news is that, in terms of income distribution, Brazil is still one of the most unequal countries in the world. The good

—

[16] From Paulo Herkenhoff, 'Introdução geral' / 'General introduction' (trans. Veronica Cordeiro), in *XXIV Bienal de São Paulo: Núcleo Histórico: Antropofagia e Histórias de Canibalismos* (exh. cat.), São Paulo: A Fundação, 1998.

news is that Brazil is still *more* equal than the world as a whole [*cut to shots of the US, Swiss and Belgian representatives*[17]], in which the top 20 per cent of the world population – primarily the US, Europe and Japan – consume 86 per cent of the resources, while the bottom 20 per cent consumes only 1.3 per cent. [*Cut back to Andrea.*] Compare that to 2.3 per cent in Brazil.

Advertising has caused expectations to go global. But affluence has not. Not everyone was invited to the party. And now, the party may be over.[18] But, according to the president of the National Institute for Land Reform in Brasília, 'We're in the international dance hall now, and we have no choice but to dance.'[19]

Reporting from São Paulo, I'm from the United States. Back to you, Gilberto.

—

5. 'The capitalist modus vivendi. Anthropophagy.'

> [*Cut to Andrea standing in the area just outside of the entrance to the Bienal. A title appearing at the bottom of the screen reads: 'Source: TV Cultura news report, September 1998'.*]

AF: This is the entrance to the Volkswagen factory of São Bernardo do Campo, quiet today as 20,000 workers take a ten-day collective holiday, to be taken out of the year's vacation time. The reason is this. [*Cut to pan of the central atrium of the Pavilhão Matarazzo.*] Demand, already weak, collapsed when the government raised interest rates to 50 per cent to protect the real. Consumers disappeared. Fiat, Ford, General Motors and Mercedes-Benz are also imposing collective vacations for their workers. [*Cut back to Andrea.*] According to the president of the auto worker's union, lay-offs cannot begin until the end of the year.[20]

—

[17] Judy Pfaff, Sylvie Fleury and Johan Muyle.

[18] See United Nations Development Program, 'Human Development Report 1998', available at http://hdr.undp.org/sites/default/files/reports/259/hdr_1998_en_complete_nostats.pdf (last accessed on 16 February 2015); Barbara Crossette, 'Most Consuming More, and the Rich Much More', *The New York Times*, 13 September 1998.

[19] Roger Cohen, 'Brazil Pays to Shield Currency, and the Poor See the True Cost,' *The New York Times*, 5 February 1998.

[20] From a TV Cultura report broadcast on the programme *National*, September 1998. See also Diana Jean Schemo, 'Brazil's Once-Robust Auto Industry Struggles as Sales Skid', *The International Herald Tribune*, 28 September 1998. In August 1998, the Brazilian Ministry of Culture released a study claiming that the cultural sector employs more people than the automobile industry and at average wages at twice the national average – although lower than in the car industry. A report on the study noted that 'since unemployment is one of the greatest fears among Brazilians, cultural activities have acquired importance in the political platforms of the candidates for the presidential elections to be held on Oct. 4'. Mario Osava, 'Economy – Brazil: Culture Creates More Jobs Than Cars', *Inter Press Service*, August 1998.

AF [*voice-over*]: [*shot of* Dangerous Relationship (Touch Me) *(1998) by Choi Jeong Hwa*] Asian economies have collapsed. [*Cut to photographs by the Russian representative Oleg Kulik*]. Russia has plunged down a black hole. [*Cut to pan of galleries containing Hélio Oiticica's* Relevos Espaciais *(*Spatial Reliefs, *1959), ending on guards.*] The question now terrifying world financial markets is whether Brazil, and with it Latin America, will be next. At stake is not only the health and wealth of national economies and stock markets. [*Cut to Andrea standing against the top-floor atrium railing*]. The future of globalisation itself now depends on Brazil. As Brazil goes, so goes the world. [*Cut back to pan of the gallery showing works by Alfredo Volpi; then works by Valia Carvalho, the Bolivian representative; and then Cecilo Thompson, the Paraguayan representative.*] When Moody's and Standard & Poor's lowered their rating on Brazil to negative – putting it in the same category as Bolivia and Paraguay – foreign capital began fleeing the country at a rate of one billion dollars per day.[21]

fig.31–32 and 35

fig.97–98

fig.88–90

[*Cut back to Andrea on the top floor. The gold statue can be seen in the background.*]

AF: *Boa Tarde* Maria. BOVESPA is suffering from a climate of complete instability today. After minimal rise of 0.12 per cent, it resumed its fall with the announcement that the United States Congress voted to proceed with impeachment hearings on the conduct of President Clinton. [*Cut to camera walking past guards, surveillance screens, plaques of sponsors and turnstiles into the 'Núcleo Histórico'.*] Analysts believe that the markets will not stabilise until programs for fiscal adjustment are announced. The finance Minster admitted today that these measures will include tax increases, but he has stopped short of announcing capital controls.[22]

[*Cut to Andrea in the Bienal's exhibition of paintings by van Gogh.*] fig.62–63 and 73

AF: The 24th Bienal continues the tradition begun in the first editions of bringing masterpieces from foreign museums to Brazil. These jewels of the Bienal are sheltered in the museological space on the [top] floor. Among the stars is van Gogh, represented with a large group of important paintings, which only arrived in Brazil after exhaustive negotiations.

[*Cut to details of works by van Gogh.*]

—

[21] Bill Wellman, 'Diary,' *The New York Times*, 13 September 1998. On 14 September, President Clinton, in a speech to the Council on Foreign Relations in New York, set out to address what he described as 'the biggest financial challenge facing the world in a half-century'. While calling for pro-growth rather than anti-inflation policies and for the reform of the international financial system, he also emphasised that 'no nation, rich or poor, democratic or authoritarian, can escape the fundamental economic imperatives of the global market. No nation can escape its discipline.' He additionally stated: 'What is at stake is more than the spread of free markets and their integration into the global economy. The forces behind the global economy are also those that deepen democratic liberties.'

[22] From a TV Cultura report broadcast on the programme *National*, October 1998.

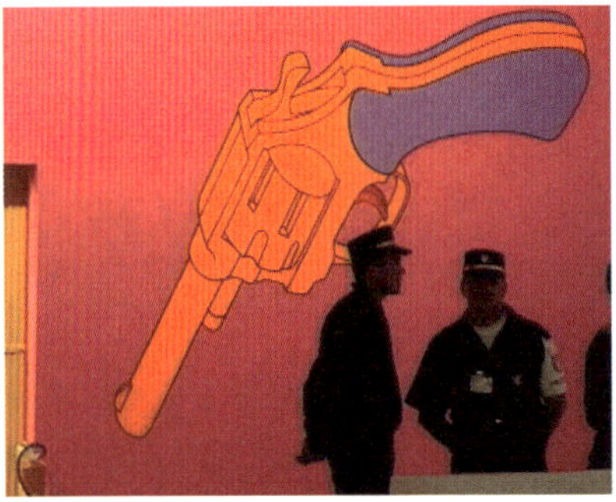

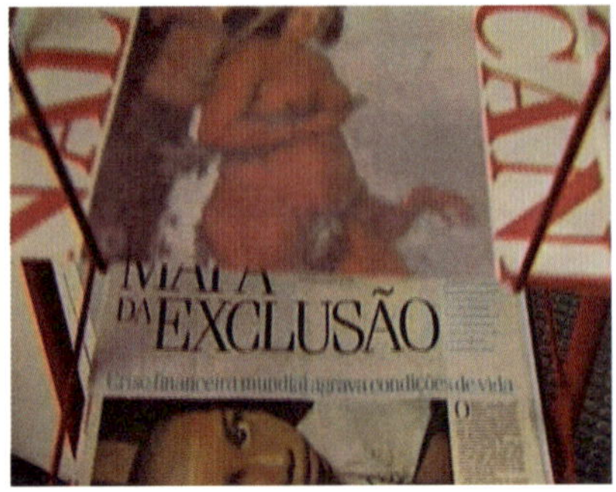

AF [*voice-over*]: International loans are extremely important to the Bienal. Without international loans of world famous art, the Bienal would not be able to raise the money necessary to meet the standards of international lenders necessary to get international loans.

[*Cut to interview with Julio.*]

JO: Of course, it's very complicated. We had to have dinners and lunch in embassies. [*Cut to a reaction shot of Andrea, then back to Julio.*] After the 22nd Bienal it was clear that people were coming here for these big names. It showed that if you bring important artists, you get sponsors. Art is an investment after all.

[*Cut to a guard opening the door to a section of the Bienal. Cut to a surprised caterer closing the door to the pre-opening cocktail party.*]

AF [*voice-over*]: The Minister of Finance is also in Washington today attending a meeting with the International Monetary Fund and the World Bank. One objective of the meeting is to show that Brazil is different from Russia and deserves the flow of international capital.

[*Cut back to Andrea with paintings by van Gogh.*]

AF: But a climate of frustration has dominated the IMF meeting here, where nothing has yet been done to stop the exit of capital from emerging markets. For Brazil, however, there's good news. The director of the IMF gave a green light to the policies of fiscal adjustment that the government promises to implement by the end of October. He praised Brazil for making moves to cut spending and adjust finances without altering exchange rates, saying these policies would bring the right reaction from international investors in these times of crisis.[23]

—

[23] From a TV Cultura report that was broadcast on the programme *National*, October 1998.

[Cut to parking lot outside the Bienal. Regina Silveira's mural of receding animal tracks can be seen on the side of the pavilion. A title appearing at the bottom of the screen reads: 'Source: TV Cultura news report, September 4, 1998'.] fig.1–3

AF: Last night at 1.30 am, 30 per cent of the ceiling of this church, an old theatre rented six months ago, collapsed suddenly, bringing almost one thousand square metres of wood, plaster and concrete crashing down on hundreds of worshippers. Some people managed to leave the building only moments before the catastrophe, alerted by the sound of creaking and the sight of cracks in the ceiling, but most were taken by surprise. All the doors were closed, making it difficult to exit. Moments of panic and chaos followed. [*Andrea passes the microphone to her right hand and extends it in front of her*]. You were inside. What was it like?[24]

[Cut to pan of the exterior of Bienal building starting at a billboard that reads 'Only anthropophagy unites us' and ending on the parking lot.]

AF [*voice-over*]: After months of negotiations, the IMF has announced a two-billion-dollar package of loans to stabilise the Brazilian economy. The release of the funds, however, depends on the further privatisation of industry in Brazil [*cut to main entrance, where a sign with the Ford logo points to the ticket office*] as well as the enactment of politically painful spending cuts.

[*Pan down an* Estado de São Paulo *newspaper rack installed in the entrance area. In addition to the supplement on the Bienal ('Cannibale') sponsored by the paper, the rack also contains other newspapers inserted for the shot, including one showing a headline on IMF negotiations above a photograph of a flooded village, and another a with photograph of a poor child below the headline 'A Map of Exclusion.'*]

While the effects of cuts in health and education are already being felt by millions of poor Brazilians [*cut to shots of guards around Bienal building*], government officials continue to award themselves maximum compensation – like the 47,000 dollars that will be paid members of congress for a special three-month session to debate spending cuts.

Government officials also continue to spend lavishly on other benefits of office. [*Cut to pan of the Bienal's Francis Bacon exhibition*]. These Persian carpets and top-of-the-line decorative accent pieces were recently purchased by the Supreme Court for a new reception area. [*Cut to installation shot of the Bienal's 'Roteiros…' exhibition, including* La DS *(1993) by Gabriel Orozco.*] According fig.28
to the president of the Supreme Court, the furnishings are necessary because visiting dignitaries frequently dropped in for cocktail parties. [*Cut to camera following Andrea through crowd in pre-opening cocktail party.*] But now, he

—

[24] From a TV Cultura report that was broadcast on the programme *National*, September 1998.

says: 'We just give them coffee, maybe a glass of juice.' [*Cut to second shot of cocktail party; camera finds Minister of Culture Francisco Weffort talking to a man in a business suit.*] Private banks in the United States and elsewhere who have lent large amounts in Brazil will be the biggest beneficiaries of any plan that stabilises the economy. It is still unclear what Brazil will offer as collateral for the loans.[25]

[*Cut to interview with Francisco.*]

AF: I'm here at the opening of the Bienal with Minister of Culture Francisco Weffort. Minister Weffort, why is supporting the Bienal important for the federal government?

FW: Well, for us, this is probably the most important exhibition of visual art that we have in the country and we are sure that this is one of the two or three most important exhibitions of visual art in the world. Public support for this kind of exhibition you have here in the Bienal is necessary for the development of the country from a cultural point of view. So we can manage with a double point of view. This is no contradiction at all.

[*Cut to Andrea against the top floor atrium railing with the gold statue in background.*]

AF: By most accounts, the 24th Bienal is the best instalment of the exhibition yet. After a year and a half of intensive work, the organisers can finally rest assured, without fear of being happy.[26]

[*Cut to interview with Jens.*]

—

[25] D.J. Schemo, 'Dry Bread for Brazil, but for Its Lawmakers, Jam,' *The New York Times*, 12 November 1998.

[26] This magnificently ambivalent phrase was the slogan of Lula, the head of the Workers' Party, during his first run for president. Lula lost against Cardoso in 1994, and again in the elections the day after the opening of the 24th Bienal. By most accounts, the noisy support for Cardoso from the 'international community' during the economic crisis – drowning out Lula's warnings that Cardoso was 'selling the country to fill the bellies of foreign banks' – contributed enormously to Cardoso's first-round victory. Cardoso visited the 24th Bienal – and met with 'business leaders' there – the day before the second-round of voting in late October. There is still much debate on the question of whether Cardoso underwent an ideological transformation in his passage from a (Marxist) sociologist to a (neo-liberal) president, or whether he simply carried through on a political pragmatism he always espoused. José Luiz Fiori has suggested that 'Cardoso is right when he says that at no point has he renounced or cast aside his sociological analysis. What he has done is perhaps more profound. He has chosen a new ethical and political option by abandoning his reformist idealism to embrace the position of his former object of study, the Brazilian business class. Simultaneously, he assumes as an unquestionable fact the current international relations of power and dependency.' J.L. Fiori, 'Brazil: Cardoso Among the Technopols', in Fred Rosen and Deirdre McFadyen (ed.), *Free Trade and Economic Restructuring in Latin America*, New York: Monthly Review Press, 1995, p.99.

AF: Well, thank you very much.

[*Camera zooms out to show Andrea and Jens shaking hands.*]

JO: Thank you very much. And thank you for the programme. [*Laughing, looking at camera.*] Thank you, TV Cultura.

[*Cut to a TV Cultura weather report. Roll credits, over weather report.*][27]

—

[27] The 24th Bienal de São Paulo closed on 13 December 1998 to generally positive reviews abroad and negative press within Brazil. The following week, MoMA in New York announced that the 24th Bienal's Chief Curator, Herkenhoff, would be the first to fill a newly created five-year curatorial position at the museum. On 15 January 1999, the Brazilian government, 'reeling under a hemorrhage of dollars from its foreign reserves in a losing battle to defend the nation's currency', lifted exchange-rate controls and allowed the real to float. BOVESPA's initial 33 per cent rally (joined by stock market rallies around the world) proved to be another instance of short-lived, speculative economic euphoria. See D.J. Schemo, 'Exchange Controls Lifted: Brazil Stocks Rise by 33%', *The New York Times*, 16 January 1999. Within two weeks the real lost half of its value, then stabilised. Despite multiplying calls for currency controls, the global economic order weathered the Brazilian crisis.

Andrea Fraser in conversation with David Morris, November 2014

David Morris: How did you come to be involved in the 1998 Bienal?

Andrea Fraser: Ivo Mesquita invited me to participate in the North American
pp.*100–13* section of the 'Roteiros...' exhibition. I first went to São Paulo in the spring of 1998, so it was a very short lead time. I actually think of it as one of my failed projects, but the whole experience was very important to me and to my development as an artist.[1]

DM: What was important about the experience for you?

AF: The concept of anthropophagy and how it was interpreted by Ivo and Paulo Herkenhoff led me to a whole new way of thinking about my own work. Ivo's selection for this section of the exhibition, which also included
fig.17–18, 63 and 34 Michael Asher, Sherrie Levine and General Idea,[2] was rooted in an interpretation of Institutional Critique and strategies of appropriation as anthropophagy. Among the many different frameworks in which Ivo and Paulo were interpreting anthropophagy was a psychoanalytic framework, and more specifically a Kleinian and object relations framework. I had read a lot of Freud and Lacan, but at the time I didn't know anyone who was reading that stuff, which had a much broader reception in Latin America than in the US and Europe. And that interpretation, which emphasises the ambivalence of incorporation and, by implication, of appropriation and critique, had a tremendous impact on me. That is, ambivalence in a strong sense, as the confrontation of opposing affects and impulses. To cannibalise may be to destroy something with one's mouth, with one's teeth, by ingesting it, but it's also to take it in and make it a part of one's self, to incorporate. That helped me understand that artistic critique, which invariably involves some form of appropriation, is never only the rejecting, destroying, aggressive fault-finding that we tend to identify as 'critical'. The attached, identificatory, desiring and incorporating investment is always there as well, and it is absolutely necessary to own that part of it.

DM: And you can locate that in your work since?

AF: Oh, absolutely. It led pretty directly to my focus on artistic ambivalence in works like *Art Must Hang* [2001], *Official Welcome* [2001] and *Projection* [2008], and to the understanding of Institutional Critique as an enactment of a love-hate relationship with art and its institutions that I developed in essays in the early 2000s. And that understanding eventually turned my thinking

—

[1] Editors' Note: The film script from Andrea Fraser's project at the 24th Bienal, with additional notes by the artist, is included in this volume, pp.248–267.
[2] EN: This section of 'Roteiros...' also included work by Janet Cardiff and Jeff Wall. See pp.100–13.

about what I did and what I wanted to do as an artist upside down. Almost everything we recognise as critical art practice is rooted in a Brechtian tradition of alienation or estrangement. Even when that estrangement is enacted as over-identification, the aim is to produce a distancing through which critical consciousness can develop. I started to realise that such distancing is part of the problem, not part of the solution! [*Laughs.*] At least, if we get stuck there. It's only a halfway point. That distancing may allow us to recognise certain impulses or structures, but the most important step is to be able to recognise them as part of ourselves, to recognise our own investments in them, to reintegrate that understanding into our actions. That's a perspective I develop in the essay 'There's No Place Like Home' that I wrote for the 2012 Whitney Biennial, which is actually the first biennial I've been in since the Bienal. In fact, it's a pretty Kleinian perspective, although one also finds it in Freud.

DM: How did you understand your own relation to this institution, the Bienal, that was in 1998 intent on devouring foreign influences?

AF: Well, the Bienal had been devouring foreign influence since its inception. I think the 24th edition was more intent on influencing foreigners. Certainly, I felt more influenced than devoured by it. In many ways, the strategies of Institutional Critique developed as attempts to resist being devoured by such institutions. They aim to appropriate rather than be appropriated. Large-scale exhibitions are difficult contexts to produce new work in. But it's not just 'the institution'. There is also the crazy competition for attention and space and resources among artists that those exhibitions entail. So, making a work *about* the exhibition was also a strategy to take myself out of that.

DM: The resulting work was titled *Reporting from São Paulo, I'm from the United States.*

AF: I developed a plan to produce television news reports about the exhibition. Originally it was supposed to be with Brazilian HBO or something, and then we had one meeting with them and I think I was not to their taste! [*Laughs.*] So I started working with TV Cultura, which is a non-profit foundation-run cultural station. I also had some existing video works in the exhibition, *Museum Highlights* [1989] and *May I Help You?* [1991]. Unfortunately, *Reporting from São Paulo…* was never broadcast or included in the exhibition.

DM: The video reflects upon the Bienal and its history and how it functions within broader social and economic conditions. I wonder how your experience as an artist working with an institution like the Bienal influenced your thinking?

AF: In a way, the Bienal was the end of my engagement with that kind of institution. I had been thinking about biennials and globalisation since the early 90s, when I did a project for the Austrian pavilion at the Venice Biennale. After the Bienal de São Paulo, I felt sort of done with that line of investigation. My approach also shifted away from site-specific engagement with specific institutions to what I call situational or relational specificity, which is more about the here and now of an encounter (a shift that was also influenced by psychoanalysis). By the late 90s, a lot of people were questioning the way artists and curators working site specifically were 'parachuting' into complex contexts and presuming to be instant experts. I do think that describes how I had been working and what I tried to do for São Paulo as well. I collected lots of books and set out to understand an incredibly huge and complex country in a few months. I finally had to recognise how absurd that was. I remember saying at some point, 'I took on Brazil and I lost.'

DM: Is that why you consider it a failed work?

AF: Partly. There's also the fact that it wasn't finished until the show closed! One of the things I aspire to in my work is to be able to identify, articulate and perform complex structures with enough coherence to enable them to become more broadly intelligible and available for reflection. I don't think I achieved that with my work for the Bienal. I'm afraid it remained quite fragmented.

DM: And you don't think the fragmentation might be a necessity of the subject matter?

AF: I suppose. If you're an artist and you're doing something that really is site specific and you really are engaging in a situation, then that situation is going to challenge and maybe transform your work and your criteria. I think that did take place for me with the Bienal, but maybe in some ways that I wasn't able to incorporate. I'll have to watch the videos again and see what I think today.

DM: What meaning do you think the 1998 Bienal has, sixteen years on?

AF: I think it had a huge impact internationally. It led to the partial rewriting of twentieth-century art history from a Brazilian perspective. It expanded international awareness of Brazilian artists and art movements exponentially. The show also still stands out in my mind as one of the most successful of the genre that I have seen. I think other curators have tried to emulate its accomplishments but I'm not sure anyone has succeeded. Paulo's genius was to find a very specific and coherent principle, anthropophagy, that could contain all the diverse parts of a huge exhibition that a curator can't control and that usually end up flying off in a hundred different directions. And what was really brilliant about his approach is that anthropophagy was both very specific geographically and culturally and also generally pertinent, and that it functioned both on the level of content and as a broadly pervasive structure that was able to frame, in a reflexive way, its own mode and field of operation. In fact, there may be very few principles like that, too few for all of the exhibitions that are being made. The truly historic exhibitions are the ones that can capture that kind of principle, and the 24th Bienal was one of them.

Dias & Riedweg in conversation with Line Ellegaard, January 2015

Line Ellegaard: Could you give me an impression of your situation prior to your participation in the 24th Bienal de São Paulo?

Mauricio Dias: I was born and studied in Rio de Janeiro. In 1986, when I was 22, I left Brazil, and after a year of travelling in Europe, I arrived in Switzerland. In 1990, I met Walter. He was working with performance and theatre then and mostly based in New York, but in 1993 we decided to start collaborating, and began a project called *Devotionalia* [1994–2003] on our own – it was not curated or commissioned by anyone – where we spent about a year with a mobile workshop in Rio working with street children in the favelas.[1] This work became very popular because there were not many people working on the street with visual art in Brazil at that time. Whilst we were working on this I sent our outline for the project to Mary Jane Jacob, who had just finished 'Culture in Action' [1993] in Chicago. A few months later, to our surprise, we received a very long fax from her inviting us to take part in 'Conversations at the Castle' in Atlanta, the exhibition she did with Homi Bhabha in 1996.[2] And actually she was the one who told Paulo Herkenhoff about our work.

Walter Riedweg: Paulo saw *Devotionalia* when it was first shown at the Museu de Arte Moderna in Rio de Janeiro in 1996. Ten years later, when Paulo was director of the Museu Nacional de Belas Artes in Rio, he opened the doors for *Devotionalia*, which by then consisted of 2280 fragile objects and casts – weighing about 2500 kilos – to become part of the national collection. In this sense, Paulo had a final and very important role in that project.

MD: But it was not until 1997, when we attended the opening of Catherine David's documenta X in Kassel, that we met. I remember very well, we were both standing at the entrance and Paulo waved at us, and I looked back to the other side thinking he was waving at someone else, because I did not know that he knew us. He laughed and told us right in that room that he wanted us to make a project for his 1998 Bienal. Shortly after we left for São Paulo.

—

[1] Editors' Note: In 1995, the artists made casts of the hands and feet of over 600 children and teenagers living in favelas in Rio de Janeiro, to function as ex-votos. Those cast were each asked to express a wish, which was recorded on video and inscribed on his or her ex-voto mold. Subsequently, the work was shown in the Netherlands, Switzerland and Germany, and workshops were carried out with children in these countries. Over the years the project has gone through numerous iterations including collaborations with social workers and NGOs. For a discussion of this project, see Suely Rolnik, 'Otherness Beneath the Open Sky: The Political-poetic Laboratory of Maurício Dias & Walter Riedweg', in *Dias & Riedweg: Possibly Talking About the Same* (exh. cat.), Barcelona: Museu d'Art Contemporani de Barcelona, 2003, pp.211–44.

[2] 'Conversations at the Castle', for the Arts Festival of Atlanta, Georgia, 28 June to 29 September 1996.

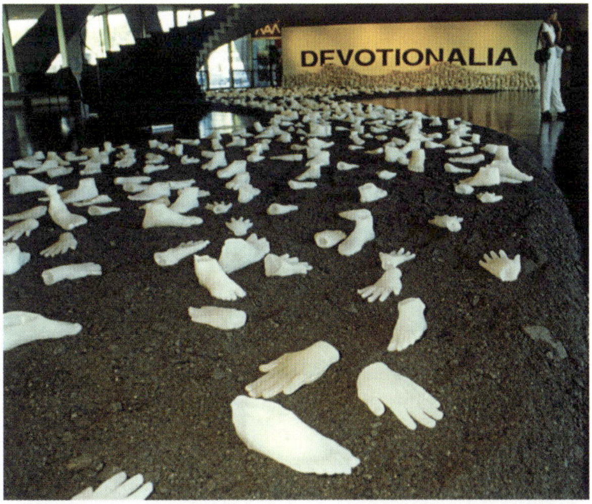

Dias & Riedweg, *Devotionalia*, 1994–2003, public art project and video installation with 2500 plaster and wax castings, Museu de Arte Moderna do Rio de Janeiro, 1995

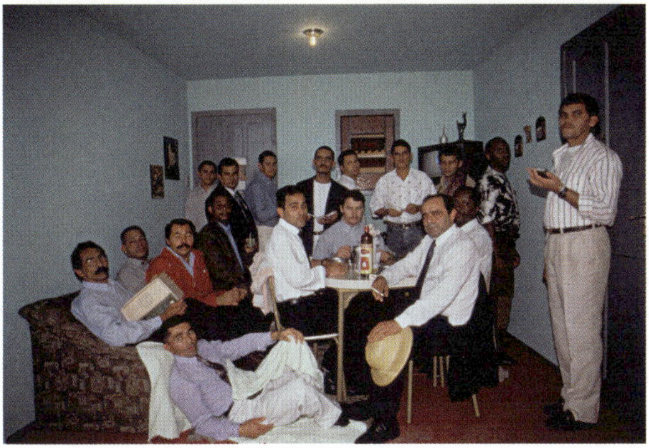

Dias & Riedweg, *Os Raimundos, os Severinos e os Franciscos* (*The Raimundos, the Severinos and the Franciscos*), 1998, public art project and video installation, video still

LE: The 24th Bienal set out to rewrite art history from a Brazilian perspective, and in this context your work appeared in the 'Arte Contemporânea Brasileira: Um e/entre Outro/s' ['Brazilian Contemporary Art: One and/among Other/s'] element. As a Brazilian and Swiss duo, how did you understand your position here?

pp.*78–99*

WR: I found that very beautiful. The Swiss had their own official representation in the Bienal that year, and they could not understand how we got to be there, or at the Venice Biennale a year later, since our work did not fit any of the criteria they put up! I remember very well there was this Swiss guy, when I met him the first time I wore a Brazilian artist badge. He looked at me and asked, 'And how is it to be a Brazilian?' [*Laughs.*] I said, 'It's fine, it's perfect! I'm still whatever I was before.'

MD: I think it had more to do with our methodology than with our national identities...

LE: The work you presented at the 24th Bienal, a multimedia installation titled *Os Raimundos, os Severinos e os Franciscos* [*The Raimundos, the Severinos and the Franciscos*, 1998], was made with doormen and janitors. Do you recall how the idea for this work came about?

fig 16 and p 273

MD: Paulo invited us to do a new project, something somehow connected to the city of São Paulo and anthropophagy. We decided to focus on a social form of cannibalism and to make a project on how the social classes may somehow eat and digest each other in the Brazilian metropolis. We were very intrigued by the fact that in São Paulo about eighty per cent of the population live in tower buildings and all of them have *porteiros,* doormen or janitors who take care of the building in terms of keeping it clean and safe. They are always at the entrances of the buildings. Yet, the people living in the buildings often do not interact with them.

We were also very curious about the fact that many of these janitors came from the Northeast of Brazil. Throughout the twentieth century (when most of these towers were built), proletarian workers from that poorer region immigrated to São Paulo to work in the construction industry and simply stayed on, creating new families and a new cultural background to the city. We noticed that many of them were named Raimundo, Severino or Francisco – three very popular names in the Northeast – and that became our criteria to approach and choose the guys we worked with.

We chose thirty different areas on the map of the city in an attempt to outline some of the social and cultural differences of this huge place, then started walking from door to door. We had this stupid question: 'I heard that there is an apartment for rent here, is it true?' The doormen would answer 'yes' or 'no', and then our second question would come immediately after: 'Ahh, you are from the Northeast, aren't you?' And he would say 'yes', and I would ask: 'Is your name Severino?' Sometimes they would say 'yes' and sometimes 'no, not at all', or 'no, it is not Severino, it is Francisco'. In this way, we invited them to take part in our art project. Depending on the interaction, we would go back the following day and start a deeper conversation focusing on their work and their interaction with the people in the tower buildings. We stayed in São Paulo for three to four months doing this daily, until we had found thirty doormen.

LE: Your final installation included gossip about the doormen played through intercoms installed on the outside of the screening space.

WR: We did that mainly in public parks and along sidewalks, asking people if they lived in a building with a doorman and if they had any stories to tell about their doorman. It was amazing. People would stand in line to listen to these little stories played out of the intercoms.

LE: Can you specify how you saw the relationship between the doormen and the locals living in the building as a form of social cannibalism?

MD: We wanted to emphasise the anthropophagical aspect of relationships between the different classes in the metropolis of Brazil in terms of alterity, in terms of otherness. In São Paulo there is a huge divide between the proletarian class – the strong presence of Northeastern people working as doormen, maids, drivers, waiters – and the locals being served by them. The interaction stopped there; there were not many other connections. On the one hand, we tried to show how identities had shifted from a geographical territory into a social territory, and, on the other, how a doorman or a maid *could or could not* interact with the people they were serving.

WR: Our work did not seek to reaffirm the social hierarchies in place and did not try to compensate for the many abuses that this society inflicts on a big part of its population by placing these subjects in a 'social project corner', where you could do something to help them or to bring them their voice. Instead, the audience was challenged to look at the *porteiros* at eye level – to see them not as objects of social need, but to really encounter them.

MD: Another peculiar aspect was how this cannibalistic relationship was somehow embedded in the architecture of the metropolis. Whereas the inhabitants of the towers lived in fancy apartments, the doormen only had a very small room, roughly four by five metres. Some of them lived there alone, some with an entire family. Except for the shower and the bathroom, everything was in this room: bedroom, kitchen and living room. Often this room was located in the garage or under the roof, and this, again, underlined the focus of our work.

LE: The last scene of the video was shot at the Ciccillo Matarazzo Pavilion. How was it to make the work with the doormen there? I'm p.*278*
also curious about your sense of how they understood your work and how they felt about the Bienal?

MD: The documentary part of this work consists of about forty minutes of video shot at building entrances – right at the sidewalk, where they worked – and partially in the spaces where they lived. Halfway through the project we identified that every doorman had a story that included an object connected to the Northeast, which culturally and politically is a very strong region in Brazil. We asked if we could borrow some of these objects, and also invited all the doormen to come together to record a final scene in the Bienal pavilion, the last five minutes of the work. It was during the 1998 [FIFA] World Cup, two months prior to the opening of the Bienal. We had to record just after one of the Brazilian matches because most of them were given time off for that. We arranged the transportation and they arrived to find a replica of the space that they lived in with the furniture we had borrowed from them. That was also when they met for the first time. One would go, 'Hello, my name is Francisco', and the others would go, 'Me too', 'Me too', and so on.

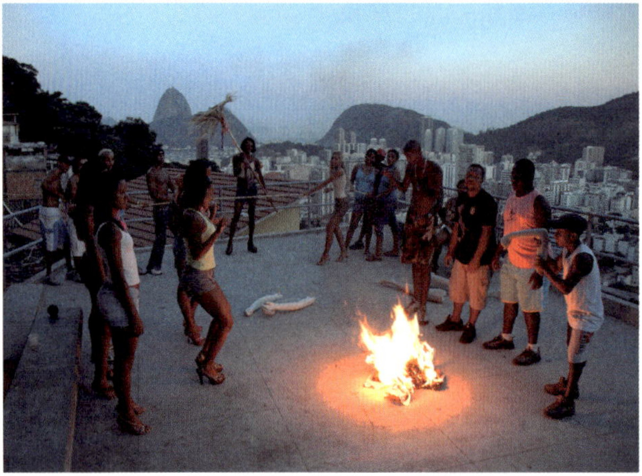

Dias & Riedweg, *Funk Staden*, 2007, public art project and video installation, video still

WR: It was very pleasant to witness the doormen learning how their names were part of our artistic conspiracy to make them partake in our project. It turned out to be a mirror exercise in a very complex sense, a reflection on who they are, who we are, and how we look at each other. This mirror motif has been present in almost all of our projects since then.

The idea to build a space, a living space of one family, also had to do with the fact that if you shoot video everything looks great, you have no real idea of the dimensions of the space. We placed a semi-transparent screen in front of the stage set, onto which we projected the video. During the last scene, the light in the back turned on and revealed the projected image to be identical with the set behind. With the change of view from the two-dimensional video projection to the actual living space, the real space then appeared amazingly small.

Using footage of the pavilion was a way of situating the audience in relation to the projected image. If you are in the Arsenale of the Venice Biennale and you look at a thing that was filmed in it, this changes the situation and adds another sense of presence for yourself looking at that thing. It was the same at the Bienal de São Paulo. It was as important to talk *about* doormen as it was to show *how* we talk about them. The privilege of art, which is important to insist on, is that we do not need to convey a specific message – we can think about *how* we communicate a message. That also includes the idea of questioning which part of this is an act and which part is truth.

LE: Did the doormen go and visit the exhibition when it opened?

WR: I remember we saw many of them with their families, and their brothers, coming to the Bienal and showing them the work and also laughing a lot watching it.

MD: The educational programme and the choice of artists opened the 24th Bienal to a wider audience. Our work was somehow a prototype of this, and although the work exposed prejudices about the doormen, they came with their families. They came to the opening, and later. They brought people from their building to see it, too, to show they were capable of subjective reflection, not only service. The local media also wrote about it, how it was the doormen of São Paulo and not the bourgeois who were portrayed in this work.

WR: Just because people have no access does not mean they have no idea. The *porteiros* knew very well that the Bienal existed even though they never had been there. The fact that they became part of it is maybe more natural than we imagine. What I like very much about Brazil is that the popular culture is imbued with immense self-esteem and has a very close relationship to poetic existence. There is an osmosis of popular culture and the intellectual and academic world, and I think it is part of the same interconnection that made the *porteiros* come to the Bienal, which then maybe again relates to the anthropophagical question – showing an interest in all that which is not ours. Today it is different. The major cultural institutions in Brazil, like the Bienal de São Paulo, have thousands and thousands of visitors every day, a huge part of which relates to schools and education. For a young person in the major cities, it is very common to go to a museum, even if he or she is not well off.

> *LE*: Do you think the 24th Bienal posed a significant challenge to dominant readings of Brazilian history and culture?

MD: Paulo's Bienal was not the first manifesto about anthropophagy in the history of Brazilian culture. There was also Oswald de Andrade's 'Manifesto antropofágo', from 1928. Although separated by decades, both were similarly effective in how they approached a postcolonial comprehension of high culture and of art history at large.

> *LE*: ...of Brazilian culture?

MD: Not just in Brazil, but how to think about culture in a postcolonial era and in a world that has been colonised and recolonised in many ways. Colonisation has been a great axis of the European economy for the past 500 years. Today we live in a globalised world, but we cannot deny that what is going on in economic terms does not differ that much from what happened in the sixteenth century when the Europeans reached the original native cultures in the Americas. The trade routes continue and the trade of people also goes on – not as slaves but as refugees. I think an understanding of anthropophagic culture in the context of immigration would be a breeze in the heads of world politicians, if they could see it as we artists see it.

> *LE*: Even if Herkenhoff was not the first to come back to this idea of anthropophagic culture, did his Bienal have an impact in the Brazilian art world, or elsewhere?

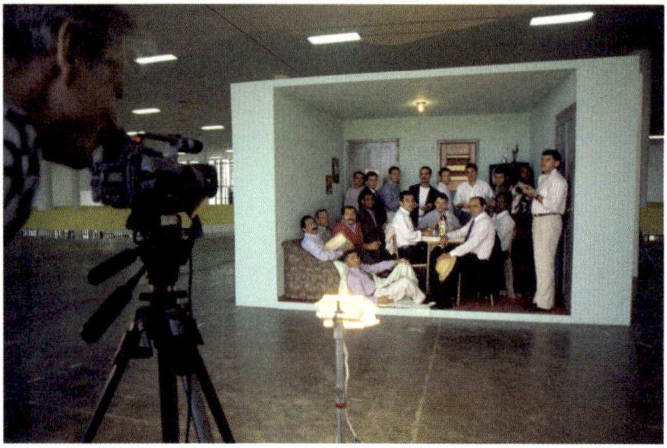

Dias & Riedweg filming the last scene of the video for *Os Raimundos, os Severinos e os Franciscos* (*The Raimundos, the Severinos and the Franciscos*), at Ciccillo Matarazzo Pavilion, 1998

MD: I think its impact might have been as strong as Andrade's 'Manifesto', because of its scale. We were just not aware of it then.

fig.62–63 and 67

I remember that there were paintings by van Gogh and Yves Klein, and many original paintings that you rarely see outside of Europe because their value is so high. Paulo showed them with pieces of contemporary Brazilian art. For instance, next to masterpieces you would find a small and ironic piece by Cildo Meireles – thus proposing another scale of art understanding. You would encounter these as pauses to think, like pauses in history or like counter-reflections. Paulo called them 'contaminations'. It was very clear and very dense. The museum that he is directing now is doing the same, just on another, extended scale. At Museu de Arte do Rio, he is making a museum with universal ambitions, where specific subject matters are presented in a type of Warburgian tradition, also on a local basis for local audiences. He often refuses to travel. Culturally this is very strong and rare, and I sympathise very much with that.

p.*276*

The 24th Bienal also coincided with a moment in which Brazil had its first generation of young artists exporting into the international art system. It was also one of the few events that did not seek to raise the differences between art markets and culturally important exhibitions. Roger Buergel, as artistic director of documenta 12 – in which we showed *Funk Staden* [2007], a video piece that directly revisits the subject of anthropophagy – largely employed such strategies. But perhaps that was different and important in 2007. In 1998, in Brazil, Paulo actually involved the art market and also invited many independent curators to participate at the Bienal. He did not become dependent on anybody. On the contrary, he was the one who effortlessly dealt the cards; he became the 'joker' leading the game.

LE: You mentioned that this experience and your participation in this Bienal was crucial for your later body of work and your career. How was taking part in the so-called Anthropophagy Biennial significant for you as artists?

MD: For Walter and me, the Bienal had a strong impact on our way of constructing a new body of work. We found a new language. I will tell you an anecdote that made it both peculiar and unforgettable for us, that not even Paulo knows about. We were very young and insecure in the art system then. We received money to do the project, had moved to São Paulo to do the work, and then our apartment was burgled and the entire sum went. We already had the outline of the concept we wanted to make with the doormen, but even our video camera was stolen, so we didn't know what to do. We talked about this to our closest friends, but we wouldn't go to the Bienal's staff or to Paulo because we were afraid that they wouldn't believe us and eventually dismiss us from the show. Instead we made the work with almost nothing and rented a flat as small as the average doorman's room. It was just one room with a shower and toilet right next to the elevated highway that people call Minhocão – the big worm – because it is loud and dusty and has destroyed the neighbourhoods it passes through. Afterwards we went back to Switzerland to teach again in order to raise money to pay for the work we did! That experience helped us better understand the reality of the living conditions of the *porteiros*.

We had always been interested in the concept of anthropophagy, even before the Bienal. We are both migrants and see the migrant as a poetic figure. Anthropophagy, and the relation to otherness, has always been part of our framework, of our thinking, not just because of our biographies but because we initially worked together teaching foreigners in the Swiss public school system. This was during the Yugoslav Wars. The schools were filled with kids from Bosnia, Serbia, Montenegro, Croatia and so on, due to the conflict. Because there were children from very different cultural and religious backgrounds in the same classroom, we had to create channels of communication where there were none. We realised we had the ability to do that through art and that became our main tool.

WR: The Brazilians are able to articulate this concept very precisely in relation to their own historical specificity. However, this anthropophagic way of thinking is not just true for Brazil, it is what happens to you if you are open and you go into a new place: it eats you up and you eat it up. For me it made total sense. When we did *Devotionalia*, I was only just learning to speak Portuguese and a street child told me, 'Now you are speaking my tongue.' I said, 'Yeah, more or less', and he said, 'Yes you do, but tell me, now that you talk my tongue are you still able to talk yours?' I found that a very good question. At that moment, I answered him, 'Sure, I still know how to talk', but later on I perceived that the question was much more profound. I no longer speak as I did before.

Afterword: For What, For Whom
— Pablo Lafuente

The questions of what and whom an exhibition is for are relatively easy to answer with a repertoire obtained from within the art system. What it might do for those immediately involved, as core participants or initiators, for art and its history, for what we might understand as relevant in what we do, as people who make it, organise it, administer it, discuss it... Answering these questions with what, from an insider perspective (artistic, professional or academic), might be considered secondary or external is a harder task, one that often goes neglected. The work that we have done with the *Exhibition Histories* project until now, in these books and the events that have accompanied them, has not exhausted these questions. Today, in retrospect, I understand the project with the help of an image, or an assumption: in the same way a game is not equal to the toys, tools or players that are involved in it, 'art' is more than the objects of art and those who make them, own them, arrange them. The choice of the word 'game' is not accidental: 'art', or what the complex, at times very concrete and at times ghostly system of art identifies as art, functions in many ways as a game. As in a game, the end is often itself, its goal self-reproduction – securing, even if as an alibi, the independence of the game from the need (or, rather, possibility) to produce anything beyond it.[1]

Being consequent with that image, the *Exhibition Histories* project has, since its beginning, attempted to address art from the moment it enters into contact with publics, through an approach that brings together different disciplines and different voices – those who were involved, and those we asked to look into what had been done and how, into the ways the curatorial, artistic or discursive work had left something behind. At the core was a belief, not always explicit or conscious, in the need to intervene into practice through discourse. Using Henri Lefebvre's words, the exhibitions we selected as case studies can perhaps be seen as 'total phenomena',[2] events from the past that make things possible in the present, and whose historical character resides in the realisation of these possibilities. The task of the *Exhibition Histories* project, then, is not only to point at these moments of realisation, but to also render some of the events' possibilities more likely.

This absence of innocence in the historiographic task, what Lefebvre calls 'objective relativism', became for me clear when working on this book on the 24th Bienal de São Paulo and, at the same time, being involved in the development of another edition of the biennial, the 31st.[3] Perhaps more

—

[1] See Roger Caillois, *Les jeux et les hommes* (1958), Paris: Gallimard, 1991.
[2] See Henri Lefebvre, 'What Is the Historical Past?', *New Left Review*, issue 90, March–April 1975, available at http://newleftreview.org/I/90/henri-lefebvre-what-is-the-historical-past (last accessed on 24 June 2015).
[3] I was one of the curators of the 31st edition of the Bienal in 2014, as part of a team that began with five people working horizontally (Galit Eilat, Charles Esche, Nuria Enguita Mayo, Oren Sagiv and myself) and expanded to include two more (Luiza Proença and Benjamin Seroussi).

importantly, in addition to becoming conscious of the intervention the book was attempting, the parameters used to assess what made that past edition relevant also shifted. Now 'possibility' could not be defined by the rules and values of the art system, by general criteria developed in relation to past practice, but rather by the particular political conjuncture of the São Paulo and the Brazilian situation. This meant, to some extent, not playing the game, or playing it wrongly.

What if this perspective was adopted when writing the history of exhibitions? What if the comprehensibility, relevance or exemplarity of an exhibition from the past were articulated in terms that are exogenous to the discourses that constitute contemporary art as we know it? What if we assume that the fundamental engine was not the interest of those 'involved' but the interest (or forced, abstract or ghostly interest) of those who are not immediately interested? Perhaps because of its strong emphasis on pedagogy, it is, I think, possible to look at the 24th Bienal de São Paulo through this lens. Although, in order to do so, we would need to undertake a series of suspensions: we would need to step aside from the history of a Bienal that likes to think of itself as the fundamental art event in Brazil and beyond, in Latin America; from the work done by a very extensive curatorial team with an intense expertise in art and its histories; from a list of works and artists that proposed something equivalent to a 'parallel' art history; and from a system of national representation that is a fundamental problematic within the history of biennials.

If we abstracted from all those points – points that this book has addressed – we could perhaps suggest a reading that is beyond the art logic, one that is instead urged by the class structure of Brazilian society and the position of what is considered contemporary art and culture within it – at the time of the 24th Bienal in 1998, but also, in slightly different constellations: at the time of the foundation of the Bienal in 1951; at the time of the publication of Oswald de Andrade's 'Manifesto antropófago' in 1928; and still, today, in 2015.

In a society with an intense and resilient class divide that overlaps with a racial divide, often in conflict with, when not camouflaged by, a dominant national narrative of miscegenation and 'racial democracy', the position and understanding of art, as a system, acquires aspects that are at least uncomfortable. The Bienal itself is here exemplary: an institution created by business elites – and still, sixty years later, 'owned' and run by them – using public funding to disseminate and promote a vanguard culture (a culture made for and embraced by the elites) to a mass audience of around half a million people who, in their majority, belong to what could be identified, in shorthand, as the lower classes.

The questions this raises – questions that could be posed to the art system as a whole, worldwide, even considering the differences between the class structures of diverse territories – are not easy to answer. How is a culture made by and promoted by the dominant class of benefit to other classes? What mechanisms of mediation need to be established in order to allow for a critical reception? Whose interests does this construction respond to, which interests does it incite or promote, and how?

Historically in the Bienal de São Paulo, and in an emphatic way in the 24th edition, the answers to these questions were articulated through a word and a practice: 'education'. Education was one of the three pillars of the 24th Bienal (together with the exhibition and the publications, all considered by the organisers of equal importance), the fundamental framework through which the construction of sense, discursively but most importantly politically, was secured. An educational impulse that, in Brazil, is a response to the perceived deficit within the general education system (one of the ongoing effects of the dictatorship that finished in 1985). For the contemporary art context in the country, and for the majority of those who run, fund and work in it, educational activity is essential: it is a constituent part of many of the initiatives, projects and institutional policies in place. For Brazilian art institutions, audience relations are not a question of marketing, as they seem to be in large institutions in, for instance, the Anglo-American context, or an issue of communicating to those already at least interested, who seem to be prioritised by most of the Western art system. It is a matter of reaching those who are far from being invested, through applying a set of pedagogical tools and with an emancipatory remit.

In Brazil, where it could be said that art's fundamental relation to audience is through education, a different game is created, where funding determines practices that are assessed through quantitative measure and a humanist ideology of individual emancipation through culture. If games operate either according to rules or by adopting fictions, in the game of 'contemporary art as education' the rules of inclusion, exclusion, formalisation and operation continue, but accompanied by a fictional narrative of the emancipation of those who are allowed only as spectators.

For the 24th Bienal, the choice of Andrade's 'Manifesto antropófago' as a leitmotif, as a curatorial method and as a topic complicated this Brazilian art-education equation (then in its initial stages) in a manner that offered a set of alternatives that are still to be explored to their full potential. Because, while the adoption of education as one of the exhibition's three fundamental pillars can be seen as responding to a historical lag, as an attempt to secure finances through the appeal of education and as an emancipatory strategy from above (the above of an art history of objects by artists, rewritten by experts), the irreverence of Andrade's thought – its playfulness, its populism and its anti-academic stance – sabotaged the machine. A partial sabotage, but one that filled the exhibition with possibilities.

pp.*114–73*

The 'Núcleo Histórico' that constituted the core of the exhibition, and which remains responsible for its reputation, was the inheritor of a populist initiative of a different kind: the historical rooms that were introduced in previous editions as an attempt to increase visitor numbers, a remedy to the limited appeal of the languages and forms of contemporary art. Paulo Herkenhoff's response was to use this platform to create an alternative history of art, one that was radical not in its elements – nothing that was included in the 'Núcleo' was too eccentric to be assigned a historical role – but that employed a grammar dictated by a modernist construction – anthropophagy, or cultural cannibalism – and a display strategy of contamination. Together, they did away with the linearity, progression and coherence of modern art history, and opened the doors for a game in which, following Andrade, anything could be done, if joy was the result. (A joy that was also the effect, in the exhibition as well as the 'Manifesto', of an intense rigour of construction.[4])

This approach didn't question *who* was allowed or able to create an emancipatory culture, but it proposed that this culture could be articulated differently, 'inconsistently', playfully, and that any hierarchy was a sterile pretence. And it created a system of mediation that helped enact this through the work of a large number of educators or mediators, the training of schoolteachers and an intense programme of guided visits. The tension was present throughout: between, on the one hand, academic texts on the wall, books in vitrines and a main catalogue that functioned like a book of art history, and, on the other, an ambition to create a situation that allowed for direct access, without the tools and knowledges of art history; between this direct access and that facilitated by the large and complex system of mediation set in place; and between the attempt to undo hierarchies within cultural materials while the long-standing institutional hierarchies persisted, especially in relation to those for whom the exhibition was intended.

Brazil had to wait until 2013 for the tension between class interests to be expressed publicly, at a large scale, in its streets – a manifestation that echoed recent, similar cries in many parts of the world. But this conflict, despite its scale and intensity, and echoes that continue two years later, still hasn't found strong echoes in the system of contemporary art, which by and large responds to the interest of the dominant classes – not just the '1 per cent', but those who are comfortable enough to access a certain level of education (that is, income). The 24th Bienal de São Paulo, in its unresolved tensions, was perhaps a test of sorts, able to question the logic of the game of art by embracing a set of mechanisms (discursive, thematic, operational) that undermined it from both inside and outside. And, as a test, it shows how those 'external' questions are consistently ignored by those who decide what and whom art and its exhibitions are for.

—

[4] A possible question is whether Andrade's modernism was, in 1998, a popular construct, one that was able to echo the culture of those who attended the exhibition from the periphery of a city with an extremely deficient transport system, and with stubborn (also material) social barriers. The leisurely aspect of the 'Manifesto' was present in the exhibition, as it is in the contemporary art system as a whole; the conflict that is present within the words of the 'Manifesto' and that could also be found within the display of the exhibition remained on the level of culture, and did not travel to class relations.

Authors' biographies

Dias & Riedweg have worked together since 1993 on collaborative and interdisciplinary public art projects, videos and performances. The duo, consisting of Mauricio de Mello Dias (born in 1964, Rio de Janeiro, Brazil) and Walter Stephan Riedweg (born in 1955, Luzern, Switzerland), live and work in Rio de Janeiro. Their work explores issues of social politics and subjectivity using experimental practices that connect the centre with the margins of urban society. They have realised art projects and exhibitions worldwide, and have participated in the biennials of São Paulo (1998 and 2002), Istanbul (1998), Venice (1999), Havana (2003) and Gwangju (2006); they also took part in documenta 12 in Kassel (2007). Major solo exhibitions have taken place at the Museu d'art Contemporani de Barcelona (MACBA), Kiasma in Helsinki and Le Plateau in Paris. Recent projects include solo exhibitions at Nikolaj Kunsthal in Copenhagen and at the Americas Society in New York, and a retrospective at Kunstmuseum Luzern in Switzerland.

Line Ellegaard is associate editor of the *Exhibition Histories* and *One Work* series at Afterall Books. She previously worked at IMO projects, an artists-led space in Copenhagen, where she contributed to the programme of exhibitions and events; in 2013, she curated the exhibition 'Reading Vogue' at SixtyEight in Copenhagen. She holds an MA in Visual Culture from the University of Copenhagen, and trained as an artist.

Andrea Fraser is professor of New Genres at the University of California, Los Angeles (UCLA). Books featuring her writings and projects include *Andrea Fraser: Works 1984–2003* (Dumont, 2003; edited by Yilmaz Dziewior), *Museum Highlights: The Writings of Andrea Fraser* (The MIT Press, 2005; edited by Alexander Alberro) and *Texts, Scripts, Transcripts* (Walther König, 2013; edited by Carla Cugini). Her performance *Not just a few of us* was featured in 'Prospect.3: Notes for Now' (2014–15) in New Orleans. Retrospectives of her work will be presented at the Museum der Moderne Salzburg in 2015 and the Museu d'art Contemporani de Barcelona (MACBA) in 2016.

Paulo Herkenhoff was chief curator of the 24th Bienal de São Paulo. An art critic and curator, he is presently cultural director of the Museu de Arte do Rio (MAR). From 1983–85, he was director of the National Institute of Fine Arts Funarte (INAP); from 1985–90, chief curator of the Museu de Arte Moderna do Rio de Janeiro (MAM); from 1999–2002, adjunct curator in the Department of Painting and Sculpture at the Museum of Modern Art (MoMA) in New York; and from 2003–06, director of the Museu Nacional de Belas Artes (MNBA) in Rio de Janeiro. Among the exhibitions he has curated are 'Guignard e o Oriente: China, Japão e Minas' (Instituto Tomie Ohtake, São Paulo, 2010), 'Guillermo Kuitca' (Museo Nacional Centro de Arte Reina Sofía (MNCARS), Madrid and Museo de Arte Latinoamericano de Buenos Aires (MALBA), 2003), 'Tempo' (MoMA, New York, 2002), 'Cildo Meireles, geografia do Brasil' (Museu de Arte Moderna Aloísio Magalhães (MAMAM), Recife and Museu de Arte Moderna da Bahia (MAM), Salvador, 2002), 'Arte brasileira na coleção Fadel: da inquietação do moderno à autonomia da linguagem' (Centro Cultural Banco do Brasil, Rio de Janeiro and São Paulo, 2002) and 'Trajetória da Luz na arte brasileira' (Instituto Itaú Cultural, São Paulo, 2001). His writing has appeared in periodicals, catalogues and books published by such institutions as Tate Modern, London; Centre Georges Pompidou, Paris; Musée d'Art Moderne de la Ville de Paris; and Fundació Antoni Tàpies, Barcelona.

Lisette Lagnado is a writer and curator, holds a PhD in philosophy from the University of São Paulo, and was chief curator of the 27th Bienal de São Paulo in 2006. She also curated 'Desvíos de la deriva: Experiencias, travesías y morfologías' ('Drifts and Derivations: Experiences, Journeys and Morphologies') at the Museo Nacional Centro de Arte Reina Sofía (MNCARS) in Madrid in 2010. Between 2001 and 2011, she co-edited the online art magazine *Trópico*. In 1993, Lagnado established the Projeto Leonilson to start the catalogue raisonné of the artist; in 1999, she was invited to coordinate the online platform of Hélio Oiticica's writings, Projeto HO, Instituto Itaú Cultural. She is currently director of the Escola de Artes Visuais do Parque Lage (EAV) in Rio de Janeiro.

Pablo Lafuente is a writer, researcher and curator based in São Paulo, where he moved in 2013 to be part of the curatorial team for the 31st Bienal de São Paulo (2014). He was previously an editor for *Afterall* journal and Afterall's *Exhibition Histories* series, and a reader at Central Saint Martins, University of the Arts London. He was also associate curator, from 2008–13, at the Office for Contemporary Art Norway (OCA) in Oslo. He has curated such exhibitions as 'A Singular Form' (Secession, Vienna, 2014), 'Beware of the Holy Whore: Edvard Munch, Lene Berg and the Dilemma of Emancipation' (Norway's representation at the 55th Venice Biennale in 2013, with Marta Kuzma and Angela Vettese), 'The State of Things' (Norway's representation at the 54th Venice Biennale in 2011, with Marta Kuzma and Peter Osborne) and 'Forms of Modern Life: From the Archives of Guttorm Guttormsgaard' (OCA, Oslo, 2011, with Marta Kuzma). He is the editor of, among other books, *A Singular Form* (Secession and Revolver, 2014) and *Whatever Happened to Sex in Scandinavia?* (OCA and Walther König, 2011).

Mirtes Marins de Oliveira holds a PhD in the history and philosophy of education. She is currently a professor and researcher at the postgraduate programme in design at the Universidade Anhembi Morumbi in São Paulo. Previously, she coordinated the MA in visual arts at the Faculdade Santa Marcelina (FASM) in São Paulo, where, between 2008 and 2013, she co-edited, with Lisette Lagnado, the publication *marcelina*. In 2014, she curated the exhibition 'contra o estado das coisas – anos 70' at Galeria Jaqueline Martins in São Paulo. Alongside curator Ana Maria Maia and historian and psychoanalyst Sybil Douek, she is a member of the Grupo de Estudos e Pesquisas em Histórias das Exposições, at Casa do Povo in São Paulo, which studies manifold aspects of the curatorial process by means of historical research on art and design shows.

David Morris is a writer, researcher and teacher. He is co-editor, with Sylvère Lotringer, of *Schizo-Culture: The Event, The Book* (Semiotext(e)/MIT Press, 2014) and has been working with the Semiotext(e) archive since 2011. He was co-curator, with Katherine Waugh and Paul Pieroni, the exhibition project 'Cracks in the Street' (SPACE, London, 2014). His writing has been published in publications including *Cabinet, Art Monthly, frieze, A Circular* and the *Los Angeles Review of Books*, as well as in exhibition texts and catalogue essays. He is an editor for *Afterall* journal and Afterall's *Exhibition Histories* series and an associate lecturer at University of the Arts London.

Carmen Mörsch is trained as an artist, educator and researcher. Her research interests include museum and gallery education as critical practice; collaborative practices in art and education; and post- / de-colonial and queer perspectives and histories of art education. She worked as a freelance gallery educator and artist-educator between 1993 and 2003. In 1999, she cofounded the group Kunstcoop©, which comprised seven artists seeking to conceive gallery education as critical arts practice. Kunstcoop© conducted the education programme of the neue Gesellschaft für bildende Kunst (NGBK Berlin) from 1999–2001. Since 2003, she has been conducting several team-based research projects, including, in 2007, the research and consultation of education for documenta 12. From 2003 to 2008, she was professor in the department of cultural studies at Carl von Ossietzky University of Oldenburg. Since 2008, she has worked as head of the Institute for Art Education (IAE) at Zurich University of the Arts.

Catrin Seefranz was educated in Latin American studies and cultural studies and is a research associate at the Institute for Art Education (IAE) at Zurich University of the Arts. She researches transcultural transfers within Brazilian modernism with a focus on critically historicising and decentring now-celebrated practices such as artistic research or education. She is also engaged in participatory, practice and art-based research into the field of higher art education and its inequalities and normativities, as well as in the transnational research project Another Roadmap. She has worked extensively in the fields of arts and culture, for example as head of communications for documenta 12 (2007) and the Vienna International Film Festival (Viennale).

Renato Sztutman is professor in the department of anthropology at the University of São Paulo. He has authored *O profeta e o principal* (Edusp, 2012); edited *Eduardo Viveiros de Castro: Entrevistas* (Azougue, 2008); published writings in academic journals and essay collections; and participated, as anthropological consultant, in creative processes of theatre and dance. His main research areas are political anthropology; the anthropology and history of lowland South American Indians; anthropological theory; and anthropology and cinema. From 1997–2006, he was co-editor of the independent journal *Sexta Feira*, and since 2013, he has been the editor of *Revista de Antropologia*, a publication of the University of São Paulo.

Selected bibliography

Catalogues for all the editions of the Bienal de São Paulo to date, as well as other publications by the Fundação Bienal de São Paulo, are available at the Fundação's website; many, including those for the 24th Bienal, are bilingual editions. See http://www.bienal.org.br/publicacoes.php (last accessed on 18 May 2015). An archived version of the official website for the 24th Bienal is available at http://web.archive.org/web/19991010090543/http://www.uol.com.br/bienal/24bienal/ (last accessed on 18 May 2015).

XXIV Bienal de São Paulo: Arte Contemporânea Brasileira: Um e/entre Outro/s (exh. cat.), São Paulo: Fundação Bienal, 1998

XXIV Bienal de São Paulo: Núcleo Histórico: Antropofagia e Histórias de Canibalismos (exh. cat.), São Paulo: Fundação Bienal, 1998

XXIV Bienal de São Paulo: Representações Nacionais (exh. cat.), São Paulo: Fundação Bienal, 1998

XXIV Bienal de São Paulo: Roteiros. Roteiros. Roteiros. Roteiros. Roteiros. Roteiros. Roteiros. (exh. cat.), São Paulo: Fundação Bienal, 1998

Francisco Alambert and Polyana Canhête, *Bienais de São Paulo: Da era do Museu á era dos Curadores*, São Paulo: Boitempo, 2004

Aracy Amaral, 'Brasil: Commemorative Exhibitions – or, Notes on the Presence of Brazilian Modernists in International Exhibitions', paper given at the conference 'Grand Expositions: Iberian and Latin American Modernisms in the Museum', Yale University, New Haven, 26 to 27 October 2001, available at http://www.lehman.cuny.edu/ciberletras/v08/amaral.html (last accessed on 18 May 2015)

Aracy Amaral and Paulo Herkenhoff, *Ultramodern: The Art of Contemporary Brazil* (exh. cat.), Washington DC: National Museum of Women in the Arts, 1993

Oswald de Andrade, *Do Pau-Brasil à Antropofagia e às utopias: Obras Completas*, Rio de Janeiro: Civilização Brasileira, 1978

Carlos Basualdo and Vincent Martin, 'The 24th São Paulo Biennial', *Nka: Journal of Contemporary African Art*, no.10, Spring/Summer, 1999, pp.58–61

Bienal de São Paulo 50 anos, 1951–2001/50 years of the São Paulo Biennial, São Paulo: Fundação Bienal, 2001

Elena Filipovic, Marieke van Hal and Solveig Øvstebo (ed.), *The Biennial Reader: An Anthology on Large-Scale Perennial Exhibitions of Contemporary Art*, Bergen and Ostfildern: Bergen Kunsthall and Hatje Cantz Verlag, 2010

Anthony Gardner and Charles Green, 'Biennials of the South on the Edges of the Global', *Third Text*, vol.27, issue 4, 2013, pp.442–55

Sara Giannini, '"J'est unt Autre": Notes on Cannibalism and Contemporary Art', in Hans Belting, Andrea Buddensieg and Peter Weibel (ed.), *The Global Contemporary and the Rise of New Art Worlds* (exh.cat.), Karlsruhe and Cambridge, MA: ZKM | Center for Art and Media and The MIT Press, 2013, pp.239–45

Paulo Herkenhoff, 'The Biennial in São Paulo, Past and Present', in Mika Hannula (ed.), *Stopping the Process? Contemporary Views on Art and Exhibitions*, Helsinki: NIFCA, 1998, pp.153–62

Paulo Herkenhoff, 'Enlightenment', in Paulo Herkenhoff (ed.) *Amazônia: Ciclos da Modernidade* (exh. cat.), Rio de Janeiro: Centro Cultural Banco do Brasil, 2012, pp.163–66

Paulo Herkenhoff and Adriano Pedrosa, 'The Brazilian Curator Private / The Carioca Curator', in *TRANS*>, no.6, New York: Passim Inc., 1999, pp.6–15, available at: http://www.transmag.org/nuevo_transmag/nuevodiseno/content/tablecontents.php?vol=TRANS%3E6&codigovol=7 (last accessed on 18 May 2015)

Sérgio Buarque de Holanda, *Raízes do Brasil* (fifth edition), Rio de Janeiro: Editora José Olympio, 1969

Carlos A. Jáuregui, *Canibalia, Canibalismo, calibanismo, antropofagia cultural y consumo en América Latina*, Madrid and Frankfurt a.M.: Iberoamericana and Vervuert, 2008

Caroline A. Jones, 'Anthropophagy in São Paulo's Cold War', *ARTMargins*, vol.2, no.1, February 2013, pp.3–36

Lisette Lagnado, 'On How the 24th São Paulo Biennial Took on Cannibalism', *Third Text*, vol.13, issue 46, Spring, 1999, pp.83–88

Edward Leffingwell, 'Report from Sao Paulo: Cannibals All', *Art in America*, vol.87, issue 5, May 1999, pp.46–55

marcelina, vol.1, São Paulo, 2008, available at http://www.sophiamarchetti.com.br/index.php/PDF/1/32/ (last accessed on 18 May 2015)

Martina Merklinger, *Die Biennale São Paulo: Kulturaustausch zwischen Brasilien und der jungen Bundesrepublik Deutschland (1949–1954)*, Bielefeld: transcript Verlag, 2013

Ivo Mesquita, Paulo Herkenhoff and Justo Pastor Mellado (ed.), *Cartographies* (exh. cat.), Winnipeg: Winnipeg Art Gallery, 1993

Ivo Mesquita and Ana Paula Cohen, 'Relatório da curadoria da 28a Bienal de São Paulo', April 2009, available at http://www.forumpermanente.org/event_pres/exposicoes/28a-bienal/relatorio (last accessed on 18 May 2015)

Gerardo Mosquera, 'Beyond Anthropophagy: Art, Internationalization, and Cultural Dynamics', in Andrea Buddensieg and Peter Weibel (ed.), *The Global Contemporary and the Rise of New Art Worlds, Hans Belting* (exh. cat.), Karlsruhe and Cambridge, MA: ZKM | Center for Art and Media and The MIT Press, 2013, pp.233–38

Benedito Nunes, *Oswald Canibal,* São Paulo: Perspectiva, 1979

Katrin H. Sperling, *Nur der Kannibalismus eint uns: Die globale Kunstwelt im Zeichen kultureller Einverleibung: Brasilianische Kunst auf der documenta,* Bielefeld: transcript Verlag, 2011

Vinicius Spricigo, *Modes of Representation of the São Paulo Biennial: The Passage from Artistic Internationalism to Cultural Globalisation / Modos de Representação da Bienal de São Paulo: a passagem do internacionalismo artistico a globalizacao cultural* (Fórum Permanente Series), São Paulo: Hedra, 2011

Eduardo Viveiros de Castro, *From the Enemy's Point of View: Humanity and Divinity in an Amazonian Society* (trans. Catherine V. Howard), Chicago: University of Chicago Press, 1992

Rachel Weiss et al., *Making Art Global (Part 1): The Third Havana Biennial 1989*, London: Afterall Books, 2011

Picture credits

All artworks © the artists

© The Estate of Francis Bacon. All rights reserved. DACS 2015 (fig.58, 62 and 73–74)

© Corneille, ADAGP, Paris and DACS, London 2015 (fig.45)

© Constant, DACS 2015 (fig.45)

© The Estate of Alberto Giacometti (Fondation Giacometti, Paris and ADAGP, Paris), licensed in the UK by ACS and DACS, London 2015 (fig.41 and 43)

© Anna Bella Geiger, courtesy Henrique Faria Fine Art, New York (fig.16 and 49)

© Donation Jorn, Silkeborg / billedkunst.dk/ DACS 2015 (fig.45)

© Sherrie Levine. Courtesy of Paula Cooper Gallery, New York (fig.63)

© Leonilson, 1957 Fortaleza – 1993 São Paulo (fig.26)

© René Magritte, ADAGP, Paris and DACS, London 2015 (fig.69 and 72)

© Esko Männikkö, courtesy Galerie Nordenhake Berlin / Stockholm (fig.30)

© Piero Manzoni, DACS 2015 (fig.66)

© Estate of Maria Martins / Nora Martins Lobo (fig.40, 46–47 and 49)

© André Masson, ADAGP, Paris and DACS, London 2015 (fig.72)

© Roberto Matta, ADAGP, Paris and DACS, London 2015 (fig.73 and 75)

© Bjarne Melgaard, courtesy Galleri Riis, Oslo (fig.31)

© Vik Muniz / VAGA, New York / DACS, London 2015 (fig.17 and 70)

© 2015 Bruce Nauman / Artists Rights Society (ARS), New York and DACS, London (fig.80 and 81)

© 2015 Robert Ryman / DACS, London (fig.68)

© David Alfaro Siqueiros, DACS 2015 (fig.75 and 76)

© Estate of Robert Smithson / DACS, London / VAGA, New York 2015 (fig.78)

© Collection of the Franz West Privatstiftung (fig.87 and 94–95)

Photography: © Rômulo Fialdini (fig.14)

Photography: © Juan Guerra, courtesy Arquivo Histórico Wanda Svevo / Fundação Bienal de São Paulo (fig.1–3, 7, 12–13, 16–17, 19–21, 23–26, 29, 38–39, 41–51, 54–82, 84–91, 93–96 and 98)

Photography: © Vicente de Mello (fig.22)

Photography: © Gal Oppido, courtesy Arquivo Histórico Wanda Svevo / Fundação Bienal de São Paulo (fig.8, 11, 27, 32, 40, 52 and 83)

Courtesy Arquivo Histórico Wanda Svevo / Fundação Bienal de São Paulo (fig.4–6, 10, 15, 18, 28, 30–31, 34–37, 53, 92 and 97)

Courtesy Iftikhar and Elizabeth Dadi (fig.33)

Courtesy Thomas Dane Gallery, London; Galerie Tschudi, Zuoz; and Kimsooja Studio, New York (fig.9)

Acknowledgements

Afterall would like to thank the authors, artists, curators and photographers for their contributions to this book.

For support in the research process that led to this publication we are additionally grateful to: Arquivo Histórico Wanda Svevo / Fundação Bienal de São Paulo; Atelier Soto; Bart de Baere; Marta Bergamin; AA Bronson; Daniela Castro; Sandra Cinto; María Iñigo Clavo; Martin Corullon; Fernanda Curi, Arquivo Histórico Wanda Svevo / Fundação Bienal de São Paulo; Fabio Cypriano; Iftikhar and Elizabeth Dadi; Catherine David; Dias & Riedweg; the Estate of Egill Jacobsen; the Estate of Eva Hesse; the Estate of Francis Bacon; Nicole Fletcher, Winnipeg Art Gallery; Fondation Giacometti; Fondazione Lucio Fontana; Franz West Privatstiftung Archiv; Andrea Fraser; Marcos Gallon, Galeria Vermelho; Cayo Honorato; Instituto Alfredo Volpi de Arte Moderna; Kimsooja; Julio Landmann; Laura Lima; Nora Martins Lobo; Ana Maria Maia; Anne Maier, Haus der Kulturen der Welt; Antonio Manuel; Júlio Martins; Marco Antonio Mastrobuono, Instituto Alfredo Volpi de Arte Moderna; Nuria Enguita Mayo; Ivo Mesquita; Vik Muniz; César Oiticica, Projeto Hélio Oiticica; Fernando Oliva; Filipa Oliveira; Rachel Pafe; Adriano Pedrosa; Ariane Figueiredo Pesquisa, Projeto Hélio Oiticica; Pedro Cid Proença; Projeto Leonilson; Tania Rivera; Royal Museum of Fine Arts Antwerp; Regina Silveira; Edgard de Souza; Marion Strecker; Delson Uchôa; and Carla Zaccagnini.

Lisette Lagnado would like to thank Tainá Azeredo, Casa Tomada; Ilana Goldstein; Shirley Paes Leme; and Isabella Prata, Escola São Paulo.

For her support of the project from the outset Afterall would like to thank Marie-Claude Beaud. Research assistance for this publication was made possible through the kind support of Inge and Philip van den Hurk.

The *Exhibition Histories* series has been generously supported by: the Academy of Fine Arts Vienna; Central Saint Martins, University of the Arts London; the Center for Curatorial Studies, Bard College; MUDAM Luxembourg, Musée d'Art Moderne Grand-Duc Jean; the National Lottery through Arts Council England; and Van Abbemuseum, Eindhoven.

Index

A
'A Cor no Modernismo Brasileiro' 22–23, 114, *130–31*
Adéagbo, Georges 100, *113*
Ades, Dawn 25, 40, 116, 149, 152
Aguilar, Nelson 45, 47, 68
Albán, Vicente 115, *136*
Álvarez Bravo, Manuel 40, 242
Amaral, Aracy 19, 32–33, 36–37, 43, 45, 116, 185
Amaral, Lilian 193–94
Amaral, Tarsila do 9, 11, 12, 18, 114, 116, *160–66*, 198, 230–32, 235, 240, 242, 246, *257*
'America: Bride of the Sun, 500 Years Latin America and the Low Countries' *41*, 40–44
Américo, Pedro *15*, 15–16, 19, 93, 115, 138
Andrade, Mário de 13, 235
Andrade, Oswald de 12–16, 19, 23–27, 29–30, 32, 34, 51, 52, 54, 56, 60, 62, 64–65, *128*, 178, 182–83, 185, 206–11, 214–15, 219–20, 222–29, 231, 234, 239, 240, 242–43, 244, 246, 277, 278, 281–83
Andujar, Claudia 78, 88, *98–99*, 240
Anthropophagy, see Andrade, Oswald de
Antunes, Arnaldo 115, *159*
Araki, Nobuyoshi 100, *111*
'Arte Contemporânea Brasileira: Um e/entre Outro/s' 10, 25, 49, 54, 64, *78–99*, 122, 261, 273
'Art in Latin America' 40
Asher, Michael 52, 79, *82*, *88*, *89*, *92*, *94*, *98*, 100, 268

B
Bacon, Francis 18, 25, 49, 114, 116, *138*, *142*, *151–52*, 237, 259, 265
Baere, Bart de 51–52, 101, 185
Bakhtin, Mikhail M. 17, 53
Balka, Miroslaw 68, *74*
Barbosa, Ana Mae 195, 200
Barr, Jr, Alfred H. 18
Barrio, Artur 18, 37, 49, 78, 114, 152
Barsotti, Hércules 115, 146, *147*
Bataille, George 13, 19, 26, 53, 149, 237, 247
Belluzzo, Ana Maria 43, 116, 132, 136, 185
Beuys, Joseph 48, 237
Bienal de La Habana 44, 56, 62, 177, 184
Bienal de São Paulo, previous editions:
1st (1951) 10n5, 11n8, 23, 30, 33, 191, 255, 281
2nd (1953–54) 8, 33, 57, *58*
3rd (1955) 34
10th (1969) 36, 178
13th (1975) 188, 192
16th (1981) 37, *38*, 178, 193
17th (1983) 37, *38*, 178
18th (1985) 29, 179, 193
19th (1987) 48n142, 193
21st (1991) 202
22nd (1994) 46n130, 253, 264
23rd (1996) 46n130, 49n143, 50, 51, 179, 193
25th (2002) 60, 188
26th (2004) 50, 60, 188n4
27th (2006) 31, 61, 178n10, 203
28th (2008) *61*
31st (2014) 59, 204, 280
Bienal do Mercosul 44, 56, 62, 204
Bienal Latino-Americana de São Paulo (1978) *36*, 37n98
Bill, Max 32, 115, 237
Blake, William 25, 115, *141*
Bo Bardi, Lina 10
Bois, Yve-Alain 26–27
Botero, Germán *42*, 232
Bourgeois, Louise 26, 28, 114, 156, 180
Bratke, Carlos 60
'Brazil: Body and Soul' 20–21
Brett, Guy 39–40, 241
Bry, Theodore de 18, 115, 260

C
Calder, Alexander 33, 237
Cannibalism, see Andrade, Oswald de
Carpeaux, Jean-Baptiste 25, 115
'Cartographies' 41–43, *42*, 236
Carvajal, Rina 43, 52, 53, 101, 185, 231
Carvalho, Flavio de 22, 114, 233
Castro, Eduardo Viveiros de 13, 26, 212–15, 219
Cendrars, Blaise 13, 114, 242
Cerviño, Rodrigo *48*
Césaire, Aimé 184
Chiavatto, Milene 195
Choi Jeong-Hwa 69, *77*, *99*, 100, *107*, *108–09*, *112*, *122*, *125*, 249
Chougnet, Jean-François 43, 116, 132, 136
Christanto, Dadang 100, *112*
Cinto, Sandra 78, *95*
Clark, Lygia 26, 28, 40, 78, 114, 115, 131, 180, 235, 238, 240, 242–43, 246
CoBrA 114, 116, *127*, 259
'Colour in Brazilian Modernism', see 'A Cor no Modernismo Brasileiro'
Concrete art 33–34, 146, 232, 247
Concrete poetry 178, 247
Constant 114, *127*
Contamination / 'contaminações' 19–20, 49–50, 114, 116, 130, 135, 137, 149, 152–54, 157, 170, 176, 180, 278, 283
Corneille 114, *127*
Costi, Rochelle 78, *88*, *90*, *94*, *99*
Craig-Martin, Michael 68, *77*, 79, *82–83*
'Cubism and Abstract Art' 18
Cypriano, Fabio 46

D
'Dada e Surrealismo' 18–19, 114, 116, *149–50*, 261
Dadi, Iftikhar and Elizabeth 100, *108*, *110*
Danto, Arthur 187
David, Catherine 21n41, 61, 101, 116, 177, 234, 272
Dias & Riedweg 78, *87*, *273*, *276*, *278*, 272–279
Dias, Antonio 114, 115, *121*, *124*, 146, *147*, *168*
Dictatorship (Brazil) 35–36, 39, 43, 178, 181, 192, 230, 252, 258, 282
documenta 34, 177, 199, 203, 272, 278

E
Eckhout, Albert 18, 20, 43, 114, 116, *132–36*, *158*, 257, 259
Ekisian, Chaké 192–93
El-Hassan, Roza 101, *104–05*
Eliasson, Olafur 68, *72–73*

F
Fernandes, Iveta 197
Ferreira, Edemar Cid 45–47, 61, 179
Flusser, Vilém 188n1, 193
Fontana, Lucio 11, 19, 115, 146, *147*, 231, 237, 240
'Formless: A User's Guide', see 'L'Informe: mode d'emploi'
Fraser, Andrea 52, 100, *248–267*, 268–70
Freeman, Andrew, see Asher, Michael
Freitas, Iole de 78, 97, 114, *129*, 238
Freud, Sigmund 16, 17, 19, 24–25, 53, 149, 211, 222, 225, 226, 229, 231, 239, 242–43, 268–69

G
Galán, Julio *42*, 243
Geiger, Anna Bella 78, *87*, 114, *130*, 231
General Idea 52, 100, *111*, 268
Géricault, Théodore 19, 25, 115, *139–40*, 180
Giacometti, Alberto 114, 116, *123*, *125*, 180, 259
Glissant, Édouard 184
Goeldi, Oswaldo 22–23, 114, 232, 238
Gogh, Vincent van 9, 18, 19, 114, 116, *142–43*, *151*, 259, 263–64, 278
Goya, Francisco de 19, 24–25, 115, *141*
Grilo, Rubem 78, *84*
Gross, Carmela 78, *82–83*, 114, 121, 129

H
Herkenhoff, Paulo 8–10, 12–14, 16–30, 34, 43–62, 64, 78, 82, 100, 116, *120*, 145, 149, 165, 170, 176–83, 186, 187, 189–91, 203, 230–47, *250*, 268, 272, 277, 282
Hesse, Eva 28n65, 114, 116, *156*, 180, 237
Holanda, Sérgio Buarque de 11, 14, 176, 187

I
'Information' 37, 39
'L'Informe: mode d'emploi' 26–27
Ioschpe, Evelyn 10, 54, 189, 197, *250*

J
Jacob, Mary Jane 116, 156, 180, 272
Jacobsen, Egill 114, *127*, 237
Jaukkuri, Maaretta 51–52, 101, 185
Jáuregui, Carlos A. 186–87
Jorn, Asger 114, *127*

K
Kahlo, Frida 40, 242, 245, 246
Kassel, see documenta
Kimsooja 69, *76*
Klein, Yves 11, 19, 115, 146, 237, 278
Krauss, Rosalind 26
Kuball, Mischa 69, *98–99*, 261
Kuitca, Guillermo 114, 116, *124*, *130*, 231, 234, 235
Kusama, Yayoi 11, 19, 115, 146

L
Landmann, Julio 9–11, 45, 50–51, 60, 179, 189–90, 252, 257
Landmann, Oscar 11, 36n97, *252*
'Latin American Architecture since 1945' 35
Leirner, Sheila 29, 193
Leonilson 48, 78, *97*, 198
Léry, Jean de 13, 18, 115, 136
Lévi-Strauss, Claude 13, 60, 216
Levine, Sherrie 52, 100, 116, *143*, 268
Lima, Laura 49, 78, *91*, *96*, *125*
Loureiro, Raul *48*
Luo Brothers 100, *108*
Lyotard, Jean-François 28–29, 55

M
'Magiciens de la Terre' 40, 43, 44, 177
Magón, José Joachim 115, *137*
Magritte, René 115, 116, *148*, *150*
Malevich, Kazimir 24, 115, 146, 232, 237
Malfatti, Anita 22, 114, 230, 246
'Manifesto antropófago', see Andrade, Oswald de
Männikkö, Esko 101, *106*
Manuel, Antonio 78, *85*, 238
Martins, Maria 11, 26, 115, 116, *122*, *128–29*, 180
Masson, André 19, 114, 149, *150*
Matarazzo, Ciccillo 11–12, 31, 35, 46, 56, 58, 59, 251
Matta, Roberto 115, 116, *151*, *153*, 240, 242
Meireles, Cildo 18, 22, 37, 39, 40, 61, 78, 97, 115, 116, *165*, *172*, *173*, 181, 183, 238, 240, 258, 278
Melgaard, Bjarne 101, *107*
Mendes da Rocha, Paulo 47, 70
Mesquita, Ivo 41, 42, 52, 61, 82, 100, 188, 192, 194, 236, 248, 268
Michel, Régis 24–25, 27, 59, 116, 138
Milhazes, Beatriz 78, 115, *164*, *169*
Military rule, see Dictatorship
Moffatt, Tracey 101, *108*
'Monocromos' 19, 23–24, 115, 116, 144–47

Montaigne, Michel de 13, 18, 19, 20, 115, 136, 222, 227
Moreau, Gustave 11, 19, 25, 115, *140–41*
Mosquera, Gerardo 44, 183–84, 241
Munch, Edvard 23, 25, 105, 115
Muniz, Vik 18, 78, *88*, *98*, 115, *149*

N
Nassar, Emmanuel 78, *86*, 232
Nauman, Bruce 26, 69, 115, 116, *158*
Neoconcrete art 27, 34, 238, 246
Neto, Ernesto 78, *92*, *98*, 115, *153*, 238
Neuenschwander, Rivane 78, 91–92, 98
Niemeyer, Oscar 10, 33, 248
'Núcleo Educação' 54–55, 195
'Núcleo Histórico' 9–30, 40, 43, 49–50, 53, 59, 62, *114–73*, 181–82, 185, 197, 257, 260, 263, 282

O
O, Honoré d' 101, *104*, *106*
Oiticica, Hélio 18–19, 22, 24, 37, 39, 40, 49, 115, *145*, *154–55*, *170*, *173*, 231, 232–35, 237–38, 240, 247, 250, 258, 263
Omar, Arthur, 78, *90*, *92*, *94*, *98–99*, *104*
'The Other Story: Afro-Asian Artists in Post-War Britain' 177
Orozco, Gabriel 101, *104*
Orozco, José Clemente 34, 40, 235, 240, 265

P
Paalen, Wolfgang 114, *149*, 242
Pedrosa, Adriano 10, 19, 24, 25, 47, 51, 53, 64, 78, 82, 180, 226n1
Pedrosa, Mário 232–33, 241, 244, 246, 247
Pfaff, Judy 69, *72–73*, *74–75*
Picabia, Francis 19, 114, 149, 206, 231
'Portinari of Brazil' 35
'"Primitivism" in 20th Century Art: Affinity of the Tribal and the Modern' 177
'Princípio Potosí' *21*
Psychoanalysis, see Freud, Sigmund

R
Ramírez, Mari Carmen 34, 39, 116, 153, 249n3
Rêgo Monteiro, Vicente do 22, 114, *130–31*, 232
'Representações Nacionais' 10, 51, *68–77*, 82, 86
Resende, José 78, 97, 115, *123–24*
Reverón, Armando 19, 23, 24, 115, 116, *144*, 232
Richter, Gerhard 115, 116, *126*
Rio Branco, Miguel 78, *95*, 101
Rivera, Diego 34, 40, 232, 240, 242
Rockefeller, Nelson A. 34–35, 251n5
Rodin, Auguste 11, 24, 25, 115, *139*
Rolnik, Suely 202
'Roteiros...' 10, 43, 47, 49, 51–53, 69, 77, 79, 82, 89, 90, *100–13*, 116, 122, 143, 165, 184–85, 265, 268
Ryman, Robert 11, 19, 115, 146, *147*

S
Sala Educação *66*, 188–89
Salcedo, Doris 101, *112*, 246
Schendel, Mira 115, *157*
'Século XIX' 24, 27, 115, 116, *136–142*
Segall, Lasar 22, 114, 131, 230
Semana de Arte Moderna 12, 59, 60
Senise, Daniel 78, *83*
Serpa, Ivan 34, 55n167
Silveira, Regina 48, *64*, 78, *82*, 265
Siqueiros, David Alfaro 34, 49, 115, 116, *153–54*, 232, 240
Skulptur Projekte Münster 199
Smith, Courtney 78, *94*, *122*
Smithson, Robert 116, *156*, 180
Soto, Jesús Rafael 115, 146, *147*, 232
Souza, Edgard de 78, *92*, *96–98*
Spricigo, Vinicius 45n129, 201

T
Tamayo, Rufino 34, 245, 246
Tarsila, see Amaral, Tarsila do
Torres-García, Joaquín 11, 33, 40, 115, *144*, 146, 231, 238, 240
Traba, Marta 41, 43, 246–47
Tropicalismo 32, 178
Tunga 20–21, 78, *91*, 97, 116, *135*, 233–34, 236, 238, 243, 246–47

U
Uchôa, Delson 116, *168*, *169*, 232

V
Varejão, Adriana 21, 49n144, 78, *93*, 116, *137*, 241, 243
Vargas, Getúlio 30, 178n9
Venice Biennale 8n1, 31, 51, 56, 58, 61, 62, 251, 269, 273, 276
Vergara, Luiz Guilherme 195–96, 200–01
Volpi, Alfredo 18, 19, 22, 116, *165–68*, 232, 263

W
Week of Modern Art (1922), see Semana de Arte Moderna
Weissmann, Franz 34, 232, 238
West, Franz 101, 116, *165*, *170*

Z
Zanini, Walter 37, 178, 193

Please note that not all artists involved in the 24th Bienal de São Paulo are mentioned here; full lists of names can be found on the title pages for each section of the exhibition, see pp.63–174.

Notes